SOUNDPIECES □
Interviews With American Composers

by
COLE GAGNE
and
TRACY CARAS

with introductory essays by
Nicolas Slonimsky and
Gilbert Chase

photographs by
Gene Bagnato

The Scarecrow Press, Inc.
Metuchen, N.J., & London
1982

Library of Congress Cataloging in Publication Data
Main entry under title:

Soundpieces : interviews with American composers.

Includes bibliographies and index.
1. Composers--United States--Interviews. I. Gagne,
Cole, 1954-   . II. Caras, Tracy. III. Bagnato,
Gene.
ML390.S668   780'.92'2 [B]   81-13520
ISBN 0-8108-1474-9   AACR2

Dedicated to Cole's Mother
and Tracy's Mother and Father,
in memory of John Ono Lennon

CONTENTS

PREFACE

This book grew out of our activities with WFUV-FM Radio when we were undergraduates at Fordham University in New York. As two "classical music" programmers, we kept introducing contemporary music into the shows, despite frequent objections and occasional censorship. Finally, a truce was drawn: We would give the dinnertime listeners music to digest by, and the station would give us our own program. Thus, "The Contemporary Composer" was born late in 1974. The twelve interviews conducted in 1975 that are included in this book were originally broadcast on that show.

In 1976, at the suggestion of Don Gillespie, we began transcribing those interviews for publication. We then conducted twelve additional interviews in 1980 and these appear for the first time anywhere in this book.

The varying circumstances that prompted the twenty-four interviews are reflected in our selection of composers. Because of our studies and the deadlines of radio, the first set of interviewees had to be located predominantly in New York City. Enjoying fewer restrictions on our time in 1980, we were able to broaden the geographic base of the book. Outside of these factors, we made our selections solely on the basis of musical considerations; we sought to include composers typifying a wide range of compositional attitudes and methods, as represented by their most respected and successful exponents. There are at least another two dozen composers with whom we would have liked to have spoken. A book of such expanded dimensions simply was not possible, and so we decided upon the twenty-four composers featured here.

Similarly, there were several considerations that informed the kinds of questions we asked. Neither of us is a musician, and so we could not discuss music in great technical detail. Our purpose in all the interviews was to give the composers an opportunity to help the greater concert-going public better understand new music. In light of this purpose, we thought of these interviews as a forum for the composers' ideas. It was our policy, therefore, to permit each composer to edit and revise both the interview and the catalog of compositions before they were published. This had the unfortunate effect, although in only a few instances, of ending the discussion of certain topics somewhat abruptly and of excluding some fascinating stories and remarks. Nevertheless, we feel that these omissions are more than compensated for by the texts' accuracy and fidelity.

Acknowledgments

There are a number of people to be thanked for their contribution to Soundpieces. To begin with, we extend our gratitude to the twenty-four composers for giving so generously of their time and energy, submitting to interviews, revising texts, and posing for photographs. No composer whom we approached ever declined to participate, and we thank them for their trust and interest. Several of the composers also assisted us in our work to interview their colleagues, and so we owe even greater thanks to Ross Lee Finney, Lejaren Hiller, and Roger Reynolds. But special acknowledgment must be paid to Milton Babbitt. From the first day we met him to the present, he has given us his concern, encouragement, support, and assistance, and we are truly grateful.

Our thanks also go to Larry Marotta of WFUV; Jim Mervis and the Volunteer Lawyers for the Arts; Robert Kimball, Lolya Lipchitz, and Mimi Johnson (who helped us contact Elliott Carter, Charles Dodge, and Philip Glass, respectively); the staff of the Lincoln Center Library for the Performing Arts; Stephen Fisher of

C. F. Peters Corp. and Arthur Cohn of Carl Fischer, Inc., for helping us compile several catalogs of compositions; Richard Markowitz and Bruce Posner, who helped us research and prepare for several of the interviews; Bill Duckworth and Cynthia Fell, who helped us in our efforts to find a publisher; William R. Eshelman, who accepted the manuscript and consistently supported our efforts to enlarge and enhance the book; Nicolas Slonimsky and Gilbert Chase, for their introductory essays, which they wrote especially for this book; and Gene Bagnato, whose outstanding portraits of twenty-three of the composers appear in the book--he dedicates his contribution to his Mother and Father with love.

One individual, however, warrants special recognition. Earlier we mentioned that it was Don Gillespie who first prompted us to publish a book. In every phase of this project Don was of invaluable help. He was instrumental in paving our way with several of the composers, as well as with Nicolas Slonimsky and Gilbert Chase--convincing all these people of our seriousness and ability, and persuading them to participate in Soundpieces. He was our liaison with C. F. Peters in the preparation of catalogs of compositions for one-third of the composers represented in this book. As musician, historian, new-music enthusiast, record and tape collector, photographer, advisor, and supporter, he proved indispensable. He is also a close, dear friend. Without him, this book would not exist. In a very real sense, therefore, Soundpieces is as much his book as it is ours.

Cole Gagne
Tracy Caras

ONWARD TO 2000

Nicolas Slonimsky

I am often asked why I do not bring up to date my Lexicon of Musical Invective. The answer is simple: music critics have lost their power of invective. They review even the most galling (to a critical mind) exhibitions of musical, or anti-musical, compositions, or decompositions as the case may be, with philosophical equanimity. Or are they afraid of landing in the new edition of my Lexicon? At least, this is the suspicion voiced by an American music critic who accused me of corrupting the morals of young composers by flaunting before them my anthology of insults, denunciations, and anathemas hurled at Beethoven, Chopin, Liszt, Wagner, and even the innocent Tchaikovsky, not to mention Stravinsky and Schoenberg. The young composers exclaim subliminally (if one can exclaim subliminally): "If music critics of the past could say such things about Chopin or Liszt, then why should we pay any attention to what they might say about us?" Thus freed from fear of critics they drop all inhibitions and compose pieces under such defiant, or simply disgusting, titles as "Masturbation" (actually a piece for piccolo solo by a British composer) or even dispensing with all titles or musical notes and confining themselves to concise instructions, such as "Urinate" (an actual title of a modern American composition with no other musical content than the gradually descending melodic curve produced by micturating in the toilet). To this list may be added "Symphony for Ten Young Penises," scored for ten young penises protruding through a paper curtain spread over the stage. It was actually performed in San Francisco.

No, none of these compositions are works by the quite respectable, perhaps too respectable, and even eminent twenty-four composers whose interviews constitute the contents of this thought-provoking and informative book to which my few observations are intended to serve as a prelude. But one shudders to think what critics whose effusions and tantrums are collected in my Schimpflexikon (too bad this synthetic word cannot be adequately translated into English) would have said about these interviewed composers,

had these critics been disinterred and given a temporary lease on
life and expression. And yet ... and yet ... one cannot help ad-
miring the purely literary skill of those malefactors of the word.
It is almost incredible to read what James Gibbons Huneker, a fine
literary man, wrote about Debussy early in this modern twentieth
century:

> I met Debussy at the Café Riche the other night and was
> struck by the unique ugliness of the man. With his long
> hair, unkempt beard, uncouth clothing and soft hat, he
> looked more like a Bohemian, a Croat, a Hun, than a
> Gaul. His high prominent cheekbones lend a Mongolian
> aspect to his face. The head is brachycephalic.... The
> man is a wraith from the East; his music was heard long
> ago in the hill temples of Borneo; was made as a sym-
> phony to welcome the head-hunters with their ghastly spoils
> of war.

What irony! Composers of today now seek inspiration and new
modalities in that East which so frightened Huneker by its sav-
agery!

Personal slurs were used freely by music critics of yester-
year. Reviewing a concert played by Chopin in London in 1841, the
critic of the Musical World notes that "the entire works of Chopin
present a motley surface of ranting hyperbole and excruciating cacophony," but finds an "excuse for Chopin's delinquencies" in that
"he is entrammeled in the enthralling bonds of that arch-enchantress,
George Sand, celebrated equally for the number and excellence of
her romances and her lovers," and then expresses his puzzlement
that she can be content "to wanton away her dreamlike existence
with an artistic nonentity like Chopin."

Composers rarely, if ever, answer their critics. Poor
Tchaikovsky in his most despondent moods could never get over
Hanslick's cruel remark that the finale of his Violin Concerto stank
in his critical nostrils, but he never struck back at the critic.
However, Max Reger, a scatologist by avocation, was moved by an
unfavorable review to fire off the following message to the offending
critic: "I am now sitting in the smallest room of my house. I
have your review in front of me. Pretty soon it will be behind
me."

It is extraordinary that throughout history, reviewers reacted
to new works using identical terms of vilification and indignant rejection, whether it was to damn Wagner in the nineteenth century or
Stravinsky in the twentieth. Consider, for instance, the last
stanzas of poems contributed by letter writers to an American
newspaper in 1884 and in 1924, the former entitled "Directions
for Composing a Wagner Overture," and the latter entitled "The
Rite of Spring." The anti-Wagner effusion concludes with the
following quatrain:

> For harmonies let wildest discords pass,
> Let key be blent with key in hideous hash ...
> And clang, clash, clatter, clatter, clang, and clash.

The anti-Stravinsky poem, composed undoubtedly by someone who just loved Wagner, contains these lines:

> Who wrote this fiendish Rite of Spring,
> What right had he to write the thing,
> Against our helpless ears to fling
> Its crash, clash, cling, clang, bing, bang, bing?

The similarity between the two poems is striking. And it was this kind of similar reactions to new music at different historical periods that gave me an idea to compile an "Inveticon," an index of vituperation by music critics. Thus we find that the description "barbaric" was applied equally to Berlioz, Wagner, Rimsky-Korsakov, Tchaikovsky, and, yes, Beethoven! And the term "cacophony" was freely used to describe the styles of composition of Chopin, Wagner, Stravinsky, and Schoenberg. Nikita Khrushchev was not exactly a professional in music criticism, but he ventured into this alien field with a rather neatly turned pun when he described the kind of music he did not like in these words: "They call it dodecaphony, but to me it is just cacophony." (In Russian the two words rhyme very nicely.)

As an ailurophile, I resent particularly the use of a cat's meow as a term of comparison for the kind of music a critic does not like. I bristle and arch my back at the description of Liszt's music in a Boston newspaper as "intolerable cacophony," depicting "every moan and howl of pain ever heard by the human kind ... interspersed by a choice selection of the various shades of expression of which the voice of the nocturnal cat is capable." I do not like the expression "catcall" either, and I find it offensive to describe unpleasant music as Katzenjammer. I find cat counterpoint in amorous congress rather stimulating. And I would not even go to Catskills on vacation because of the felinocidal implication of the name.

* * *

"The Composer Speaks!" These proud words could come to fruition only with the wide use of journalistic interview, and particularly with the advent of the tape recorder. Before that, biographers and historiographers had to rely on letters written by composers, or second-hand reports by friends and admirers. I was very fortunate in eliciting from Schoenberg in 1937 a detailed, and a very personal, declaration of the meaning and technique of his "method of composition with twelve tones," as he termed it. I published Schoenberg's letter in my book Music Since 1900. In it he wrote, significantly, "I hate to be called a revolutionist, which I am not. What I did was neither revolution nor anarchy. I possessed from my very first start a thoroughly developed sense of form and a strong aversion for exaggeration. There is no falling into order, because there was never disorder. There is no falling at all, but on the contrary, there is an ascending to higher and better order. "

My correspondence with Charles Ives and Edgard Varèse is also remarkable in that despite the almost total rejection of their works by the musical establishment, both were convinced, in their different ways, of the rightness of their ways. Ives was particularly incensed by an editorial published in the Boston Herald by the dean of American music critics, Philip Hale, entitled, "Mr. Slonimsky in Paris, " which chided me for selecting works by Americans who are generally regarded as "wild-eyed anarchists. " This editorial appeared almost exactly fifty years ago, and it already sounds incredible in its mistaken judgment. "If Mr. Slonimsky had chosen a composition by Loeffler, Hill, Deems Taylor, Foote ... his audience in Paris would now have a fairer idea of what Americans are doing in the art. "

In a way it is fortunate that Beethoven was quite deaf, and had to resort to "conversation books" to communicate with friends and visitors. The types of questions addressed to him are most revealing, even though we have few answers in writing from Beethoven himself. Take, for instance, this exchange of information about Napoleon in 1819, when Napoleon was still living. Two publishers, Bernard and Peters, came to see Beethoven, and Bernard said (or rather wrote in a conversation book):

"Seyfried received a commission from Napoleon on St. Helena to write a mass. "

[Peters:] "Correction, not Seyfried, but Eibler. They are looking for a choral group. Canné is under consideration for the post of choral conductor to go to St. Helena. He asks six thousand thalers a year for it. "

[Bernard, addressing Beethoven:] "For such a famous person as Napoleon you should be the one to write a sacred work. "

[Peters:] "Napoleon was a supporter of arts and sciences. "

This conversation proves, if proof was needed, that Beethoven had a high regard for Napoleon, and confutes the fable about Beethoven's tearing up the title page of the Eroica after Napoleon proclaimed himself Emperor while exclaiming, "So he is a tyrant like all of them!" The conversation books also illustrate Beethoven's gullibility. Bernard told him about a Dr. Mayer who maintained a "sulphur vapor installation using vibrations, " and who already cured several persons of deafness. Beethoven duly notates this information: "Dr. Mayer, Landstrasse, Elisabethener Haus, No. 317. His machine cures rheumatic ear infections, hardness of hearing and deafness by electric vibrations. " Another typical notation in Beethoven's handwriting: "Composers here play lottery every day and win a lot of money. The five pairs of numbers that win the largest prizes are 28, 878; 22, 803; 26, 119; 73, 180; 139, 452." For a biographer interested in Beethoven's eating habits, there is an interesting remark in a conversation book by one Friedrich Karl von Savigny, a lawyer: "You are an ichtyophage, a fish eater."

Just imagine the musicological, not to mention human satisfaction if Beethoven could be interviewed, and if he would drop his inhibitions when cajoled by an experienced investigative reporter! First, a musicological question to soften his defenses: "Ludwig van, excuse the familiar address, did you follow the descending chromatic bass, when in the very opening of the Waldstein Sonata you modulated from the first inversion of the tonic triad in C major straight into the tonic triad of B flat major, a modulation Haydn would have certainly disallowed? And in many other instances, when in lieu of approved modulations, why did you drop a chromatic lead and simply regard the new key thus formed as a fait accompli? And did you deliberately write so high in the 'Ode to Joy' in order to emphasize the joy of freedom and the total independence from the limitations of the human voice? And did your growing deafness really affect your vocal writing?" Then on to more personal questions: What was the meaning of the cryptic reference in the Heiligenstadt Testament to Dr. Schmidt who alone knew the nature of Beethoven's deadly malady which was the primary cause of his deafness? Was it "the ominous lues," that is, syphilis, that was mentioned numerous times in the Beethoven literature? The suspicion seems to have been confirmed when Beethoven's body was exhumed in 1863, and the cranium was found to have collapsed, a strong indication of tertiary syphilis. Was it knowledge of that "horrible secret" that made Beethoven so shy in expressing his love to several ladies in Vienna of whom he was fond? And then the final question: Was the "immortal beloved" to whom he addressed his passionate, but unmailed, letter a certifiable person or a figment of his feverish imagination seeking love that was forever denied him?

My favorite avant-garde composeress almost solved all questions about Beethoven, musicological and psychological, by summoning his disembodied spirit at a séance held in London on October 3, 1968. Ludwig van even agreed to play his Piano Sonata No. 33 for her, which proved to be astonishingly dissonant in texture. She recorded her conversation with Beethoven, and his playing, but when I begged her to let me hear the tape, she refused; she had given Beethoven her word of honor that the recording would never be made public.

Tchaikovsky would have been a marvelous subject for an investigative interviewer. He was quite outspoken about his abiding problem, homosexuality, in his letters to his similarly inclined brother and biographer Modest, and he referred to it in his diary with a surprisingly prophetic Freudian term, "it." His great epistolary friend Nadezhda von Meck would also have been profitably interviewed about the reason why she cut short her correspondence with Tchaikovsky: Did she find out the truth about him? That is the most likely guess.

Brahms could have been asked a direct question, just to lay to rest the absurd speculation about his affair with Clara Schumann: "Are you a virgin?" Brahms would have undoubtedly answered in the affirmative.

Candid interviews with great composers during their lifetimes would have been of immense value if for no other reason than to clear the air of fantastic rumors. Salieri did not poison Mozart. Tchaikovsky did not commit suicide when threatened with legal action and possible imprisonment by the uncle of a young man whom he seduced.

Biographical literature on composers is infested with such nonsense. If I may be allowed a digression into a political field, my favorite theory about the death of Kennedy is that he was told by his physician that he was suffering from Addison's disease, which would within a short time render him physically incapable of carrying out his duties as President; the bronzed coloration of his skin was a tell-tale symptom of the gravity of his condition caused by progressive atrophy of the adrenal cortex. Kennedy then decided to plot his own assassination, in order to go out in style. He had a mistress who was also a girl friend of a Mafia chieftain; in the greatest secrecy he met with two Mafia hit men (Giancana and Roselli, both subsequently murdered, were his choices) and promised to give them an unconditional pardon for their previous misdeeds if they would go along with his plan. Oswald was selected as a patsy; he was provided with a gun and told to pretend to fire it from the window of his place of work. After Oswald found out what happened he panicked and killed a policeman in trying to escape. In the meantime the real assassins were placed in proximity to Kennedy's motorcade and were given the exact schedule of Kennedy's travels. Kennedy refused to have a protective bubble over his limousine; the rest is history. The "Addison Conspiracy" as the affair became later known was never divulged by the Kennedy intimates who found out about it, for such an admission would have ruined Kennedy's image as a hero and a martyr. This is not my own invention, but a theory given me without any restrictions by a medically educated friend, and I am herein publicizing it because I do not intend to make it into a million-dollar best seller. Any reader of these lines is free to use it.

*　　*　　*

The present book, consisting of twenty-four interviews, is of the highest documentary value. The composers represented are all looking towards the future in their intellectual and technical ideas and methods. They are all free from restrictions as far as musical material and its application are concerned. If Hanslick, the nemesis of Wagner and Liszt, could be returned to the realm of the living, he would have damned them all as creatures of hell. But what

he abhorred as the music of the future is already the music of the
past for the twenty-four composers herein assembled. What is
fascinating about them is that their music, teleologically regarded,
does not represent an unflinching arrow in the direction of increased
complexities, piling up of dissonances upon more dissonances. They,
each one of the twenty-four, are totally liberated composers; they
are also liberated from the contracting sphincter of conventional
modernity which demands that music of today must be ugly. Far
from it. They, most of them, seek celestial harmonies through
terrestrial means, and if these sounds strike the untutored ear as
strange, it is not the fault of the composers. As a result of this
total liberation from all constraints, modern music, and specifically
that of the twenty-four in this book, achieves an unprecedented
breadth of expression, from dodecaphonic and integrally serial to
the frugal and even parsimonious in the use of component melodic,
harmonic, and rhythmic particles. Yet there are signs and portents
that mark the works of these composers as unmistakably of the
modern times--for instance, a virtual abolition of key signatures and
a reluctance to use formal harmonic and melodic sequences. But if
a count of dissonances was to be made in each work of these modernists, then to everybody's surprise it would be found that there
are fewer discords per capita among them than in the works of
Richard Strauss! And some of them deliberately shun dissonances
by evoking the sounds of nature and experimenting with the monophony of so-called primitive people. There are also instances of what
I would like to call premeditated serendipity, the use of objets
trouvés, by inserting ostentatiously out of context, bits of Mahler,
and even Chopin. To some listeners, this is a type of provocative
stultification that is even more offensive than piling dissonant Ossa
upon the heterophonic Pelion (to borrow Homer's metaphor) in order
to scale the heavens. Zeus became incensed, and made Olympus
tremble with his thunder to dislodge the intrusive mountains. Well,
all the thunder of music critics would not move the modernists of
today.

If actuarial tables are to be trusted, most of the twenty-four
will reach the year 2000 in perfect health and capacity to produce
more music. Will they change their present persuasions? Schoenberg said, "One always returns," to justify his unexpected diversion
to tonality, complete with a key signature, in a piece designed
specially for performances by school students. Stravinsky made an
equally unexpected switch towards serialism in his last years. The
attraction that the modalities of the East, and particularly of India,
exercise on modern musicians has already made them adopt the
principle of iterative processes, and greatly expanded their use of
free rhythmic motion. The time arrow is reversed when musicians
return to ancient ways of music making, revived in the aleatory
guise of the present. The ideal of artistic synthesis, in which song,
dance, narration, silent meditation, and sacred ritual are accompanied by audience action, is the animating goal of many musicians
of today. Music of silence is one of the aspects of this synthetic
art. Some of this may appear to outsiders as a sort of abecedarian
abracadabra, a mystic evocation of modalities that are as elementary
as ABC.

What is the future of computerized music? In order to judge the authenticity of such music, Turing's test must be rigorously applied: A composer in charge of a musical computer must avoid programming it in specific details; rather the machine must be made to act in musical terms that cannot be distinguished from the crea- tive process. Stochastic methods come closest to satisfying the Turing test; the genuineness of its results can be gauged by the psychological surprise on the part of the programmer at hearing the music produced by the computer that is unfamiliar to him.

There is no need for looking into the crystal ball to discern the future of electronic music. It is already here; electronic instru- ments have come a long way from their unicellular ancestor, the Theremin, in their capacity to produce tones of any frequency, in- cluding fractional intervals.

The most important question, however, remains unanswered: Will the audiences of A. D. 2000 turn a deaf ear to the music of that year? Or will Homo Musicalis finally reach the evolutionary point in time when contemporary music will give unalloyed pleasure, ap- pealing to senses? An educated guess is that music and the un- tutored ear will meet halfway; composers will gradually depart from pedantic observance of established methods and techniques, and audi- ences will become accommodated to the New Sound of 2000.

INTRODUCTION

Gilbert Chase

Back in that dark and turbulent decade called "The Sixties" I put together a book titled The American Composer Speaks, ranging in time from 1770 (William Billings) to 1963 (Earle Brown). Obviously, the title was more metaphorical than literal, since the earlier composers were dead and could not "speak," while the contemporary ones had expressed their views and ideas in print. There was, however, one notable exception: that of the great New Orleans jazz musician Ferdinand "Jelly Roll" Morton (1885-1941). In May and June of 1938, folklorist Alan Lomax made the giant historic step of recording a series of interviews with Morton, which took place in that shrine of classical music, the Coolidge Auditorium in the Library of Congress. So, thanks to that unprecedented initiative, the voice of a great black composer and pianist (often accompanied by his music) actually "speaks" to us from the past, prompted and stimulated by questions from Alan Lomax. True, he eventually put the results of the interview into a book titled Mister Jelly Roll--so we are back to the medium of the printed page, and an enduring heritage that Marshall McLuhan referred to as "the Gutenberg galaxy."

But that kind of cross-over--from tape to print, from reel to reading--has now become a common practice. Even if print is substituted for speech, the mental dialogue remains effective between speakers and readers. In recorded and transcribed interviews, such as we have in the present collection, the interviewers also serve as intermediaries between the readers and the speakers. Their questions and comments offer signposts and guidelines to keep the reader alert and receptive--as though he or she were indeed present at the interviews. Characters and quirks, attitudes and opinions, ideas and judgments, affinities and discrepancies, are spontaneously revealed when a question has been set in motion. Precisely because Gagne and Caras, unlike many reviewers, reject an adversary stance, prompting rather than provoking their subjects, the reader feels drawn into a conversation rather than a polemic.

1

The composers interviewed in this volume cover in their work approximately six decades of the twentieth century, from 1920 to 1980, beginning with Roger Sessions, who was born in 1896, and Aaron Copland, born in 1900. They and their colleagues, such as Roy Harris, Walter Piston, Henry Cowell, and Virgil Thomson, have been called "The Generation of 1920." That decade was indeed a decisive turning point in the evolution of American musical composition. In the previous decade the hitherto overwhelming impact of Germany had begun to be challenged by input from France, Russia, and the Far East. The Russian Revolution of 1917 prompted an influx of composers from that area, anticipating a similar migration to America as the aftermath of Hitler and the Nazis coming to power in Germany. The latter development brought to the U.S.A. such innovative and influential composers as Arnold Schoenberg, Ernst Křenek, and Paul Hindemith. World War II brought from France the composer Darius Milhaud, who taught many Americans at Mills College in California. The American musical scene had become irrevocably international and would continue to be so even while developing distinctive contours and configurations.

In this context the careers of Sessions and Copland offer interesting contrasts. Both were born in Brooklyn; but there the similarity ends. Sessions' family was of old New England stock, and soon after his birth his parents returned to their home ground. Their intellectually precocious son enrolled at Harvard when he was fourteen, and after graduating went to the Yale School of Music to study composition with Horatio Parker. Soon afterwards he found his ideal teacher in the Swiss-American composer Ernest Bloch, whose influence was decisive. He later traveled widely, spending about eight years in Europe; but, unlike Copland, he made a living mainly as a professor at various universities, chiefly at Princeton and the University of California at Berkeley.

In contrast, Copland's family were of Russian-Jewish descent, and the Brooklyn neighborhood where he grew up, "peopled largely by Italians, Irish, and Negroes," was scarcely the path to Harvard or Yale--though one might say that it was more typically American. In any event, he evinced musical talent, took lessons in piano, harmony, and composition, and in his teens simply decided that he would be a composer. His formal education ended with high school; the next step was to go to Europe for further musical study. In the aftermath of World War I, not Germany but France was the place to go, and by the summer of 1921 Copland was at Fontainebleau. There he met Nadia Boulanger, the teacher who was to become (as Virgil Thomson said) "The Mother of Us All" for several generations of young American composers-in-the-making. In his interview Copland tells us about that decisive moment in his life--including the unprecedented experience of studying composition with a woman!

Ross Lee Finney (born 1906) also studied with Boulanger and gives credit to her teaching; but he was in his late teens, and subsequently felt she was too motherly, or "protective." He then went to Vienna to study with Alban Berg and became involved with twelve-tone composition (also called "serialism"), which influenced many American composers of this period, including Copland and Sessions. Later he began to use electronic tape, which he regarded as leading to "totally new concepts of time" in musical expression.

With all these innovative trends, Finney never forgot his "grass roots" in North Dakota and his love for folk music. This background is evoked in such titles as Landscapes Remembered and Summer in Valley City. He tells us that he has "always sung folk songs with guitar," and that Landscapes Remembered is based on the tune of "O bury me not on the lone prairie." Much of his later music is symbolized in the title of a recent composition: Variations on a Memory.

Very few of the composers represented in these interviews (unlike Roy Harris and Virgil Thomson) have been concerned with using American folk-popular music. The notable exception is Copland, whose musical Americana, ranging from jazz to cowboy songs and from ballets to film scores, is comparable in impact only to that of Charles Ives. In contrast, Elliott Carter (born in 1908) repudiated the "populist" trend of the 1930s and went on to develop theoretical concepts and formal configurations that eventually placed him as one of the leading innovators of the twentieth century. Nevertheless, it is interesting to note that in his interview, discussing the use of "metric modulation," Carter tells us that he was "deriving this whole method from jazz." He goes on to say that there were some jazz configurations where "the melody would move rapidly from very slow things, giving it the impression of improvisation which I seek in my music." The key word in that statement is "impression," which signifies an idea, not a fact (or an act).

Like Sessions, Carter takes a dim view of electronic music, chiefly because he doesn't like "the feeling of not having any contact with a living musician." He does, however, praise the works that combine live and electronic music, such as those of Mario Davidovsky. During his formative years Carter was very close to Ives and readily acknowledges the influence of that great American innovator.

At Harvard, Carter majored in English and the literary factor is evidently important in his musical thought, although mainly as a symbolic analogue. The music always comes first. Carter's compositions are considered "difficult" by many listeners (as well as musicians!), no doubt because of his systematic inventiveness and urge for innovation. Yet he has persistently sought to clarify his intentions verbally in lectures and writings--and now he does so again in the interview for the present volume. The reader should be encouraged by what he says therein: "My music sounds like confusion, but if you hear it more often it isn't so confused as you think!"

Another composer who has experienced considerable difficulty in establishing a rapport with so-called "music lovers"--i. e. , the concert-going public (with radio and recordings as supplementary media) addicted to the "classics" and imitations thereof--is Milton Babbitt (born 1916). Our interviewers sort of put him on the spot by immediately asking him about his notorious article titled, "Who Cares If You Listen?" (1958). Whereupon Babbitt promptly states that this was not his title: It was foisted upon him by the editor of the magazine in which it first appeared.

As he tells us in the interview, the title of the article as submitted was "The Composer as Specialist"--which, far from attracting wide attention, would have turned off most readers. Anyhow, when asked what he had precisely in mind, he replied: "If you're not going to take our activities in as serious and dignified a manner as we take them, then of course we don't want you to listen." That still seems a bit up-tight, and in any case it gives a misleading impression of Babbitt's personality and manifold interests, ranging from popular songs to jazz. A case of split personality? I think not; rather a man of zestful character who refuses to recognize a barrier between spontaneous humor and recondite intellectualism.

It is indicative of Babbitt's open-minded character that he formed a close friendship with Gunther Schuller, a highly trained composer and conductor whose main interests are in jazz and ragtime. There is also his tour de force of writing a jazz piece, All Set, which not only combines jazz references with twelve-tone writing but also presents a pun in the title, because "set" is another designation for the tone row. What can be definitely said is that most of Babbitt's music is much less difficult and abstruse than his theoretical writings. A suggestion is offered: Take the music and let the theory go.

Unlike their predecessors, many contemporary composers have felt the urge to formulate new concepts and systems as a basis for their creative work. For example, George Rochberg (born 1918) has sought to evoke a "New Image of Music" via a process that he calls "spatialization." He was actually trying to characterize much of the new music of the 1960s. As he explains: "It was the acoustical or sonic aspect of the philosophic or psychological impulse that was driving composers toward spatial realization." But he adds that by the Seventies all this had become "ancient history." It appears that the lay listener, who might previously have envisaged musical styles or periods by centuries, must now think in terms of decades.

By 1980, Rochberg was having doubts concerning "spatialization" because of its tendency toward "shapelessness"! He sees "a need for clarity, for logic in the progression of ideas--whether they're musical, verbal, symbolic, or pictorial." Where does this leave the "average" listener? Rochberg is not much concerned with that type: "You always want the ideal listener who knows what you're dealing with." Hence, "give me the experienced listener every time." He frankly confesses that he's "totally elitist"--which means appealing to the select few rather than the unenlightened many.

In earlier times there was much talk about the "theory" of musical composition, but now the "in" word appears to be "philosophy." In the excerpt above Rochberg talks about the "philosophical impulse" that drives composers in a certain direction, and the first question that our interviewers put to Lukas Foss was: "Do you see yourself as a philosophical composer?" The reply: "Certainly not, no." Perhaps it was enough to be the son of a professor of philosophy! (Foss was born in Berlin in 1922 and came to the U.S.A. in 1937.) In reply to the leading question he simply adds that he is "literary-minded." This trait is revealed not merely in setting poetic texts to music per se, but rather in choosing texts that have an overall thematic significance. An example is Time Cycle for soprano and orchestra or chamber group (1960; 1961). The underlying literary context is the 'time motive," as each poem refers to time, clocks, or bells. Another example is Fragments of Archilochos for chorus and chamber ensemble (1965), with male and female speakers. The poetic fragments are literally tossed around in various changing contexts.

Foss was an innovator in non-jazz ensemble improvisation, which he also describes as "instant composition." But he refuses to be bound by any style or type; so he also did a piece called Non-Improvisation! He wanted to write "dangerous music" and he felt that "successful improvisation simply cannot afford to be dangerous." He remarks that each kind of innovative music can degenerate into "safeness," and that is what he is determined to avoid. He would like to be among those "who have one big foot in the past and one big foot in the future."

Ralph Shapey (b. 1921) started life in Philadelphia, where he received his basic musical training. At the age of sixteen he was first "turned on" to contemporary avant-garde music by hearing a performance of Schoenberg's Violin Concerto. As he later told an interviewer: "I was enthralled, and I was completely taken by the magnificence of it--that music for the first time could speak on the level that I heard in my mind."

As his subsequent career reveals (and the present interview confirms), musical ideas were to enter Shapey's mind--and exit therefrom--in a variety of modes and guises. He took what suited him from the complex theories of Schoenberg, as well as from his first teacher of composition, Stefan Wolpe. He was also deeply influenced by the greatly innovative compositions of Edgard Varèse, whose music he often conducted. Shapey's orchestral work Ontogeny (1958), not only has a Varèse-like title, but also features the "sound-color" effects, the rhythmic complexity, and the percussive timbres that characterize the compositions of Varèse. This trend is continued in such works as Dimensions (1960) and Incantations (1961), in which the human voice (soprano) is treated like an instrument, singing syllables instead of a written text.

As demonstrated in the interview, Shapey is highly opinionated and volatile in his moods--also intemperate in his speech to the point of Rabelaisian invective. The keynote appears to be frustration; but eventually his music will be judged on its own merits.

John Cage (born 1912) has scarcely one toe in the past-- and indeed might be tagged as a "Futurist." As he told his interviewers: "I'm always more interested in what I haven't yet written than in what I've written in the past." Invention, intuition, innovation--these are his guiding signs. His affinities with composers of the past are few but significant: most notably with Satie and Mozart. However, Cage cannot really be understood simply as a composer, a musician. His verbal communication in print is prolific and far-reaching, ranging from mycology to Zen Buddhism. His vade mecum for determining directions and configurations in both his music and his life is the I Ching (Chinese Book of Changes). (1951). It has served as a means for ordering "chance operations" in his music, beginning with Music of Changes (1951).

In a 1937 lecture titled "The Future of Music: Credo," Cage predicted that "the use of noise to make music will continue and increase until we reach a music through the aid of electrical instruments which will make available for musical purposes any and all sounds that can be heard." He began to compose works for a wide variety of percussion instruments, beginning with First Construction (In Metal) (1939), which included four automobile brake drums. He regarded percussion music as "a temporary transition from keyboard-influenced music to the all-sound music of the future."

Cage soon became involved with electronic composition, as well as with a wide variety of multi-media projects. This led to his collaboration with Lejaren Hiller (born 1924) in a sensationally complex work titled HPSCHD (computer language for "harpsichord"), composed at the University of Illinois in 1967. This originated in Cage's fascination with a piece supposedly written by Mozart titled "Introduction to the Composition of Waltzes by Means of Dice." The lure, of course, was that of a chance operation. The challenge was to transform the idea into a complex, multi-media, audio-visual composition, within the context of a calculated chaos. The result was both sensational and controversial.

Lejaren Hiller was originally trained as a chemical engineer but also studied music with Sessions and Babbitt. When he first joined the faculty at the University of Illinois he taught chemistry while continuing to write music on the side. He was also interested in working with computers and synthesizers, and the breakthrough came in 1955, when he and a partner created the first computer-generated composition: the Illiac Suite for string quartet. In spite of--or perhaps because of--the notoriety evoked by this "non-human" composition, Hiller had difficulty in being accepted as a legitimate professor of music; but this eventually happened, with productive results that he relates in the interview. His key statement as a composer he expresses thus: "I'm independent, and write the way I want to regardless of what is supposed to be proper and respectable."

Morton Feldman (born 1926), with Earle Brown and Christian Wolff, was one of the composers influenced by Cage in the 1960s, though later he went his own way--in many directions! In the interview he paraphrases Cage's description of experimental composition as "an act of which the outcome is unknown," and uses that to justify his dislike of electronic music. As he says: "After my first adventure in electronic music, its outcome was foreseen." So he went on to compose less foreseeable music.

While Cage held court in New York City during the 1960s, the Midwest was opening new vistas in the avant-garde scene through the multi-media activities of the ONCE Group at Ann Arbor, Michigan, in which musicians mingled with film-makers, theatrical designers, and visual artists. Among the participating musicians were Robert Ashley, Gordon Mumma, and Roger Reynolds.

Readers of the interview with Robert Ashley (born 1930) will readily understand that he was the most "far out" member of the ONCE Group, precisely because he was into so many radical innovations that drastically changed (some would say "distorted") all accepted views of what constituted a "composition." Instead of themes, forms, and developments, his basic elements were sight, space, sound, and movement. For example, Ashley's in memoriam ... Kit Carson (opera) was described as "audio-visual-theatrical 'pop-art.'" Ever since those early years, Ashley has continued to be a radical innovator in the field of mixed media, culminating in such works as Music with Roots in the Aether (video portraits of composers and their music), the Piano Sonata (subtitled "Christopher Columbus Crosses to the New World in the Nina, the Pinta, and the Santa Maria Using Only Dead Reckoning and a Crude Astrolabe"), and Perfect Lives (Private Parts), which was influenced by the Tibetan Book of the Dead. As he explains: "The idea of Perfect Lives--the dramatic idea, the narrative idea--is that the performers are describing characters who are represented by the performers." In the description of this work, as throughout the interview, Ashley's link with jazz is repeatedly emphasized--on the whole, an amazing maze!

The career of Roger Reynolds (born 1934) is comparable to that of Lejaren Hiller in one respect: both were trained in technology before turning to a musical career. Reynolds' field was that of engineering physics, in which he obtained his degree at the University of Michigan, followed by employment in the missile industry--which he did not find rewarding. He had learned to play the piano and felt that music might be a satisfying career, so he returned to Michigan and enrolled as a student at the university, taking a course on "composition for non-composers," taught by Ross Lee Finney. At first the going was rough, but he came through and was grateful for Finney's excellent teaching, with its "indomitable pragmatism." He also studied with the Spanish composer Roberto Gerhard, who was then on the faculty at Michigan. But it was a late start, and he tells us that he didn't actually compose anything until he was twenty-five.

Reynolds was fortunate in being able to join the ONCE Group, which proved to him that "you can do virtually anything if you have enough energy and capable friends." Creatively, the prime benefit was to grasp "the flexibility of various media--the knowledge that very diverse values could work in easy conjunction." This principle he applied with remarkable results in a multi-media theater piece titled The Emperor of Ice Cream (after a poem by Wallace Stevens), written for the ONCE Festival in 1962. Thereafter he continued to be increasingly innovative and inventive in the use of multi-media works, while also producing many impressive compositions for orchestra and other instrumental and vocal combinations, often with literary or symbolic implications. In 1973 Reynolds became director of the newly founded Center for Music Experiment and Related Research at the University of California in San Diego, and in 1975 he published an influential book, Mind Models: New Forms of Musical Experience.

In the 1960s many of the avant-garde composers whom we have mentioned began to take a keen interest in the music of an American expatriate living on the outskirts of Mexico City, Conlon Nancarrow (born 1912). As he tells us in the interview, he had no formal musical studies other than a course in strict counterpoint with Roger Sessions, and at an early age he became involved with jazz: in many ways an ideal combination. His career as a composer was interrupted when he joined the Republican side in the Spanish Civil War against Franco. Upon his return to the U.S.A. he was regarded as a persona non grata and when he wanted to travel was refused a passport. So Nancarrow settled in Mexico; but before leaving the United States he had acquired a copy of Henry Cowell's book New Musical Resources, which gave him new ideas of what could be done with rhythm and complex time patterns. Previously he had been introduced to Far Eastern music by attending performances of the Shankar Ballet from India, and then he went on to explore Balinese and African music, always with a fascination for rhythmic complexities. Add to this the memory of a player piano (or "pianola") from childhood, and we get to the crux of the unique type of musical composition that finally made him famous.

It all began when Nancarrow decided to use the player-piano roll and mechanism as his primary medium for composition. This involved a specially made punching machine that enabled him to place notes accurately on the piano rolls, with complete control of time and space. Beginning tentatively with some jazz-and-blues pieces in 1949 (he called them "Studies"), he went on to more extended and complex "Studies," including some for two pianos. All this required an immense amount of time and skill and patiently dedicated labor. By the 1970s, disc recordings of the "Studies" were available, and he became an admired hero of the avant-garde, who enthusiastically beat a path to his doorstep.

We have noted the crucial influence that Cowell's New Musical Resources had on Nancarrow, and this is a reminder that for the first time in our musical history American composers were assimilating new ideas from their native predecessors instead of relying heavily on European influences. The three American composers who had the most innovative impact in this direction were Charles Ives, Henry Cowell, and Harry Partch (1901-1974). The last-mentioned had a direct and decisive influence on two of the composers interviewed herein: Henry Brant and Ben Johnston.

Henry Brant (born 1913) speaks of "a miserable and incompetent academicism" that surrounded the teaching of composition in America around 1929-1930. True, he received some informal input from Antheil, Riegger, and Copland that was useful, but the decisive turning-point came when he met Partch in 1938. The latter, a Californian, had invented both a new system of composition and a marvelous array of new instruments (which he built himself) for performing his microtonal pieces. By this time Brant was also using some unconventional instruments, so there was an immediate rapport with Partch, which was extended further by Brant's acceptance of microtonality.

In 1949 Partch had published a treatise titled Genesis of a Music, in which he totally rejected the European system of twelve notes to the octave. As Brant says: "Harry Partch did not leave musical materials and institutions the way he found them. He decided that Western music needed completely new musical resources and he began all over again as though the tradition had never existed." He adds: "I was impressed and still am."

It follows from what has been said that Brant attaches great importance to microtonality in the compositional process. As he states: "I still think that's the way matters have to go," and he advocates a system based on quarter tones.

Another aspect of his compositional process that Brant discusses is that of spatial distribution, or "directional sound"--also referred to as "antiphonal placing"--for the conception of which he gives full credit to Ives. As he explains, there are practical problems in distributing the various performers within the area of a conventional concert hall or auditorium--and it was even worse outdoors! He sees "a technological crisis in space music," which can be resolved only by changing the dimensions of our concert halls, together with "new instruments for the outdoors, the simultaneous collaboration of ensembles of musicians from different cultures, multi-track recording equipment up to seventy-two channels, and perhaps a few devices for safely, swiftly, and noiselessly lifting and transporting musicians about the hall as they play." He still believes that Ives and Partch are the tutelary spirits who might make such a transformation possible.

Ben Johnston (born 1924) is another composer who felt that "twentieth-century tonal music doesn't have a lot to offer," and as an alternative turned to the microtonal system. Again the catalyst was Partch, when Johnston discovered the Genesis of a Music after some unsatisfactory study in conventional composition. He immediately wrote to Partch, who invited him to come and work in his California digs. The stay lasted six months, after which Partch got him into Mills College, recommending him to study with Milhaud. But the crucial event was his meeting with Partch and his commitment to microtonal composition. As he tells us in the interview, he also did a great deal to help Partch, especially by bringing him to the University of Illinois. Further study with Cage ensued, followed by a fling with electronics; but the influence of Partch proved stronger, and the result was a Sonata for Microtonal Piano. As he tells us, it took five years to write this--including a retuning of the piano, and then getting the tuning in his head!

The preoccupation with microtonality by no means implies that Johnston has a "single-track" mind--far from it! The interview speaks for him in the context of continual "reaching out" for new configurations, as in the experimental vocal piece Visions and Spells, or the controversial Quintet for Groups. He is firm in his conviction that "just intonation" (as contrasted with the "equal temperament" of traditional tonality) will eventually prevail. He doesn't want the simplest or most obvious system but instead one that is capable of "dealing with subtleties of relationship" in creative composition.

George Crumb (born 1929) has the unique distinction among prominent American composers of having been born and raised in West Virginia--which has left at least some token mementos in his music. For example, in Ancient Voices of Children (1970) he includes a "musical saw" and in Music for a Summer Evening (Makrokosmos III) (1974), a stone "jug." Although these are not exclusive to his home state, they are certainly typical. When queried in the interview about the possible effect of his background, he replies with symbolic images that are typical of his approach to composition: "An echoing quality, or an interest in very long sounds, haunting sounds, sounds that don't want to die, this is all part of an inherited acoustic, I think." Later he goes on to say that any sound is possible--and this is an important key to his music. Although he uses some amplification, he is not partial to electronic music per se. He prefers live action, as in Echoes of Time and the River: Four Processionals for Orchestra (1967), in which the musicians are directed to whisper and shout, to whistle, and to walk around the stage. His compositions, in effect, are a kind of time-space scenario, including surrealist effects. Several of his best-known works use settings of poems by the Spanish poet Federico García Lorca, with whose haunting images he formed a lasting affinity.

Since the visual element is so important in Crumb's compositions, he was not attracted to electronic music, as we have noted. However he praises Mario Davidovsky for his "elegant" manner of "combining live instruments with the electronic sounds." Davidovsky (born 1934, in Argentina) was immediately "turned on" when he heard the first available recordings of electronic music, and when he came to the U.S.A. in 1958 he met Milton Babbitt, who offered his advice and encouragement. Two years later he began to work at the Columbia-Princeton Electronic Music Center and soon established a reputation in that field. But (as he tells us in the interview) he found something that was not advantageous in electronic music--namely, the sound! He goes on to explain that "the genuine value in electronic music concerns such aspects as the control of dynamics in time." He was also bothered by the elimination of live performers; so he solved that problem by starting to compose for a combination of electronic sounds and live performance. After 1965 he made no more purely electronic pieces, and in 1975 he began to compose non-electronic music. Davidovsky obviously values freedom more than theory.

Throughout this Introduction we have referred to electronic music from various aspects and points of view but the uninitiated reader may be left in doubt about its intrinsic functions and operative processes. Those seeking enlightenment will find it in the interview with Charles Dodge (born 1942), whose explanations and descriptions are set forth clearly and comprehensively, ranging from the RCA Synthesizer and the digital computer to "speech synthesis" and experimental video programs for television, culminating with a "kind of electronic soap opera"!

The electronic experience continues with Jacob Druckman (born 1928), who early on discovered that "Electronic music is a great debunker of the vanities that composers hold." That alone is sufficient to justify its existence. Even when he was writing his String Quartet No. 2 as a "serial" (twelve-tone) piece, he felt the influence of electronics. His experience with the latter, however, was not entirely satisfactory, because he preferred "the actuality, the physicality of human beings" and "the physical presence of a person in a theater." He is in fact very much attracted to the theater and looks forward to the time when "I'll be up to my ears in opera"--with or without electronics.

To the long list of male interviewees there is an exception in the person of Barbara Kolb (born 1939), who studied composition with Lukas Foss and Gunther Schuller, and in 1969-1970 was in residence at the American Academy in Rome. She is not committed to electronics but has used tape in several pieces. As indicated in the interview, she is interested in manipulating "a gradual change of pitches over a slow period of time," combined with different speeds. She uses tape eclectically; for example, in a piece for two pianos she uses a tape that includes mandolin, guitar, marimba, and vibraphone. Kolb also tells us that she is "very much influenced by jazz"--which appears to be a constant factor in a great deal of contemporary American composition, as these interviews reveal again and again. In stating that Soundings is one of her works that she likes best, she attributes this to "the influence of jazz."

Charles Wuorinen (born 1938) got involved with electronic music when he was a student at Columbia University studying with Otto

Luening and Vladimir Ussachevsky, two pioneers in that field. But, as he indicates in the interview, he soon lost interest in that medium because he felt it was too limited and static. He is very much involved with the performance of "live" music and rejoices in "the amazing appearance of so many really expert young players" who have come to the fore. He believes that we are "living in one of the greatest ages of performance, if not the most distinguished that has yet appeared for Western music."

A prolific composer, Wuorinen tells us that as of 1975 he had written 110 works! Four of these, including Time's Encomium (1969), used the electronic medium. He seldom repeats himself, but is continually seeking (and achieving) new configurations and syntheses. He acknowledges the creative influence of Schoenberg and Stravinsky, especially the latter. But he sees no dichotomy between the twelve-tone system and the traditional tonal system. He believes that it is "an old-fashioned, Romantic notion" for composers to regard themselves as "path-breakers who move into an ever-expanding frontier," and that they should instead regard themselves as "inheritors of an unbroken, whole, and wholesome artistic tradition in which we simply continue." This is a noble vision, and there are many composers who do regard themselves as continuators of the "Great Tradition." But there are perhaps many more who believe that in a new Era of Technology, when even children play with computers, and audio-visual, multi-media devices become household objects, there can be no valid turning back to the past. Transformation and invention replace tradition and continuity. Some composers, like Wuorinen, will try to bridge the gap; others may be attuned to the sounds of Outer Space.

Steve Reich (born 1936) doesn't like "the way electronic music sounds," so he has sought ways and means to produce and communicate other kinds of music. In 1970 he predicted, "The pulse and the concept of a clear tonal center will re-emerge as basic sources of new music." He felt at the time that the "dominance of a non-rhythmic atonality" as represented by the twelve-tone system had run its course and already belonged to the past. He believed, "To ape another culture of another time has to have a certain sterility as a result." This he regarded as retrogressive because it ignored the vital sounds, such as jazz and rock-'n'-roll, "that surrounded America from 1950 through 1980." This is a key statement, to which we will return later.

Unlike some composers who had to tread a labyrinth before finding their true path, Reich found his directions early on: at the age of fourteen, when he first heard the music of Bach and Stravinsky--and of Charlie Parker and Miles Davis, playing bebop. As he tells us: "That nexus of tastes--Baroque music, Stravinsky, and jazz--stayed with me ever since." Reich has drawn on other sources, such as music of Africa and the Far East, but these are not the "deep structures" of his work. He considers himself as being "obviously a Western composer." At the same time, he cherishes his Jewish heritage and in recent years has turned to settings of Hebraic texts.

Most of Reich's music, beginning in 1966, has been presented to the public by his own ensemble, varying from twelve to eighteen performers. His music has a great appeal for young people, perhaps because (as he said) "My music has a beat, and perhaps you can even dance to it."

Philip Glass (born 1937), like Reich, has worked with his own ensemble in a drastically innovative context. But before he got into that there were long years of study and teaching in the academic mill. On the plus side, he acknowledges the benefits of his study with Boulanger and Milhaud: From the former he learned techniques and from the latter the "tricks of the trade." The turning point came in 1966, when he took lessons on the sitar with Ravi Shankar and on the Tabla with Alla Rakha. This opened up a new (and very old!) concept of rhythm, based on working with small units continually regrouped in predetermined patterns. He then took the crucial step of establishing his own performing group for presenting his new compositions, beginning with Music with Changing Parts (1970) and Music in Twelve Parts (1974), the latter lasting from four to six hours! The "repetitive structures" and "static dynamic level," all devoid of thematic content, drew more "rotten eggs" than applause--at least in some circles. Because they aimed to eliminate "memory and anticipation"--the heart and core of musical appreciation in the classical tradition--these compositions were regarded as radically subversive.

Nevertheless, Glass persisted and eventually established a large following both in America and abroad. He also became the business manager of all his enterprises, including the publication of his music and the performances of his operas. The latter proved to be especially rewarding both creatively and financially. His most famous opera, Einstein on the Beach (with Robert Wilson), was performed with sensational success at the Metropolitan Opera in New York (December 1976).

I find it interesting to note that several of the composers interviewed referred to jazz as a significant factor in their creative development. While it is true that they are only a minority, what makes their references to jazz important is that the composers in question represent such a wide diversity of theoretical views and compositional processes. From Copland to Reich, jazz proves to be a persistent factor in American musical composition of the twentieth century.

photo: Gene Bagnato

Robert Ashley was born on March 28, 1930, in Ann
Arbor, Michigan. He is a graduate of the University
of Michigan and the Manhattan School of Music. His
composition teachers included Ross Lee Finney, Roberto Gerhard, and Leslie Bassett. Ashley is currently the head of the Center for Contemporary Music
at Mills College in Oakland, California. He has one
son by his first marriage. In 1979, he married Mimi
Johnson, who has participated in the performance of
many of his pieces.
In 1961, Ashley co-founded the legendary ONCE
Group. With the ONCE Group he began his unique,
ground-breaking achievements as both a composer and
a performing artist of theatrical music, vocal music,
and the live performance of electronic music. With
the possible exception of John Cage, no composer has
challenged the definitions of music as radically as
Robert Ashley. Equally impressive is his success in
persuading audiences of the validity of his redefinitions.
The authors interviewed Robert Ashley in his Manhattan apartment on July 7, 1980. Speaking with him
was as fascinating and absorbing as the experience of
hearing him perform his works. Being aware of the
important work he had done in interviewing composers,
both in print and on videotape, it came as a pleasant
surprise to the authors that he responded to their work
with respect and enthusiasm.

Q: In an interview in 1967, you said that your music teachers had
impeded you and even lied to you. Do you still think that is an accurate evaluation of your formal musical studies?

ASHLEY: Sounds like I was exaggerating, as usual. But I must
have been talking about what they had to teach with, what the idea
of music was. I don't think it was an inadequacy of anybody as a
person or as a teacher.

There was definitely not very much music in my childhood.
I had the experience of growing up in the Midwest--a sort of out-
post, away from a culture that had much music in it. I think your
culture has to reach a certain point in recognizing itself before you
can stop imitating another thing, before you can stop trying to im-
prove yourself according to some other standards. In the way I
grew up I don't think there was very much respect for contemporary
music or for the idea that you could be a living composer. It seems
like that respect and that idea are really spreading fast now.
There's been a lot of improvement in my lifetime.

I can't remember the situation of that interview, but when I was taught music, it was the idea of imitating some very exotic tradition, something that had nothing to do with my reality. The tradition happened to be European, but it could have been anything else. It didn't have anything to do with my everyday reality with music. Even in college, the highest level where you continue to be a student (formally), you still can run into that idea--that you're supposed to be imitating something else.

Q: You found this idea even in your composition classes?

ASHLEY: I didn't really take composition classes. As an undergraduate I didn't study composition at all, excepting just one semester, casually. I wasn't a "composition major," as they say. When I was in school, I was trying to be a piano player. It wasn't until I finished studying concert piano playing that I realized that that music wasn't interesting to me, that it didn't have any reality for me. Then I had to start inventing my own idea about music; and it was at the time of that breach that I went back to Ann Arbor with the intention of studying composition. It wasn't until I got there and saw what was required for a university degree that I realized that I had made a mistake. I worked for a couple of years with Leslie Bassett and Ross Lee Finney, but I don't think I made much improvement by their standards. Roberto Gerhard was there for one year and was most encouraging to me personally. I ended up giving a lot of my attention to psychoacoustics and speech research.

Q: Do you regard your participation in the ONCE Group as your real musical education, at least as far as composition is concerned?

ASHLEY: Oh, yes, definitely. I was very lucky to meet, at the right time in my life, people who were very encouraging to me. I just happened to meet a bunch of people who were independently doing very encouraging work, even before it formally became the ONCE Group. For instance, I met Gordon Mumma through a sculptor named Milton Cohen, who was doing very amazing work with light sculpture; it was through his idea--and this was in 1956--of having live electronic music with light sculpture that he introduced me to Gordon. To be able to work with Milton was a very inspirational thing for me. He was already working with a designer named Harold Borkin, and meeting Harold was also very important. It was a combination of the people working with Milton and the people who were working with Mary Ashley in her performance art and three other composers I met in Ann Arbor--Roger Reynolds, George Cacioppo, and Donald Scavarda--who started the ONCE Festival. And out of the ONCE Festival the legendary ONCE Group was born.

Q: Did you formally organize yourselves into the ONCE Group in order to give performances of the music each of you was writing?

ASHLEY: The idea of being able to have music played was involved with the idea of playing your own music. The only people I've ever been interested in, the only people I've ever been affected or influenced by, are people who make their own music. The idea that you can just sit down and make music is very different from accepting certain performing institutions (orchestras, string quartets) and other institutions (publishers) that are intermediaries for your ideas: You write a piece of music and then you give it to somebody and they give it to somebody else and finally it gets played. This idea had no interest for me whatsoever; it still doesn't. It's not based on any political point of view; I'm just personally not interested in music for those older institutions. It never sounds like music to me.

Q: Have you used this approach as a teacher at Mills College?

ASHLEY: Mills is an extremely famous place for new music, and justifiably so. It just happens to be one of those places where there seems to be some sort of extraterrestrial force operating. There's always been new music there: John Cage, Harry Partch, Henry Cowell--all worked at Mills. And then they were followed in turn by Milhaud, who was there until I arrived. But when I arrived there, Mills was still operating on the idea of the intermediary system: People would write scores, show them to Milhaud, and he would arrange to have them played. He must have been a pioneer in encouraging people like Brubeck, and encouraging others to play with electronic music, because it meant a direct participation. But still it was only a concert or two in the fall and one or two in the spring; the programs would be something like Stravinsky, Milhaud, Somebody, and then maybe a graduate student. So the only change I've made is the idea that you're supposed to perform music all the time; basically, the main thing that composition students do at Mills College now is to make music that they perform for an audience. That's the only responsibility a student there now has; there's no intermediary system working there anymore.

Mills is an extraordinary place in that respect, and I believe that's why it's famous recently for so many active and successful young composers who have studied there. For its size (or maybe because of its size), the role of Mills in the history of American contemporary music is astounding. And I must say, too, that that role was developed almost entirely during the career of Margaret Lyon as head of the Music Department. She is an amazing person in her respect for originality and in the courage she had during the many years she was department head. What has developed at Mills is a system where the composer can hear something like hundreds of new pieces every year. I don't think I'm exaggerating again.

When I was a student in New York in the early 1950s--and this is true of everybody my age (it's something that I talked to Phil Glass a lot about in the interview of Music with Roots in the

Aether)--I went to three or four deeply impressive concerts. But they were the only concerts of new music the whole season--I mean literally, literally the only concerts. There was a series at the uptown "Y" that Milton Babbitt produced: Three or four concerts with Bethany Beardslee and Jacques Monod. They were playing Berg and Webern and some of Babbitt's pieces, which I love-- fantastic pieces. Those were immensely important concerts. There were also one or two things that David Tudor did, or there'd be a composer's-forumlike thing. Some concert that would have a Wallingford Riegger piece was an outstanding occasion.

Now, as you know, there are fourteen thousand new music things happening every night of the week. It's a totally new world, a totally different point of view. There's such an abundance of music now that it's hard for me to believe that not very long ago there wasn't very much. I'm proud to have been involved with the beginnings of it. I would give more credit in particular to people like Cage and Tudor: just amazing pioneers in inventing the idea of a personal music. That change is a huge one, it's an amazing change in point of view, and it has taken American music out of its dark ages. I don't think one can exaggerate that at all. It has caused a crossover of popular music and so-called concert music, which is going to change the audience for new music entirely. Younger composers are going to be more and more involved in that audience change, I think. It's just a natural consequence of people making music. It's amazing to think that the people of the United States went for a long period of time when there was a terrible discrepancy between what you imagined musically and what you heard.

Q: Do you think that one of your most important achievements as a composer has been helping to conceive and perpetuate this new tradition?

ASHLEY: Yes. It was inevitable; I'm just happy that I caught on. A lot of people didn't catch on.

Q: How would you describe your development as a composer up through the time of your involvement with the ONCE Group?

ASHLEY: I learned music from listening to jazz. But I realized at a certain moment of my life--when I was in my early twenties-- that music was not as abstract as I had imagined. In order to play jazz, one had to be able to speak the language of the people who play jazz. And that meant from the start, almost exclusively, that you had to be black. In other words, the stories that were told by jazz music were stories that I didn't grow up with; they weren't my stories. So I stopped trying to play jazz. Then I went through exactly the same experience with European music;

I was introduced to Beethoven when I was eighteen, and I spent about a six-year period in that romance. But then at a certain point I realized that neither was I European--and especially not European from the nineteenth century. That ended that.

I made an electronic music studio with whatever stuff I could get together; in becoming a composer, that was the first thing I decided to do. And I designed my own personal studio in the direction of real-time music (I don't think the word "improvisation" is right), the direction of playing music. There always are two points of view that influence every composer--two directions: one toward more and more premeditation or precontrol, and one toward invoking whatever you think the energies of being spontaneous are. You can see that, it's like the left and right hands. It was very interesting to work with Gordon Mumma because he definitely went toward the other point of view, toward premeditation--and with great success, I would say.

You only know how to deal with your imagination through the techniques that you've acquired. My early pieces that were scored (on paper), my works prior to the larger pieces made specifically for the ONCE Group as a performance ensemble--from the Piano Sonata (1959) through The Wolfman (1964), which was the last piece of that time that I wrote down--basically were all ways of trying to understand so-called jazz techniques, or the techniques that came out of thinking about jazz and spontaneity, and how those techniques could be applied to stories that I understood--my stories. So all those pieces--in particular the Piano Sonata, Maneuvers for Small Hands, the in memoriam set, the Trios, The Wolfman--were about technique; they were research into what I knew about music and research into my ideas. In other words, I was trying to find out what were the formal elements of those ideas and what were the inexpressible elements. I was trying to figure out how to make procedures that would invoke spontaneity.

For musicians and audiences--not just the performers but the listeners, too--there's an attraction toward known materials, because of the idea that in mastering these materials you can, in action, transcend the materials. It's like playing baseball. Once the rules are perfectly clear for all of your actions and all the consequences of all these actions; once everybody totally understands all of the metaphor, then you can get some sort of mastery over the actual technique of the action that you're undertaking, and you enact the moment of being "released" from all your training. (That's a psychological theater that definitely accompanies the performance of music.)

The trade-off against that idea is the idea of the materials having a more symbolic meaning, that they're more personal; and that symbolic meaning is revealed in the uniqueness of the materials. So you have, on the one hand, materials that are so well known they have no meaning whatsoever; the only meaning is in watching those materials being enacted. (For instance, there's a

strong argument for the experience of watching a great pianist play
the C Major scale as fast as he or she can.) On the other hand,
there are materials that have so much symbolic meaning that you
can't even see the performer for the materials. The performer
"disappears." I think this is the ideal we look for in seeking
"spontaneity." I would say that The Wolfman is an example of
this other extreme, the newer, the more personal. Because there's
no tradition for that kind of performance, because the materials
are unfamiliar they so dominate the performance that it's almost
impossible to recognize the performer in the context of those materials. It's my experience when I perform The Wolfman that almost no one distinguishes what I'm doing; it's almost impossible
because they're so involved with the materials themselves. So as
a consequence, listeners almost always misread the actions. Literally, they don't recognize how the sounds are being produced.

When so-and-so plays Mozart, his job is to make his performance sound as much like Mozart as he can. But his job is
equally to dazzle you with his technique. We all know what that
means in every dimension, bad or good--that's the one extreme.
But in concert music now there's almost no body of experience
that includes the present. In other words, the techniques are not
understood (something like The Wolfman is, after all, only fifteen
years old). Because there's so little experience in general with
new ideas, there were unbelievably bad performances of The Wolfman by other people--just unbelievably bad. And I never could
figure out why, since it's so simple. I've figured out only recently that it's because The Wolfman represents that other dimension
of music where the materials are everything. I could never understand that. I still barely understand it; it's very mysterious to me.
But I think there is definitely a trade-off between the newsworthi-
ness of musical materials--how recent they are, how contemporary
they are, how original they are--and the ability of those materials
to be understood in performances.

With the ONCE Group, I found that I could make pieces without going through an intermediary, or at least without going through
an intermediary of notation. I could make music that didn't have
to be formalized, and so the agreements that I made with people
about performance could be much more casual. In other words,
there could be a greater expression of fluency on the part of the
performer, and as a consequence, much more input into my imagination. I didn't have to finalize any idea before I expressed it,
and this left a huge latitude for interpretation in the performance
sense. That latitude was naturally of benefit to me--a great benefit. It was like jazz but without any of the connotations of the black
experience or whatever. Totally without any of those connotations,
but still in that realm of a more spontaneous version of music.
That became more interesting to me, more profoundly interesting,
than any possibility for a third party doing my music.

Q: In light of your work in this more spontaneous form of music,

was it difficult for you to go back and complete your Piano Sonata
in 1979? Did it seem too removed from everything that you now
wanted to uncover in music?

ASHLEY: The technique of the Piano Sonata is a perfect example
of the problems that composers talk about when they talk about notation. The technique of the Piano Sonata cannot be represented
gracefully in conventional notation; conventional notation doesn't accommodate that particular idea because it's a jazz idea. Since the
gestures are all jazz gestures, there's no reason why a notation
that's based on another kind of music should accommodate them.
It was about four years from the time when I actually made up the
piece and started playing it (from notation that no one else could
read), and the time that I actually notated it (after talking about it
with a lot of different piano players, and having a lot of people help
me with the notation). It took me about four years to notate the
first unit, the first part of the piece. And by that time I had even
stopped playing the piece myself, and I just didn't want to think
about the notation of the other two units. (I had originally intended
for there to be three units to the piece.) So I never got around to
it. And it was only when "Blue" Gene Tyranny said he wanted to
record it that I realized that I had to sit down and actually write
the thing out. But there was no problem in writing out the second
and third units because those problems had been worked out in the
first unit.

I told "Blue" Gene the image of the piece (which is subtitled: "Christopher Columbus Crosses to the New World in The
Nina, The Pinta, and The Santa Maria Using Only Dead Reckoning
and a Crude Astrolabe"), which was the image of the three ships,
the flagship and the two "shadows" of the flagship; the second part
is a shadow of the first part seen in one direction, and the third
part is the shadow of the same first part seen from another direction. The second and third parts are not meant to have any
chronological order; the first part comes first, but you can play
either part two or part three next. So when I was telling "Blue"
about the image of the flagship and the two ships following it, he
got the idea of recording all three at the same time--that was his
idea, to combine parts two and three and play it against part one
again, to see if you could get that image of the "shadows." I
think it's really [done] convincingly there. He plays it just magnif-
icently on the recording--a fantastic performance. But he actually
added the last movement. That was the only way the piece changed
between 1959 and 1979.

Q: In 1968, Larry Austin quoted a letter of yours about a concert
that you and Gordon Mumma had given in Los Angeles. Your comment was: "They'll probably invite you to play there eventually.
When they do, do something outrageous." Did you in fact say that?

ASHLEY: Oh, I always say that. Oh, God--I mean, it's only interesting to do something outrageous. I only hope I haven't lost the touch!

Q: Was that advice peculiar to the L.A. music scene, or is it indicative of a general approach for dealing with audiences?

ASHLEY: Los Angeles has the movies, so music in Los Angeles was always subservient to the movies, at least socially, and you feel that. Performing music there always seemed--still does, as a matter of fact--like you're doing a soundtrack for something. Whenever you perform music in Los Angeles, it's always incidental music, and I can't figure out why. I think it's just in the nature of the way it goes together out there.

Q: Isn't there a problem in having as your main objective simply shocking an audience? That kind of thing tends to date pretty rapidly.

ASHLEY: There's a long tradition for "shocking" audiences, and I don't think that's necessarily bad. I think that you tend to modulate what you do according to some mysterious sense of how you think the piece should make its "appearance," historically. When you start working on something, you're always trying to figure out how the initial appearance works with what happens after. You can weigh the scales totally in one direction, or totally in the other direction: You can choose not to put any "attack" on the piece whatsoever. There are lots of examples of that: people who work totally as recluses, totally concerned with an eventual history of the piece. And you can go to the other extreme and deal with the piece as though it didn't have any duration in history.

Modernism is involved with the idea of the newness of something. There's a long history of how important the initial value of a piece is. In other words, the person who decides to give a piece a very short history is not doing anything unusual; it's part of what we all do, don't you think? If I thought that you were going to hear something I wrote or something I made only once, then that would make it different, I think, than if I thought you were going to hear it two times, or five times, or a hundred times. I think that's the way it works. I think that somehow you choose how many times you expect the audience to hear a particular piece of music. I don't know why you choose it--for personal reasons or whatever. The form of the piece has to do with that decision.

Q: Do you think that that decision is always within your control?

ASHLEY: No. But I think you have a lot of control over it; you don't have all the control over it, but you have a lot of control over it. I think it's within your control as much as your personality is within your control; it's almost exactly the same thing.

Q: How much French should one know in order to fully appreciate Automatic Writing?

ASHLEY: The text is made from English, exactly in the process of automatic writing: The English words were the closest that I could come, after working in it for a long time, to involuntary speech. And so the English has a lot of the characteristics of involuntary speech. The person who translated it, Monsa Norberg, really understood that aspect of it, I think. (I don't know what form involuntary speech takes in French; in English it has a lot to do with syllables.) The French is not involuntary speech; it's just a literal translation of the form of English involuntary speech. So, in effect, you don't have to know any French. You can almost understand it by listening to the English. Or you could get the translation simply from a dictionary. You could literally just look up the words.

I was working with involuntary speech as a sound for a few years, and finally did a recording--a very high-quality recording of my own involuntary speech. But I wanted to remove the quality of "intimacy" from that recording. I wanted it to be heard as "involuntary," rather than just "intimate." Because--just because I did; for whatever reasons I made up in my head, I wanted to place that characteristic of involuntary speech at a certain distance from the listener. After about a year, I had an idea about how to do that with a synthesizer and a digital switching device that Paul De-Marinis had built for me. After working that out, then, I had a tape with two characters on it: the involuntary speech and the synthesizer character--which was, amazingly, involuntary in a complementary fashion, technically: I designed a circuit to do one thing, and when I set it up, it did exactly the opposite. I mean a total antithesis of what I understood the circuit would do. (It's still very mysterious to me; to this day I don't understand why the circuit worked that way, and I know something about what I'm doing.) So when I heard that antithesis, when I heard that quality, it was really a shock; it was like the entry of a second character into a play. I used that tape with the speech and the synthesizer for a piece of video music called Title Withdrawn. Title Withdrawn is one of the video tapes in Music with Roots in the Aether.

Q: Why did you incorporate a French translation of your own involuntary speech into Automatic Writing?

ASHLEY: Music with Roots in the Aether opened in Paris, and for that opening I felt that I should put French on Title Withdrawn. I don't know what made me feel that, since the sound of the English is the important thing, but I felt like I should put French on it. So I asked Monsa Norberg, who speaks eloquent French, simply to make a translation of the involuntary speech. She made the translation from the text I transcribed. In other words, I wrote down what I had said in English, including all the interruptions: just a few words, dot, dot, dot, a few words, dot, dot, dot. She did exactly the same thing in French; in other words, she just translated phrases as best she could, even though, out of context, they didn't take precise translations.

I didn't have time to do the recording of the translation until I got to France. I did the recording in a very small office, sort of the day before the premiere of the piece. And the technical situation was such that when Mimi Johnson was doing the reading of the text, she couldn't hear the English version; I was wearing headphones and I would point to a certain phrase when it came up, and Mimi would read it. Because her inflection was unpremeditated, just because of that situation, it was like a different version of the same quality that I'd been listening for in the original tape. It was totally accidental, just a technical thing, but it was a wonderful thing to happen.

Then I started thinking about the actual subject that I had discovered in the text of the involuntary speech: The text was all about "fourness." In other words, the subject of Automatic Writing is "fourness"; it's all about the quality of "fourness." So I got fascinated with the idea that there were meant to be four characters in the piece. I had the involuntary speech sound that had been processed; then I had the synthesizer sound, which was involuntary in another way; then, when I heard Mimi's inflection of the French, because of that crude recording situation, it was like a third character had been introduced into the play--they all had the same qualities about them. So I started looking for the fourth character, because that had been predicted by the text. I fooled around, looking for that fourth character for about two years. I mean, I had no idea what the instrument would be. I finally did it on the Polymoog. I worked at that character on the Polymoog for about a month. I had an opportunity to make another record for Lovely Music and I wanted to do Automatic Writing, so I just started working, seeking out that fourth character on the Polymoog. When that character appeared, it appeared with exactly the same unpremeditated quality that the other three had, so I knew then the piece was finished.

Q: Why did you choose not to say any of this in some kind of liner notes with the recording?

ASHLEY: It's pretty hard to say. It's hard enough to write down a grocery list, much less tell an idea.

I was just talking about this with Peter Gordon the other

day. Liner notes go in and out of fashion. Liner notes are coming back in. I totally love wonderful liner notes, but it's so hard to write them. There are bad liner notes; that's why they go out. I'd love to write good liner notes but it's too hard; it takes years and years and years.

Q: What was the origin of Perfect Lives (Private Parts)?

ASHLEY: Perfect Lives (Private Parts) is connected with Automatic Writing, as a matter of fact. I mean, it began within that same period when I was performing Automatic Writing. I performed what became Automatic Writing (on the record) under many different titles, but always performing the piece as a group of simultaneous monologues. Mimi and I did the first performance in France. (I think I called it then Exposure in Little Light; the title always had something to do with the visual part of it.) Then I did it a few times alone, and I did it many times with Gordon and with Alvin and David. Maybe altogether I performed it fifteen or twenty times in front of different audiences in different ways.

So I was working on the idea of involuntary speech in performance, and during that same time, I got involved in a project to do a movie based on music. A friend, Phil Makanna, had said, "We should write a movie," and he was going to try to produce the movie. I was interested in doing some sort of opera, using a recorded medium. I wanted to pick up from where I had been with the ONCE Group with the narrative or operatic style of piece; I hadn't had a chance to do anything like that for about five years-- the time I was working at Mills. But I didn't want to go back to doing stage pieces as such; it didn't have any appeal. I wanted to do an opera in a recorded medium, so I started writing a "treatment" for a screenplay because I thought I could get it produced. I had developed a whole bunch of imaginary characters--but they were more like ways of speaking than like personalities. There were certain phrases that identified the certain characters in my mind. So I had all this stuff that was sort of rattling around in my mind.

Then, when I was working on Music with Roots in the Aether, I was living in New York and didn't have any musical instrument. All the rest of my life, as far as I can remember, I'd always had some sort of musical instrument, but I found myself for months without a musical instrument. So I started doing things with my voice--I'd talk to myself. I started trying out this idea to try to talk about something or write about something for just as long as I could focus on the image, and no longer; that is, never to go back to an idea. So I started doing improvisations of speaking that I associated with these characters. It's very rudimentary stuff. I would just do these as long as I could remember them. You know, I might be able to remember a minute or two minutes; I was just trying to make up some sort of modern talk, riff, or whatever you call it, that I would say to myself. Then I would just type it out. I would never go back and revise that; I'd just type out what I had said.

So I had this sheaf of these short songs--I don't know what else to call them--and then I had a chance to do the first record for Lovely Music. And that was the only thing I had--I wasn't ready to do Automatic Writing, and I didn't have any other materials that I had been working on. So I went to California with this pack of materials and I just pulled out certain groups of these short songs that made up two characters--or what I thought were two characters--and I read them into the tape recorder. I practiced just going through them, end to end, in the same way I had been saying them to myself. (This was after a lot of experimentation: I had tried to get Mimi to read some of them, and I had tried to get other people to read some of them.) I was just fooling around with this idea of short vocal pieces, or speech pieces. I recorded them and then I did a kind of chamber music setting of them. I asked "Blue" Gene to invent with me a special kind of piano playing--what everybody calls "cocktail style." It's not really cocktail style at all; it's a different style of "recorded" piano sound. And he very graciously consented to get involved in that kind of experiment.

The movie project never worked out, but after we did the record I started working on Perfect Lives seriously, and then there were a bunch of coincidences that made the piece possible. In particular, The Kitchen asked me if I would do a piece for television. So I had to figure out some way of being able to transform the materials I had made--all those short songs--into a piece that I could present on television, and I got the idea of working in "templates." The idea is that each of these seven half-hour songs, the episodes of Perfect Lives, is made up of some number of shorter songs. Those short songs govern all of the other aspects of the piece--the character of the playing, the orchestration, the video imagery-- making them a kind of template, in the sense that a template is a "profile" and also a pattern to reproduce parts with a similar form. So the working of the "template" is in the notion of how long something lasts and how complicated it is--how dense it is--and whether the actual song image is within a frame or whether it's unframed, whether it's right to the edge or almost to the edge--all those different qualities that a song can have. And those qualities, that is, the "template" of the piece, are reproduced in all of the separate parts: that is, my singing, "Blue" Gene's playing, Jill and David's responses, the mixing, the video, etc. The way I can describe the piece now to "Blue" Gene or to Peter or to Jill and David or to John or to Carlota or to Mary or to Jackie or to Mimi is in terms of those short songs. (All collaborators on Perfect Lives (Private Parts): Peter Gordon, Jill Kroesen, David Van Tieghem, John Sanborn, Carlota Schoolman, Mary Ashley, Jackie Humbert, Mimi Johnson.)

Q: Should we see the new version of "The Backyard" that will be

released by Lovely Music as a replacement of the old version, or
are there now at least two legitimate versions?

ASHLEY: There are at least two versions. I think there may be
a lot of versions. This is something that I haven't thought out for
myself very well. Because it's an opera, because it has that form
of story telling--not so much story telling as character descrip-
tion--I've been thinking that there are actually different ways of
realizing the "templates." What we're doing now might be only
one version of the piece. I would be interested to see if I could
think of those same songs for, say, computer-generated sounds.

Q: Was the very different vocal quality that you give the reading
of the text in the new version created on the basis of the latitudes
offered by the "templates," or were there other reasons for wanting to say it differently?

ASHLEY: The way I did it the first time began with just the sound
of my voice; it was just my voice and a click track in a little, tiny
room. As I said before, I started working on the idea of the piano
sound with "Blue" Gene after I had recorded the voice tracks. That
was three years ago, too, and I had a totally different idea about
what I wanted the piece to sound like. That was in the summer of
1977. So it was a totally different version of what I thought the
sound of the piece should be. The version that I just finished of
"The Backyard" (that is, the version for the television production)
is done not only in the context of all the other instruments that are
on the twenty-four-track tape, but also in the context of doing the
other six songs of the opera in a recording studio, day after day
after day after day after day. But they both follow the "templates."
There's no way that they would not be governed by the idea of a
"template." I can't think of the piece except as a series of short
songs governed by the "templates." I'm pretty sure that "Blue"
Gene and everybody else thinks of it in the same way. As for the
changes that come out of different performances, I tend to think
of something, a decision I'm making now, not in terms of a goal
that might come much later, but only in terms of what I'm trying
to do at the moment. In other words, it's only my experience of
going through something X number of times that has any meaning,
that gives the first idea any relationship to the last.

I'm positive that the effect of the form of Perfect Lives
(Private Parts) is the accumulation of a bunch of short stories--
by short I mean like a minute or two. I'm positive that's the way
people listen to it. I'm positive because I believe it intuitively,
and also because of what people have told me: They say, "I can
always hear the first two parts, but I can never hear the third
part." I know exactly what they mean. They'll describe exactly
three or four "templates" that they listen to every time, but they
don't listen to the ones in between. Somebody will say, "I've been

listening to your record for a long time now, and I always hear
this part," and they'll describe three or four short songs within
"The Backyard." They don't hear the other ones. And they'll
say, "I tried so hard, but I can't hear the other ones." It's true;
it's like an accumulation of very short stories.

Q: What are some parts that most people remember from "The
Backyard"?

ASHLEY: Well, everybody I know likes "Dear George." For a
while. I've never met a person who didn't like "Dear George." Everybody likes "Giordano Bruno."

Actually, people have told me things they don't like, but I
block those out. I can't remember what they were.

Q: Is it true that the Tibetan Book of the Dead is a basis for
Perfect Lives (Private Parts)?

ASHLEY: Yes, but not the "inspiration"--just the formal model.
Did you ever read the Tibetan Book of the Dead in the Evans-
Wentz edition? There are three or four very elaborate explanations of the Book of the Dead from different cultural points of
view. It's not just from the Book of the Dead but from reading
those other ideas about it that you realize how it's almost an exact replica of a lot of things that we think.

The idea of the Tibetan Book of the Dead, as I understand
it--I'm not an expert--is that when a person dies, according to
that tradition, the person passes through certain stages of trials.
The Book of the Dead is a series of descriptions of the problems
that the spirit will face, warnings meant to be spoken into the ear
of the person who's just died. That idea seems profoundly helpful
to me, and very civilized. We have been taught to believe that
you're gone when they unplug you at the hospital; you're dead.
Whereas evidence all over points to the fact that you die gradually.
Even in Western medicine, now, there is the idea that the last
sense to go is hearing. It's the last one. There are all kinds of
ideas about how long the sense of hearing lasts, but apparently it
lasts a long time. So the idea of the Tibetan Book of the Dead is
that when the person dies, you immediately start talking them
through their next experiences--you're guiding them.

So I thought about the idea of the urgency of the text of
Perfect Lives: urgency in the sense that it allows for only the
most skeletal kinds of repetition for understanding. It not only
doesn't observe the most common rules of musical repetition, but
it even stays in an area that's beyond the conventions of speech.
In other words, in song, in traditional singing, you repeat the same

thing many, many, many, many, times. In conventional speech, you repeat the same thing fewer times, but you're at least repeating until you're assured in some way that either you understand it or the listener understands it.

I got interested in this idea and the idea of transcending the materials in the way we were talking about earlier--transcending them through a display of technique. In the case of Perfect Lives, since the materials are so dense and urgent as speech, that meant displaying technique in materials which would allow for no repetition at all. And I think I got the idea for that from reading--from just thinking about--the Tibetan Book of the Dead. It's a very urgent kind of speech because the time schedule is very tight, so to speak. Also, I think the Book of the Dead is very much about characters.

Perfect Lives is not a parody of the Book of the Dead; I don't mean for the relationship to be frivolous at all, but it does use other aspects of the Book of the Dead in a very simple, almost unquestioning way. I'm referring to the formalistic proportions--the numerology. It seemed to me that if I were using the functional elements as I understand them from that particular book, then I could use some of the formalistic elements at the same time, and sort of invoke their magic. So I decided that I would use the numerology of the Book of the Dead, as best I understood it, in my work. If there's any relationship between that numerology and that form, then I should be obliged to try out that relationship. If as long as humans have been alive there have been certain numerological proportions involved in that kind of singing, then I should investigate them.

Q: It seems that almost all your music has emphasized performance as a social function, specifically in terms of the tensions between individual freedom and responsibility to the group. Does a large work like Perfect Lives (Private Parts), on which you've spent several years, seem to you a significant success in resolving that tension?

ASHLEY: Oh, no. It's a different version of the same tension. It's just a different version of the same piece.

The idea of Perfect Lives--the dramatic idea, the narrative idea--is that the performers are describing characters who are represented by the performers. The characters do not interact, so the performers can develop the "templates" independently of one another. In other words, it's not a matter of the singer and an accompaniment to the singer, or, conversely, the idea of integrating the voice into the orchestra--neither of those ideas is of interest to me at all. The idea that voices should be like instruments, or the idea that there should be accompaniments to voices--those ideas are not interesting to me. The idea of "private parts" is that, for instance, the character of "Buddy"--that is, the "part"

of the solo piano player--is a reflection of the "templates,"
totally independent of the other characters or "parts" that appear
in the piece. Those parts are all invented privately; they're totally independent of each other. This is a technique or approach
that I associate with jazz.

    The idea in jazz, for instance, that if you put together an
orchestra it's a group of characters, is a really powerful idea.
Some jazz ensembles are almost "operas" in the sense of the development of the various characters in the group. It's totally different from the idea that the composer invents characters and then
"characterizes" them; for instance, to say, "Well, this imaginary
character can be defined by: She always wears short skirts, she
always acts silly, she always sings in a high range, etc." That's
a traditional technique in opera--like the way Wozzeck is made.
In Perfect Lives I pick somebody to play a character and let them
develop that character themselves. I'm much more interested in
the possibilities in this idea. It's not a totally original idea, but
it's definitely a departure from traditional ways of opera. Any version of Perfect Lives only looks like the four people who are onstage. Everybody's totally individualistic to the point of being private.

Q: What are you working on now, besides the videotaping of Perfect Lives?

ASHLEY: I would like to make pieces for television. I'm interested in the idea of opera on television, or music on television. I
don't know whether I can make it work; I think I can make it work.

    When you say what you're working on, it always sounds so
silly, but what I'm thinking about now is how to talk about the idea
of "The Law." I'm really interested in the idea of The Law. I
would like to make a piece about The Law and how people understand what The Law is. I'm trying to figure out some way to realize that piece. I'm thinking about making a long song about The
Law and what the tone of voice or tone of attention is when you
think about The Law. In Perfect Lives, I've been trying to make
seven different tones of voices that will be quite distinctive charac-
ters--you know, in the way that you describe a tone of voice as
being "ironical" or "affectionate" or whatever, without any particu-
lars in mind. It seems like there are so many tones of voice that
one can have.

Q: Is the new version of "The Backyard" based on this idea of
adapting a specific tone?

ASHLEY: Yes. I think it's going to be different in the television
version too. I think there are going to be many different versions.

It's so interesting to me. I don't understand it at all. I totally do
not understand it. The idea that people could get a totally different
feeling from exactly the same materials, as far as I'm concerned,
is what I've been aiming at my whole life.

CATALOG OF COMPOSITIONS

1957	Film Music for The Image in Time	Visibility
1959; 79	Piano Sonata (Christopher Columbus Crosses to the New World in the Nina, the Pinta, and the Santa Maria Using Only Dead Reckoning and a Crude Astrolabe)	Visibility
1960	Film Music for The Bottleman	Visibility
1960	The 4th of July for tape	Visibility
1961	Something for Clarinet, Pianos, and Tape	Visibility
1961	Maneuvers for Small Hands for piano	Visibility
1961	Public Opinion Descends Upon the Demonstrators electronic music theater	Visibility
1962	Details for two pianists	Visibility
1962	Detroit Divided for four-channel tape	Visibility
1962	Complete with Heat for orchestra instruments and tape	Visibility
1962	Fives for string quintet, two pianos, and percussion	Visibility
1963	Trios (White on White) for various instruments	Visibility
1963	in memoriam ... Esteban Gomez (quartet) for four players	Visibility
1963	in memoriam ... John Smith (concerto) for three players and assistants	Visibility
1963	in memoriam ... Crazy Horse (symphony) for twenty or more wind or string or other sustaining instruments	Visibility
1963	in memoriam ... Kit Carson (opera) for eight-part ensemble	Visibility
1963	Boxing sound-producing dance	Visibility
1964	The Wolfman Tape	Visibility
1964	Film Music for Jenny and the Poet	Visibility
1964	The Wolfman for amplified voice and tape	Visibility
1964	Kittyhawk (An Antigravity Piece)	Visibility
1964	Combination Wedding and Funeral electronic music theater	Visibility
1964	Interludes for the Space Theater sound-producing dance	Visibility
1964	The Lecture Series electronic music theater (Co-composer: Mary Ashley)	Visibility
1965; 78	Waiting Room (Quartet) for any number of wind or string instruments	Visibility
1965	Film Music for My May	Visibility
1965	Orange Dessert electronic music theater	Visibility

1965	Untitled Mixes (Co-composers: The Bob James Trio)	Visibility
1965	The Entrance for organ	Visibility
1965	Unmarked Interchange electronic music theater (Co-composers: The ONCE Group)	Visibility
1966	Night Train electronic music theater (Co-composer: Mary Ashley)	Visibility
1967	Frogs for voices and tape	Visibility
1967	She Was a Visitor (from That Morning Thing) for speaker and chorus	Visibility
1967	That Morning Thing opera for five principal voices, eight dancers, women's chorus, and tapes	Visibility
1968	The Trial of Anne Opie Wehrer and Unknown Accomplices for Crimes Against Humanity electronic music theater	Visibility
1968	Film Music for Overdrive	Visibility
1968	Purposeful Lady Slow Afternoon (from The Wolfman Motorcity Revue) electronic music theater	Visibility
1968	The Wolfman Motorcity Revue electronic music theater	Visibility
1969	Film Music for Portraits, Self-portraits, and Still Lifes	Visibility
1970	Morton Feldman Says sound-producing dance	Visibility
1970	Illusion Models hypothetical computer tasks	Visibility
1970	Film Music for Battery Davis	Visibility
1970	Fancy Free, or It's There for male speaker and four cassette-recorder operators	Visibility
1972	String Quartet Describing the Motions of Large Real Bodies for string quartet with electronics	Visibility
1972	In Sara, Mencken, Christ, and Beethoven There Were Men and Women for voice and electronics	Visibility
1973	Revised, Finally, for Gordon Mumma for pairs of bell-like instruments	Visibility
1974	How Can I Tell the Difference for violin (or viola), electronics, and tape	Visibility
1975	*[Over the Telephone] remote/live audio installations	Visibility
1975	The Great Northern Automobile Presence lighting accompaniment for other people's music	Visibility
1975	*[Night Sport] simultaneous monologues	Visibility
1976	What She Thinks (from Music with Roots in the Aether music theater on video tape	Visibility
1976	Music with Roots in the Aether video portraits of composers and their music--seven two-hour programs for television	Visibility

---

*The various performances of this piece were named according to the place of the performance and the production techniques.

1976	<u>Title Withdrawn</u> music theater on video tape	Visibility
1978	<u>Ideas from The Church</u> for magnetic tape	Visibility
1978	<u>Interiors Without Flash</u> for magnetic tape	Visibility
1979	<u>Automatic Writing</u>	Visibility
1980	<u>Perfect Lives (Private Parts)</u> opera in seven thirty-minute episodes for television	Visibility

photo: Gene Bagnato

Milton Babbitt was born on May 10, 1916, in Philadelphia, Pennsylvania. He received his B.A. from New York University and his M.F.A. from Princeton. Babbitt studied composition with Marion Bauer and Roger Sessions. He is currently on the music faculties of both Juilliard and Princeton. In 1939, Babbitt married Sylvia Miller. They have one daughter.

For more than three decades, Babbitt has been working at the forefront of the twentieth century's two major musical innovations: serialism and electronic music. He has been a co-director of the Columbia-Princeton Electronic Music Center since its establishment in 1959, as well as a consultant in the creation of the Mark II RCA Synthesizer. With this machine, Babbitt has composed several landmark works, some totally electronic and others for combination with live performers. Babbitt's work in the purely instrumental realm reflects the rhythmic and temporal concerns of his electronic music. In his extension of serial procedures from pitch to time, Babbitt has written a body of work unprecedented in its complexity--a virtuosity of composition, which can be successfully realized only by a virtuosity of performance.

Milton Babbitt was interviewed on August 24, 1975, at the Columbia-Princeton Electronic Music Center in Manhattan. The range of Babbitt's interests and expertise seems without limit, and so any conversation with him can only be uniquely fascinating and rewarding. However, when this quality is coupled with his genuine warmth and interest in others, then time spent with Milton Babbitt becomes something very special.

Q: We'd like to start by discussing your article, "Who Cares If You Listen?"

BABBITT: I'd be delighted to start there, because almost inevitably, people who have had very little opportunity or desire to hear, see, or think about my music have, at least, heard of this bloody article. That is not my title, and that's a perfect example of certain aspects of the content of the article itself.

I gave a lecture at Tanglewood in 1957 about the state of the contemporary composer. The then-editor of High Fidelity heard it and asked me to write it down. I had been improvising it and didn't want to write it down, but they had a copy of the tape, and asked me if I would take it and put it in some kind of publishable shape. The title of the article as submitted to <u>High Fidelity</u> was "The Composer as Specialist." There was no imputation whatsoever of "who cares if you listen," which as far as I am concerned conveys very little of the letter of the article, and nothing of the spirit. Obviously the point was that I cared a great deal who listened, but above all how they listened. I was concerned about the fact that people were not listening. But theirs of course, was a much more provocative title, and journalists are concerned to provoke, and do.

I'm very distressed by this, because inevitably the article is what I'm known by, and I don't really care to be known at all if I have to be known by that. The piece was reprinted twice in anthologies, and I asked in both cases that my original title be restored, along with some of the sentences. Some of the sentences had been changed in <u>High Fidelity</u>, not because of my alleged obscurity, but because at the last moment some new advertisements came in, so they just cut a few phrases and sentences to make room. That is the story of "Who Cares If You Listen?" my most celebrated achievement.

Now, of course, I don't mean to disavow the article--not all of it--by any means. Some of it is unintelligible because of the cuts, but I am not apologizing for or disclaiming the article; I am deeply concerned about the title and what it signifies, because most people don't go beyond the title.

Q: Could you tell us precisely what it was that you had in mind then, and how you feel about those ideas today?

BABBITT: It wasn't "who cares if you listen." It was this: If you're not going to take our activities in as serious and dignified a manner as we take them, then of course we don't want you to listen. I don't offer my music for the approval or disapproval of those who have no serious concern to find out what we do in our music, or why we're doing it. It is certainly not music for the unlettered, nor is anything most of my colleagues do for the unlettered. If you want to find out what we're doing and how we're doing it, we'd be only too happy to tell you about it. That article was a very simple, brief introductory attempt to do so.

There was a time when we thought that perhaps we could gain some kind of appropriate position among intellectuals in other fields by appealing not to their capacity to hear the soundness of our music -they have little musical background--but by the sense of our words. Of course, it turned out that our words went as unheeded as our music went unheard. If anything seems to offend people more than taking music seriously, it's taking talking about music seriously. The result was that people whom we thought would at least recognize that we were trying to be responsible and informative were irritated by our insistence that any music was to be taken seriously. Most of my colleagues in other fields regard music as something that is obliged to provide them with some sort of surcease from the demands of their really important pursuits.

It's not my paranoia. I have two kinds of colleagues: professional colleagues in a place like Juilliard, and academic colleagues in a place like Princeton. If I begin to say the things that my compositional colleagues are obliged to discuss we sound either patronizing or paranoid. We're neither; we're simply discussing what are our immediate professional concerns. "Who cares if you listen" appears to convey the notion that it makes absolutely no difference to us. It makes all the difference in our world. The reason I have so little time to compose is because not many people can or do listen.

Q: A lack of time in the sense that if people listened you could support yourself by your music and wouldn't have to spend your time teaching?

BABBITT: Exactly. But not just teaching, none of us really minds teaching. On the contrary, we're stimulated by students. But we're stimulated by certain kinds of students, at a certain level. We're not stimulated by being on committees, or the other nasty work that occupies about three quarters of our time. Young American composers have been for many years, and still are, the most responsible, the most able, the best-informed young composers in the world. Of course one is stimulated by contact with them--and I'm sure nobody knows more stimulating young composers than I do. But the fact of the matter is that that's not what teaching usually consists of, and that's not what much of the academic racket consists of.

I'm not baiting the academic. Some composers say, "Well, look, I'm a composer, and I don't really belong in a university." Then you ask, "What are you doing here?" and they respond, "I have to be here in order to eat." I can't imagine a more pertinent sense of belonging than the fact that it makes it possible for you to survive and do the little composing you can do. Just because things could be better doesn't mean they couldn't be worse. And they have been worse. Back in the thirties they were worse; there were very few academic jobs and therefore very few composers.

Q: In the article, you compared the development of music to the development of physics, saying that the layman couldn't be expected to understand or appreciate what an informed professional would hear.

BABBITT: That's not unreasonable. By the way, the comparisons with physics also have been misunderstood; I wasn't comparing the fields, the content of the fields, but rather the states of the fields. There was a time, for example, when the educated man read what was called philosophy, the serious philosophy of his time. Do you know anybody who reads serious philosophy these days? Their notion of serious philosophy may be Eric Hoffer, or Mortimer Adler, or Ayn Rand, or no one. Do these people read Quine or Montague, or even Bertrand Russell or Austin? No. So from that point of view there is a suitable comparison, not between the contents, but the states of the field.

Consider what musical education consists of. I see people who come from the Midwest, which I think educationally is probably the bottom of this nation--on the basis of the evidence I see (California is in other ways quite close). The South is not as good as it was in my time, because at least we got a good, old-fashioned, classical education. The truth of the matter is that we receive musical illiterates into our universities. When I say "musical illiterates," I'm not being contentious; I'm just describing a state of relation to music: the inability to read, hear, or remember music.

How, then, can they come in and hear music which is founded on a whole complexly evolved tradition of music, without any preparation? I don't mean only or even primarily formal preparation, but informal conditioning, the preparation of having lived with this music and listened to this music as a primary activity. Not as something which, if you listen to it at all, you listen to only while you're doing something else more demanding. This is not the way we composers think of music. When we're writing music, we're not thinking about something else. We're not writing easily grasped and forgotten entertainment music, of course not. I've written entertainment music--apparently not many people found it entertaining, but it was supposed to be entertainment music!

Obviously, they can't expect to be interested in my music when they know so little of the music on which it's founded. I don't care what one thinks these days of Ulysses or Finnegans Wake, but the enjoyment derived therefrom cannot be derived by someone who doesn't know other literature and languages. I'm not making comparisons just with Joyce, I'm making comparisons with works that have had great intellectual success (or at least succès d'estime).

It was simply a question of who is listening to this music, and why they make presumptions about it and us. In other words, I could be very nasty and say, "Why should we stoop to conquer the masses; why shouldn't the masses aspire to comprehend the condition of our music?" (That's terribly oversimplified.) There was that presumption that those dangling imperatives and detached normatives could be asserted by music audiences and so-called music "critics" as perfectly reasonable evaluations of serious composers' activities.

I think there was a misconception about the whole situation, that we were saying, "Look, our music is just like all the great music of the past; it has no particular problems." But it does; music changed. It changed significantly and demonstrably some seventy years ago (that's one obvious date). Music changed in a very decisive way, and in ways that created difficulties not only for the listener, but for the performer and above all the composer. It's a different relationship to the whole tradition of music from the one a composer had in 1850. It's ridiculous to pretend, "Oh well, this is just a temporary aberration, you're dramatizing your position, and in a hundred years you'll see that it was all really the same." We've lived half a hundred years already, and it has not been the same. Schoenberg hasn't become part of the repertoire. If one dares to say, "Well, that's Schoenberg's fault," how is it Schoenberg's fault? I can demonstrate what I find valuable in his music, and I defy you to demonstrate what you find valuable in the audiences that still don't listen.

Q: The basic purpose of this interview is to give you a chance to help people understand your music.

BABBITT: There are enormous hazards in a composer attempting to invoke words in explication of his music. Obviously, the words themselves, if they're going to have any genuine correlation with the unfamiliar musical event, are going to be very unfamiliar. I'm going to have to depend on concepts that derive from musical and analytical processes that will be at least as unfamiliar as my music.

The things that I could say about my music are likely to be overladen with misunderstandings. For example, I could say that all of my music is twelve-tone. What does that possibly mean? It possibly means that someone will connect it with all of the misunderstandings and all of the bad books on the subject. "Twelve pitches where you can't repeat one until all have been stated" or "whatever goes up may go sideways," and a heap of other such imperatives and permissives, which if they were the conditions for music to be characterized as twelve-tone music, then a twelve-tone work would not be discoverable anywhere in the world of serious music.

On the other hand, I don't wish it to be presumed that the question of "twelve-tone" is an irrelevant one. Very often, the attitude seems to be that to inform the audience that the piece is "twelve-tone" is downright anti-social and undemocratic. To be sure, the listener doesn't have to be aware that it is twelve-tone, but those fundamental relationships which are available within any twelve-tone piece are going to provide the basic musical relations. If he construes this piece in a different way, fine, let me hear how he does it, but don't let me hear him say that the music doesn't make any or much sense, and then have him explain with respect to a completely inappropriate language frame.

It's the difference between hearing a triad and hearing that it is a triad. I imagine that many people who listen to the Eroica Symphony do not realize that what they hear in the beginning is what we normally come to call a "major triad." But what they are hearing is still a "major triad." The man on the street is not aware of the problems of grammaticality, and how difficult it is to speak of grammaticality, but he speaks and understands grammatical English. So the question of internalized twelve-tone properties is very important. But how could he hear these relationships in any satisfactory way if he's heard perhaps one twelve-tone piece, and no late Beethoven String Quartet?

It's a critical problem, and I don't mean to minimize it. My problem is not, as I see it, my saying to somebody, "Look, you don't know this music, therefore don't listen." On the contrary, mine is: "Listen, but don't worry about whether or not the music sounds coherent to you the first time you hear it. What about the first time you hear a sentence in Hungarian--assuming that you're interested in listening to and learning Hungarian." The music is in a different language in a reasonably metaphorical sense.

Q: One of the things that tends to frighten a lot of people is electronic music.

BABBITT: It frightens people because there is where the misunderstandings and misapprehensions are perhaps the greatest. The moment somebody utters "electronic music," I am terrified to suspect that they're thinking in terms of a music, a kind of music, a style or idiom, a mode of composing, all of which, of course, have nothing to do with the case; electronic music can be the most banal "pop" or the most intricately sophisticated. It's all made with the same medium, the most tolerant and admittant of media.

Suppose someone were to say to you, "Do you like orchestral music?" It would be perfectly reasonable to say, "Do you mean Tchaikovsky, or Morton Gould, or Kostelanetz arrangements, or Schoenberg?" You name it. By the same token, you have even more of a right and need to qualify with electronic music because the very vastness, the very flexibility of the medium imposes least on the composer by way of style or idiom--whatever those vague terms might signify. So therefore, when we talk about electronic music, we're talking only about a medium. But a medium in which the composer's decisions are confided to a machine which happens to produce sound in terms of tubes, transistors--electronic modes from which the music must issue from a loudspeaker, rather than from an instrument which produces sounds by being plucked or struck or bowed.

Q: What would you say was the value of electronic music for you as a composer?

BABBITT: That I can answer much more easily, because the possibilities of the medium represent very different things for very differently inclined and disposed composers. To begin at my beginning, I was involved in this activity back in the late thirties, at the time of the hand-written soundtrack. In my case, I was interrupted by the war. In the cases in Europe, it was interrupted by even more catastrophic events.

Those composers who were first attracted to the medium were so because of deep-seated musical needs. Those musical needs were usually associated with composers who were "serial" composers. The reason for that was a very simple one. In twelve-tone music, what one was dealing with was an interpretation of an ordering of pitch classes, which is often interpreted compositionally as an ordering in time. Schoenberg at one point talked of how his musical pitch notions were supplanting those structural functions of tonal music. Someone asked him about the rhythmic aspect, and he said, "We don't need a new rhythmic system because we never have had a rhythmic system." This may seem a naive and distressing statement, but you can see what it signifies. There's no conservatory or college in the Western world that doesn't offer alleged courses in harmony and counterpoint, but analytically, not very much [is offered] on rhythmic structure. Somehow, there's the idea that we don't know or have to know very much about rhythm. We don't really understand very much about how you get from this place to that place rhythmically in a Mozart symphony. We think we understand something about how you get from this harmonic area to that one, but not why he doesn't juxtapose this "rhythm" with that, or what the stages are in going from one rhythmic state to the next.

So when we were suddenly confronted by the mysteries of the temporal dimension, and recognized that this dimension was, next to the pitch dimension, the most susceptible to musical structuring, we began to realize two things. First of all, that the performer's relationship to the temporal aspect was very different from his relationship to the pitch aspect. Any untutored idiot can strike an "A" on the piano, and--in some sense--that can be extended to the most accurate and able performance. After all, you simply learn to put your fingers at a certain place at a certain time. But the temporal aspect has to be realized by the performer. He has to remember, he has to recall, he has to judge, to measure. There's no little key he can press and say, "This will last an eighth of a second." Performers were and are much less equipped rhythmically than in other regards. When you extend that inadequacy to ensemble rhythm, that's where the crucial problems are always the greatest in performances of contemporary music. So it was in the temporal domain, above all, not only conceptually and from the performance point of view, but also in the realization that there was one of the most significant discrepancies between what you could discriminate aurally and that which could be controlled precisely by the performer.

When we speak of the new resources of electronic music,

people think we're talking about the timbral resources. I'm talking about the temporal resources, but I'm not speaking about unrealistic electronic speeds or differentiations. Electronic speeds are far faster than the ear's capacity to assimilate; electronic instruments are capable of differentiations which far exceed the ear's discriminative capacities. Those don't interest us as such--though we have to know them. But there is an enormous area between what a pianist can provide temporally for the listener and what these electronic "instruments" can provide.

The synthesizer permits me to hear what I'm doing as I do it, and that's terribly important, because we have so little notion of what we can and do hear, as human beings and as trained human beings. Here is a good place to stop for that question, "But what about the human element?" If the questioner is ignorant, this question is most interesting. If the questioner is hostile, it's most offensive. The answer is that never before has a music been so completely dependent upon human capacities, because those uninformed machines can do that and only that which a composer specifies in every precise detail. Never before did one's ideas have to be notated so precisely, clearly, completely, and accurately; it was neither necessary nor possible in the past. Moreover, since these machines can produce "anything," the only boundaries are the humanly meaningful. What we must know now is, beyond the capacities of the machines, how do we hear? what do we hear? and that asks us questions about all kinds of music, both electronic and non-electronic.

For us, therefore, it was what we could do in the temporal domain, how we could control it, how we could decisively define our ideas. The concern for me was how I could realize certain notions that I was only trying to satisfy in my instrumental music. There's also that wonderful sense of doing everything yourself, of being master of--and therefore responsible for--everything. I hope, by the way, that people realize that we're by no means totally satisfied with the medium yet; it's just begun. A few tired people have been working with it for almost two decades with very little money and very little assistance. If this activity had received the support that computer activity has had lavished upon it, we'd have much better instruments now.

Q: Do you prefer to compose exclusively electronically, or for combinations of tape and live performers?

BABBITT: It really depends on the piece. I've written both, and right now I'm in the process of writing a concerto for violin and a small orchestra of about twenty-two instruments with electronic tape. I must respond to you in the tired fashion, that the trouble with writing electronic pieces is the amount of time it takes.

Last December I finished composing a piece for piano and electronics. I wrote out a score, both for the piano and the electronic synthesis. Then I began synthesizing. A piece for synthesized sound takes at least twice as long to complete as a piece for instruments alone because of the electronic realization. After it is composed, it must be realized. I'm about to write a work for voice and two pianos. The performers wanted tape with it, but I just don't dare. Life is too short. I'm commissioned to write a chamber opera with tape--it was supposed to have been finished about two or three years ago, but I don't know when I'm going to be able to finish it, just because of the time involved.

It takes an enormous amount of time and physical effort. I punch every bloody hole myself, I record myself, I mix myself, I do it all myself. If someone should say, "Why don't you have an engineer?" the answer is twofold. One, who would pay for him? Two, it would take him much too long. An engineer is certain to make mistakes that a musician immediately catches by ear. I do enjoy it all up to a point. I don't enjoy it at all beyond that point.

Q: Could you tell us about your studies with Roger Sessions? What do you feel was most valuable in them?

BABBITT: I went to the Washington Square College at N.Y.U. for a very specific reason. In 1933, Marion Bauer had written a book called Twentieth Century Music. At that particular moment, I was trying to decide where to transfer (from a university which shall remain unmentioned because I consider it an unmentionable university). I wanted to study contemporary music, and Marion Bauer was at Washington Square College. Her book actually had musical examples from Erwartung and Pierrot Lunaire of Schoenberg, and I thought, "Well, this is where I have to be, with anybody who even knows that these pieces exist!"

So I went there to study with Marion Bauer, who was a wonderful woman, in certain respects a very knowing woman and a great help to me. By a marvellous coincidence, there was somebody else there named Martin Bernstein, who was just beginning to teach. He was, I think, a first generation German, with an extraordinary knowledge of the language, and had gotten to know Schoenberg, who had just a few months before landed here in New York with his family. Bernstein persuaded Schoenberg to agree to write a commissioned piece for the N.Y.U. String Orchestra, the Suite for String Orchestra. (As it turned out, the first performance was with Otto Klemperer and the Los Angeles Philharmonic.) Schoenberg also agreed to teach at N.Y.U. for 1934-35. Unfortunately, in the summer of '34 he decided that his bronchitis made it impossible for him to spend another winter here, so he moved to California. But I had gotten to know Schoenberg slightly, and found myself talking to people who had known Schoenberg.

When I graduated from N.Y.U. in '35, the question was, with

whom would I study? Roger Sessions had just returned from Europe, where he had spent the last eight years. His reputation was as a "Stravinskian intellectual." He was regarded as a cerebral composer: "one who knows a great deal about music, but whose music doesn't have heart or poetry," you know all those sorts of things. So I thought that was the man for me. Marion Bauer thought so, too, and she arranged for me to meet with him, and I studied privately with him for three years.

Roger wrote one of the first articles in English, of any significance, on the work of Schenker, and we analyzed Schenker analyses together. I told him I wanted to begin at the beginning again; we did species counterpoint together, we did analysis together. We became great intimates. The result was that three years later I joined him at Princeton. So my whole musical life is very much indebted to Roger.

When I began to study with Roger--and I don't think he'd mind my saying this--he was fundamentally anti-Schoenberg. He liked certain works of Berg, had no regard for Webern at all--and that I could understand and still understand. He was most interested in Stravinsky. I don't say that he was that fond of Stravinsky. There were certain works he was very fond of, but the Piano Concerto, which he knew very well, he basically didn't like very much.

We were very involved in looking at these pieces. You have to remember that not one of these works was recorded. Nothing of Schoenberg's middle period or later was available on records; none of the more recent Stravinsky. Not even the scores were available. We looked at the Piano Concerto in an arrangement for two pianos. You couldn't infer what was going on instrumentally, or much of anything else. The generation before mine knew Le Sacre du Printemps only in one way, as a four-hand arrangement.

In any case, Roger's musical evolution came very gradually, and so by the late forties he was writing what you would wish to characterize as twelve-tone music. We interacted on each other very much. We probably disagree profoundly--I hope so, because if we don't then one of us is unnecessary. The fact is we're still very close friends.

What he meant to me was virtually everything. He represented, to me, the first American I had met who knew European contemporary music. He knew the figures of contemporary music at that time, he had talked and worked with them and wasn't intimidated by them. That was very important. Remember the position we were in. In '34, '35, most Americans who went to Europe to study were regarded as innocents abroad and weren't taken very seriously: amusing, generous barbarians. We felt that very strongly and resented it deeply; it was untrue, pretentious vilification. We were not completely unconvinced that Mein Kampf had the effect it did in Germany because of all the other pretentious tripe which they took seriously there.

Remember, this was the time of Nazism, and I'm a Jew. You lived with this and it changed your whole relationship to life: the barbarities that were going on there and the lack of response here. We lived with all of this. Every day we saw tragedy, tragedy such as you could not believe and we could not believe.

Schoenberg came over very early; he had lost his professional life but not his life. By '36, '37, and '38, however, suddenly the whole evolving process of contemporary music was transplanted to this country. Bartók, Schoenberg, Hindemith, Stravinsky, Rathaus, Křenek--there was not a single European musical figure who was not functioning and teaching here. Many of these people were not Jewish; there were all kinds of crucial issues involved here.

So these people arrived here and changed our lives in fundamental ways. The whole intellectual atmosphere was altered. We were the reservoirs, we were the receptacles of this whole tradition which we had been standing outside of. Here was Bartók at Columbia, Schoenberg at U.C.L.A., Hindemith at Yale, and by the same token, Schenker was imported. The explosion was simply fantastic. Above all, it had psychological spin-offs that might not be so obvious. It was not merely that we could learn from the Schoenbergs and the Hindemiths and the Bartóks; it was that suddenly we were no longer in any sense irrelevantly awed by them. We suddenly realized they had their failings, they had their weaknesses, we were strong in ways in which they weren't strong, we were weak in ways in which they were strong. We came from different backgrounds, different cultures, different educations, and in many ways we could cope with them quite confidently.

Q: Could you tell us about your background in jazz and popular music?

BABBITT: My background in popular music really is from childhood. My specific relation to popular music stops around 1935. My strong field in popular music is from 1926 to around 1935. When I was a child, I was arranging it, playing it, living it--in the South, remember, where there's very little of anything else. So therefore, if, as it's alleged, I know the lyrics of every popular song between '26 and '35--it's almost true, not every song but most of them--I didn't learn these things, I lived with them.

My relation to it then became very casual. During the war I was virtually out of music entirely, and after the war I came to New York and tried to decide what the devil I was going to do. I tried film scores, but decided that this world was not for me; I'm not up to that physically, I can't stay up all night and write music. I wrote the music for a musical comedy originally designed for Mary Martin, but then I had enough.

But real jazz I kept up with. By "real" I mean what is normally called jazz, ranging from dixieland to bop, and that I knew well. When I left college here at N.Y.U. and was studying with Roger Sessions, I lived on West Tenth Street, a half block from "Nick's." After the war it became a corny place to which I never went, but then it was called "Nick's" and was the jazz place, mainly dixieland. (In fact, Mel Powell, when he was fifteen years old, used to play between the sets there.) I knew the people there well, and kept up with jazz--not pop music--between '35 and '38. But by then my interest was historical--I still have lots and lots of old records. But my relation to jazz was this: I never was interested in it for more than about thirty minutes at a time. That was my real problem, I'd just get bored and start looking for more interesting things.

Q: Something like All Set seems to derive from the jazz of the fifties.

BABBITT: Oh, I was very much into that, and it's through Gunther Schuller. Gunther came from an absolutely "classical" background. He got into jazz through mainly black performers of bop in the late forties; first as a horn player.

Gunther and I met each other through our admiration for Schoenberg, but he discovered my background in jazz. I could recall old tunes for him and perhaps help him with certain things, because he was very deeply into jazz even before writing his book. I knew the "pop" repertory and he didn't, and we'd both go and hear a lot of jazz together.

In the late forties, Barry Ulanov was one of the editors of Metronome. He was very much into jazz, but his knowledge of jazz was essentially less musical and more literary. We spent a lot of time together in those days, and he kept me up with jazz. His great man was Lenny Tristano, then the most advanced and sophisticated "bop" pianist.

So I did keep up with that, and was very much interested in bop and whatever one wishes to call it, post-bop, through about 1954 or 1955. All Set was originally written for the Brandeis University Arts Festival in 1957. Six of us were commissioned to write jazz pieces, three jazz people, and three basically non-jazz people. I wrote that piece out of my jazz experience, and there are jazz gags and inside references within this very twelve-tone piece, references to well known jazz works and jazz terms, but those are inside gags. I have no relation now in any obvious sense to what goes on in popular music, although I still feel a very strong relationship to certain kinds of jazz and popular music.

Q: Have you ever considered composing an aleatoric score?

BABBITT: You'll have to tell me what that means. I'm not engaging in verbal games. I don't know what it means to say that

one gives the performer "more choice," by "aleatoric" means.
You don't give the performer more choice, he has no more "choice"
than with any other piece, and probably fewer choices. He can
comply only with the notation; if his pitch specifications, for instance, are only for "high," "middle," and "low," then the music ex-
hibits only three functional pitches, and--so--only three pitch intervals.

Every piece "sounds different" every time it's played. One
viola player has a different wave form on his E than another one
on his, and a different one for each occurrence of the "E." Now
comes that celebrated "philosophical" issue: Is it the same piece?
To the extent that it complies to the same notation it is the same
piece. The "same" pieces of the so-called aleatoric composers
are the same pieces, because presumably what is construed as
structural and entifying remains the same. The difference between
the E of this violist and the E of that one I probably cannot con-
strue as structural. All you need recognize is that it's an E on
the viola and not an E on the piccolo, assuming the music is structured to the perceptional utmost.

Here we get back to the electronic medium, because the central property of the electronic medium is that anything which can
be perceived and differentiated can be structured. I can structure
and use referentially the difference between one wave form on an E
and another perceptually different wave form on an E. I have that
degree and range of determinancy and uniformity that I do not have
with performances by live performers. The issue is simply, what
music am I going to write? to what extent am I going to structure
this event as and in music? I dare to aspire to make music as
much as it can be, rather than as little as one obviously can get
away with music's being, under the current egalitarian dispensation.

Q: One of the major complaints that has been leveled against electronic music by composers is that the composition is frozen into
only one version and can permit no nuances of interpretation from
one performance to the next.

BABBITT: There are at least three or four necessary answers to
that. I'm sorry to hear that a composer has said that; I wouldn't
mind if a music critic had said that. First of all, if what is being
asserted is that the only interest in their music are those trivial,
non-structural differences from performance to performance, then
they'd better put more music into their music. I assume that what
you hear in successive performances of a piece is how you hear
more and more, how you grasp this continuous unfolding of the
piece, the cumulative containment that you can scarcely infer on the
first hearing, or the second.

As you hear the larger and deeper levels of a piece, then
maybe eventually you will exhaust it. We find certain pieces ex-
haustible--we may be wrong--and some, inexhaustible. If you keep

discovering new things in a work every time, I don't think that's because of the decision of the performer to play louder or softer. Of course, rarely, a great performer will help us to see things in the music by reinforcing certain compositional aspects which the composer did not. For example, the music of Chopin does not display a very detailed use of dynamics. Performers have learned to impose those details, and to clarify their conceptions of the piece. But if the only interest in successive performances are those non-structural frivolities which a performer decides to indulge in, then there can't be very much in the music.

I would answer the following, that this is exactly the point. The electronic work does remain the "same," and therefore every single detail of the music is an element of the accumulating, contained whole--if you change one thing, then you've changed the piece. What is interpretation? Interpretation is the changing of at least one dimension of the music, usually the dynamic, timbral, or rhythmic. I would like to think of a music where if you so change, you change the total piece in some demonstrably significant way. Now I've said more about my music than I've probably ever said before.

Q: In your notes to Vision and Prayer, you describe how the structure of the poem suggested certain hexachordal and trichordal structures. Could you tell us how important the words were as poetry, how their meanings may have shaped the musical relationships?

BABBITT: That's a toughie, because the answer should be long and detailed. Of course, when I talked about that work, I talked about the things that were easiest to talk about; the poem has a special shape on the page, the syllables (except for one place where he miscounts) proceed one, two, three, four, etc. Those were suggestive, as were the rhyme schemes and the stanza relations. (This was, by the way, the second version of Vision and Prayer. I wrote one in '54 for piano and voice, and in a rather nebulous way it became the basis for this one. So I thought about that poem for a long time.)

I don't know whether you've read any explications of that poem. I always find those so inadequate; I read them in the hope that I'll learn something useful, and I almost never do. The answer is a very simple one: I can't answer your question very simply. I certainly worked very hard on the rhythmic dispositions, all the things which I spoke about in the notes, but it would be ridiculous for me, for example, if when the text says "christen down the sky," I didn't have certain kinds of implications of textures.

You've asked me a very crucial question in my life right now. I'm desperately looking for texts. I have been looking for texts for months. I have to write a piece for Bethany Beardslee and two pianos; it's going to be a Requiem for her husband, and I've been trying to find a text. I have terrible troubles locating texts. I settled on that Dylan Thomas poem only after many misgivings, because of its special shape. I feel much more at home poetically in German. I don't find many poets in English whom I'd like to set--including people whom I admire and enjoy enormously otherwise.

Outside of Hopkins--I've set two of his sonnets and may set another one or two--I find it dreadfully hard to find poetry in English, whereas I find so much poetry in German that I don't know where to start, and I don't want to start. I've done it once, with Stramm in the Du cycle. I could name right now ten German poets whom I would love to set. Therefore, the answer is that in setting "Vision and Prayer" I was much more concerned with the sonic, rhythmic, and syntactical aspects than with the ideational aspects.

The only other poet whom I've set in English has been William Carlos Williams. I've done three pieces--one with tenor and two with soprano--where the voice is an instrument without text. I wish I could find texts.

John Hollander wrote Philomel for me. He's probably that poet who knows most about music--he's almost a professional. He's written a great deal about the relation of music and verse in English poetry. I must say that there are a few things in Philomel which I find very hard to take as poetry for setting; it's a little too literal and self-referential, the rhyme tricks--I was confounded by them at first. I cut a couple of things which I thought were a bit much for singing. Nevertheless, that is very close to the kind of thing I would like to find, because I must work with something which has a very strong and novel sonic structure.

CATALOG OF COMPOSITIONS

1935	Generatrix for orchestra	MS
1940	Composition for String Orchestra	MS
1940	Music for the Mass I for mixed chorus	MS
1941	Music for the Mass II for mixed chorus	MS
1941	Symphony	MS
1941	String Trio	MS
1946	Three Theatrical Songs for voice and piano	CF Peters
1947	Three Compositions for Piano	Boelke-Bomart
1948	Composition for Four Instruments	Presser
1948	String Quartet No. 1	MS
1948; 54	Composition for Twelve Instruments	AMP
1949	Film Music for Into the Good Ground	MS

Year	Title	Publisher
1950	Composition for Viola and Piano	CF Peters
1950	The Widow's Lament in Springtime for soprano and piano	Boelke-Bomart
1951	Du for soprano and piano	Boelke-Bomart
1953	Woodwind Quartet	AMP
1954	String Quartet No. 2	AMP
1954	Vision and Prayer for soprano and piano	MS
1955	Two Sonnets for baritone, clarinet, viola, and cello	CF Peters
1956	Duet for piano	EB Marks
1956	Semi-Simple Variations for piano	Presser
1957	All Set for alto saxophone, tenor saxophone, trumpet, trombone, contrabass, piano, vibraphone, and percussion	AMP
1957	Partitions for piano	Lawson-Gould
1960	Sounds and Words for soprano and piano	EB Marks
1960	Composition for Tenor and Six Instruments	AMP
1961	Composition for Synthesizer	AMP
1961	Vision and Prayer for soprano and synthesized tape	AMP
1964	Philomel for soprano, recorded soprano, and synthesized tape	AMP
1964	Ensembles for Synthesizer	AMP
1965	Relata I for orchestra	AMP
1966	Post-Partitions for piano	CF Peters
1966	Sextets for violin and piano	CF Peters
1967	Correspondences for string orchestra and synthesized tape	AMP
1968	Relata II for orchestra	AMP
1969	Four Canons for SA	Broude Brothers
1969	Phonemena for soprano and piano	CF Peters
1970	String Quartet No. 3	CF Peters
1970	String Quartet No. 4	CF Peters
1971	Occasional Variations for synthesized tape	CF Peters
1972	Tableaux for piano	CF Peters
1974	Arie Da Capo for five instrumentalists	CF Peters
1975	Reflections for piano and synthesized tape	CF Peters
1975	Phonemena for soprano and synthesized tape	CF Peters
1976	Concerti for violin, small orchestra, and synthesized tape	CF Peters
1977	A Solo Requiem for soprano and two pianos	CF Peters
1977	Minute Waltz (or 3/4 $\pm$ 1/8) for piano	CF Peters
1977	Playing for Time for piano	Hinshaw

1978	My Ends Are My Beginnings for solo clarinetist	CF Peters
1978	My Complements to Roger for piano	PNM, Spring-Summer 1978
1978	More Phonemena for twelve-part chorus	CF Peters
1979	An Elizabethan Sextette for six-part women's chorus	CF Peters
1979	Images for saxophonist and synthesized tape	CF Peters
1979	Paraphrases for ten instrumentalists	CF Peters
1980	Dual for cello and piano	CF Peters

HENRY BRANT □

photo: Gene Bagnato

Henry Brant was born on September 15, 1913, in
Montreal, Quebec, Canada. He studied privately with
George Antheil, Aaron Copland, and Wallingford Riegger, and at Juilliard with Rubin Goldmark. In addition to his work for the concert hall, Brant achieved
considerable success scoring and arranging radio
broadcasts and films. He has taught at Columbia,
Juilliard, and, most recently, Bennington College.
He is divorced and has three children.

Brant's early works were written in a modern
tonal idiom and reflected his interest in jazz and popular music. In the early 1950s, his work with polyrhythms and polytonality led him to antiphonal music.
As he became increasingly involved in the implications
of spatial separation in music, Brant's pieces became more and more ambitious. Still present from
his earliest pieces, however, are his unusual instrumental combinations and his engaging sense of humor.

This conversation with Henry Brant took place
during his brief stay with friends in Manhattan on
November 20, 1980. One cannot help instantly liking
and being drawn to Brant. His unaffected wonder and
delight in making music carries over into his dis-
cussions of music. His youthful qualities are in
part accentuated by his casual dress--especially his
well-known and ubiquitous cap, which he wore throughout the interview. The enjoyment in interviewing
Brant that morning was topped only by the experience of a live performance of his spatial music that
same evening--the composer conducting, still wearing his cap.

Q: We'd like to begin with your early concept of "oblique harmony." Does this idea have any use for you today?

BRANT: I don't really think so. Let me first try to give you an
idea of how squalid the scholastic teaching of composition was
around 1929-1930. A miserable and incompetent academicism surrounded it. People who couldn't write an idiomatic Palestrina mass
or Bach motet were teaching counterpoint; people who couldn't write
a convincing passage in the style of Schumann or Chopin were teaching harmony. What they "taught" was scholastic jabber, having
nothing to do with genuine essays in the styles. There were also
the real composers, distinguished personalities like Copland, Riegger, Bloch, or Ruggles, who took an interest in advising and helping young composers whose talent they found promising. I had been
strongly urged to study with some of the academic pedagogues; I

did so under protest. Simultaneously I pursued my true studies, under the guidance of Copland, Riegger, and Antheil. Since harmonic dissonance was still looked upon by many musicians (even Schoenberg) as something that needed defense, if not apology, I decided to invent my own academic system, mostly to annoy my stuffy, conservative, scholastic teachers. My idea was that the eye would see violent, incomprehensible dissonant textures on the page, the ear would hear likewise if the music were played, but by turning the page slantwise a completely bland parade of innocent consonances would appear, none of which could possibly reach the ear in performance! As a curiosity I showed some of this "oblique harmony" music to Henry Cowell; he immediately felt that I should pursue the concept further, and so to encourage me he not only published the "oblique music" in New Music, but arranged for performances in New York, Boston, and several German cities! I can say at this distance that the "oblique harmony" isn't really carried out consistently at all, and so it has baffled everyone who has attempted to analyze it ever since.

Q: We read that you were involved with some of the earliest performances of Harry Partch's music.

BRANT: I think this was in 1938. Otto Luening knew Partch's music, and I think it was through him that Partch came to meet Douglas Moore at Columbia University. Douglas Moore thought I might be able to help and Partch and I met in Moore's office. I was immediately interested, and I spent two months studying Partch's system and learning to play his Chromelodeon, a 43-pitched-to-the-octave keyboard instrument. I also recruited Alix Young Maruchess, an admirable violist and viola d'amore player, and she learned to play Partch's big harp, the Kithara. After about forty rehearsals, the three of us presented an all-Partch concert for the League of Composers which produced a gratifying furor of excitement and indignation. Harry Partch brought a hammer, a screw driver, and a pot of glue onto the stage with him. He had to use these homely tools many times during the concert because the adapted instruments we played on were the original, homemade models. Around that time, I was also playing my tin whistles and Persian oboes and double flageolet, so Partch also wrote two pieces in which I played these instruments. One was Yankee Doodle Fantasy and the other was Two Settings from Joyce's Finnegans Wake. (That double flageolet is now in the Metropolitan Museum, and it was probably the only time this instrument was played publicly in New York.)

Harry Partch did not leave musical materials and institutions the way he found them. He decided that Western music needed completely new musical resources and he began all over again as though the tradition had never existed. His theories and inventions were no mere window dressing. I was impressed and I still am.

Q: Has microtonality had much importance to you as a composer?

BRANT: Yes. I think that that's the way matters have to go; twelve notes to the octave are, first of all, arbitrary and, secondly, not enough. But what I want is to have more than twelve notes that are all just as safe and secure as those twelve. I don't like the idea of having to find the microtones by sliding around--I think of ways of building quarter-tone woodwind instruments with extra keys. Although it sounds like a very stodgy, mechanical way of doing it, I've come to the conclusion that quarter tones are probably the best way. Quarter tones will add twelve new pitches, and what'll happen with them will be what happened with the twelve old chromatic pitches, which were all approximate but close enough to the desired non-diatonic pitches to be very convenient. My guess is that eventually, and fairly soon, we'll have twenty-four notes to the octave, all built in with a reliable mechanism; and on all our standard Western instruments. Otherwise, we're going to have to cope with thousands of systems, all equally beautiful, but none of them accurately playable. I think the situation is analogous to the one that Bach faced: He wanted to be able to use non-diatonic tones with freedom and security, but instead of insisting on the 150-odd pitches which were theoretically implied in his time, he settled on twelve approximate notes, of which only the octaves are in tune. I believe this situation is about to be re-enacted with quarter tones.

At present I use microtones in my music in the same ways other people do: I use them in any old way I can get them, whether it's by slides or by approximations of desired microtonal pitches, or by jazz techniques. They're all good, they're all expressive. The only thing I'm concerned with is that microtones should be produced with some control, so that you know what you're getting. I've been able to encourage cellists and bass players to invent specific fingerings for quarter tones. Not by sliding with one finger, but by using a different finger for each note, and they can do this accurately, with some trouble. Of course trombonists can produce quarter tones by using half positions. In my piece for eighty trombones, Orbits, there's a place where I get eighty-note chords: Each of the trombones plays a different note, forty of them are playing quarter tones. Mechanically, this is no problem; it's the intonation of the notes that is unfamiliar (although I'm sure it will not be difficult to get used to). What happens now in playing a big tone cluster of chromatic quarter tones is what used to happen when you had big chromatic tone clusters of half tones; I remember this forty years ago, with brass instruments. In a tone cluster of six adjacent semitones, a musician who had a semitone on each side of his own assigned pitch would tend to shy away from fighting that pitch through the surrounding dissonant friction, and instead gravitate towards a unison with one of the pitches adjacent to him.

Q: Rural Antiphonies of 1953 was your first antiphonal composition. Do you see this as a break with your earlier compositions, or do you think that it evolved naturally out of them?

BRANT: Both; more an amalgam than a break. Think back to
1950: The customs in composing Western music were appallingly
rigid and conservative. You didn't hear of Boulez or Stockhausen
very much; Penderecki, Ligeti, or Takemitsu not at all. The composers whose names were known wrote exclusively in bars, with
the musicians all situated in the same location, and all playing in
the same tempo and without microtones. That's only thirty years
ago. I felt it was constrictingly rigid; I wanted to have a lot going
on at once, and with rhythmic freedom as well as control. My
only model was Ives, whose music I had known for a long time.
So I tried writing eight or ten simultaneous, contrasted, contrapuntal lines, still in bars or with the musicians all placed together
as usual. I found that I was running into trouble: The musicians
could play the notes all right, but you really couldn't identify the
details in the compound result. Ten lines were too many for intelligibility. Range was also a problem: Most of the music then
existed in five octaves, with an octave extension at each end which
was not used too much. It was unusual to have contrapuntal lines
at the extreme top and bottom; this was known, but it was not often
done. And even including those "extreme" ranges, I had a terrible
time trying to avoid collisions over the same octave range. But
there didn't seem to be a necessary reason why music should be
limited to even twelve horizontal events at once. Why not more
than twelve? The ear never said, "I refuse to listen." And I
had never taken seriously the old idea that the human ear could
not completely follow polyphony in more than three real parts.
What is "completely follow"?

    I realize that I had hit a crisis with pieces like my Sym-
phony for Percussion, which in places contained more horizontal
parts than I knew how to make clear. Then, at Juilliard, I studied
and performed The Unanswered Question, and other ensemble pieces
of Ives. I saw that he was getting at the problem of greater polyphonic complexity in two ways: by physically separating the players, and by having them not maintain rhythmic ensemble. At that
time, it seemed to me that these solutions were somewhat casual
and slovenly, because my training had been like everyone else's--
getting the music locked into the jail cells of bars and uniform
tempi. So I attempted to find a way to apply Ives' two ideas in
a more organized manner, and modified to the extent that every
detail in the music must be easily and accurately playable, a restriction which Ives had never worried about. My first effort was
Rural Antiphonies. Since then all of my spatial pieces have been
guided by these two Ivesian principles. Implicit in this way of doing things is that you can not only simultaneously combine as many
musical elements, as much subject matter as you want, but you
may combine different styles simultaneously. Stravinsky and others
had produced contrasting styles in quick succession, but one at a
time--one style, then another, then another. Ives discovered spatial ways to present several styles all at once, by sequestering
each style in a different physical location. (In all my own spatial
works, I follow this procedure strictly.)

    Teo Macero's Areas, written and performed in 1952 when he

was studying at Juilliard, requires five separated jazz ensembles, and includes improvisation as well as notated material. I consider it an important landmark in the recent history of spatial music.

Q: What has been the performer's attitude over the years toward playing your antiphonal music?

BRANT: We're now talking about a thirty-year period. The first thing musicians wanted to know in 1950 is what they still want to know: whether what they're doing makes a difference in the total effect; if they play well, will it be substantially different than if they just play so-so? Once they're assured that both these things are true, there isn't much resistance. At first, there was also the problem that musicians are trained to listen to each other. When they were situated all over the hall, they'd strain to hear what the rest were doing and would try to see how they were supposed to fit in. One consequence of the Ivesian ideas of performance that we've been talking about is the technique of not listening to the other players while you perform: If you listen then you'll try to "fit in," which is what I don't want. Much of the time in my spatial music, I wish to avoid metric and stylistic relationships between the separated groups. At first, it was very difficult to get this concept across; now it's much less difficult because there's been such a lot of unorthodox music composed and performed since 1950, although not precisely along the lines I describe.

Q: A number of your spatial pieces have been recorded. Do you feel that these pieces are significantly compromised if that's the only way that someone hears them?

BRANT: Yes, I do feel that way, but with one exception: Most people have a two-speaker stereo, and I've written some pieces for two groups only, front of the hall and back of the hall, specifically to accommodate the limitations of two-channel playback. If these are recorded (usually against the engineer's serious objections) with only one group at a time in the hall or studio, and then later put together so that there is no spill from one channel to the other, then on playback you get a fairly accurate impression of the spatial separation (if, of course, you separate your loudspeakers as much as possible). But even now, with recording equipment so much improved, this kind of recording is considered a very peculiar way of working. Engineers assure me that they can get something much closer to the separation I want if everything is recorded in the room all at once. The result of this is a mixture coming from both speakers, which occasionally produces an illusion of space. I hate recording illusions. Anything that uses a spatial setup more complicated than two groups only can't be managed with a two-speaker system. We hear of quadraphonic recording with four-speaker playback, but for me that makes as little sense as two; I'd have to write pieces for exactly four groups, because a piece for three groups isn't any more precisely projected, spatially, on four speakers than a piece for five groups is. Normally, a piece of mine has many more widely separated sources of sound than two, or even four--I often use eight or more. The piece that I mentioned for eighty trombones has just been recorded. In performance the trombones are arranged in a huge three-quarter circle and the spatial effects are based on this plan. The recording gives the pitches and the tone qualities of the trombones with considerable fidelity, and it does suggest a spatial arrangement in their placement, but when the sound accumulates around the room circularly (a very direct and vivid sensation when experienced live), the recording process is not able to make this effect substantially evident.

Recently I have been using multi-track equipment for non-spatial music comprising many unrelated elements. One instrument at a time is recorded alone on a separate track. This produces optimum recording results in terms of distinctness, clarity, and freedom from distortion, and here my Ivesian procedure of rhythmic non-coordination finds a new practical function.

Q: In the past, you've written about the difficulties in performing your spatial music outdoors. Have you had any success in resolving this problem?

BRANT: No; total failure. There are too many invariables. Spatial music is difficult enough to perform even in closed spaces, where the sound can't get out of the room and wind and traffic noises can't get in; even then, in a hall with favorable acoustics that are evenly distributed, there can be surprises. In a multi-sound-source piece, it may not always be clear where the sound is coming from; the acoustics of many halls are apt to play this kind of spatial trick. Out of doors, there's no control whatever, except in very favorable places--perhaps a town square in Italy would have a minimum of wind resistance, or a Roman amphitheater designed by Vitruvius might offer clear acoustics. But in this country, what are the developed, open spaces likely to be? Parking lots, shopping malls, mobile-home courts, industrial parks, municipal-building complexes, art center plazas, or cemeteries. My worst failure, my most humiliating musical experience, came when my The Immortal Combat was presented in the plaza outside the three big theaters at Lincoln Center in New York. I'm glad this took place because it showed me how poorly equipped indoor instruments are to deal with the urban outdoors. Despite the undaunted excellence of the playing, a fountain, a roar of Sunday traffic, and a thunderstorm wiped out my piece almost immediately.

My Bennington colleague Gunnar Schonbeck, an extremely imaginative and resourceful instrument builder as well as musician, is ready to undertake the construction of acoustic instruments--

which will not be amplified--as powerful as tugboat whistles, able to compete with any outdoor urban noise. In sound, these instruments will resemble giant trombones, oboes, and kettledrums. My next outdoor spatial piece will use instruments of this kind.

Q: You've often commented on the distinct advantages of the spatial distribution of musicians, particularly emphasizing its clarification of multiple tempi and its unique sensual impact for an audience. But beyond these advantages, can it be argued that the element of spatialization is of a fundamental musical importance equivalent to the elements of pitch and time?

BRANT: I think so. You can start with the proposition--one very difficult to controvert--that all music is space music. You need a place to put the players and their instruments, a place for the sound to vibrate and to reach the ear. This is scarcely arguable--space is a fundamental musical fact. Remove space, and you have neither tempo, rhythm, nor tone quality. The only difference between Ives' use of space (which is the one that I follow) and the symphony concert's is that the latter handles space in a rigidly conventional way. The way I do it also has its conventions, however. One is that it's indoors; aside from that, my spatial conventions are much more varied than those of the symphony concert because it is my objective to use the space itself as an expressive musical resource. But even if we were talking about a completely imagined music, in which there's not a sound made or actually heard, it would be difficult to imagine any sound with no space for it to be in.

Q: Do you think that spatial distribution is essential only for your kind of music, which involves the simultaneous musical events? Would Beethoven have been helped by the availability of spatial resources?

BRANT: No; the classical instrumental repertoire was written for a precise use of space: the conventional one. I've made experiments to test its premises. If you play a Bach fugue with the four players each in one corner of the hall, the harmony is substantially weakened. The contrapuntal lines become more independent, and precise ensemble becomes more difficult. But even if the ensemble problems can be solved, the individual lines separate from each other in a way that Bach surely did not intend, and they take on an odd, disembodied character when so heard. And certainly it is no service to his music to weaken the harmony.

It's a practical question above all. Spatial separation is essentially a contrapuntal device; it makes counterpoint more distinct. It destroys harmony and ensemble, and it enhances the polyphonic contrast between widely separated groups. The Renaissance and Baroque concept of separated groups for echo music is of limited utility because of the generally unclear spatial result--often you can't tell where the echo is coming from, but I suppose that's in the nature of reverberating echoes. But unless echo is the intention, then the only point in using widely separated spaces, involving the entire hall, as sound sources, is for contrast; if there's no contrast intended between the spatially separated performing groups, then the space is merely going to make the music unintelligible. Space removes relationships; if you want relationships, then don't use spatial separation. If you want something unified harmonically, rhythmically, in its tone quality, in its style, then put the performers as close together as possible. I've made experiments with a string quartet, moving them closer together than normal, with their heads almost touching, and the ensemble was improved.

Q: Do you have much interest now in writing a piece either for a solo performer or for an ensemble that would not be spatially distributed?

BRANT: The competition, from both living and dead composers, is too great for a solo piece; it's also too great for an ensemble that doesn't use spatial separation. What would I write? A string quartet? Besides, I think that particular combination is lopsided. For thirty years I've been trying to devise a rational string quartet; it should be one violin, one viola, one instrument that doesn't exist--a tenor violin, which I'm trying to develop--and cello. Assuming that I had this ideal string quartet, look what I'd be competing with! What chance have I of making any kind of a string quartet that anybody's going to listen to after he's heard Bartók, Berg, and Beethoven? A wind quintet is an ensemble that makes no sense except spatially because there are five contrasting tone qualities. The brass quintet is also lopsided; I couldn't make it work without revamping it. A brass quintet that had B flat flugelhorn, E flat flugelhorn, baritone horn, euphonium, and tuba would be in evenly balanced combination--as would a quartet of saxophones, for which I've written a non-spatial piece. In short, for a non-spatial piece, I would only settle for real equality of timbre in the combination, and no approximate substitute. There is one such combination that's hardly ever heard: the vocal quartet, SATB. But with that, all I have to do is hear a piece of Palestrina or Josquin properly performed to realize that I haven't much chance of competing in that medium either.

Q: As both a pianist and a conductor, you've performed a good deal of Carl Ruggles' music. Did he attend your Vermont premiere of his Sun-treader?

BRANT: Almost. He was in a hospital and he wanted to come, but at the last moment his medical advisor said, "No, you can't go." They wired the concert into his room, so he got at least a rough idea. I came to see him every day after rehearsal. He was heavily sedated, but he wanted to be awakened, and would question me in detail about the rehearsal, and then give me very precise advice, singing phrases in a rough, husky voice. He urged me to add more instruments on a unison line if I thought it necessary (in one place I added extra trombones), and to make certain that the vertical major 7ths and minor 9ths were as dissonant as possible--"not like sick octaves." This was in the last year of Ruggles' life.

At one point previous there were three scores of Sun-treader which didn't seem to agree because Ruggles had revised them at various times. I prepared a version that incorporated all three, and I believe it is this text which is now generally used. Ruggles explained to me that he had expanded the orchestration of many of his pieces and that he preferred his later versions. Men and Mountains was originally for about twenty instruments--personally, I still like the first version.

What I got from Ruggles for my own music was quite specific. He despised a melody comprising only three or four notes. According to him, a melody isn't a melody until it goes on for eight or ten bars. He also had the idea that single-line melody should be irregular and not symmetrical, although it should have identifiable outlines. On one Vermont occasion in autumn, he said, "Go outside and bring me some maple leaves." He put them on top of each other and said, "You see, they're all maple leaves; they all have the same configurations, the same number of points. But you show me a single one that is exactly regular and symmetrical. That's melody." His concept seems so different from the premises of the Viennese tone-row school, and to my mind it is very much finer. In saying that, I'm not saying anything against the great things that Schoenberg or Berg accomplished with their tone rows; I'm thinking of the depressing way in which some of their followers have tried to make an Ultimate Credo out of what is really a very low order of composing technology. I think that Ruggles' extended-melody conception of the twelve pitches is the one to emulate--although he himself regarded pitch per se in much the same way as the Viennese tone-row composers.

Q: We understand that before you write a piece, you prepare a prose report in which you make a detailed outline of all the parameters of the piece. Is this the same thing as what you call "instant composition"?

BRANT: The prose report to which you refer is a method I now use for any kind of composing. Its purpose is to make the writing of music easier, quicker, more secure and with less wear and tear on the nervous system, and all this without sacrificing either quality or complexity. It may include conventional notation and/or drastically abbreviated notation via written instructions, but in all cases the procedure is one of planned control, not improvisation. I use the term "instant composing" to describe works which use a minimum of conventional notation; but in all cases I devise a catechism, asking myself questions which gradually limit and define the final result. I am not permitted to postpone the answer to any question or to bypass the question. At the point when I feel able to write down the music by simply following my list of answers, using these as my complete plan of composing-action, my actual notating starts. If I find that I'm not ready to begin because some needed information is missing, I ask myself more questions. But I am not allowed to change any of my answers. Carrying all this out needs a certain amount of cold blood, because otherwise doubts and questions may arise, resulting in the temptation to make changes. The whole idea rests on total commitment to a single, unaltered concept and a willingness to accept the consequences of literally fulfilling all the original instructions to the bitter end. (I am perhaps making this sound a lot grimmer than it really is, but the program outlined above is how I actually do my composing.)

It took me a while to arrive at this way of doing things, which partly depends, for its workability, on the complete avoidance of the piano as a composing tool. I believe I stumbled on prose report-instant composing quite by accident. For many years I was a commerical musician, and I relied on the piano as everyone else did (although they seldom admitted it). On one occasion, around 1944, I had to do an overnight rush job of radio composing. My eyes were tired and it was already midnight, past the New York curfew for playing musical instruments. In desperation I wrote down my first, very crude instant music-prose report, which amounted to a scheme for dictation. I phoned my copyist and said, "OK, write this down; you're making the score." I dictated everything to him over the phone, note by note; he wrote it all down in score form and extracted the parts. At nine o'clock the next morning, I entered the studio in fear and trembling, believing that the gibberish I had dictated would be the certain end of my career. I made a shaky upbeat, but what I heard surprised no one; it sounded exactly like the same kind of music I would have written anyway. So now nothing will ever make me go back to the old way. In any case, my purpose in writing music is not to experience hot-blooded feelings myself, but to upset the feelings of others!

Q: Notes for most of your works usually include a programmatic or extramusical description. Are these your afterthoughts, or are they part of the basis of the composition?

BRANT: Afterthoughts, usually having nothing to do with the music. Sometimes, for a commissioned work, I announce the title before I've begun the music, so that it can be available for advance publicity.

Q: What are you currently working on?

BRANT: I think I'll have to answer that one obliquely. No two of my spatial pieces use the same number or formations of participating instrumental or vocal groups, no two have the same stylistic amalgam or the same spatial plan. All are designed to be workable in whatever kind of performing space is available. Nine times out of ten that turns out to be a conventional concert hall, large, medium, or small. It's becoming clear to me that there's something radically the matter with the traditional hall; for a new musical expression we need a new kind of hall. It should be a portable, collapsible, demountable, wooden concert hall, with movable walls, ceilings, floors, ramps, stages. So that you could pack the whole thing into one or two of those great big trucks and drive it from place to place. I envisage a hall without fixed chairs, able to accommodate an audience of about 500 people comfortably, with all the listeners free to move about silently during the music. Fixed chairs are the spatial composer's worst enemy; they prevent him from deploying the spaces in the hall in musically expressive ways, and these fixed chairs prevent the audience from perceiving spatial relationships from different locations. And these fixed seats inevitably lead to fire laws to protect the fixed audiences.

Let's now pretend that I am a wildly successful spatial composer, and that my spatial orchestral music and operas are played all over the world every hour on the hour.

Once I ventured away from the stage, I would still be limited to the "legal" spaces in locating my musicians and singers throughout the halls, which is to say I would still be working with the same kinds of dark, cramped, constricted areas as now--with boxes, ramps, places behind or under balconies, catwalks, and aisles. The only rational solution I can see is a new kind of music theater, and it must be portable because such auditoriums are not going to be built in every town. (I understand that Boulez's hall at the IRCAM has movable walls, but that they can't be moved during performances, and can be reset only between pieces!) Well, if the Ives Memorial Portable Spatial Hall ever gets built, changes in the dimensions and shape of the building will have to be possible during the course of the music, so that changing musical textures can be planned in terms of changing acoustics.

In such a new hall there must also be ways of moving the performers as they play. Up until now, I've been principally limited to composing what is in effect static space music. Presently, it is hazardous for the performers to try to move while playing, in a concert hall, in any location other than the stage. Also, they can't physically move fast enough for the motion of sound to be acoustically emphatic. (All this implies live, not electronic, music, and no amplification.) Try now to imagine an ascending passage with a crescendo with the player physically lifted as the music rises! What could be more natural and compelling! I've heard this effect approximated in an experiment which, crude though it was, gave an unmistakable indication of the potency of the added spatial factor.

I suppose what I'm talking about is a technological crisis in space music. Practically speaking, the problem of designing a portable hall with flexible dimensions and devices for moving musicians swiftly and safely is primarily an architectural and engineering task, and secondarily, it is obviously a substantial funding project.

There are other crises. One of them is the speed and thoroughness with which the institutions of the nineteenth-century Western music have congealed--by this I mean the Victorian concert hall and opera house, and the Wagner-Tchaikovksy symphonic instrumentation. I admit the enormous advantages of standardization. But if this twentieth-century institutionalization of nineteenth-century musical customs and resources remains as it is, substantially rigid, it will lead to an exclusive concentration on the music of the past--this is already an accomplished fact. It is difficult to blame the orchestras and opera houses for so seldom performing new works, when, in so many cases, the music we now produce doesn't really suit these old institutions.

In my next pieces I hope to have some new resources to work with; new instruments for the outdoors, the simultaneous collaboration of ensembles of musicians from different cultures, multitrack recording equipment up to seventy-two channels, and perhaps a few devices for safely, swiftly, and noiselessly lifting and transporting musicians about the hall as they play. The portable hall, which I regard as the top priority for composers at this time, is not likely to become a reality overnight. I invite communication from all composers interested in this project.

CATALOG OF COMPOSITIONS

Several catalogs of Henry Brant's music have been published, including music composed as early as 1929. Brant has withdrawn from performance, for the time being, much of his output composed prior to 1950, about seventy works. All the works listed below are obtainable for performance, and are given here in two categories: non-spatial (mostly composed before 1950) and spatial (mostly since 1950).

Non-spatial Works

1931; 56; 79	Angels and Devils for solo flute and flute orchestra	MCA Music
1932	Mobiles for flute	MCA Music
1932; 54	Partita for Flute and Piano	Carl Fischer
1932	Music for a Five and Dime for E♭ clarinet, piano, and kitchen hardware	Carl Fischer

1933	Double-crank Hand Organ for two pianos and percussion	Carl Fischer
1934; 55	Requiem in Summer for woodwind quintet	Carl Fischer
1938	The Marx Brothers for tin whistle and chamber ensemble	Carl Fischer
1938	Whoopee in D Major for orchestra	Carl Fischer
1938	Concerto for Clarinet and Orchestra	Carl Fischer
1940	Concerto for Violin and Orchestra	Carl Fischer
1940	Rhapsody for Viola and Orchestra	ACA
1940	Variations on a Theme by Robert Schumann for two pianos, trumpet, and timpani	Carl Fischer
1941; 70	Concerto for Saxophone or Trumpet and Chamber Orchestra	Carl Fischer
1945	Dedication in Memory of Franklin D. Roosevelt for orchestra	Carl Fischer
1945	Statements in Jazz for clarinet and dance orchestra	Carl Fischer
1945	Symphony in B Flat	Carl Fischer
1946	Jazz Clarinet Concerto for clarinet solo with dance orchestra	Carl Fischer
1946	Imaginary Ballet for piccolo, cello, and piano	Carl Fischer
1947	The Three-Way Canon Blues for voices a capella	Elkan-Vogel
1949	Street Music for winds and percussion	Carl Fischer
1949; 57	All Souls' Carnival for flute, violin, cello, piano, accordion	Carl Fischer
1949	Madrigal en Casserole for chorus and piano	MCA
1950	Millennium I for eight trumpets, chimes, and glockenspiel	Carl Fischer
1953	Signs and Alarms for woodwinds, brass, and percussion	Carl Fischer
1953	Stresses for piano/celeste, harp, and strings; for trumpet, piano, percussion, and strings	Carl Fischer
1954	Ice Age for Ondes Martenot or clarinet, piano, and percussion	Carl Fischer
1954	Galaxy 2 for woodwinds, brass, and percussion	Carl Fischer
1962	Sky Forest--Jazz Fugue for accordion quartet	Pagani
1975	From Bach's Menagerie for 4 saxophones	Carl Fischer

Spatial Works

1953; 68	Antiphony One for five orchestral groups	Carl Fischer

1954	Millennium II for soprano, brass and percussion	Carl Fischer
1955	December for soprano, tenor, male and female speakers, large and small choruses, woodwinds, brass, percussion, and organ	Carl Fischer
1955	Encephalograms II for soprano and seven instruments	Carl Fischer
1956	On the Nature of Things for string orchestra, solo winds, and glockenspiel	Carl Fischer
1956	Grand Universal Circus for eight solo voices, chorus, and sixteen instruments	Carl Fischer
1957	Hieroglyphics I for viola with timpani, chimes, celeste, and harp	Carl Fischer
1957	Millennium III for six brass and six percussionists	Carl Fischer
1958	In Praise of Learning for sixteen sopranos and sixteen percussionists	Carl Fischer
1958	Joquin for piccolo and six instruments	Carl Fischer
1958	Mythical Beasts for soprano or mezzo-soprano and sixteen instruments	Carl Fischer
1958	The Children's Hour for six voices, chorus, two trumpets, two trombones, organ and percussion	Carl Fischer
1959	The Crossing for tenor and five instruments	Carl Fischer
1960	Atlantis for mezzo-soprano, speaker, mixed chorus, orchestra, band, and percussion	Carl Fischer
1960	Quombex for viola d'amore, music boxes, and organ	Carl Fischer
1960	The Fire Garden for soprano, small chorus, and chamber ensemble	Carl Fischer
1961	Barricades for oboe or soprano saxophone, tenor, clarinet, bassoon, trombone, piano, xylophone, and strings	Carl Fischer
1961	Fire in Cities for chorus, two pianos orchestra, and eight timpani	Carl Fischer
1961	Violin Concerto with Lights for violin, ten instruments, and lights	Carl Fischer
1962	Headhunt for trombone, bass clarinet, bassoon, cello, and percussion	Carl Fischer
1963	The Fourth Millennium for two trumpets, horn, euphonium, and tuba	Carl Fischer
1964	Dialogue in the Jungle for soprano, tenor, five woodwinds, and five brass	Carl Fischer
1965	Odyssey--Why Not? for solo flute, flute obbligato, and four orchestral groups	Carl Fischer

1967	Verticals Ascending for two bands	MCA
1968	Chanticleer for clarinet, piano, percussion, and strings	Carl Fischer
1969	Windjammer for horn, piccolo, oboe, bass clarinet, and bassoon	Carl Fischer
1970	Kingdom Come for orchestra, circus band, and organ	Carl Fischer
1971	Crossroads for treble violin, violin, mezzo violin, and viola	Carl Fischer
1972	The Immortal Combat for two bands	Carl Fischer
1973	An American Requiem for woodwinds, brass, percussion, organ, church bells, and optional soprano	CF Peters
1973	Divinity for harpsichord, two trumpets, two trombones, and horn	Carl Fischer
1973	Sixty for three bands	Carl Fischer
1974	Nomads for three soloists, voice, percussion, brass, and orchestra	Carl Fischer
1974	Prevailing Winds for wind quintet	Carl Fischer
1974	Six Grand Pianos Bash for pianos, percussion, piccolos and two brass	Carl Fischer
1974	Solomon's Gardens for seven solo voices, chorus, and three instruments	Carl Fischer
1975	A Plan of the Air for SATB soli, organ, winds, and percussion	Carl Fischer
1975	Curriculum I for baritone and eight instruments	Carl Fischer
1975	Homage to Ives for baritone, piano, and three orchestral groups	Carl Fischer
1976	American Commencement for brass and percussion	Carl Fischer
1976	American Debate for winds and percussion	ʹCarl Fischer
1976	American Weather for voices, trumpet, trombone, chimes, and glockenspiel	Carl Fischer
1976	Spatial Concerto (Questions from Genesis) for piano solo, eight sopranos, eight altos, and orchestra	Carl Fischer
1978	Antiphonal Responses for three solo bassoons, piano, orchestra, and eight instruments obbligati	Carl Fischer
1978	Cerberus for double bass, piccolo, soprano, and mouth organ	Carl Fischer
1978	Curriculum II for small orchestral groups	Carl Fischer
1978	The $1,000,000 Confessions for brass quintet	Carl Fischer
1979	Orbits for eighty trombones, organ, and soprano	Carl Fischer
1980	The Glass Pyramid for voice, strings, solo winds, and percussion	Carl Fischer
1980	The Secret Calendar for orchestral groups	Carl Fischer

JOHN CAGE □

photo: Gene Bagnato

John Cage was born on September 5, 1912, in Los Angeles, California. He studied composition privately with Richard Buhlig, Adolph Weiss, Henry Cowell, and Arnold Schoenberg. In addition to teaching at various schools and universities at different points in his career, Cage was the musical director for the Merce Cunningham Dance Company from 1944 to 1966.

Several of Cage's early works were serial. He soon left this method of composition behind and embarked on a series of pieces for percussion and for prepared piano, which reflected his disinterest in harmony and his increasingly sophisticated rhythmic sense. These works, along with Cage's interest in Zen Buddhism, led him by the early 1950s to create methods of composing that would free his music from the taste, memory, and personality of its composer. For almost thirty years, he has remained at the forefront of indeterminate composition; in both his music and his writings, he is its most eloquent spokesman.

The authors spoke with John Cage on March 30, 1980, at his Manhattan home. Although suffering with the latest strain of flu that was then making its way through New York, he gave no sign of irritation or impatience at the prospect of enduring yet another interview--always treating his interviewers with courtesy and respect. Cage has the rare ability to direct his attention undividedly to the matter at hand. This quality in turn gave a sense of importance and intimacy to his every response.

Q: We'd like to begin with your works from the 1930s and '40s. Do they seem remote to you now? Did you have to unlearn from them in order to compose your indeterminate works of the last thirty years?

CAGE: I suppose the answer to both those questions is yes. I'm always more interested in what I haven't yet written than in what I've written in the past--particularly that long ago. Although now so many people are beginning to play the old music, and they invite me to the concerts, so I hear it a good deal. Some of the pieces are good and some of them are not. There are two that are quite popular that I think are good pieces: Credo in Us and the Third Construction. I think the Second Construction is a poor piece. I wasn't quite aware that it was poor when I wrote it; I thought it was interesting. But it has carry-overs from education and theory; it's really a fugue, but of a novel order. In this day and age, I think fugues are not interesting (because of the repetition of the subject).

Q: Are you distressed that the interest in these works might be at the expense of your more recent works?

CAGE: No, I don't think that that's the case because some people play the newer music too. In particular, the recent études for piano and for violin interest many people. So I don't think that there's any problem.

My basic attitude toward all this is that I have my life, and my music has its. The two are independent of one another. I'm of course interested in the life of my music, but after a while I'll die and it'll have to take care of itself, so I'm trying to let it take care of itself to begin with.

Q: In your recent music, do you feel a carry-over from one piece to the next?

CAGE: No, another thing happens with me. I work in many ways in a given time period. And not only do I make music, but I write texts, and now I make etchings. I do all of these things in different ways. Some ideas that I have I drop, and others I pick up from the past, and so on. So it's not a linear situation. It's more like overlapping layers. For instance, at one extreme you have the Freeman Etudes for violin, which are very determinate; they are written down in as exact a notation as I can make. (That was at the request of Paul Zukofsky, with whom I've been writing them.) But at the same time I'm developing an interest in improvisation, which is probably freer than anything I've done before (including the indeterminate music).

Q: In 1949 you went to Europe for a few months, and shortly after your return you began to use the I Ching in your composition. Had you encountered things in Europe that led you in this direction?

CAGE: No, it was rather my study of Zen Buddhism. At first, my inclination was to make music about the ideas that I had encountered in the Orient. The String Quartet is about the Indian view of the seasons, which is creation, preservation, destruction, and quiescence; also the Indian idea of the nine permanent emotions, with tranquility as the center. But then I thought, instead of talking about it, to do it; instead of discussing it, to act it. And that would be done by making the music non-intentional, and

starting from an empty mind. At first I did this by means of the
Magic Square.

The third movement of the String Quartet uses a canon for
a single line, and it's a kind of music which doesn't depend on
one's likes and dislikes; it's the following willy-nilly of a ball which
is rolling in front of you. But there are at least two pieces that
are a transition: the Sixteen Dances and the Concerto for Prepared
Piano and Chamber Orchestra.   Both of those use a chart like the
Magic Square. They established moves on it which distinguished,
as I recall, one phrase from another. It can be used compositionally to make differences by changing the move that's made on the
chart. Instead of having numbers, as the Magic Square would, the
chart of course had single sounds, intervals, and aggregates. The
aggregates and intervals are made on either one instrument or several.

It was in the course of doing such work that Christian Wolff
brought me a copy of the I Ching that his father had just published.
I saw immediately that that chart was better than the Magic Square.
So I began writing the Music of Changes and later the Imaginary
Landscape No. 4 for twelve radios. The reason I wrote that was
because Henry Cowell had said that I had not freed myself from
my tastes in the Music of Changes. It was my intention to do that,
so I wrote the music for radios feeling sure that no one would be
able to discern my taste in that. However, they criticized that
too because it was so soft. So I just kept on going in spite of
hell and high water.

Q: In the late forties and the early fifties, you were an outspoken
admirer of Webern's music, but by the late sixties you remarked
in an interview that you'd rather walk out of the concert hall than
listen to it. The question is really in two parts: 1) Could you explain this loss of interest, and 2) have you had a similar reaction
over the years to Erik Satie's music?

CAGE: No, I was always devoted to Erik Satie's music, and I
still am. You don't really have to be interested in it in order to
enjoy it. Whereas in the case of Webern, I think you're obliged
to be somewhat interested.

Q: You mean interested in the construction of it?

CAGE: And all of the ideas and everything. Otherwise, I don't
think it's that seductive. Certainly some pieces are not at all.
Whereas Satie is. The fact that he's interesting even though he
is charming makes him for me still very lively. I think he's one
of the liveliest musical figures, certainly of this century.

Long ago I wrote that text comparing him with Webern.

Maybe if I paid more attention to Webern now I would like him again, but I don't feel any need for it. But the remark against him is simply against any use of music that you already know, and an insistence on the music that you haven't yet heard--or as I said earlier, the music you haven't yet written. Many people collect music that they like and surround themselves with it. I do the reverse: I don't keep music around me; instead, I keep noise.

Q: You use the I Ching to make choices in composition. Is this use of it separate from the book's guiding or spiritual purposes?

CAGE: Yes. It's not entirely separate from it, but I don't make use of the wisdom aspects in the writing of music or in the writing of texts. I use it simply as a kind of computer, as a facility. If I have some question that requires a wise answer, then of course I use it that way. On occasion I do. But if I want to know which sound out of 100 sounds I'm to use, then I use it just as a computer.

Q: Is this considered an improper use of the book?

CAGE: By some people, I think, who are superstitious about it. The mechanism by means of which the I Ching works is, I think, the same as that by means of which the DNA--or one of those things in the chemistry of our body--works. It's a dealing with the number 64, with a binary situation with all of its variations in six lines. I think it's a rather basic life mechanism. I prefer it to other chance operations. I began using it nearly thirty years ago, and I haven't stopped. Some people think that I'm enslaved by it, but I feel that I am liberated by it.

Q: Your music wasn't published until Peters gave you an exclusive contract late in the 1950s. How did your signing with them come about?

CAGE: I was living in the country then, and I had quite a problem supplying copies of my music to people who wanted to have it. I first took all of my music to Schirmers, and Mr. Heinsheimer said my music would only be a headache for them. The only piece he liked was the Suite for Toy Piano, but he said, "Of course, we'll have to change the title." So I said, "There's no need for you to do that, I'll just take my music away," and I took it back to the country.

People kept writing to me and asking me for copies, and I kept on writing music. Finally, one day--it was while I was writing the incidental music for Jackson Mac Low's play called The Marrying Maiden--I put my pen down, and I determined not to write another note until I found a publisher. So I picked up the Yellow Pages and I ran down the list of music publishers, and I stopped at Peters. The reason I stopped there was because some-one--I think someone in some string quartet--had said that Mr. Hin-richsen was interested in American music. So I simply called and asked to speak with him. He said, very cheerfully over the phone, "I'm so glad that you called. My wife has always wanted me to publish your music." That day we had lunch and signed the con-tract.

He was such a fine man. Wonderful. It's so sad that he died. But the family is devoted to his work.

Q: Do you think it was primarily an aesthetic decision on their part? Was it that they realized that you were being approached more and more frequently to have your music performed?

CAGE: No. Perhaps Evelyn Hinrichsen was interested in my music, but Walter Hinrichsen was devoted to music publishing. One of his great virtues was that he made no effort to censor, or to like or dislike the music. He felt that his function was not that, but was to publish it. If he decided to publish something, he didn't ques-tion it. I think it's for that reason I have an exclusive contract with them. He accepted everything I had done, and gave me carte blanche. I can do anything I want. That was not my privilege un-til I was nearly fifty years old, and that's true in both writing mu-sic and in writing texts. Now it's true that anything I do do is used in this society. Formerly it wasn't true. Walter Hinrichsen was the first to open that door.

Q: How did your collaboration with Lejaren Hiller on HPSCHD come about?

CAGE: I was Composer in Residence at the University of Cincin-nati, and he asked me if I wanted to work with computers. I said that I would be interested, but I couldn't program and didn't intend to learn how. He said that he'd provide a programmer. Would I come? I'm not clear whether he asked me in the first year for two years or for one, but it turned out to be two years, although he left during the second year. So I proposed two projects. One was HPSCHD and the other was a piece I haven't yet realized, which is Atlas Borealis with the Ten Thunderclaps. (It's to be like a storm.) Both projects were ones that seemed beyond facilities outside of computers.

Jerry accepted all of that. But when I got to Illinois, the programmer that he'd chosen for me was nowhere to be found. So I spent about two weeks doing nothing, and Jerry finally said that he would do the programming. And then the moment he began to

do it, it was clear that his ideas and mine would have to work together. So I proposed that it be a collaboration.

We worked very easily together. I'd always been interested
in his work because he has such an unpredictable imagination.

Q: A few years ago, several orchestras across the country played
your Renga with Apartment House 1776. It usually provoked a rather vicious reaction from at least a good portion of the audience.
Did you anticipate such a response?

CAGE: No. I thought it would be a cheerful piece, and that it
would be celebrative of the bicentennial--which I think it is. I'm
always surprised that more people didn't recognize it as having
that character. But many people faced with sad music laugh, and
faced with witty music start crying, and so forth. It seems to me
that music doesn't really communicate to people. Or if it does, it
does it in very, very different ways from one person to the next.

Many people became annoyed, I think, simply because I superimposed the spiritual songs of four different peoples. Yet if
you engaged them in a discussion on ecumenical thought, you'd
probably find that they agree with the idea that there are different
ways of approaching God.

It was not bad in Cleveland or in Boston. It was bad in
New York, Chicago, and Los Angeles. That's largely because of
the orchestras, which are not good orchestras. There are good
people in each of the orchestras, but there are a large number of
people who aren't good, who don't play faithfully what they are giv-
en to play. Faced with a music such as I had given them, they
simply sabotaged it.

Q: It sounds like the same things that happened with the New York
Philharmonic and Atlas Eclipticalis.

CAGE: Yes, of course it is. The New York Philharmonic is a
bad orchestra. They're like a group of gangsters. They have no
shame: When I came off the stage after one of those performances,
one of them who had played badly shook my hand, smiled, and said,
"Come back in ten years, we'll treat you better." They turn things
away from music, and from any professional attitude toward music,
to some kind of a social situation that is not very beautiful.

In the case of Atlas, they destroyed my property. They
acted criminally. They would tear the microphones off the instruments and stamp on them, and the next day I would then have to
buy new ones to replace them for the next performance. It was
very costly. And they weren't ashamed.

Q: In light of your musical differences with Pierre Boulez, do you feel he performed properly?

CAGE: Well, Boulez and I have had a difficult friendship, one might say, but a long one. I met him over thirty years ago. He gave me the manuscript of the Second Piano Sonata. So although we don't see eye to eye, we nevertheless have a window or a door open on the other one, with a kind of sympathy. The situation between us was greatly caricatured by Joan Peyser in her book about Boulez which is, I must say, a very bad book.

Q: So he did well with your work, but the orchestra was just intractable?

CAGE: He did as well as he could do. He couldn't do very well, and the orchestra certainly could do very badly. He had worked with the Apartment House aspect of the piece, and did that very beautifully. I've since followed all his directions for the instrumentation of the quartets. The assistant conductor prepared the orchestra, and he had done it very well. But when Pierre heard the sliding tones--he hates sliding tones--he insisted that they be removed from the piece. He said that without consulting me. The sliding tones are essential to the orchestra part because they make it sound like nature. (Seiji Ozawa had done that so beautifully.) But Boulez insisted that instead of sliding, they make it like an arpeggio. It was perfectly awful. I couldn't countermand what he had said at the last minute; there would have been complete chaos in the orchestra.

Q: Do you consider works such as Branches and Inlets to be an extension of something that you were doing in Cartridge Music, or does the inclusion of natural objects have a significance that makes the works totally different?

CAGE: No, they're a move in the direction of improvisation.

Q: You've frequently spoken out against improvisation, because it relies so heavily upon habit and personal taste.

CAGE: I'm finding ways to free the act of improvisation from taste and memory and likes and dislikes. If I can do that, then I will be very pleased.

In the case of the plant materials, you don't know them; You're discovering them. So the instrument is unfamiliar. If you become very familiar with a piece of cactus, it very shortly disintegrates, and you have to replace it with another one which you don't know. So the whole thing remains fascinating, and free of your memory as a matter of course.

In the case of Inlets, you have no control whatsoever over the conch shell when it's filled with water. You tip it and you get a gurgle, sometimes; not always. So the rhythm belongs to the instruments, and not to you.

Cartridge Music has several people performing programs that they have determined by means of the materials. But one person's actions unintentionally alter another person's actions, because the actions involve changing the tone controls and the amplitude controls. So you may find yourself playing something and getting no sound whatsoever.

Q: At what stage are the Freeman Etudes now?

CAGE: The first sixteen were finished, and then Zukofsky discovered that I had learned a little bit too much about what was violinistic. When I had a B above the treble clef, it could be played on any one of the four strings. But if it seemed to me to be more appropriate to the first or the second string, I would then not involve the third or the fourth string in the chance operations. When he discovered that, he suggested--and I agreed--to go back over the string indications to find out again what string should be used when it was at all physically possible. Then I go over it with him again, and where it's literally too difficult, just impossible, then he refuses the chance operation. He accepts some and refuses others, so it never gets to be a pure chance situation. But it goes more toward that than it did.

So they're being revised. The first six are finished, and two more have been revised but not yet copied. Then we'll go on through to the sixteenth. I've begun work on the last sixteen.

It's given Zukofsky notions of things that could be done that he didn't know about. I'm keeping a record of all of his answers to my questions, and he proposes to go over them and publish them.

Q: Could you tell us what else you're working on now?

CAGE: Right now I'm just proofreading and making a final copy of the Third Writing Through Finnegans Wake. I'll be working on the Fourth. I have enough material for another book. Probably too much. Then I have a new piece called Themes and Variations which is finished. I have another, shorter text called James Joyce, Marcel Duchamp, Erik Satie: An Alphabet.

I'm tempted to write a large number of songs that come out of Thoreau on the melody of the Pastorale in the Socrate of Satie.

Q: Would it be accurate to say that there is a polemical feature to your work as a composer? Are you more interested in changing the way music is perceived by audiences, performers, and composers than you are in changing the shape or history of music itself?

CAGE: I think there is a didactic element in my work. I think that music has to do with self-alteration; it begins with the alteration of the composer, and conceivably extends to the alteration of the listeners. It by no means secures that, but it does secure the alteration in the mind of the composer; changing the mind so that it'll be changed not just in the presence of music, but in other situations too.

Q: You've commented that most audiences go to a concert with the feeling that something is being done to them, instead of going with the attitude that they have to take an active role. Could you be more specific about what you think they should be doing?

CAGE: The two things that they shouldn't be doing are the things that they generally think they should be doing: one is responding emotionally, and the other is responding in terms of relationships of sounds. I don't think either one should be done.

A great deal of the education has taught them to do just what I've said they shouldn't do. So then the average person goes on to say--or at least is quoted as saying--that he doesn't know anything about music (as the educators suggest that he should do), but that he knows what he likes. So he searches to see whether he likes something or not. Then the first time he's rubbed the wrong way, he says, "I don't like it." That can be because something is too loud, or too dissonant, or too this, or too that.

A mind that is interested in changing, though, such as the mind of Ives, is interested precisely in the things that are at extremes. I'm certainly like that. Unless we go to extremes, we won't get anywhere.

Q: A great many people would be baffled by the suggestion that they should respond neither emotionally nor intellectually to music. What else is there?

CAGE: They should listen. Why should they imagine that sounds are not interesting in themselves? I'm always amazed when people say, "Do you mean it's just sounds?" How they can imagine that it's anything but sounds is what's so mysterious.

They're convinced that it's a vehicle for pushing the ideas of one person out of his head into somebody else's head, along with --in a good German situation--his feelings, in a marriage that's called the marriage of Form and Content. That situation is, from my point of view, absolutely alarming.

I had just heard The Messiah with Mrs. Henry Allen Moe, and she said, "Don't you love the 'Hallelujah' Chorus?" and I said, "No, I can't stand it." So she said, "Don't you like to be moved?" and I said, "I don't mind being moved, but I don't like to be pushed."

Q: What do you think the harmful effects of that marriage are for an audience?

CAGE: What it does is bolster up the ego. It is in the ego, as in a home, that those feelings and ideas take place. The moment you focus on them, you focus on the ego, and you separate it from the rest of Creation. So then a very interesting sound might occur, but the ego wouldn't even hear it because it didn't fit its notion of likes and dislikes, its ideas and feelings. It becomes not only insensitive, but, if you persist in annoying it, it will then put cotton in its ears. So if it isn't sufficiently insensitive to the outside, it will cut itself off from possible experience.

Q: Is it possible to listen to The Messiah in such a way that the sounds can be taken simply as themselves?

CAGE: I think so. But you'd have to listen to a lot of other music at the same time, in some kind of Apartment House situation. Then it might be very entertaining. You can get rid of intention by multiplying intention. That's what's at the basis of my work with Musicircus, which is in Apartment House.

Q: A number of years ago, you made this comment about the use of aleatory in basically controlled compositions: "I think we're in a more urgent situation, where it is absolutely essential for us to change our minds fundamentally." You've just been restating that idea now. Do you think that much progress has been made toward fundamental change like that?

CAGE: No. I'm not at all as optimistic about these ideas as I was formerly. The reason is that the social situation is in a more critical stage. I see music, unfortunately, and the arts generally as insufficient in altering the minds of a sufficiently large number of people. We are under the control of precisely the things that the arts would like us to become free of; and we are under that control almost hopelessly. I hate to say something like that because I haven't much training as a pessimist. But I think it's evident from the media and the news that something like that is happening.

We know that we should be doing differently than we're doing if we're to continue on the planet, but nobody acts to make that change come about. Some do, but not enough. We continue the incredibly mad use of fossil fuels, yet we've known for a long time that it's just a question of years before there won't be any. As Fuller has pointed out, those are capital energy sources, and when the capital is gone there isn't any more. On top of which, the use of those things pollutes the air and makes it impossible to breathe in a healthy way. And then to use those very things that are worst for us as the cause for wars between us, involving further uses of energy--it's just madness. And music has little effect upon this situation.

Q: Could it?

CAGE: Theoretically, it could, but it doesn't work according to the theory. The theory being that of Marshall McLuhan: We have extended the central nervous system and therefore the whole society is a single human being with its mind exteriorized, and we know that minds can change, therefore it could conceivably change.

Perhaps it will change, ultimately, but it will change after some awful pain, which will be a world pain. Then people will finally realize that something has to be done. But the Lord knows what form that pain will take.

Generally, society works on the assumption that power is what is necessary, whereas what is necessary is intelligence. Power is not of importance, because power ultimately decays, and another power takes its place. I think we still don't realize that we are now weak on the world scene. But we are. And yet we still think that we have some strength. Furthermore, we think we're the best people. It's all foolishness, and music hasn't been able to change those thoughts.

I think that in a real crisis situation, people do change. I think they're too comfortable; they're not sufficiently troubled. I changed my diet four years ago to the macrobiotic diet, and I did it because I had pains which the doctors couldn't remove. Within a week of the changed diet, the pains went away; also my arthritis, for which I'd been taking twelve aspirin a day for fifteen years. So I was able to change; not only my mind, through the use of chance operations and such things, but my body, through the alteration of what I put into it--which only stands to reason. But before that, I insisted on going on eating the dairy products and meat and all the animal fats, which are destructive of the body--and which always destroyed the rich bodies of the earth; it was the poor bodies that were always obliged to be healthy, through the eating of beans and rice.

Q: Do you think that, as the years go by, more people will compose with the methods you've brought forth?

CAGE: No, I think we're going in a multiplicity of directions. If I performed any function at all, it's one that would have been performed in any case: to take us out of the notion of the mainstream of music, and into a situation that could be likened to a delta or field or ocean, that there are just countless possibilities.

Q: And you think that would have happened anyway, without your music?

CAGE: I think so. I think that our ideas that seem to be novel are merely ideas that one or another of us is about to have. At the time that I was using the Magic Square, Wyschnegradsky on the other side of the Atlantic was also using it, and I had no connection with him. At the time that Edison invented the electric light, someone else did it too but didn't get to the post office soon enough!

CATALOG OF COMPOSITIONS

1932	Twenty Years After for voice and piano	Henmar
1932	Is It As It Was for voice and piano	Henmar
1932	At East and Ingredients for voice and piano	Henmar
1933	Solo with Obbligato Accompaniment of Two Voices in Canon, and Six Short Inventions on the Subject of the Solo	Henmar
1933	Sonata for Clarinet	Henmar
1933	Sonata for Two Voices	Henmar
1934	Composition for Three Voices	Henmar
1934	Music for Xenia for piano	Henmar
1934; 58	Six Short Inventions for Seven Instruments	Henmar
1935; 74	Two Pieces for Piano	Henmar
1935	Three Pieces for Flute Duet	Henmar
1935	Quartet for Percussion	Henmar
1935	Quest for piano	Henmar
1936	Trio for Percussion	Henmar
1938	Metamorphosis for piano	Henmar
1938	Five Songs for Contralto and Piano	Henmar

1938	Music for Wind Instruments	Henmar
1939	Imaginary Landscape No. 1 for records of constant and variable frequency, large Chinese cymbal, and string piano	Henmar
1939	First Construction (In Metal) for percussion sextet	Henmar
1940	Second Construction for percussion orchestra	Henmar
1940	Bacchanale for prepared piano	Henmar
1940	Living Room Music for percussion and speech quartet	Henmar
1941	Double Music for percussion quartet (Co-composer: Lou Harrison)	Henmar
1941	Third Construction for percussion quartet	Henmar
1942	Imaginary Landscape No. 2 (March No. 1) for percussion quintet	Henmar
1942	Imaginary Landscape No. 3 for six percussion players	Henmar
1942	Credo in Us for percussion quartet (including piano and radio or phonograph)	Henmar
1942	The Wonderful Widow of Eighteen Springs for voice and closed piano	Henmar
1942	And the Earth Shall Bear Again for prepared piano	Henmar
1942	In the Name of the Holocaust for prepared piano	Henmar
1942	Primitive for prepared piano	Henmar
1943	Amores for prepared piano and percussion	Henmar
1943	Tossed As It Is Untroubled (Meditation) for prepared piano	Henmar
1943	Totem Ancestor for prepared piano	Henmar
1943	She Is Asleep for voice, prepared piano, and twelve tomtoms	Henmar
1943	A Room for piano or prepared piano	Henmar
1943	Our Spring Will Come for piano	Henmar
1944	The Perilous Night for prepared piano	Henmar
1944	A Book of Music for two prepared pianos	Henmar
1944	Prelude for Meditation for prepared piano	Henmar
1944	Root of an Unfocus for prepared piano	Henmar
1944	Four Walls for voice and piano	Henmar
1944	A Valentine Out of Season for prepared piano	Henmar
1944	Forever and Sunsmell for voice and percussion	Henmar
1944	Spontaneous Earth for prepared piano	Henmar
1944	The Unavailable Memory of for prepared piano	Henmar
1945	Daughters of the Lonesome Isle for prepared piano	Henmar
1945	Mysterious Adventure for prepared piano	Henmar
1945	Three Dances for two prepared pianos	Henmar
1946	Ophelia for piano	Henmar

1946	Two Pieces for Piano	Henmar
1947	The Seasons ballet for orchestra or piano	Henmar
1947	Music for Marcel Duchamp for prepared piano	Henmar
1947	Nocturne for violin and piano	Henmar
1948	Sonatas and Interludes for prepared piano	Henmar
1948	Dream for piano	Henmar
1948	Experiences No. 1 for two pianos	Henmar
1948	Experiences No. 2 for voice	Henmar
1948	Suite for Toy Piano or Piano	Henmar
1948	In a Landscape for piano or harp	Henmar
1950	String Quartet in Four Parts	Henmar
1950	Six Melodies for violin and keyboard (piano)	Henmar
1950	A Flower for voice and closed piano	Henmar
1951	Concerto for Prepared Piano and Chamber Orchestra	Henmar
1951	Imaginary Landscape No. 4 (March No. 2) for twelve radios	Henmar
1951	Sixteen Dances for flute, trumpet, violin, cello, and percussion	Henmar
1951	Music of Changes for piano	Henmar
1952	Waiting for piano	Henmar
1952	Imaginary Landscape No. 5 for tape using any 42 phonograph records	Henmar
1952	Seven Haiku for piano	Henmar
1952	Two Pastorales for prepared piano	Henmar
1952	Williams Mix for tape	Henmar
1952	Water Music for a pianist	Henmar
1952	For M.C. and D.T. for piano	Henmar
1952	4'33" tacet, for any instrument or combination of instruments	Henmar
1952; 61	Music for Carillon No. 1 (2-Octave Version)	Henmar
1952; 61	Music for Carillon No. 1 (3-Octave Version)	Henmar
1952; 61	Music for Carillon (Graph) No. 1	Henmar
1952	Music for Piano 1	Henmar
1953	Music for Piano 2	Henmar
1953	Music for Piano 3	Henmar
1953	Music for Piano 4-19 for piano solo or ensemble	Henmar
1953	59½" for a string player	Henmar
1953	Music for Piano 20	Henmar
1954	Music for Carillon Nos. 2 and 3 (Graph)	Henmar
1954; 58	Music for Carillon (2 Octaves) No. 2	Henmar
1954; 61	Music for Carillon (2 Octaves) No. 3	Henmar
1954	34'46.776" for a pianist	Henmar
1954	31'57.9864" for a pianist	Henmar
1955	26'1.1499" for a string player	Henmar
1955	Music for Piano 21-36; 37-52 for piano solo or ensemble	Henmar
1955	Speech for five radios and news-reader	Henmar

1956	27'10.554" for a percussionist	Henmar
1956	Radio Music for one to eight radios	Henmar
1956	Music for Piano 53-68 for piano solo or ensemble	Henmar
1956	Music for Piano 69-84 for piano solo or ensemble	Henmar
1957	Winter Music for one to twenty pianists	Henmar
1957	For Paul Taylor and Anita Dencks for piano	Henmar
1958	Variations I for any number of players and any sound-producing means	Henmar
1958	Aria for voice	Henmar
1958	Solo for Voice 1	Henmar
1958	Concert for Piano and Orchestra (solos for piano and 13 instruments)	Henmar
1958	Music Walk for one or more pianists	Henmar
1958	TV Koln for piano	Henmar
1958	Fontana Mix for tape	Henmar
1959	Sounds of Venice for solo television performer	MS
1959	Water Walk for solo television performer	Henmar
1960	Theatre Piece for one to eight performers	Henmar
1960	Music for Amplified Toy Pianos	Henmar
1960	Music for "The Marrying Maiden" for tape	Henmar
1960	WBAI material for making a mechanical program	Henmar
1960	Solo for Voice 2	Henmar
1960	Cartridge Music for any number of players and loudspeakers	Henmar
1960	Where Are We Going? And What Are We Doing? for tape	Henmar
1961	Variations II for any number of players and any sound-producing means	Henmar
1961	Music for Carillon No. 4 for a 3-octave electronic instrument with accompaniment	Henmar
1961	Atlas Eclipticalis for 1 to 86 players	Henmar
1962	0'00" (4'33" No. 2) solo to be performed in any way by anyone	Henmar
1963	Variations III for one or any number of people performing any actions	Henmar
1963	Variations IV for any number of players, any sounds or combinations of sounds produced by any means, with or without other activities	Henmar
1964	Electronic Music for Piano	Henmar
1965	Rozart Mix for tape	Henmar
1965	Variations V audio-visual performance	Henmar
1966	Variations VI for a plurality of sound systems	Henmar
1966	Music for Carillon No. 4 for a 2-octave electronic instrument with accompaniment	Henmar

1967	Music for Carillon No. 5	Henmar
1967	Variations VII	Henmar
1967	Newport Mix	Henmar
1968	Reunion	Henmar
1968	HPSCHD for 1 to 7 harpsichords and 1 to 51 tapes (Co-composer: Lejaren Hiller)	Henmar
1969	Sound Anonymously Received	Henmar
1969	Cheap Imitation for piano	Henmar
1970	Song Books (Solos for Voice 3-92)	Henmar
1971	62 Mesostics Re Merce Cunningham for voice	Henmar
1971	WGBH-TV for a composer and technicians	Henmar
1971	Les Chants de Maldoror Pulverises Par L'Assistance Meme pour un public francophone de pas plus de 200 personnes	Henmar
1972	Cheap Imitation for orchestra (24-95 players)	Henmar
1972	Bird Cage for tape	Henmar
1973	Etcetera for orchestra (with or without 3 conductors) and tape	Henmar
1974	Score (40 Drawings by Thoreau) and 23 Parts for any instruments and/or voices and tape	Henmar
1975	Etudes Australes for piano	Henmar
1975	Lecture on the Weather for twelve speaker-vocalists (or instrumentalists) with tape and film	Henmar
1975	Child of Tree (Improvisation I) for solo percussionist using amplified plant materials	Henmar
1976	Branches (Improvisation IA) for percussion solo, duo, trio, or orchestra (of any number of players) using amplified plant materials	Henmar
1976	Renga for any 78 instruments and/or voices	Henmar
1976	Apartment House 1776 for any number of musicians with live or recorded Protestant, Sephardic, and American Indian songs, and Negro calls and hollers, to be played with or without Renga	Henmar
1976	Quartets I-VIII for an orchestra of 24 instruments; 41 instruments; 93 instruments	Henmar
1976	Quartet I for concert band (39 instruments) and 12 amplified voices	Henmar
1977	Cheap Imitation for violin (Edited with Paul Zukofsky)	Henmar
1977	Inlets (Improvisation II) for three players of water-filled conches and one conch-player using circular breathing and a recording of the sound of fire	Henmar

1977	Pools (Improvisation IIA) for soloist using water-filled conch shells	Henmar
1977	Telephones and Birds for three performers	Henmar
1977	49 Waltzes for the Five Boroughs for performer(s) or listener(s) or record maker(s)	Henmar
1977	Quartets V and VI for concert band (39 instruments) and twelve amplified voices	Henmar
1978	Chorals for violin (Edited with Paul Zukofsky)	Henmar
1978	Freeman Etudes I-XVI for violin	Henmar
1978	A Dip in the Lake: Ten Quicksteps, Sixty-two Waltzes, and Fifty-six Marches for Chicago and Vicinity for performer(s) or listener(s) or record maker(s)	Henmar
1978	Etudes Borealis I-IV for cello solo and for piano solo	Henmar
1978	Letters to Erik Satie	Henmar
1978	Variations VIII for no music or recordings	Henmar
1978	Some of the Harmony of Maine (Supply Belcher) rewritten for organist and three assistants	Henmar
1979	Hymns and Variations for twelve amplified voices	Henmar
1979	___, ___ ___ Circus on ___ title article adjective title of a book means for "translating" a book into music	Henmar
1980	Improvisation III	Henmar
1980	Improvisation IV	Henmar
1980	Litany for the Whale	Henmar

ELLIOTT CARTER □

photo: Gene Bagnato

ELLIOTT CARTER

Elliott Carter was born on December 11, 1908, in
New York City. He received his B. A. and M. A.
from Harvard, where his teachers included Walter
Piston and Gustav Holst. From Harvard he went to
Paris, enrolling at L'Ecole Normale de Musique as
well as studying privately with Nadia Boulanger.
Carter is currently on the faculty of The Juilliard
School of Music. In 1939, he married Helen Frost-
Jones. They have one son.

Carter's early works were written in a tonal, neo-
classical idiom. His development of metric modulation in the late 1940s led him into a music of extreme
rhythmic complexity. At the same time, his music also became increasingly chromatic and dissonant. Since the 1950s, Carter has been composing
in his own style of atonal chromaticism; it is a body
of work that has made him one of the most highly
regarded of living composers.

Cole Gagne interviewed Elliott Carter on August
10, 1975, at his home in Katonah, New York. The
experience was much closer to visiting family than
to interviewing a stranger. Both Mr. and Mrs. Carter are possessed of a genuine, fundamental warmth
and friendliness. As a result, the author left that
day with more than he brought, the gifts ranging from
a record to a bag full of parsley from their garden.

Q: What are your feelings toward your neo-classical works of the
thirties and forties? Do you think that there's a break from them
to such later pieces as the First String Quartet?

CARTER: Not at all, no. I feel that they move bit by bit from
one to another. I think that the neo-classical scores are transition-
al scores. The Piano Sonata--which is sort of a tonal work--and
the Cello Sonata--also a neo-classical score--are really step-by-
step introductions to the First String Quartet. I feel that all of
my scores shouldn't be suppressed. I don't know exactly how much
I like them--sometimes I'm more impressed by them than others
are, that's all I can say.

Q: This is going to be old hat for you, I know, but I can't talk to
you and not mention metric modulation. It's actually three questions: How did you come up with it, precisely what is it, and what
is its value for you?

CARTER: I can't explain how I came up with it. It appeared in my mind at the time that I was writing my Cello Sonata, which was in 1948. But it's obvious that this is not a new thing with me. There are examples of it in the last Beethoven sonatas, and there are even examples in very early music, where there were changes in rhythm and polyrhythms superimposed on each other. Certainly in the Elizabethan madrigals there's some of that, but even before then, in the fourteenth century, composers enjoyed writing all sorts of tricky rhythmical things.

A lot of this was known to me, but it didn't occur to me to write a piece that employed this thoroughly until my Cello Sonata. In that work, I made an analogue to the key changes, a kind of modulation from one speed to another, step by step. The whole Cello Sonata starts and ends with the same speed, and it goes through a great variety of speeds that are all strung together one right after the other. One speed emerges from the other, so you can't tell in certain passages which speed the piece is in. There are superimpositions of one speed over another, and one becomes more dominant than the previous one, and that leads into the next section. That's really what the whole substance of it is.

There are examples of this in the music of Schoenberg--it was never used thoroughly by Schoenberg--and even in Alban Berg, but it was never used to the extent that my music uses it. They just have it at moments, even in some of Stravinsky. When I finally began to think more about this, it seemed to me to be a summation of all the different efforts that modern music had been making in the matter of rhythm--the various changings, going from slow to fast or from fast to slow, having irregular rhythms like Stravinsky, accents on sevens and fives and threes, and alternations. One could make a complete connection between all the different possibilities modern music had been developing. It seemed to me a conclusion that everybody was trying to find, and I felt that I had found it.

The method has been expanded, especially in more recent works, so that it combines speeding up and slowing down with regular speeds going on at the same time, all kinds of things. There's one other person that has developed this rather elaborately, and it's partially in collaboration with him that I have worked this out. That's a man who lives in Mexico City, named Conlon Nancarrow, who's written quite a lot of pieces for player piano. They do this mathematically. They are very amusing pieces, mostly jazz derived--some of them very clearly so. I felt that I was also deriving this whole method from jazz. There are tendencies, especially in the jazz of the time that I was very interested in it, where the rhythm was straight and went along regularly, and then the melody would move rapidly from very slow things to very fast things, giving it the impression of improvisation which I seek in my music.

Q: You've said that you particularly like it when the musicians have studied long enough and are able to play the piece as if it's being improvised.

CARTER: Yes. People are always saying that now my music is so mechanically notated that it's become impossible for the performer to interpret it, that every note--and it's true--that every note of my music seems to have a mark on it. On the whole that doesn't seem to change the approach of performers, for one performer will play my piece very differently from another. My feeling is that I'm trying to give them a more precise direction, and then allow their imagination to play. If they don't make any sense out of it, then it won't make any sense. They have to somehow understand what the musical intention is, and this is just a way of making it more precise. It's like using a larger vocabulary if you were writing prose or poetry, rather than a very small one.

Q: It would seem that with your interest in different tempi that electronic music would be a big help. You could have a perfect control over the speeds.

CARTER: I've got a funny feeling about that because of this friend of mine who's written so many pieces for player piano. They are so mechanical. He's really carried it out to a degree that I've never heard in electronic music. This mechanistic aspect is something I don't like. To me, the performance of music depends a great deal on the imagination of the performer, and I see my music as something that is going to be played by people, and something that is going to interest them. I find that one of the greatest problems with electronic music is the feeling of not having any contact with a live musician, and I don't feel that the music is somehow so interesting that it captures my imagination and makes me forget that. Of course, in the movies, or on records, you aren't aware of this, because you get the sense that there's a physical person playing the piece. But in electronic music you feel that it's all coming from some place that doesn't seem to have very much life in it--in the detail, the sense of the sound. Sometimes the imagination of the composer is very fanciful, and at times that's very interesting. I think that the works that have combined both live music and electronic music, such as the works of Mario Davidovsky, solve this in many ways, and I think a lot of it is very beautiful.

Q: I was just going to bring that up. Have you ever considered incorporating the two?

CARTER: It's hard for me to learn about a new technique. I realize it would take me years to learn how to deal with electronic music in a way that would be satisfactory to me. I have students that have shown me about it and have done a great deal with it,

and I find that it would be just too damn much work. I have so
many pieces that I want to write, and I would not like to start
learning all over again. I'm learning enough about things as it is
just writing my own music, and I can't picture the idea of stopping
that and sitting down and learning all about computers, or other
electronic devices. It would be too frustrating at my stage.

Q: In your comments about your different works, I notice that you
frequently refer to literature and cinema. I'm thinking about St.
John Perse's Vents with the Concerto for Orchestra, or Lucretius
and Alexander Pope with the Double Concerto, or the First String
Quartet, in which you compare its beginning and end to Jean Coc-
teau's The Blood of a Poet. Are these basically just metaphors to
help the listener, or do these different art forms play a role in
your composing?

CARTER: I don't think that they play the role that you would imagine, but they do play a role in my music. They don't play the
role of being the primary thought. That is, I did not sit down to
write a piece that was going to be like The Blood of a Poet, or
like Vents. These things came to mind after I began writing the
music. There are many other things that probably come to mind
as I write my music, but these became important because they
were similar to certain ideas in the music. But the music always
came first. I'm very concerned with modern painting and modern
literature, I always have been all my life, and so these are all in
my head, and they have an effect, there's no doubt about that. But
I don't think they ever have a generative effect. They're sort of a
crutch that helps me clear up some of the intentions that I have in
the piece.

Q: I understand that you were originally an English major at Harvard.

CARTER: That's right.

Q: What turned you around into music?

CARTER: I was always interested in music, and I had wanted to
go into music before I got into English literature, but there were
two problems. First of all, in 1926 to '30, when I was at Harvard,
the Harvard music department disliked contemporary music very
much. I was too young and inexperienced to understand that maybe
it was important to learn older music before you learned new music,
and the department was just unsympathetic to what I wanted to do.
I wanted to understand why Stravinsky and Schoenberg and Bartók
wrote the music they did, and they couldn't understand why anybody

would want to do that. So therefore I decided that I should study something else.

I got so much out of being at Harvard. The Boston Symphony was extremely active in playing contemporary music at that time. Even their Pops concerts at that time were conducted by one of the leading Italian modern composers, Alfredo Casella. He used to play a great deal of his music at the Pops, so we used to hear all kinds of things. Nicolas Slonimsky was also living in Boston at the time that I was a student. He did a great deal to publicize the works of Ives and Varèse, and we used to hear those there. So to be in Boston at that time was a very lively thing musically. There were also people around the college who were very interested in this. I was very interested in contemporary literature and painting, and there were many people who were interested in that too. James Agee, for instance, was one of my college friends, and we were very interested in all of this, you see.

I could have gotten up and gone somewhere else, although at that time in the United States there was very little interest in teaching contemporary music anywhere, so it would have been the same if I had gone to another place. The only places at that time where you could learn about contemporary music were either Paris, where I finally went with Nadia Boulanger, or with Schoenberg in Berlin-- and I didn't speak German decently enough at that time to want to go there. I was also old enough to have felt rather strongly about the war, and wasn't very sympathetic to the Germans.

Q: I understand that Walter Piston and Gustav Holst were something of an exception on the Harvard faculty.

CARTER: Yes, that's right. Walter Piston, while I was a student at Harvard, came back from studying with Nadia Boulanger and was an assistant in the music department, and he was much more interested in contemporary music. But he's always been very conservative in his point of view. He was very helpful to me, I must say. Gustav Holst was an exchange professor for six months, and he was of course also a very conservative composer, but he was interesting.

Q: How did you finally get to work with Nadia Boulanger?

CARTER: I was an undergraduate in English, but I went into music as a graduate student, because I really had always studied it and taken courses in it. I was very interested and really wanted to be a musician. When I received my M.A. at Harvard, Walter Piston advised me to go and study with Nadia Boulanger. In fact, I had even talked to Ives about it--I saw a lot of him at that time--and it seemed that that was a reasonable thing to do. Now, there were other people. Henry Cowell was teaching something about contemporary music out in California. Just after I left to go and study with Nadia Boulanger, Schoenberg came to the United States. Things might have been slightly different if there had been a change of one year.

Q: How important was working with Boulanger for you?

CARTER: Oh, very important. She was of course very devoted to Stravinsky's music in particular. It was a great revelation to have someone explain that all those wrong notes were right!

Q: The different instrumental personalities in your Second String Quartet remind me of Ives' Second Quartet, and its use of confrontation and dialectic. Has much of Ives' technique found its way into your music?

CARTER: It's rather complicated to say. I don't think you could ask any artist about his influences. Obviously, I have not sat down and said to myself, "I will write something that is like Charles Ives." It never even occurred to me to do that at any time--except when I was a student, I sometimes wanted to write like Stravinsky or Bartók. But it never occurred to me to do that later on.

I've always known these pieces of Ives, and certainly the influence of his music at times is great. Particularly when I was teaching at Columbia around 1947 or '48. I arranged to have the first performances of The Unanswered Question and Central Park in the Dark at a festival there, and I have all that correspondence with Mr. and Mrs. Ives about that. That obviously influenced my First Quartet, which quotes a theme from Ives in the beginning. It was something I'd thought of, I felt that I owed something to him, and so I quoted a little piece of his music.

Q: What about other members of the American Five--Ruggles or John Becker or Wallingford Riegger. Do you have a high regard for their music?

CARTER: I don't know John Becker very well. But I know Carl Ruggles very much--I know his music and I like it, and I can say that it's interested me a lot. I don't know if Wallingford Riegger influenced me or not. I find his music has had its day, and I think it's awful that it's been so neglected. I wrote very good reviews, especially of the First String Quartet of Wallingford Riegger, which interested me a great deal at the time. I've never heard it since, but I think it's a very good work. I must say I like Riegger very much. I especially like his Dichotomy. Some of the other works seem to me less successful.

Q: To get back to the Second String Quartet: each of the instruments has a different personality. What dictated the personalities that you gave the instruments? Was it their individual characteristics more than the work's musical necessities?

CARTER: It's pretty hard for me to remember that. I would say that it was more or less playing on the notion that we talked about a bit before: the notion of strictness and regularity as opposed to improvisation and freedom. I think I chose a repertory of characters in which there were various degrees of freedom and strictness; I invented characters around this. I think what started it originally was a musical idea: how one could make textures in which there would be two or three, or even at maximum four (which would seldom happen) very distinct events occurring, which would all be quite clear to the listener. It was out of this that a plan began to evolve in which there would be really quite strikingly different kinds of characters. It was thinking of this, more than actually deciding on some kind of story, that made me choose the characters--but that's at a much later stage. The choice of the type of characters came after the idea of how you would keep these people separate, how you would keep each one quite clear. The idea that one like the cello would move by very small steps rhythmically, so that it would get slower and faster in small degrees while the first violin would jump from very slow notes to fast ones--well, this immediately would suggest certain kinds of emotional feelings to me, you see.

Q: Is the auditory scenario more of a metaphor to explain the music after the fact, or do you really have certain dramatic concepts in mind as you're composing?

CARTER: It isn't thought of after the fact, it is thought of during the time that it's happening. I don't think that the scenario or any kind of thing like that starts with me until after the piece is underway, until after I've decided what the musical materials are and have tried to write some of it. Then all this begins to become much more clarified. I think one of the problems about being an artist is always that the artist has to clarify his intentions, and know what it is he's trying to do. Works that don't have that kind of clarity of intention I think inevitably become very weak and silly. You have to know what kind of quality you're trying to present. Part of the whole process of clarifying is finally to invent a scenario--in my case, very often a kind of social scenario, sort of an analogue of the behavior of people. By the same token, the performers become the people with the actual performance.

Q: I'm curious as to how you compose such highly chromatic, non-tonally oriented music without a system like dodecaphony.

CARTER: The choice of using twelve-tone music or not occurred to me quite a long time ago, when I first began to be interested in twelve-tone music. It became something I thought a lot about when many people began to write it after the war--I'd even though about it a lot before then. I tried to write it, and found that I was not able to solve my problems and do what I wanted to do. So I decided that it was silly to add another kind of problem to something that was already difficult enough to manage.

Now, my music does have a rather strong bias towards systematizing--as you can understand, for instance, in the Second Quartet. Each one of the instruments for a good part of the time plays all the various material that it has within a certain range of intervals. The cello has minor sixths, for instance, and perfect fourths. A great deal of its material is built out of that--that's very restrictive indeed. The same is true of each one of the instruments, and none of them have the same thing. This was one of the modes of keeping them apart. Now, to have decided to give a repertory of certain sounds to one instrument and another, and then to solve that with the twelve-tone system--I would've had to have had a computer. I didn't do it that way. I sat down and simply worked out little sample passages that would do this, and when they didn't work I tried other ones, and gradually I taught myself how to write a piece that would have this technical requirement enough of the time so that it would be fairly audible to a listener who knew what was happening. Also, it had to have an expression that gave each one of these voices a kind of liveliness. This took a good deal--sort of like playing tennis, you finally get to know how to do it after you've done it a lot. It took training to work it out so I could do it without feeling that I was constantly being constricted by the various things that I was trying to do. Mainly, it consisted of accumulating a large number of examples of little things--any old thing that comes into my head that will fit this particular scheme like a puzzle. After a while I learned how to do that. A lot of the examples were of no use, they were just sort of trials.

Q: Earlier, you mentioned the importance of clarifying your artistic intentions. Is it this need for clarity that has kept you from using aleatoric techniques?

CARTER: Well, yes, it's partly that. I feel about aleatoric music in general that it always borders on something very nondescript. Anything that doesn't have a clear-cut intention behind it will, in the end, always produce something which is very obvious. It will sound like confusion, just a rather simple kind of confusion. My music sounds like confusion, but if you hear it more often it isn't so confused as you think!

Q: I've found that I listen to many of your works in almost the same way in which I listen to a Richard Strauss tone poem. Your notes for them very clearly map out what's happening, particularly

with difficult pieces like the Concerto for Orchestra or the Third
String Quartet. Eventually, after several listenings, the road maps
become less necessary and you can just listen to the music.

CARTER: It's important to have those road maps for the people
who don't know what's going to happen, because it can be profoundly confusing. I think that it would be confusing to me to hear someone else doing something which I didn't know about. I've had the
experience of being very confused by some kinds of contemporary
music, the first time I heard it, and then gradually coming to understand it. Like Boulez's Le Marteau Sans Maître, which I heard
for the first time in 1955. I thought it was very interesting, but
I didn't understand what it was all about, exactly. Maybe we didn't
have a good performance of it, I don't know. But after a while,
over four or five years, it all began to seem very sensible to me.

Q: Does that bother you when you compose? Do you think that
you can't write a certain passage because an audience will not comprehend what you're doing, or do you take it for granted that if
they're interested enough they'll put in the effort to understand?

CARTER: I don't think about it quite that way. The censorship
that I exercise on my own music is the censorship of difficulty of
performance: two instruments playing two rhythmic patterns that
nearly coincide but not quite; I tend to try to avoid that. I try to
make it quite clear that they are not coinciding, and that everybody
else can hear it in just what degree. So I'm always having to re-
write passages that have some sort of little mathematical pattern,
in order to fix it up so that you can hear that these are really separate. It's troublesome. I've found that if they're almost together
too much of the time, they play it together. The listener doesn't
know they're not, and thinks that they should be together and hears
it that way. That's the kind of censorship I exercise largely, aside
from the ones of making the instruments play things that make instrumental sense of one kind or another.

But as far as the listener goes, I take myself as the listener.
What I think I'd like to hear, I feel other people might like to hear--
that's about all I can say.

Q: In the Third String Quartet you superimpose the different movements. Why did you decide to forgo a more linear progression?

CARTER: In the earlier works, I was very interested in writing
pieces that had a continuous line from beginning to end, like one
big process. Then, especially with the Third String Quartet, I
realized that the sense of abruptness, of sudden change, had been
eliminated from the earlier works. Everything was sort of sliding

from one thing to another. So it occurred to me that it would be very interesting to write a work which really had sudden things happening all the way through it. Therefore, I jumbled up the movements so that no movement succeeds another movement in the same way. That is, if "b" follows "a" the first time, "c" will precede "b" the next time. The order is always unpredictable. That's taking just one of the two duos, this holds true for both. The principle of continuity is that one duo goes on and on playing while the other one suddenly switches from one thing to another.

Q: The Concerto for Orchestra also superimposes its different movements.

CARTER: Well, that I conceived of as one continuously happening thing of all the same character, with things fading in and out which you would notice. Primarily, the concept was that all of this was going on all the time, that it was like nature. It was just like a continuous process of nature, and I was simply bringing to the listener's attention various facets of this.

The poem suggests this. You know, there were some people that just hated the poetry, and they said to me, "Why did you ever have anything to do with it?" And in a way, I came to dislike the poetry a little bit myself; it's so bombastic. In some respects the music is not a direct expression or an analog of Vents at all. It's only vaguely like the poem as I see it. It has other things that are very different. As I pointed out, there are certain things like it. But I disliked very much the excessive primitivism of the poem. There's a very arty kind of primitivism that keeps coming back, and it's very impressive in a way. It's not something I like, and I don't subscribe to it; I even find it disturbing emotionally. It seems to me wrong to take this kind of false primitivism and glorify it; it seems to me dangerous, and rather fascist in intention. That became more and more obvious to me as I went on. What interested me in the poem was the idea of the wind, but the other side of it, the side of the excessive violence was something that I found a little bit extravagant and a little false, as far as I was concerned.

Q: Does the Concerto for Orchestra still please you today? It's certainly one of your most difficult orchestral scores, if not the most. Do you think it's one of your best?

CARTER: Oh, yes. I think it's a fine work. One of the things is it's very difficult to play it well. We're going right now on tour to perform it. They're playing it at the Edinburgh Festival--Boulez is conducting it all around Europe. When it's done very well it's very impressive--to me, anyhow.

One of the problems that militates against its being played

well is that with the concert conditions as they are, the orchestra plays it two or three times and that's all. Now, you really need to play it twenty times and finally get to know it. But this can never happen; because of the orchestral repertoire a thing like that gets put aside and shows up again maybe once in a while, but so seldom that there's no hangover from one performance to the next.

Q: I was struck by the fact that after the choral pieces of the forties you've written no music for voice. Is that just a matter of commissions, or is that preference?

CARTER: Mainly, it's a matter of the fact that the choral and vocal music that I wrote mostly around 1942--the songs which I wrote in 1942, and the choral music which I continued to write up until around 1947--were always sung so badly. I decided that it was too discouraging to write choral music, especially as my style began to develop much more elaborately than either the choral music or the vocal music. I decided that it would be just folly to try and write things of the kind that I wanted to write for voice, since the easier pieces were sung so poorly. Now, people are beginning to sing the old songs--and well. Susan Wyner's been going around singing the Voyage and the Whitman song, and those have come out beautifully, so I'm thinking of writing some more songs.

As far as choral music goes, I find that the problem with writing choral music in the United States is that you have to write for an amateur chorus. The professional chorus hardly exists. There is one in Chicago, and it's a big event when you get a piece played because it's so complicated to make the arrangements. Nobody wants to do it. The Chicago Symphony is doing Roger Sessions' When Lilacs Last in the Dooryard Bloom'd next year, but it's taken years for anybody to get around to doing it. They did it up in Cambridge fairly well last winter, but he'll have three performances and that's all. He's very lucky; it's a very good work. But most people who write anything that makes any demands on the chorus either get a lousy performance or they don't get any performance at all. It's too discouraging. Especially when you're a person such as myself, who has circulated a lot. I've been to Europe at different times and I've heard the most difficult things played and sung beautifully. I realize that this is impossible for me to get in the United States, and I can't write for a European performance; that's too silly, because you get that one performance and that's it.

Q: Do you find that professionalism has increased over the years, that music that couldn't be done well some years ago can now get better performances?

CARTER: Oh yes, in instrumental music it's developed enormously. The difference between the way people play my First String Quartet is very obvious. There's that old record of the Walden Quartet playing it, and then the new record of the Composers Quartet, and it's very different indeed--although both of them played it pretty well. The Walden Quartet played it remarkably well, considering that it was the first time that anybody had ever played it, that any-body'd played anything of that difficulty. This is true of the two Juilliard performances of my Second String Quartet, for instance. There's an old one on RCA Victor that's out of print now, and the new one on Columbia Records, and they're very strikingly different. It shows that the Quartet itself has somehow developed. Mainly, they're no longer so hectic and nervous. They go crazy, you know, thinking that they may never be able to get through it at the first performance, and then later it all seems to be easy. Well, not so easy!

Q: Not impossible.

CARTER: Not impossible. And not nerve-racking--which is the bane of contemporary music performances, with these people hys-terically trying to keep their places.

CATALOG OF COMPOSITIONS

1933	Incidental Music for Philoctetes	MS (withdrawn)
1936	Incidental Music for Mostellaria	MS (withdrawn)
1936	Tarantella for men's chorus and piano four-hands or orchestra	AMP
1936	Pocahontas ballet for piano	MS (withdrawn)
1937	Let's Be Gay for women's chorus and two pianos	MS (withdrawn)
1937	Harvest Home for mixed chorus	MS (withdrawn)
1937	To Music for SATB	Peer
1938	Heart Not So Heavy As Mine for SATB	AMP
1938	Prelude, Fanfare, and Polka for small orchestra	MS (withdrawn)
1938	Tell Me Where Is Fancy Bred for alto voice and guitar	AMP
1939	Canonic Suite for four alto saxophones	BMI (withdrawn)
1939	Pocahontas ballet for orchestra	AMP
1939; 62	Suite from Pocahontas for orchestra	AMP
1940	Pastoral for English horn (or clarinet or viola) and piano	Presser
1941	The Defense of Corinth for speaker, TTBB, and piano four-hands	Presser
1942; 54	Symphony No. 1	AMP
1943	The Rose Family for medium voice and piano	AMP

1943	Dust of Snow for medium voice and piano	AMP
1943	The Line Gang for baritone and piano	MS
1943	Voyage for medium voice and piano	AMP
1943	Warble for Lilac Time for soprano (or tenor) and piano; for soprano and chamber orchestra	Peer
1943; 61	Elegy for viola and piano	Peer
1944	The Harmony of Morning for SSAA and small orchestra	AMP
1944; 61	Holiday Overture for orchestra	AMP
1945	Musicians Wrestle Everywhere for SSATB (a cappella or with string accompaniment)	Presser
1946	Elegy for string quartet	Peer
1946	Piano Sonata	Presser
1947	Emblems for TTBB and piano	Presser
1947	The Minotaur ballet for orchestra	AMP
1947	Suite from The Minotaur for orchestra	AMP
1948	Woodwind Quintet	AMP
1948	Sonata for Cello and Piano	AMP
1950	Eight Etudes and a Fantasy for woodwind quartet	AMP
1951	String Quartet No. 1	AMP
1952	Elegy for string orchestra	Peer
1952	Sonata for Flute, Oboe, Cello, and Harpsichord	AMP
1955	Variations for Orchestra	AMP
1956	Canonic Suite for four clarinets	AMP
1959	String Quartet No. 2	AMP
1961	Double Concerto for Harpsichord and Piano with Two Chamber Orchestras	AMP
1965	Piano Concerto	AMP
1966	Eight Pieces for Four Timpani	AMP
1969	Concerto for Orchestra	AMP
1971	String Quartet No. 3	AMP
1971	Canon for 3: In Memoriam Igor Stravinsky for equal instrumental voices	AMP
1974	Brass Quintet	AMP
1974	A Fantasy About Purcell's Fantasia Upon One Note for brass quintet	AMP
1975	Duo for Violin and Piano	AMP
1976	A Mirror On Which To Dwell for soprano and chamber orchestra	AMP
1977	A Symphony of Three Orchestras	AMP
1978	Syringa for mezzo-soprano, bass, and chamber orchestra	AMP
1980	Night Fantasies for piano	MS

AARON COPLAND □

photo: Gene Bagnato

Aaron Copland was born on November 14, 1900, in Brooklyn, New York. He studied harmony and counterpoint with Rubin Goldmark. In 1921, Copland went to Paris where he became the first American to study composition with Nadia Boulanger. He returned to America in 1924. Copland has taught at The New School, Tanglewood, and Harvard.

In his early compositions, Copland used elements intrinsic to American jazz. Other works were characterized by their Hebraic quality or their affinity for a highly dramatic and grandiose manner of expression. By the 1930s, he was writing in a lean, austere, and highly complex style. But when Copland began to accept commissions for motion picture and ballet scores in the late 1930s, the resulting compositions were generally characterized by a more accessible style. After World War II, Copland's music demonstrated his interest in serialism. As with all his music, any style or technique employed remains subservient to his unique musical profile. In his career as composer, performer, and teacher, Copland has achieved an unassailable stature as America's most beloved and renowned composer.

To speak with Aaron Copland, the authors traveled to his home in Peekskill, New York, on January 6, 1975. They found Copland to be a gracious man, one given to direct expression of his ideas. Moreover, they were surprised and gratified to learn of his concern and curiosity about their musical interests. Especially characteristic of the interview with Copland was a strong reluctance to leave his company.

Q: Your Piano Variations of 1930 has been described as an early demonstration of your interest in serial technique. Can you tell us why there was no further exploration of this method in your music until the Piano Quartet of 1950?

COPLAND: I don't think that while I was writing the Piano Variations I was thinking serially. The interest in serial music really dated from later. The Variations dated from 1930, and by 1940, I think, I began to get more interested in the possibilities of twelve-tone technique. We had heard more twelve-tone music by that time, we were more familiar with it. After all, Schoenberg was living in America, out in California, and there was a great deal more literature about the method. We heard more of the music of the twelve-tone composers, so that it seemed to open up possibilities that were not inherent in the regular tonal system.

Q: For a time, your music seemed to move away from the more complex and problematic style of the Piano Variations to a more accessible style, to works like the three great ballets.

COPLAND: Well, it's a little bit difficult to think back that far-- forty years ago--and to remember quite the way one's mind was working at that time. But I think most composers tend to explore certain things that interest them in their composition, for a while. Then they feel they've exhausted that--as far as they themselves are concerned--and they would normally look around for something else to do.

Also, outside influences have something to do with it. If a dancer comes to you and says, "I would like to commission you to write a score for a ballet," and you say, "Well, where does the ballet take place?" and she says, "In the Appalachian Mountains," naturally you're not going to write a twelve-tone score--under nor- mal circumstances. Therefore, some of my music which is a bit more direct and accessible had its origin in requests, either for ballet music, or film music, or stage music. The origin of the work would have been some non-musical medium which needed mu- sic, and that naturally makes you think along different lines.

Q: Do you feel that a work like the Piano Variations sacrificed emotional expressivity for a more rigorous or abstract quality?

COPLAND: I don't like the word "abstract" too much. I don't think it really is abstract. I think it's full of feeling, but not, I hope, of an obvious kind. In other words, it's more severe in the thing it's trying to say. I wouldn't be able to put into so many words what the nature of the severity is, but it's rather hard-bitten. The pianists who play it know they're supposed to strike the notes not in a Chopinesque way, but with a more modern kind of sonority. This should be looked for in the playing of the Piano Variations. I think of it as one of my best works, actually. Why it should have happened at that particular time I no longer remember. But after all, in 1930 I was thirty years old. I had had ten years of writing music, in the twenties, and I was looking around for a new way of expressing what I wanted to say, and for some reason or other, that work turned out to be rather severe and not so easy for a gen- eral public to absorb on one single hearing.

Q: When you compose, does a question like accessibility with the audience concern you, or do you set out to satisfy yourself, hoping that enough people will be able to follow what it is you're doing?

COPLAND: You mustn't forget that music takes its origin in a composer's mind in terms of specific <u>musical</u> ideas. You don't sit down there coldly and say, "Well, what sort of a piece ought

I do now?" You could do that, of course, but more normally--
somehow, suddenly, a musical idea occurs to you; either a whole
phrase, or three notes, or a series of chords, something that
seems pregnant with possibilities for development. That's where
a piece takes its origin. Once you have the kinds of ideas that
fascinate you, you're no longer in a position to decide the nature
of the animal. It's going to take its essence from the musical
ideas that occur to you. That's why you're a composer, because
you don't sit there thinking thoughts, you sit there thinking notes
which then tell you what their character is like, and on the basis
of which you decide whether you think you can really develop those
ideas and make a whole piece out of them. Some musical ideas
are too short, they don't seem long enough to carry you through
ten minutes of music, so you have to start searching about for
other ideas; contrasting ones that seem to fit with the original
ones. It would be very difficult to generalize in a way that would
cover all cases--impossible, I'd say. But every composer knows
immediately--I hope he knows--when he has a series of notes or
chords, or a section of a piece, or some sort of notion that that
thing I can develop; I can make a piece out of that, that's really
good, where did I get it?

So you don't sit down coldly, unless, as I say, you've been
commissioned by somebody to do a work. I won't say that you sit
down to fulfill the commission in a cold manner, why should you?
But you really shouldn't accept the commission unless you have a
feeling at the very start that you could write that sort of piece. I
had written a certain amount of music based on Americana before
Miss Agnes DeMille thought of asking me to do the music for her
ballet Rodeo, and also before Miss Martha Graham thought of asking me to do the music for the ballet which she wanted to create
called Appalachian Spring.

Q: So you feel that, to an extent, the pieces surprise you, that
you know only so much from the ideas when you begin as to whether
the work will be severe or very direct?

COPLAND: That's right. Especially when you collaborate with
someone else. After all, the ballet choreographer hasn't even created the ballet yet. They can't create it until they have the music.
They don't know what kind of music you're going to give them. So
it's a wild chance they're taking when they ask you to do a musical
score for them.

I remember, in connection with Appalachian Spring, that after
Miss Graham gave me the few pages of prose outlining what she
thought would be the action of the ballet, and the nature of the work,
I went off to Mexico to write it. I came back just in time for the
premiere performance at the Library of Congress Auditorium in
Washington. The first thing I said to Miss Graham was, "What did
you call the ballet?" and she said "Appalachian Spring." I said,

"Oh, what a nice name, where'd you get it?" and she said, "It's the name of a poem by Hart Crane." I said, "Does the poem have anything to do with the ballet?" and she said, "No, I just like the name, so I used it." I tell that story because so many times people come to me and say, "Oh, I can just see the Appalachian Mountains when I hear your music, and I can feel spring," as if I had begun with that title as a kind of inspiration.

Q: Do you prefer not to give titles to your music, for fear of giving the listener less to do?

COPLAND: It depends on the nature of the work. Some pieces don't suggest a title of any kind--it seems to be a sonata to me. It's a sonata, or a symphony, and you don't feel the need of a specific series of words that, in a sense, limit the nature of the piece. You hope that people will be able to sense the character of the work from the nature of the music itself, and that the title really shouldn't have very much to do with it. In some cases it could be a help, of course, but by and large, composers have written quartets, trios, sonatas, which don't tell very much about what's going to happen in the piece itself.

Q: With something like Music for a Great City, did the music dictate its title to you?

COPLAND: Music for a Great City was written as film music. It was not written as a piece of concert music. I derived, from the film music I wrote, a suite of movements which I then called Music for a Great City because the film took place in New York City, for the most part.

I would think that listeners should be a little wary about what they conclude from the title given to a piece. Sometimes they're a help, sometimes I think they sort of get in the way. Most composers feel that listeners should really gather the nature of the work they're hearing from the work itself, rather than getting hints from the title.

Q: What about a work like Inscape? Was that really an afterthought, or had you been involved with the poetry of Hopkins while composing?

COPLAND: I don't really remember when I happened on that. I had been reading him, and I was an admirer of his--and still am-- and the word "inscape" suddenly seemed to me to be a title that could very well be used on a piece of music. It suggests the idea of a whole landscape, that is, a thing you might travel through, like

you travel through a piece of music, but it's a kind of inner landscape, it doesn't have any actuality in the outside world, and it
speaks a musical language at the same time. There's something
about the word "inscape" that seems to me to apply to that piece.
Not in too specific a way, but in a general way.

Q: You've been quoted as saying that Inscape is a reflection of the
tension of present times. Do you feel that the tension is achieved
simply through your use of twelve-tone technique, which still disturbs a lot of people, or will Inscape still create the same effect
when serial music becomes more accepted?

COPLAND: No, I think the tension is inherent in the nature of the
chordal structures, and in the general character of the piece.

As I say, you mustn't really attach too much significance to
a title. All it is is a suggestive word. A word like "inscape"
couldn't possibly cover all the things that would happen in a twelve-
or fifteen-minute piece. It seemed to me to apply to music almost
better than to words, because music is more vague as to what it
really means, vaguer than actual words are. The idea of a scape
of any kind, a landscape, or an inscape, or an escape, seemed to
lend itself very well to a musical piece.

Q: Both Inscape and the Connotations for orchestra have the same
quality of tension. Could you explain why these recent works are
composed in this manner?

COPLAND: No. It's just that we contemporary composers have
been given a harmonic language far more complex by its nature
than that of the composers of the nineteenth century. The fact that
we have now the capability of using these much more complex chords--
many of them more dissonant than nineteenth-century chords--
gives us a vocabulary that they didn't have the benefit of. It's
as if musical history hadn't yet produced the possibilities of
making use of such chords, and of having people find them not just
dissonant, but dissonant with a meaning, and pleasant--in the sense
of highly expressive, though of a dissonant nature. That fact alone
gave us the possibility of working with series of such chords, which
wouldn't have been possible for the nineteenth-century composers.
It's only possible for us through the gradual evolution, through the
nineteenth century, of harmonies that became more and more complex.

Audiences of today, by now--after all, it is 1975--really
ought to be "hep" to what the composers have been doing since the
year 1900. They've been getting more and more sour, sometimes,
in their music, and more intensely edgy, and just not so mellif-
luous all the time. People always tend to think of music as a
pleasant art, you can relax to it--for the tired businessman to

enjoy when he comes home, in order to forget about the strains of the day. But the composer, when he's writing his music, is the tired businessman, straining to express what he has to say. If it's well done, it shouldn't come out tired-sounding. It should come out sounding highly expressive. You see, we have access to a musical vocabulary which the nineteenth century didn't have. It would be silly to try to ignore that and make believe it wasn't there.

Q: Music for a Great City is not a serial work.

COPLAND: No, it isn't at all.

Q: Yet it's as powerful and uncompromising as a piece like Inscape. Since you can use an atonal idiom without serial technique, what would you say is the value of serialism for you?

COPLAND: I hadn't thought of Music for a Great City as being that atonal. You're describing a piece I don't completely recognize. I think of that as much more accessible than a piece like the Connotations for orchestra or Inscape. It's rather hectic at times, because I was picturing New York City streets in part of the film, but I don't think it quite matches up to the other two works from the standpoint of sheer dissonance.

Q: Still, though, how would you say twelve-tone music appeals to you?

COPLAND: You're talking a little bit about the past now. Twelve-tone music is not as new as it once was. We've had about seventy years of it, so that I don't think it quite holds the fascination for composers that it had during the post-Schoenberg period, right after he died. I doubt whether it will be so passionately worked with by composers as was true for our own century. But that's guesswork, of course.

Any new development like that in musical history tends gradually to take its place in a normal fashion with the passage of years. Then something else new and startling arrives, which also has to be ingested and digested, and made part of the musical language. People think of music too often as a set kind of art, invented nobody knows quite when. But we composers who work in it all the time are very aware of its belonging to culture as a whole, which tends to change from generation to generation. Man experiences new things, the world becomes different all the time, and music changes along with all those happenings. But the big public always wants to be lulled by it, as a nice, pleasant, consoling, entertaining music that they've become accustomed to. But we composers don't think along those lines. That's where the rub comes, that's where the trouble starts.

Q: Do you think that electronic music is another such phase that will eventually take its place in the art as a whole?

COPLAND: I've never worked in any way with electronic music, so I'm really an amateur in relation to it. I've often thought that one of the great drawbacks of electronic music is the fact that it has to be put on tape. You rarely have it produced live. The minute you put a thing on tape, you're stuck with it. It's always going to be that same tape and that same sound, and the electronic composers are going to be the first ones to get bored with hearing their music without that great advantage of interpretation that we concert composers have. Sometimes it's a great disadvantage, but anyhow it keeps the music alive in a way that no tape machine can. Therefore, I have the feeling that they're going to have to get around that in some way. They'll have to either add a live performer along with it, as some of them have done, or play the tape slower or faster and change the character that way. But that is a great drawback. On the other hand, naturally, you can produce musical effects not otherwise producible, and that is a great advantage. Those men and women who have worked in the medium are obviously fascinated with it, and I would expect a real contribution to musical art in the end.

Q: Is it this problem of freezing the music that has kept you away from electronic composition?

COPLAND: No, I don't have any talent with electricity. I feel lucky if I push a switch and the light goes on.

Q: Have you ever considered incorporating chance techniques into your music?

COPLAND: Apparently not, since I haven't ever done it. But I can see the advantage, of course, of including such possibilities in a piece of music. You take your chances. The aleatoric section may be a complete flop with one performer, and something terrific with another performer, so it's not what you might call a sure medium, but it does add a resource to a score that wouldn't be there if no use were made of it.

Q: Are you working on a piece at this time?

COPLAND: Theoretically I am, but I have slowed down a bit.

After all, you know, I'm in my seventies, and you don't just go breezing along as you did when you were sixteen. So it's only natural that I haven't been producing as much as I used to. I never was a very prolific composer, as a matter of fact. If I did one or two, or even three pieces a year, that was a lot, if they were serious and lengthy pieces. It's only natural, I think, as a man gets older, that his creative powers are not exactly what they were when he was twenty.

Q: Have you gotten many commissions for the bicentennial?

COPLAND: Well, I haven't lacked offers of commissions! And if I do a piece, I'm not free to talk about it now.

Q: Are there certain composers today whom you particularly admire, and feel should be getting a larger audience?

COPLAND: You mean younger composers? Yes, sure, there are always younger fellows coming up. I happen to be an admirer of the music of Jacob Druckman. He teaches at one of the universities here, and he's begun to be played in a serious way by the Philharmonic and the bigger organizations.

There's another younger man, in his thirties, David Del Tredeci. He comes from California, and has a German mother and an Italian father--which is a good combination to have if you're going to be a composer. He's a very musical guy. He's already written music that I find very good indeed, and I'm sure you'll be hearing about him.

Q: Some of your music has been choreographed. Do you like writing music specifically for dance?

COPLAND: Oh, yes, it's fun to have a ballet made to one's music, because you never can figure out in advance how it's all going to work out. Some parts may seem much better combined with the music than other parts. Sometimes, if you don't have a really good choreographer, it can be very disappointing. On the other hand, sometimes, if your choreographer is very imaginative in the use of music, you think, oh, gee, I didn't realize this music could get dressed up like this through the action onstage. It lends itself to a lot of different kinds of interpretations. Nowadays, for example, with a work like Appalachian Spring, it is very difficult for me to think of that music without seeing in my mind's eye the dancing that goes with it. You have to see a ballet a fair number of times in order to be able to remember all the different things that go with it, but there aren't very many Martha Grahams in the world, with that much personality and imagination, and the American quality which she gives most of her things--so that was a very lucky chance indeed.

Q: In doing film scores, you're very much in the same position as the choreographer, because you can't go to work until somebody else has given you the material which you have to adapt to. Did you find that work exciting?

COPLAND: It is very exciting for a movie composer to create the music after he's seen the scene--because you can't create it before you've seen the scene, you wouldn't know how to time it to make it match the action. To have it actually played by an orchestra and then added to the film can be very exciting, because it really does make the scene come alive in a way which it just isn't without the music. All you have to do is turn the music switch off, and you see the scene dead, so to speak. You turn the switch on, and suddenly everybody seems to be twice as alive as they were a moment ago.

I had great fun writing film scores out in Hollywood. But I was there only occasionally. I never had a permanent job in a movie studio, so I didn't turn scores out by the dozens. I only scored five or six films in all, and each time the director was a gifted man, interesting to work with. Of course, you get a very complete idea of how music can be used effectively when you actually hear your music in conjunction with the picture for the first time. At first, you see the film without music, of course, and so you can only imagine what kind of music is needed for a certain scene. Then you finally write the music that you think would serve the purpose, and then you have the excitement of seeing the two things come together. Of course, sometimes, if you're very disappointed, you can redo it. But for the most part I had very good experiences, and I worked with different kinds of stories: some in the West, some in New York City, one foreign one--the Russians and Germans at war with one another. That, too, helps to freshen one's style. The score I did for The Heiress, for instance, pictured Washington Square in the 1870s or '80s. It needed a completely different kind of music from, let's say, Of Mice and Men, which I also composed--a cowboy picture with horses in it, having nothing whatever to do with Washington Square.

Q: Do you think that the music for Something Wild or The Red Pony, which you made into orchestral suites, was better than the music for The Heiress or Of Mice and Men, which you didn't subsequently use?

COPLAND: No; I think the ability to make an orchestral suite from cinema music is just a lucky chance. You can't figure that out in advance. The fact that a film doesn't lend itself to the mak-

ing of a concert suite might even make it seem more important in
its use in the film itself. After all, it was created for that purpose in the first place, and it's not its fault that it can't be turned
into concert music. Some films have musical sections which are
too short; you'd have to develop them in symphonic style if you
wanted to make use of them. There might be any number of reasons why a score that satisfies you fully in its use with the film
would not seem to be so satisfactory by itself in a concert hall.

Q: You're most well known, of course, for your more traditional
scores. It even comes as a surprise to some people that you've
written music like the Piano Variations or Inscape--the side of
your music which we're focussing on with this interview. Does it
bother you that people tend to think of your music mainly in terms
of the more accessible pieces?

COPLAND: One likes to be known for all the different things one
does. One doesn't like to be pigeonholed, and credited for being
able to do one thing in music very well, and have other pieces
which you think are quite different in nature ignored. So the wider
a public one is able to attract to one's music, through the different
kinds of music one writes, the better, from a composer's standpoint. I wouldn't want to be thought of as a mere purveyor of
Americana, for example, nice as that may be from one aspect.
There are other things in the world besides Americana which interest me also. One tends, as a creative artist, to be pigeonholed
too easily; it's comfortable to be able to put a creator in a slot
and feel, well, we know about him. Anything that can work against
that notion, I'm all for.

Q: Earlier, you said that the character of your initial ideas dictate the basic nature of the musical piece. Does this apply to the
question of instrumentation as well?

COPLAND: Basically, I believe it's there at the inception. You
may not know precisely what instruments in the orchestra you're
going to make use of. But by its very nature, you would probably
know that certain musical ideas seem to suggest various possibilities of orchestral color, giving it much more bite, or magnificence, or whatever the word may be, than if you were just going
to make a piano piece out of it.

Q: What prompted you to orchestrate the Piano Variations?

COPLAND: I don't any longer remember exactly why I orchestrated them. Somebody must have asked me to do an orchestral piece
and I couldn't think of one, and I said, "Well, will you take an

orchestration of a piano piece?" It seems to me that that was the origin of it, but I'm not certain.

I think the two works side by side would give off a rather different impression, actually. I think the orchestral version of the Variations would tend to be less hardbitten. There's something about an orchestra that suggests roundness of tone, even when it's meant to be rather severe. You get a sense of fullness that you don't get from piano tone. It was the sense I had that I would be getting a different emotional connotation out of the orchestration that made me think it was possible to orchestrate that piece. After all, I didn't orchestrate my Piano Sonata, and I didn't orchestrate my Piano Fantasy, but I did feel that I could achieve it with the Variations.

Q: Could you tell us about the importance of your studies with Nadia Boulanger?

COPLAND: In a sentence?

Q: Two if you want.

COPLAND: Mlle. Boulanger was a very extraordinary musician, that's the first thing. I think it was her sensitivity to music which seemed to me so valuable. Especially to a young student who isn't really quite sure himself as to the value of what he's doing. He doesn't have enough perspective on himself yet, or enough experience to be able to know the good from the bad in what he's created. To have a feeling that you were bringing your work to somebody highly sensitive to music, who knows better than you what the inherent possibilities of these phrases are--because very often you don't bring a completed piece, you just bring an idea for a piece-- that kind of guidance and assistance is of course invaluable to a young composer starting on his way.

Don't forget, it took a certain amount of courage in the early twenties for a young composer to decide to study composition with a woman. I don't want all the women's lib people to get excited, but the fact of the matter is, for some extraordinary reason which nobody seems to be able to explain, although there are great women performers in music, great pianists and singers, etc., the history of music simply doesn't name anyone who is in the Beethoven class. There must be some very profound reason. I can't think of what it may be. I'm sure it'll change. For the nineteenth century you could mention a few women composers' names, but I certainly don't happen to know their music.

Mlle. Boulanger was in that case, in my mind, a terrific exception, not because she composed herself, but because she had that kind of sensitivity to music, which could tell you which the good parts were, and which the less good parts were, and what the possibilities were of the sketches you brought to her. So you felt you were in very sure hands--hands that you could trust to guide you along the paths that were needed.

CATALOG OF COMPOSITIONS

1920	The Cat and the Mouse for piano	B&H
1920	Poem for high voice and piano	B&H
1921	Pastorale for high voice and piano	B&H
1921	Four Motets for mixed chorus	B&H
1922	Passacaglia for piano	Salabert
1923	As It Fell Upon a Day for soprano, flute, and clarinet	B&H
1924	Symphony for Organ and Orchestra	B&H
1925	Grohg ballet for orchestra	MS
1925	Cortege Macabre from Grohg for two pianos	B&H
1925	Dance of the Adolescent from Grohg for two pianos	B&H
1925	Two Choruses for Women's Voices ("The House on the Hill" and "An Immorality")	EC Schirmer
1925	Dance Symphony	B&H
1925	Music for the Theatre for small orchestra	B&H
1926	Two Pieces for violin and piano	Schott
1926	Concerto for Piano and Orchestra	B&H
1926	Sentimental Melody for piano	B&H
1927	Song for medium voice and piano	B&H
1928	Two Pieces for string quartet; for string orchestra	B&H
1928; 72	Vocalise for high voice and piano; for flute and piano	B&H
1928	First Symphony	B&H
1929; 55	Symphonic Ode	B&H
1929	Vitebsk for violin, cello, and piano	B&H
1930	Piano Variations	B&H
1931	Incidental Music for Miracle at Verdun	MS
1932	Elegies for violin and viola	MS
1933	Short Symphony (Symphony No. 2)	B&H
1934	Statements for orchestra	B&H
1934	Hear Ye! Hear Ye! ballet for orchestra	MS
1935	What Do We Plant? for SA and piano	B&H
1936	Two Children's Pieces for piano ("Saturday Afternoon Music" and "The Young Pioneers")	Carl Fischer

1936	El Salon Mexico for orchestra	B&H
1937	Sextet for clarinet, two violins, viola, cello, and piano	B&H
1937	Music for Radio (Saga of the Prairie) for small orchestra	B&H
1937	The Second Hurricane high school opera	B&H
1937	That's the Idea of Freedom for SATB	Summy-Birchard
1938	Billy the Kid ballet for orchestra	B&H
1938	Billy the Kid Suite for orchestra; for two pianos; for piano	B&H
1938	Waltz and Celebration from Billy the Kid for violin and piano	B&H
1938	An Outdoor Overture for orchestra; for band	B&H
1938	Lark for baritone and SATB	EC Schirmer
1939	Incidental Music for Five Kings	MS
1939	Incidental Music for Quiet City	MS
1939	Film Music for The City	MS
1939	Incidental Music for From Sorcery to Science	MS
1939	Film Music for Of Mice and Men	MS
1940	Film Music for Our Town	MS
1940	Our Town Suite for orchestra; for two pianos	B&H
1940	Quiet City for trumpet, English horn, and strings	B&H
1940; 52	John Henry for small orchestra	B&H
1941	Piano Sonata	B&H
1941	Episode for organ	HW Gray
1942	Las Agachadas for mixed chorus	B&H
1942	Lincoln Portrait for narrator and orchestra	B&H
1942	Rodeo ballet for orchestra	B&H
1942	Four Dance Episodes from Rodeo for orchestra; for piano	B&H
1942	Music for the Movies for small orchestra	B&H
1942	Fanfare for the Common Man for brass and percussion	B&H
1942	Danzon Cubano for two pianos; for orchestra; for piano	B&H
1943	Film Music for The North Star	MS
1943	Song of the Guerillas for baritone, TTBB, and piano	B&H
1943	Sonata for Violin and Piano	B&H
1943	The Younger Generation for SATB; for SAB; for SSA; for SA; for girl's chorus	B&H
1944	Appalachian Spring ballet for thirteen instruments; for orchestra	B&H
1944	Letter from Home for orchestra	B&H
1945	Appalachian Spring Suite for orchestra	B&H

1945	Film Music for The Cummington Story	MS
1946	Third Symphony	B&H
1946	Hoe Down from Rodeo for violin and piano	B&H
1946	Hoe Down and Saturday Night Waltz from Rodeo for two pianos	B&H
1947	In the Beginning for mezzo-soprano and mixed chorus	B&H
1948; 77	Midsummer Nocturne for piano	B&H
1948	Film Music for The Red Pony	MS
1948; 67	The Red Pony Suite for orchestra; for band	B&H
1948	Concerto for Clarinet and String Orchestra (with harp and piano)	B&H
1948	Four Piano Blues	B&H
1949	Film Music for The Heiress	MS
1949; 73	Preamble for a Solemn Occasion for narrator and orchestra; for orchestra; for organ; for band	B&H
1950	Piano Quartet	B&H
1950	Twelve Poems of Emily Dickinson for medium voice and piano; (Eight Songs arranged for voice and small orchestra)	B&H
1950; 52	Old American Songs for medium voice and piano; for medium voice and orchestra	B&H
1950	Simple Gifts for girl's chorus; for boy's chorus	B&H
1950	Long Time Ago for SATB	B&H
1952	The Little Horses for TTBB; for SSA; for SA; for girl's chorus	B&H
1954	The Tender Land opera	B&H
1954	Dirge in Woods for high voice and piano	B&H
1955	Canticle of Freedom for SATB and orchestra	B&H
1956	Variations on a Shaker Melody for band	B&H
1957	Piano Fantasy	B&H
1957	The Tender Land Suite for orchestra; for SATB and orchestra	B&H
1957	Orchestral Variations	B&H
1957	Incidental Music for The World of Nick Adams	MS
1959; 62	Dance Panels ballet in seven sections for orchestra	B&H
1960	Nonet for three violins, three violas, and three cellos	B&H
1961	Film Music for Something Wild	MS
1962	Connotations for orchestra	B&H
1962	Down a Country Lane for piano; arranged for orchestra	B&H
1964	Music for a Great City for orchestra	B&H
1964	Emblems for symphonic band	B&H
1966	In Evening Air for piano	B&H
1967	Inscape for orchestra	B&H
1969; 75	Inaugural Fanfare for winds, brass, and percussion	B&H

1969	Ceremonial Fanfare for brass ensemble	B&H
1969	Happy Anniversary for orchestra	B&H
1971	Three Latin American Sketches for orchestra	B&H
1971; 78	Duo for Flute and Piano; for Violin and Piano	B&H
1971	Threnody I: Igor Stravinsky in memoriam for flute, violin, viola, and cello	B&H
1972	Night Thoughts (Homage to Ives) for piano	B&H
1973	Threnody II: Beatrice Cunningham in memoriam for alto flute, violin, viola, and cello	B&H

photo: Gene Bagnato

George Crumb was born on October 24, 1929, in
Charleston, West Virginia. After receiving his B.A.
from the Mason College of Music in Charleston,
Crumb went on to study at the University of Illinois
and the University of Michigan, where he received
his doctorate while studying under Ross Lee Finney.
In addition, Crumb spent one year in Berlin as a
Fulbright fellow at the Hochschule für Musik, studying with Boris Blacher. Since 1965, Crumb has
taught at the University of Pennsylvania. In 1949,
he married Elizabeth May Brown. They have three
children.

Whereas Crumb's earlier works might include
influential strains of Hindemith or Bartók, his later
compositions speak with an assured voice that is entirely Crumb's own. The majority of his works written over the past twenty years have been scored for
chamber ensembles that frequently employ an unusual
array of instruments and require special performance
techniques that sometime extend into theatricality.
Out of such diversified means, Crumb has created
a unique and coherent sound world.

The authors spoke with George Crumb at his
home in Media, Pennsylvania, on December 8, 1975.
The entire interview took place in the presence of
his two aging dachshunds, who refused to abandon
him to the company of strangers. A soft-spoken,
ingenuous man, Crumb finds it difficult to verbalize
at great lengths about his music. Yet one cannot
meet and speak with him without gaining a greater
understanding of his music.

Q: We were wondering if you could tell us about your student days.
We're particularly interested in your studies with Ross Lee Finney.

CRUMB: I've always considered Ross Lee Finney to have been my
most important teacher. I had other teachers, but I felt that I
learned a lot about compositional technique from him. He taught
his students to be very self-critical, something I appreciated.

Actually, my own style matured later. I had left the University of Michigan, and it was some years later that I found my
own style. Finney's influence was not so much stylistic, rather
just a solid grounding in the mechanics of composition.

Q: In the Makrokosmos I, you have Finney's initials after the

"Crucifixus." Was that just an afterthought, or did you have him in mind all along?

CRUMB: Well, although I was searching for enough initials, I had him in mind from the beginning. It's incredible. In trying to match up all the zodiac signs for two complete sets, I found that I was running out of friends and acquaintances. I discovered that, for some reason, most people in music tend to cover about six of the signs. The others are very rare. I don't know why that is. For example, the sign Virgo is very poorly represented. I think Schoenberg does fall under that sign--which is enough to redeem that sign!

Q: Can Makrokosmos I be seen as a work comparable to the Elgar Enigma Variations, where there's an attempt to portray different people, or are the initials you give to each piece simply dedications?

CRUMB: They are in the nature of dedications. In some cases, I suppose, I actually tried to reflect the psychology of the person. There was a certain influence of that type, but I certainly wasn't very consistent in the matter.

Q: Are we speaking about "The Phantom Gondolier," which is inscribed "G. H. C."?

CRUMB: I'm not sure about that one! Originally, I did want to make the work an enigma of sorts. I guess by now some of the signs are pretty well known. It's easy for people to look up birth dates and guess initials.

Q: In your student days and with the works before Night Music I, did you write in the more traditional forms?

CRUMB: I had a rather traditional background. I started writing music when I was a kid ten or eleven years old. I was rewriting Mozart, because that was the sound that was in my ear. I wrote little sonatas, rondos, variations--all of the tonal forms. Later on I tried to use sonata form in some larger pieces--which I suppose were influenced primarily by Bartók. But since the early sixties I've used freer forms.

Q: Are you highly critical of your earlier works?

CRUMB: I feel that all of my music up to the early sixties is not really my own music.

Q: You've been quoted as saying that the more traditional forms that grew out of tonality were no longer applicable for today's music, but that the more primitive forms were still useful. Other composers argue that, with the dismissal of tonality, more rigorous and complex forms--total serialization, for example--are needed in order to compose. Why do you think that simpler forms are valuable?

CRUMB: I'm not sure that "simple" is the correct adjective. I think the forms tend to be freer. Many of the older sophisticated forms, such as sonata form, I feel really depended on tonality. This was the magic substance that held the form together. It's true that some composers nowadays are working with highly integrated large-scale forms, but I think here, too, in most cases, these forms tend not to be traditional, but rather come from the materials themselves. I'm thinking now of the twelve-tone composers who are working today.

Q: Weren't you a twelve-tone composer for a while?

CRUMB: Not really. I never completed a work that was consistently twelve-tone. There was some of the influence in a student work called Variazioni for orchestra. The theme itself was a twelve-note series, and some of the variations drew from that source, but there was nothing at all that was highly structured in the work, in that sense.

Q: Can you say what it is about serialism that you find incompatible with your musical ideas?

CRUMB: No, I don't think I could define that. I think every composer tends to write the music that he has to write, the music that he can write. This was a technique that I couldn't use in a personal way. Perhaps because the major influences on my music would be Debussy, Ives to a certain extent, Varèse a little bit, Bartók certainly. There is also, I suppose, Webern, but somehow the side of Webern's music that influenced my own music was not the pitch organization per se, but rather the whole timbral, gestural aspect.

Q: Aside from the more obvious things--the musical saw in Ancient Voices of Children, or the motto Montani semper liberi in Echoes of Time and the River--is there a genuine importance for your music in your West Virginia background?

CRUMB: I think that for every composer there's a natural acoustic which he inherits. If you come from Kansas, you have a certain acoustic in your ear. If you come from Charleston, West Virginia, located in a river valley with sizable hills around--that's an altogether different acoustic. This must influence a person in very subtle ways, but I think it's in my music. An echoing quality, or an interest in very long sounds, haunting sounds, sounds that don't want to die; this is all part of an inherited acoustic, I think.

Q: Were the popular forms of music, or the church music you grew up with in your ear too?

CRUMB: Yes, I'm sure. In fact, I was exposed to the same hymnology that Ives was--the revival songs included. Being American, as you know, it's hard to avoid any of the types of popular music that surround us, so this was in my ear.

Q: In the CRI recording of Night Music I, you're the conductor. In some performances of Night of the Four Moons, you've taken the banjo part. Would you prefer to take a more active part in the performance of your music?

CRUMB: No, I have no real motivation to be a performer. I used to participate a little more in playing the piano in some contemporary music performances, mostly of other composers' music. For example, I was in Buffalo during the first year of the contemporary music project there, and I was involved in some performances as a pianist.

The banjo thing, I guess, was a sort of practical necessity, since most banjo players don't really read music. I learned subsequently that any cellist can easily learn the part. I knew the part from writing the piece. I had to have my own banjo in order to know the possibilities of the instrument, since there's no tradition for the instrument in concert music.

Q: You couldn't see yourself performing Makrokosmos I in Carnegie Hall?

CRUMB: No, no. In a case like that, there are so many really excellent pianists. I would feel very shy about that sort of thing.

I've never performed any of my own piano music, but I guess I've played most of it working it out. When I write for the piano I tend to work at the piano. If it involves solo pianist, it seems natural to sit at the piano and improvise along with the composition. The "improvisation" becomes an integral part of the composition.

Q: What was your first introduction to Lorca's poetry? It's obviously been very important in your music.

CRUMB: I first got familiar with some of his poetry in the late fifties. Even at that time I planned one day to use some of the poems. Of course, it was only in 1963 that I did set two of the poems in Night Music I--which, although basically an instrumental piece, does include the two Lorca settings. That led to other works. I saw other poems I wanted to get into.

Q: Most of your Lorca settings utilize a female singer. The exceptions are the baritone in Songs, Drones, and Refrains of Death and the boy soprano in Ancient Voices of Children. Is there something in Lorca that makes you do that, or is it simply a matter of the greater availability of good female vocalists?

CRUMB: I think that's the main reason, simply that there are more female performers involved in that style of singing. This may change in time, but I think it is the situation now. There are, of course, a few excellent contemporary baritones, but perhaps for every baritone there would be ten or twenty sopranos involved in new music.

It's a question of flexibility, too, I suppose. It would seem that the female voice might be more flexible by nature for this type of music--although I've heard excellent baritones who have trained their voices to cope with the type of timbral and rhythmic flexibility that exists in my music.

Q: Could Songs, Drones, and Refrains of Death have been written for a female voice?

CRUMB: No. In that work, somehow, I really heard a male voice from the beginning. The work seemed to demand that specific timbre.

Q: Could you tell us how you first began working with Jan DeGaetani?

CRUMB: I guess the first occasion was the performance of the first two books of Madrigals. They were written in '65, and Jan performed them the following spring, in '66. That was my first introduction to Jan. Then I got the sound of her voice in my ear. I was of course impressed with all the beautiful things she does, and this flexibility she has, and used this in Ancient Voices, which was specially written for Jan.

Q: That must influence the way in which you're going to compose.

CRUMB: Yes, I think one's writing is definitely influenced by a certain performer which one has in mind. I think that's probably a healthy influence. It can help to keep the music sort of real if you imagine it being performed by a person you know.

Q: What precisely was it about DeGaetani that affected the writing of Ancient Voices of Children? Was it just that you knew that you could demand a greater virtuosity?

CRUMB: Yes, that's one aspect. Also the timbral flexibility. I'm also impressed with the very dark timbre of her voice. I tend to think that this particular timbre fits Lorca very well. It's that quality I see in his poetry. I hear a dark timbre in his Spanish words.

Q: One of the things that DeGaetani does in Ancient Voices is sing directly into the piano. This raises rather a curious problem. We've read that in performances of Night Music I, some people laugh at the sight of a gong being immersed in water. The visual element is certainly quite important in a number of your works-- the masked performers of Vox Balanae, for example--but are there times when the visual element is a drawback? Did you ever wish that the audience couldn't see what was going on, that they could only hear the music?

CRUMB: I suspect that by now, audiences are no longer quite so distracted. So much has been required in the music of contempor- ary composers. I personally don't think that anything that's integral to the music should be distracting in performance. On the contrary, I have felt that any performance has its built-in choreography. Even with traditional music. I feel this strongly in a Beethoven String Quartet. The very gestures that are involved in realizing the score create a kind of choreography. I find this quality exciting in mu- sic. Of course, it's something that is missing in recordings.

It's part of the magic of music. I find it in Chopin's piano music. Just playing the music requires the pianist to make certain gestures. Obviously, given the range of the piano keyboard, he must make some movements, even the most discreet performer. This gestural element becomes part of the music for me.

Q: So even the works without specific theatrical overtones suffer when they're only heard?

CRUMB: As a recording? Yes. As valuable as recordings are--

and I believe they're most valuable--there is this loss. I've found, too, that in recordings of my music it's very difficult to get the dynamic extremes. I suppose I must suffer more than most other composers, because my music ranges from a whisper--which is just about the most difficult thing to pick up in a recording--to sharp points that tend to make the needle jump off the dial. The mix-down always seems to involve a compression of the dynamic range. I guess this is true of any recording, but it particularly affects my music very much. It wouldn't affect the Brahms Third Symphony that much, since that work has a narrower dynamic range.

Q: This matter of dynamics is certainly one instance where your music displays its relationship to the music of Gustav Mahler.

CRUMB: Yes, that's true, Mahler has this enormous range. I guess with Debussy the range tends to be infinite on the piano side, but his music tends not to lean as heavily on the loud side. Works like the Nocturnes or La Mer have very loud passages, but in those works he doesn't go quite so far in the other direction either, so that there is still a more traditional dynamic range.

Q: Do you feel a very strong kinship to Mahler and his music?

CRUMB: Yes. I've always loved Mahler's music. Even as a student--much before the Mahler revival of the last few years--I was quite interested, even though there were only poor recordings available in some cases, or no recordings at all of certain symphonies. I got to know some of his works through four-hand versions and through the scores. I was delighted, later on, when the symphones had a kind of resurrection, and Mahler received his just due.

I feel that the aspects of his music which have influenced me are his incredible sense of time, his textures, even certain melodic cells, I suppose.

Q: Perhaps also in terms of a respect for the vast potential of sound. Mahler loved to utilize instruments and melodies normally considered too banal or vulgar for use in a concert hall.

CRUMB: Yes, that's very true. Also the juxtaposition of seemingly contradictory musics--the military band music, all the various styles. I think this characteristic intrigues many composers nowadays, since the whole question of style has become an important aspect of new music, that is, the synthesis of varied, or even opposite types of music.

Q: Earlier, you were discussing the visual aspect of all music in performance. This element is of course absent with electronic music. Does this make you less inclined to compose electronically?

CRUMB: Yes, that of course is a basic difficulty with electronic music. A composer normally depends on the performer to introduce an element of bravura--which I'm using in a very general sense, to include not only pyrotechnics, but just the sense of electricity generated by the performer. Of course, beautiful sounds exist in electronic music, but the lack of this kind of bravura has to be compensated for by a compositional bravura--which makes it more difficult to write, I would think. I've often thought that Bach would have been a great electronic composer, since his music is full of compositional bravura. As we know, you can play his music in any medium, it can be electronically synthesized, and it still holds up as music.

Of course, some composers would compensate for this by combining live instruments with the electronic sounds. Most notably Mario Davidovsky, who has such an elegant sense of idiom, and writes so beautifully, I think.

Q: Is the absence of the visual the only drawback, or are there other problems that keep you away from composing electronically?

CRUMB: I guess I really haven't felt the necessity. There are so many possibilities with traditional instruments which probably never will be exhausted. I feel no instinctive urge to work with electronic sounds, although I think my music has probably, to a certain extent, been influenced by these sounds.

Q: In Black Angels, you have an alternate version of the Pavane. Why did you decide to include that option?

CRUMB: It occurred to me after I composed the Pavane that there was another possible way of realizing my conception. The ossia version involves a continuous glissando--a series of minute, microtonal descensions. It's very difficult to do in actual performance, therefore it's rarely played. The version in the body of the score is more frequently taken.

Q: It's been said that the Vietnam War and the climate it created here played a large part in the nature of the music of Black Angels. Would you agree with that?

CRUMB: I think so, yes. That was, of course, a very dark time.

One lives in the world, and these things influence the music one writes. I tried to make the work reflect a more universal sense of tragedy. Sometimes I think there's a danger in tying art to a specific thing, no matter how urgently it demands expression in its own right. I feel that an artist would tend toward the more universal statement. Perhaps it's not one war, that war, but war in general, the human condition.

Q: Earlier you said that for a piano piece, you composed at the piano. So many of your scores require an enormous battery of percussion instruments. Do you have most of them at your disposal, or do you pretty well have all the ranges and sounds in your mind?

CRUMB: No, I wouldn't have all of the instruments! I think composers tend to store sounds. They learn the possibilities of instruments, or they recall a sound which exists in another composer's work. To be honest, I suppose, I'm not quite always sure about a possibility in some cases; I write the sound I want and hope it works! Sometimes it doesn't, and I have to revise a little; but I find that doesn't happen too frequently, because one learns by experience.

Q: Does teaching take away more than it gives back to you, or do you find that it's valuable for you to teach?

CRUMB: Well, I think of teaching as something quite separate from composition, even though I'm involved in teaching composition; I have some private students, and I'm also involved in classes on analysis of new music and old music. Occasionally, I will get some ideas or stimulus from the students--and maybe occasionally they'll get some from me--but I think of it as kind of a separate thing. One doesn't collide too much with the other.

Q: Is it disadvantageous simply as a drain on your time and energy?

CRUMB: No, I haven't really felt this. My schedule is not tremendously demanding. I think that I would write either a lot of music or very little music, quite independently of what my commitments are in teaching.

Q: A number of your works have been choreographed. Have you seen any of these productions? Do you like it when your music is choreographed?

CRUMB: I did see the choreography of Black Angels, and I was quite impressed. I must confess, I have no real insight into dance as a form. I'm really not very knowledgeable, and I'm rather surprised that certain works of mine have been used that way. I thought that the Butler production of Black Angels was impressive though-- for what that's worth!

Q: In your remarks in the score of Ancient Voices of Children, you say that the instrumental passages can be performed with a solo dancer. Why did you include that possibility?

CRUMB: Well, that just occurred to me while I was writing the piece. The work's rarely done with a solo dancer. It's usually done without dance at all, of course, although it has been done as a complete ballet in several cities.

Q: In the music that could be considered your mature style, there's only one work for orchestra: Echoes of Time and the River. Why has so little of your music been for orchestra?

CRUMB: I don't know. I suppose my ideas seem better adapted to the more flexible medium of chamber music. But I hope to get back to orchestra. I've been involved with it recently.

Q: Flexible in what sense?

CRUMB: I was thinking of ensemble and rhythm. As you know, a considerable rhythmic flexibility is demanded by many new scores, and naturally ensemble is easier to control in a chamber situation. There are ways, of course, of compensating. I guess I haven't been as inventive in this area. I would like to solve that problem for myself.

Q: The only areas where you haven't been active are choral and opera. Would you like to work in either of those two mediums?

CRUMB: I would certainly like to write choral music one day. I suppose opera is something I leave open, too. I think opera would be very difficult. I tend to be a little frightened at the possibility of ever doing that. The example of Wozzeck is frightening, it's such a tremendous piece. One feels that Berg has kind of wrapped up all the possibilities. I'm sure that's not true, but it just seems that way to composers. Some of them do write operas, but there's nothing that comes close to the Berg, really--for me.

Q: Could you tell us what you're working on at the present?

CRUMB: I'm involved with another chamber work. One for orchestra, also. I prefer not to speak too much about works in progress because I find that I'm always changing things around! It's completely fluid, it seems, until I draw the double bar.

Q: Some composers feel that any sound, by itself, constitutes music, whereas others insist that it's only in the interrelation of different sounds that music occurs. Do you feel an affinity more to one side than the others?

CRUMB: Any sound, I should think, is possible. It has to be integrated, it has to make sense, and that brings us to considerations of texture and the total conception of a piece. I'm not saying necessarily that a piece of music must have a narrative quality, as in a Beethoven symphony. But still, I feel the whole is important, and that any element must somehow relate to the whole.

Q: You wrote a credo for your publishers, C. F. Peters: "Music might be defined as a system of proportions in the service of a spiritual impulse." Could you elaborate on that for us? What kind of spiritual impulse?

CRUMB: I guess I was using "spiritual impulse" in a very broad sense. You could substitute "the expressive side of music," or "what music means beyond the pure mechanics." In regard to the whole statement, I guess I wanted to say that music has its structural side, and it has its expressive side, and I think they're both important.

Q: You're actually rather a controversial figure in music today, and one always hears the same two charges leveled at you. The first is that you aren't blazing enough of a trail for younger composers; if you were a great composer, you would come up with some sort of school or system that other people could utilize. The second complaint is that the nature of your music does not change sufficiently from one piece to the next, and that you're running the danger of simply repeating yourself. Do these issues bother you at all?

CRUMB: To take the second thing first, the idea of repeating one's self and defining how narrow or wide a style is, I suppose that my own music would tend to be more narrow than wide. But I think the music of Varèse is extremely narrow. I think the music of Webern is very narrow. Perhaps the most incredibly broad composer was Beethoven--he invented more basic types than any other composer who ever lived. No one person should have invented so much, such a variety of types! But with other composers, there's

much more carry-over from one work to the next. I feel this in
Mahler, in the sense that he really wrote one "larger symphony."
I feel this also in Debussy. I think composers are of different
types.

Q: Webern may be narrow in a certain sense, but for a lot of people he opened the doors to a whole new realm of composition.

CRUMB: Perhaps this is out of one's control. I don't think you
write music either for pedagogical reasons or in hopes of opening
up possibilities per se. I think you write what you have to write.

CATALOG OF COMPOSITIONS

1954	String Quartet	MS
1955	Sonata for solo cello	CF Peters
1959	Variazioni for orchestra	CF Peters
1962	Five Pieces for Piano	CF Peters
1963	Night Music I for soprano, percussion, and piano-celesta	Belwin-Mills
1964	Four Nocturnes (Night Music II) for vio- lin and piano	CF Peters
1965	Madrigals, Book I for soprano, contra- bass, and vibraphone	CF Peters
1965	Madrigals, Book II for soprano, flute, and percussion	CF Peters
1966	Eleven Echoes of Autumn, 1965 (Echoes I) for alto flute, clarinet, violin, and piano	CF Peters
1967	Echoes of Time and the River: Four Processionals for Orchestra (Echoes II)	Belwin-Mills
1968	Songs, Drones, and Refrains of Death for baritone, electric guitar, electric contrabass, electric piano, electric harpsichord, and percussion	CF Peters
1969	Madrigals, Book III for soprano, harp, and percussion	CF Peters
1969	Madrigals, Book IV for soprano, flute, harp, contrabass, and percussion	CF Peters
1969	Night of the Four Moons for alto, alto flute and piccolo, banjo, electric cello, and percussion	CF Peters
1970	Black Angels (Thirteen Images from the Dark Land) (Images I) for electric string quartet	CF Peters
1970	Ancient Voices of Children for soprano, boy soprano, oboe, mandolin, harp,	

	electric piano, toy piano, and percussion	CF Peters
1971	Vox Balanae for Three Masked Musicians for electric flute, electric cello, and electric piano	CF Peters
1971	Lux Aeterna for Five Masked Musicians for soprano, bass flute, sitar, and percussion	CF Peters
1972	Makrokosmos, Volume I (Twelve Fantasy-Pieces after the Zodiac for Amplified Piano)	CF Peters
1973	Makrokosmos, Volume II (Twelve Fantasy-Pieces after the Zodiac for Amplified Piano)	CF Peters
1974	Music for a Summer Evening (Makrokosmos III) for two amplified pianos and percussion	CF Peters
1976	Dream Sequence for violin, cello, piano, percussion, and glass harmonica	CF Peters
1977	Star-Child: A Parable for Soprano, Antiphonal Children's Voices, Bell Ringers, and Large Orchestra	CF Peters
1979	Celestial Mechanics (Makrokosmos IV): Cosmic Dances for Amplified Piano-Four Hands	CF Peters
1979	Apparition: Elegiac Songs and Vocalises for Soprano and Amplified Piano	CF Peters
1980	A Little Suite for Christmas, A.D. 1979 for piano	CF Peters

MARIO DAVIDOVSKY ☐

photo: Gene Bagnato

MARIO DAVIDOVSKY

Mario Davidovsky was born on March 4, 1934, in
Medanos, Buenos Aires, Argentina. In Argentina, he
studied composition with Guillermo Graetzer, Teodoro
Fuchs, Erwin Leuchter, and Ernesto Epstein; in the
United States, with Otto Luening and Aaron Copland.
Davidovsky has taught at the University of Michigan,
the Di Tella Institute of Buenos Aires, and Yale Uni-
versity, and presently teaches at City College of the
City University of New York. In 1961, he married
Elaine Blaustein. They have two children.

Although Davidovsky has established himself as a
composer of both purely electronic works realized on
the RCA Synthesizer and of purely instrumental scores,
it is his series of Synchronisms, works combining
live performers with tape, which are the most widely
known and highly regarded of his compositions. Combining a logical structuring with a sensitive use of
color, the Synchronisms have wedded together these
media with a success that has yet to be surpassed.

The authors spoke with Mario Davidovsky on
June 9, 1975, in his Manhattan home. After becoming acquainted by trading stories about respective
schools, the interview was made in a relaxed and
cogenial atmosphere.

Q: In the first part of this century, the music of many major composers such as Schoenberg and Bartók reflected ties to distinct cultural and ethnic traditions. Your music, however, does not sound
"South American." Do you feel there is still such a thing as a
"native strain" today?

DAVIDOVSKY: I am South American to the extent that I was born
there. I am first generation Argentinian and I was very close to
the values of a European family and culture. So even though I
was born and raised in Argentina, and culturally I identify with my
native country, the European background of my family was a very
important input in my total education.

Today, regional differences are generally disappearing more
and more. We are in the midst of a homogenized culture where
tendencies are years beyond being regional. Of course, if a composer is still using materials of a "folkloristic" origin, the differences will be right there at the surface. Those composers involved
in total serialization, or electronic music, or in any form of chance
composition, would not have differences that one could detect.

Q: Were you first introduced to electronic music after you came to the United States?

DAVIDOVSKY: No. In South America I was introduced to it when I heard the first available recordings. I was terribly impressed by them. In 1958, I had the good fortune of having some of my music played at Tanglewood. Aaron Copland was rather favorably impressed with it. At the time, I was a young kid--twenty or twenty-two. So we got in touch, and he invited me to come to the States. I came to Tanglewood and, at that time, Milton Babbitt and Lukas Foss were on the faculty. I expressed my interest in electronic music, and Babbitt told me of the imminence of the creation of the electronic music center--they were going to get, or had just gotten, a grant. He advised me to wait for one or two years until they could set up the laboratory. So I went home to Argentina and came back in 1960.

Q: What was it about the electronic medium that first excited your interest?

DAVIDOVSKY: I guess that I was essentially impressed by the strangeness and the oddity of the sound itself; I was first attracted, really, by the mere surface of the sound. At that time I was not aware of what the clear or genuine possibilities of the medium were. It was just a very different and extremely fascinating sound.

Q: Besides the new sound dimensions, what do you consider are the advantages of electronic music?

DAVIDOVSKY: I think that if there's something that is not advantageous in electronic music, it's the sound. At first you can be shocked or fascinated by it, but this quickly wears off, simply because electronic music is always played through loudspeakers, and loudspeakers tend to equalize sounds. I don't think there's so much variety as you still have in orchestral sounds--theoretically, yes, but in reality, no. The differences within the electronic music tend to really disappear when the sounds are put in the context of a composition.

The genuine value in electronic music concerns such aspects as the control of dynamics in time. For example, you can control a crescendo or a diminuendo in time with a precision that is not available anywhere else. Since you are not limited by the anatomy of an individual player, you can use the most sophisticated dynamics in the most incredible situations. You could have a tremendously fast succession of sounds--imagine a performance of Paganini's Moto Perpetuo in which every single note has a substantially different dynamic. In other words, the first note would be fortissimo, the second note pianissimo, and so forth. You also have access to generating speeds and successions of attacks that are not available in conventional music. If these elements happen to be of extreme importance in terms of what you are trying to articulate musically, then you can see why you better do it in the laboratory; people playing instruments simply could not do what is needed. So there's an example in which the idiosyncrasy of the electronic medium can be of interest for a very particular musical idea. There are other aspects, such as those concerning articulation procedure, where you can predetermine articulative procedures in electronic music with a precision that, again, is not really available otherwise.

Q: You've composed purely electronic works as well as pieces combining electronic sounds with live performers. Do you prefer one approach over the other?

DAVIDOVSKY: I did not write any purely electronic pieces after 1965. In 1961 or '62, I was very, very interested in the combination of live instruments with tape, for several reasons. At that time, one of the many aspects of electronic music which I was bothered by was its elimination of the performer. I was rather philosophically bothered; I asked myself what would happen if music is going to be frozen and not subjected to any possible reinterpretation. Today, I think that, essentially, the question is naive. But at that time, I intended several approaches to compensate for the lack of a performer. One approach was to reincorporate the performer into the electronic sound, or to bring the electronic sound into the realm of traditional sounds. The combination was successful, and I received many commissions for pieces combining instruments and tape. So it was a combination of my own choice and the circumstances.

Q: In your notes to the Synchronisms No. 1, you mention that there exists a slight chance element in that the performers will not always play exactly in time with the tape in one performance as they will in another. Did you purposely introduce such a chance element as something which might compensate for the frozen aspect of electronic music which you mentioned earlier?

DAVIDOVSKY: What you say is true for the earlier Synchronisms, numbers one, two, and three. When I wrote them there was very little tradition in that form of composition. So far as I was concerned, I had to start from scratch. There were so many problems that, right now, seem simpler because a certain tradition has been established. At the time, having a tape recorder, a machine, running against a human being playing an instrument was very problematic. There was a lack of real experimentation in the field which could determine to what extent precision was possible.

As it turned out, I underestimated the ability of performers; they can be terribly precise. There were certain things that I was very suspicious of, and avoided doing at that time. But through experience, I found out how it was possible to realize them successfully. So in the beginning I found an enormous amount of problems in terms of synchronizing polyphonically the tape and the instrument. This did not hold true for the later works--the piano piece, the percussion piece, or some of the others that I did. In other words, the tape functions like another voice within the composition. The only chance element existing between the recorded voice and the rest of the instruments would be equal to the amount of chance involved when two violins are playing the same piece. It's not a compositional chance element; it's a chance inherent to the live performance.

Q: In combining tape and live instruments, what were some other aspects that you had to take into consideration?

DAVIDOVSKY: One thing I considered was how to get a coherent sound out of the combination of both media. The Synchronisms No. 1 used a flute because the flute is a relatively simple sound to combine with electronic sounds. Another real reason is that at Columbia University I was very close to Harvey Sollberger, a magnificent flutist with a remarkable, personal way of playing that instrument.

Q: In what respect was the flute sound simple to combine with the electronic sounds?

DAVIDOVSKY: In terms of color. These early Synchronisms differ from my later ones, in which the electronic sounds tend to produce an "instrumental" sound on the tape. The electronic sound is more clearly articulated than in the early pieces, simply because the devices available in the seventies were not available in the sixties. Now you can electronically produce a shape of a sound that you couldn't produce in the sixties (or which was extremely difficult to produce). In other words, every sound has an attack: It remains for a while, and then it will decay. To do that now with electronic sounds is very easy. In the sixties working in the kind of laboratory that I was working in, the only way of doing that was by using razor blades--by editing. The technology available determined accessibility to certain sounds.

When I spoke earlier about my reasons for combining electronic sounds with a flute, I did not mean that I made electronic sounds sound like a flute. Rather, I tried to produce a type of sound that would complement the flute, a chamber-like sonority around the flute which would not be, acoustically speaking, antagonistic.

Q: Do you think that the time you spent working with electronic music changed the way you composed a non-electronic piece such as Inflexions?

DAVIDOVSKY: Well, you have to think in these terms: Imagine if you abandon the material you are using to produce your work, and for four years you go into quite a different material. After living with it for a long period of time, you then go back to the previous one; you are necessarily going to be influenced because your whole memory has been invaded with an element that has become part of your total recollection of sounds. So, all the experiences that you had in electronic sounds have to come out one way or another. I think that, especially, the percussive character of Inflexions is something I would not have tried in that kind of language before I had experience with electronic music. It's almost as if you were a wood sculptor who then decided to work in granite. Obviously, you have to completely change the structure of your thinking if you are going to think coherently in terms of stone. Then, when you go back into wood you will, naturally, try to think coherently in terms of wood, but all your experience in the other realm is going to show up somehow.

Q: In an interview made a few years ago, you expressed dissatisfaction with the incorporation of theatrical elements into music. Are your feelings still the same?

DAVIDOVSKY: I guess, properly phrased, yes. You see, mixed media, as a proposition, started with Greek theater. As a proposition, it is of enormous interest. But whatever I saw in the field, I found very poor. It never really worked properly. The idea is still fascinating, but I never saw anything that really convinced me. It's still a wonderful idea to discuss over a cup of coffee.

At one point, I did write a lot of music for art movies and short films. Especially in Argentina, where there was a very active group of young filmmakers involved in art films and short films. I also wrote ballet suites in Argentina, but actually they should be considered pure pieces of music.

Q: Your Electronic Study No. 3 is dedicated to Edgard Varèse. Had you ever met Varèse?

DAVIDOVSKY: I worked with Varèse. As a matter of fact, in my second or third year at Columbia I became his technician. Every day around one o'clock Varèse used to come to work in the laboratory. He had a health condition--he could not stand air conditioning. The room was windowless and very close, so the air was rarefied and he could stay for only two hours. I worked there for him for more than one year. I would help him find patchings; he would be very specific in describing the type of sound he would like to get, and I would just help him find it. By this time, Varèse was already seventy-five or seventy-six years old. I had a really great time working with this extraordinary man.

I completed my third Study at the time of Varèse's death, and I wanted to pay this tribute to a man who was a great composer and a close, warm friend.

Q: Earlier, you mentioned Aaron Copland. Did you find him to be interested in electronic music?

DAVIDOVSKY: Once, years ago, I remember trying to convince Mr. Copland of the value of, at least, experimenting in electronic music, even if you couldn't write great music with it. He came once or twice to the laboratory and I spent a few hours demonstrating things and discussing things with him. I think that, probably, if electronic music had been available at another point in Mr. Copland's life, he would probably have used it. You could say the same thing about composers such as Sessions or Carter. They are perfectly aware of and interested in the field, but they themselves are not interested in actually using it.

Q: Was Copland very critical of your music?

DAVIDOVSKY: I worked with him only a short time, when I was at Tanglewood. In terms of practical guidance he was terrific-- very, very direct and always to the point. It was a tremendously profitable experience. His major criticism of my music was that it sounded as if it derived too much from Central European sources. I guess this implied that, at the time, I subscribed to twelve-tone technique.

Q: Have you moved past serial technique?

DAVIDOVSKY: I never wrote what's known as serialized music. I do use sets; but the processes of unfolding notes derive from within the context of the particular piece I'm working on at the moment.

Q: Has teaching affected the way you compose?

DAVIDOVSKY: Yes, because whenever you try to communicate an idea at that very deep level, the act of articulating clarifies your own thinking. Also, working with a bright, young composer creates a feedback relationship. Sometimes, I look at the score of one of my students, criticize certain points, and then offer five possible solutions to a specific problem. Then the student comes back next week with a sixth solution better than the others. Eventually, when you work with a very talented student, this will happen. You suggest something, and the suggestion works as a trigger for other associations and solutions. In that process, and in other ways as well, you are obviously enriched.

Q: Does the question of audience accessibility concern you when you compose?

DAVIDOVSKY: The audience is really an abstraction. When I write music or when anybody else writes music, you are your own audience at the moment. It's really impossible for me to think in any other terms if I am deeply involved with a musical idea. Think of yourself writing a sonnet or a poem. You are trying to build an entity that makes sense within itself, to create relationships that are organic--to create a small universe. The audience is really not part of that process. This does not mean that composers don't want to be successful, or that they don't want to be adulated by audiences standing and cheering. Sure, we all want that, we like to be successful. But this does not in any way determine the choices you will make unless you are writing a certain kind of music, one which is successful only if it's commercially successful. My success is measured only by the success of the piece itself, not by the success of the piece in terms of the critical or the audience reception. In my mind, there is no way of making peace with this situation. They are two completely different things. You obviously hope that your music projects, and that people apprehend it; that's of fundamental importance. But this hope does not in any way determine that I will use a trombone doing such a thing or the tuba doing another thing in order to make the piece succeed.

I think it's a great virtue to write music that is accessible and simple. Simplicity is a great virtue. But what I was just explaining has nothing to do with simplicity. This problem has always existed in music. There were always very few people who spent the time educating themselves in order to gain access to this language. We do have a small audience. But I don't think you can make compositional decisions by thinking what the audience reaction will be.

Q: Could you tell us what you're currently working on?

DAVIDOVSKY: Well, for the next two years, I will be working on non-electronic music. I just finished a piece for woodwind quintet and tape, and a piece for orchestra and tape. Right now, I'm writing a piece for four singers and chamber ensemble based on the Song of Solomon. Immediately after that, I have to write a string quartet for the Juilliard String Quartet. Then, I have to write a chamber piece for twenty instruments.

For the piece based on the Song of Solomon I am using the original language, Hebrew. I haven't written vocal music for about fifteen years. I considered myself completely untalented for writing for voice; I had a block when it came to thinking about the human voice. But right now I'm having a great time doing the piece. I am going to use three poems for the composition. The piece should be about thirty minutes long, and could be minimally staged. I mean "staged" in a very simple sense: All of the singers will play percussion instruments.

I had a great time reading all of the commentaries that I could grab hold of concerning the Song of Solomon, in the hope of discovering more contrasting elements that would be musically suggestive to me. I plan to use musical materials of very diverse origins--some of these suggestive of medieval procedures, some of Judaic cantillation. Hopefully, I'll succeed in writing a piece of "divertimento" character.

CATALOG OF COMPOSITIONS

1954	String Quartet No. 1	MS
1954	Concertino for Percussion and String Orchestra	MS
1955	Quintet for Clarinet and Strings	MS
1955	Suite Sinfonica Para "El Payaso" for orchestra	MS
1956	Three Pieces for Woodwind Quartet	MS
1956	Noneto for Nine Instruments	EB Marks
1958	String Quartet No. 2	NY Public Library
1959	Serie Sinfonica 1959 for orchestra	NY Public Library
1960	Contrastes No. 1 for string orchestra and electronic sounds	MS
1961	Electronic Study No. 1	EB Marks
1961	Planos 1961 for orchestra	NY Public Library
1962	Electronic Study No. 2	EB Marks
1962	Trio for Clarinet, Trumpet, and Viola	NY Public Library
1963	Synchronisms No. 1 for flute and electronic sounds	McGinnis & Marx
1964	Synchronisms No. 2 for flute, clarinet, violin, cello, and electronic sounds	McGinnis & Marx

1965	Synchronisms No. 3 for cello and electronic sounds	McGinnis & Marx
1965	Electronic Study No. 3	EB Marks
1965	Inflexions for chamber ensemble	EB Marks
1966	Junctures for flute, clarinet, and violin	EB Marks
1967	Synchronisms No. 4 for male or mixed chorus and electronic sounds	EB Marks
1968	Music for Solo Violin	MS
1969	Synchronisms No. 5 for percussion ensemble and electronic sounds	EB Marks
1970	Synchronisms No. 6 for piano and electronic sounds	EB Marks
1971	Chacona for violin, cello, and piano	EB Marks
1972	Transientes for orchestra	EB Marks
1973	Synchronisms No. 7 for orchestra and electronic sounds	EB Marks
1974	Synchronisms No. 8 for woodwind quintet and electronic sounds	EB Marks
1975	Scenes from "Shir-Ha-Shirim" for soprano, two tenors, bass, and chamber orchestra	EB Marks
1976	String Quartet No. 3	EB Marks
1978	Pennplay for sixteen players	MS
1980	String Quartet No. 4	MS
1980	Consorts for symphonic band	MS

CHARLES DODGE ☐

photo: Gene Bagnato

Charles Dodge was born on June 5, 1942, in Ames,
Iowa. He received his B.A. from the University of
Iowa where he studied composition with Richard Her-
vig. His other composition teachers have included
Gunther Schuller at Tanglewood, and Jack Beeson,
Chou Wen-chung, and Otto Luening at Columbia Uni-
versity. Dodge studied electronic music with Vladi-
mir Ussachevsky and computer music with Godfrey
Winham. Dodge has conducted research in computer
music and speech synthesis at the IBM Thomas J.
Watson Research Center, the Bell Telephone Labora-
tories, and at the University of California, San Diego.
He has taught at Columbia and Princeton, and presently
teaches at Brooklyn College. He has two children by
his first marriage. In 1978, he married Katharine
King Schlefer.

Although Dodge has written purely instrumental
works, he has devoted the greater part of his career
to computer music. A leading force in this area of
electronic music, Dodge has spearheaded research in
computer speech synthesis. The compositional results thus far display imagination, sure craftsmanship, and a gift for humor. They have already opened
doors to valuable new methods of electronic composition.

The authors spoke with Charles Dodge in his Manhattan apartment on August 31, 1975. Much to their
surprise, he seemed initially uncomfortable in the
presence of the tape recorder. But during the course
of the interview, his friendliness prevailed as he
thoughtfully discussed his complex work in computer
music with a refreshing enthusiasm and clarity.

Q: Your electronic music utilizes a computer. Could you explain
the difference between composing with a computer and composing
with something like the RCA Sound Synthesizer?

DODGE: The RCA Sound Synthesizer is a piece of electronic mu-
sic-producing equipment which has no memory. It's simply a device which will make the electronic sounds that are encoded on a
sheet of paper, much like a piano roll has encoded in it a piece of
music to be played on a player piano. The Synthesizer, you know,
is a unique instrument. There's but one RCA Sound Synthesizer in
existence today, and it's the one that Milton Babbitt uses.

The digital computer is a much more generally available

142

musical instrument than the RCA Sound Synthesizer. A wide variety of manufacturers' computers have been used to produce electronic sounds. All that's required to get a digital computer to make an electronic sound is something called a digital-to-analog converter, which transforms the output of the music synthesis program--which is a stream of numbers--into a fluctuating voltage. As with the RCA Sound Synthesizer, computers can be made to make stereo electronic sound, to make full frequency sound, in a wide variety of different kinds of sounds. But the digital computer is a more general purpose sound synthesis medium than the RCA Sound Synthesizer for the reason that it has a memory. In addition to the tools by which it's programmed--punch cards, or teletype, or cathode ray tube--the computer can store sets of instructions for the processing. It therefore enables one to do a much wider variety of things. You can, for example, create most of the standard kinds of electronic sounds on the computer at the one extreme, and at the other extreme you can do things like synthesize the sound of people talking and singing.

The computer's generality provides for the possibility of encoding the works of Bach, and creating computer performances on them ad infinitum--ad nauseam. Once the basic melody, harmony, and rhythm of a work is encoded, that work can be interpreted in many different ways, with perhaps even minimal instructions. Once the notes were decided upon for the composition, you wouldn't have to re-encode the composition each time you wanted to make a slight change. By using a well-known music synthesis language, MUSIC IV, on the computer at Columbia, you can change the tempo of a passage by changing one instruction. You could play the work that you had encoded more slowly or more rapidly just by changing one card.

Q: As opposed to going there and redoing each note at the new tempo?

DODGE: That's right; you'd already have the notes residing on some memory device, and then it would be a matter of calling them up and changing one thing in the program to get a quite different sound. Similarly, you can change the timbres without changing the rhythms, or without changing the tempo. There are really two features of the sound synthesis language that we use. One is dubbed the score, and that's generally the pitches-in-time of the composition. The other is dubbed the orchestra, the types of electronic sounds to carry those pitches and rhythms. The two overlap in certain ways so that you can make changes in one that affect things in the other.

Q: How did you become involved with computers and with electronic music in general?

DODGE: I studied music in quite a traditional way at the college in Ames, Iowa: piano teachers, and violin teachers, and woodwind teachers. In high school, I played a lot of jazz; I played the saxophone and had my own band. Gradually, I became more and more interested in writing concert music. I'd always written music from the time I was young, but more pop music: songs and jazz tunes, and the like. As I got farther along in high school I became interested in writing string quartets and pieces for orchestra, things like that, and I left Ames to study at the University of Iowa in Iowa City, as an undergraduate. There I found a marvellous teacher in the person of Richard Hervig, who's now head of composition there. He taught me a tremendous amount about writing music. When I finished at Iowa, I came to Columbia University to study instrumental and electronic music. I took an electronic music course-- I think in my second year of graduate study--and found that there was a great disparity between the means and the ends of electronic music. I was accustomed to being able to think in terms of the orchestration of my musical ideas for traditional instruments, and I found that there was no analogous feature in the electronic music studio that enabled me to think of my compositions in terms of texture and line. I had to become a carpenter on the side in order to realize my musical ideas. I found that very unsympathetic with my musical thinking, and was quite discouraged with electronic music until I went to Tanglewood.

I had been a student at Tanglewood in 1964, and then was commissioned to write a work for the twenty-fifth anniversary of Tanglewood in 1965. One of the other commissionees was J.K. Randall, from Princeton, who was writing computer music. He played a tape which he had realized on his university's computer and converted to analog form at Bell Labs. In discussing computer music with Jim Randall, I saw that there needn't be this disparity between means and ends in electronic music. I was just using what was for me the wrong kind of equipment. So the next year I registered for the electronic music course at Columbia, but by an informal arrangement took the computer music course at Princeton with Godfrey Winham. I found right away that my musical thinking and the kind of thinking that went into realizing music on tape were very close. I fancied electronic music through computers in a way that I had never found possible in the traditional electronic music studio, and I've been working with computers, then, since 1966.

Q: Could you tell us about your studies with Darius Milhaud?

DODGE: Milhaud was the guest composer at the University of Iowa in the spring of 1961, my freshman year at college. I had been writing a lot of music that year, and some of it was played for him. He was encouraging, and asked me if I would like to come to Aspen summer music school to study with him. My parents paid for my tuition and room and board in Aspen, Colorado for the summer of '61 in order to study with Milhaud.

I found the experience of staying in Aspen and having contact with other young, aspiring professionals from around the country to be more valuable than the study with Milhaud personally. He was quite ill that summer and was unable to meet many of his classes. As a result, it was a time for finding myself in the prospect of having a career as a professional musician. I found that my education, although parochial, was not that bad, and that I had learned quite a bit in the years that I had been studying music. My experience at Aspen served to show me that there was a larger music world in which I could feel comfortable.

Q: Do you find any genuine problems in composing computer music?

DODGE: There have been numerous difficulties with computer music over the years, but a number of these difficulties have been satisfactorily solved. There are still difficulties with the medium, but I'm confident that they, too, will be solved.

In 1966, when I began computer music at Princeton, the procedure for hearing a piece you were writing for computer was the following: You'd go to the computer center at Princeton and punch IBM cards for a few hours, and try to be as careful as possible not to make mistakes in the punching. The collected cards would then be submitted to the central computer on campus, and you'd come back the next day to see if the job had worked properly. If you had not caught all the typos, you'd have to go back to the key punch and work through that, and then submit the job again and wait for the next day. If, on the next day, the job had been completed successfully, you then went to the telephone and called Bell Labs. There's a very nice lady there who was in charge of scheduling the digital-to-analog conversion facility for the Bell Labs at Murray Hill. She would schedule an appointment to use the digital-to-analog conversion system sooner or later, depending on the use of the Bell telephone system itself. So that might be the next day, but it was more likely the next week. Occasionally it was the next two or three weeks, if there was some major project being worked on by the researchers at Bell Labs, or if the machine was broken, which also happened--with frustrating regularity.

Typically, the matter of time lag could be from a few days to a week. That problem has been significantly reduced over the years, and in 1971, Columbia got its own digital-to-analog conversion facility, thus reducing the amount of time required for the digital-to-analog conversion from a week to the next day. Recently, in the last eighteen months, at Columbia the turn-around time has been reduced even farther. Now I can sit in my laboratory, type instructions into the computer, wait a few minutes for them to be processed, and hear the musical result. It takes only five to ten minutes, and, depending on the length of a specific assignment, sometimes less than a minute. So now we have immediate feedback on our musical ideas, an essential condition for effective music making. It's unthinkable to work on synthesizing speech without being able to get immediate feedback on the sounds. It's hard enough to deal with abstractions of musical timbre and rhythm, but it is impossible to deal with something as specific as the sound of a natural language without this feedback.

Now, there is still this matter of a time delay of a minute or two or five or ten, and that problem is being solved in new developments in computer hardware, which enable one to sit at a computer console and play one's music in real time, the way you would a piano or organ.

Q: How do you feel toward the traditional complaint which is leveled against electronic music: that the composer is left with one frozen, finished product?

DODGE: It's true that one's electronic music exists in a frozen, fixed way, but with the computer this isn't as serious as it is with other media in electronic music, for the reasons that I mentioned earlier. Once the composition exists in the computer's memory, it can be reinterpreted by different people, or by the composer on different occasions. The same composer in a different frame of mind may interpret the same composition in quite different ways. There are those computer musicians who are looking forward to the day when they'll be able to give live performances on their digital computers. That day isn't so very far away.

Q: Do you still write non-electronic scores?

DODGE: Very few. I've found myself in the position of being something of a pioneer--although I don't know that I like that word--in computer music. It's been very time-consuming. I've had to solve technological as well as artistic and compositional problems along the way, and I just haven't had the time to write much instrumental music. Extensions for trumpet and tape, realized in 1973, is my solitary instrumental effort in recent years.

Q: How well does your early instrumental work Folia still sit with you?

DODGE: I heard it quite recently, and I enjoyed listening to it. I think the piece is rather successful. It sets out to do a particular sequence of things, and it does them. You can't ask much more from a piece of your own music. It's the work of a young composer, but one who had quite a bit of experience by the time that he wrote it, and who was very insistent upon trying to communicate his compositional ideas.

Q: Would you prefer to write more music for both electronic sounds and traditional instruments?

DODGE: Extensions is the only piece I've done like that. That piece mixes two completely opposite kinds of sounds. The trumpet was very tuneful and lyrical, and the tape was very mechanical and increasingly difficult to grasp. Overlapping the two at that place in the piece and combining these opposites was one of the purposes of the composition.

That work was created on commission, and I think if it hadn't been commissioned I wouldn't have written it. My ideas these days are moving much more along the lines of the electronic medium, and less along the lines of instrumental setups. It may just be a matter of my time. I just don't have time to think along those lines--or at least I don't have enough thoughts that seem to warrant moving along those lines. My thoughts are concerned with analyzing and synthesizing speech, and synthesizing video programs to go with the speech, and secondarily, analyzing the sounds of musical instruments, mainly to help students along those lines.

The project that I'm engaged in now is as an artist-in-residence at WNET-TV. I'm producing experimental video programs to go with the synthetic voices.

Q: Abstract visuals?

DODGE: No. I think that one of the interesting things about the video medium is that you can do with it what you can do with synthetic speech. That is, you can go from a quite realistic picture to something that's an unrecognizable jumble of color and form. Just as with the synthetic voice you can go from something that sounds like my normal speech to something that sounds completely unreal.

Q: Exactly how do you synthesize speech?

DODGE: The type of speech synthesis I do is called synthesis by analysis, and it works this way: A voice is recorded speaking the passage that you want to synthesize. That recording is subjected to a process called analog-to-digital conversion, which transforms the fluctuating voltage on tape into a sequence of numbers inside the computer. That sequence of numbers then represents the waveform of the voice speaking the sentence that was recorded. Since it's a sequence of numbers, it can be subjected to numerical analysis. So the next stage is to analyze the digitized voice, and to mathematically determine its frequency content and its resonance structure. (The analyzer returns a set of values--parameters--for the voice for every one-hundredth of a second of the speech.)

At this stage one can resynthesize the voice and, depending on the success of the analysis, the result will sound more or less like the voice that was recorded in the first place. Now, the point is that once the voice has been analyzed into its components, I can change those components before I resynthesize the voice. It enables me to do things that you can't do with standard tape techniques. With the synthetic voice, you can, for example, change the speed of the voice without changing the pitch. You know how, with tape, if you speed up the tape or slow it down significantly, you lose intelligibility. With the synthetic voice that's not the case. Similarly, you can change the pitch of the voice without changing the speed.

For the first time, we have in electronic sound the possibility of making something extremely concrete--that is, English communication of words--which can be extended directly into abstract electronic sound. In the past, there's been quite an abutment between the two. On the one hand, you've had music such as Milton Babbitt's, with its sophisticated differentiations of timbre, pitch, and time; and on the other hand, you've had musique concrète, consisting of reprocessings of sounds made with microphones. The synthetic speech process combines the two in quite an interesting way. It bridges that gap between recorded sound and synthesized sound.

Q: In the first Speech Songs, the synthetic voice still seems to have a mechanical accent.

DODGE: The Speech Songs were done at the Bell Labs during 1972 and early 1973, and used for the first three songs a technique of speech analysis called formant tracking. The formant tracking program necessarily results in a mechanical-sounding speech. The fourth Speech Song sounds extremely natural, due to a brilliant breakthrough in speech analysis on the part of Vishnu Atal, a researcher in speech at Bell Labs. Since that time, I have created my own speech-synthesis and speech-analysis system at Columbia, in which the speech quality is extremely natural. With the new system, it's possible to analyze female voice as well as male voice, and to change the pitch of the synthetic voice over a very wide range without destroying the intelligibility.

Q: The original method could not do a female voice?

DODGE: No, the formant tracking would work only on male voice. It was a feature of the technique. Whereas, after the linear predictive coding techniques of Vishnu Atal were devised, there's no significant difference in quality between male or female, or child's speech. With the formant tracking, whenever you put the pitch up into the female range, it just sounded like a boy whose voice hadn't changed. Now, with the new techniques, it's possible to preserve speaker identification over a broader range of pitch.

Q: You talked about breaking the voice down into its components and then resynthesizing it to get the finished product. Was it a matter of trial and error, or could you get immediate feedback?

DODGE: The Bell Lab system that I used had the possibility of immediate feedback, so that I always heard the result of the alteration that I made through synthesis within a matter of minutes. It was a most efficacious environment for working on speech.

Q: If you can synthesize speech, isn't it conceivable that you could do this with a violin or a trumpet?

DODGE: Yes.

Q: It seems that the prospects of this technique are unlimited.

DODGE: They are. We're working on that now. I have a student who is writing an opera for his dissertation, and part of the plot involves a magic violin. We're hoping to be able to analyze and synthesize a violin that will be able to do things that are unreal.

Q: It would seem that you could ultimately make completely elec-tronic performances of orchestral music. No composer would ever have to worry about scoring a piece for too large a group of play-ers, or about writing music that would be too virtuosic.

DODGE: This is certainly one of the implications of the research in this area. It's something which I think will probably not be worked out by us, because we're not engineers as much as artists. When I say "us," I refer to myself, my colleagues, and my students. The purpose of our research is to provide aesthetic experiences which couldn't be had by other means; and, as such, to help people come to grips with the implications of technology. Having artists work in areas of technical sophistication is probably quite important for our culture. So I'm not going to spend my time making a syn-thetic orchestra to rival well-trained instrumentalists.

Q: Earth's Magnetic Field exploits its stereophonic capabilities, as do many current electronic works. How important is this for the piece?

DODGE: Its importance lies in creating a spatial dimension. I'd say that the first side of Earth's Magnetic Field, the setting of that index of the effect of the sun's radiation on the magnetic field that surrounds the earth, is the main business of the piece. After that the movement of the sounds between the loudspeakers is an additional layer of activity, one which could be dispensed with, without destroying the structure of the piece.

Q: Could you tell us about The Story of Our Lives?

DODGE: The Story of Our Lives was the first work that I did with my own speech-synthesis system at Columbia. I call it my own, but it was created with the help of a number of individuals who should get credit. Howard Eskin, the manager of systems programming at Columbia Computer Center and professor of electrical engineering, was a great help in creating the speech-analysis system, particularly the pitch-tracking scheme. Godfrey Winham, of the music department at Princeton, and Kenneth Stieglitz, of the electrical engineering department at Princeton, contributed essential parts of the system, as did Richard Garland of the Nevis Labs. One of the things that technological art in the late twentieth century entails is collaboration, working with people in other disciplines to make something that no single individual could put together very well. I have the musical ideas for what I want the system to be able to do, the engineers have some ideas about problems they'd like to solve, and we all get together and make the kinds of collective decisions that are necessary to put together something that's of use and value to all of us.

The Story of Our Lives is based on a poem of the same name by Mark Strand. (It's published in a volume of poetry by Atheneum Press called The Story of Our Lives.) Mark and I are old buddies from the Midwest. His first teaching job was at the University of Iowa, where I was an undergraduate. If we didn't meet then, we at least were aware of each other's existence, and we did eventually get to know each other in New York City. I followed his work in poetry quite closely, and was very taken by "The Story of Our Lives" when it was first published in The New Yorker. It's the story of a man and a woman who are sitting in a room reading a book, and the book they're reading is the story of their lives. As they read the book, the book says that they are reading the book. It's like looking in a mirror of their lives, one they can't stand to look in, and at the same time one they can't avoid.

The problem in composing was to take this poem--which was that situation seen from the man's standpoint--and to musicalize it in such a way that the woman became equally important. The way I did that was to treat the first stanza as an exchange and repetition over the lines between the man and the woman. In the middle part of the work, the man has a solo in which he fantasizes ways of getting out of the situation. He talks about moving into another life, another book, and that he's worried about how his life is indistinguishable from the book. Also, in that middle portion of the work, the passages from the book are read in an unreal voice, one in which a synthetic voice is given a complex electronic sound for its characteristic timbre, rather than a simulation of the vibratory effect of the glottis.

In the last part of the work, the man and the woman get back together again to obsess about the hopelessness of their situation, but this is offset by a greater and greater emphasis on the book. Passages from the book get longer and longer; they're treated in first two and then three voices. At the very end, there's a bow to radio soap opera of the 1940s, in which the Hammond organ-like sound that's been hinted at through the book voice actually comes out in an unmodified form; a surrealistic Hammond organ. There are other references to the techniques of soap opera throughout The Story of Our Lives. Soap operas are a lowbrow way of finding expression for your emotions, finding an outlet for these feelings that we all have. I think it was very important to Strand at the time that he wrote "The Story of Our Lives" to set the terrifying emotions that he had, in a way that other people could appreciate.

Q: And the raw material for the work was simply you and a woman reading the poem?

DODGE: That's right. My friend Dana Lichty and I read the poem.

Q: What of your second major synthetic-speech composition, In Celebration?

DODGE: In Celebration is a setting of a poem from the same collection by Mark Strand. The music combines choral writing with solo speech and song in a way not too terribly far removed from late sixteenth-century Italian madrigal. Of course, you get a wider variety of vocal articulations here. For example, there are passages where people speak. In fact, the climax of In Celebration is a speaking chorus repeating the lines about what the celebration means: "By giving yourself over to nothing you shall be healed." It's a choral section which is done without the artifice of adding pitch to the spoken word; it just takes the established contour of the spoken voice and repeats that. All of these choral effects are done by mixing different versions of the synthetic voice on the computer. The poem was read into the computer once, and from that all of the different versions of the lines that you hear were derived after analysis. It was completed quite recently, in July of '75.

Q: What are your current projects?

DODGE: A synthetic speech work which is a setting of a radio play by Samuel Beckett called Cascando is my major compositional project. That piece will combine synthetic speech with computer-synthesized sound. I'm also making the scenario for the visualization of The Story of Our Lives. I'm making a visual program to go with that. It's kind of an electronic soap opera.

Q: And that will be shown on WNET?

DODGE: I don't know if it will ever get shown or not, but I'll have the result of my work on tape. It's my first effort, and I think the first effort anywhere to combine synthetic voices with synthetic visual images, and there's probably a lot there that I can't predict. Luckily, I have a Guggenheim Grant to spend my year investigating such things, so I won't be teaching so much as performing research in these new areas, and hopefully creating works of art for television--a long neglected, if understandably neglected, medium.

CATALOG OF COMPOSITIONS

1964	Composition in Five Parts for cello and piano.	ACA
1964	Solos and Combinations for flute and/or oboe and/or clarinet	ACA
1965	Folia for chamber orchestra	ACA
1966	Rota for full orchestra	ACA
1970	Changes for computer-synthesized sound	ACA
1970	Earth's Magnetic Field for computer-synthe-sized sound	ACA
1972	Speech Songs realizations in computer-synthe-sized speech of poetry by Mark Strand	ACA
1973	Extensions for trumpet and tape	ACA
1974	The Story of Our Lives realization in com-puter-synthesized speech of poetry by Mark Strand	ACA
1975	In Celebration realization in computer-synthesized speech of poetry by Mark Strand	ACA
1976	Palinode for computer and orchestra	ACA
1978	Cascando electronic musicalization of the radio play by Samuel Beckett	ACA
1980	Any Resemblance Is Purely Coincidental for piano and synthesized voice on tape	ACA

JACOB DRUCKMAN ☐

photo: Gene Bagnato

Jacob Druckman was born on June 26, 1928, in Phil-
adelphia, Pennsylvania. He received his B.S. and
M.S. from The Juilliard School of Music, where he
studied with Peter Mennin and Vincent Persichetti.
Druckman also studied with Tony Aubin at L'Ecole
Normale de Musique, and with Aaron Copland at
Tanglewood. Druckman is currently teaching at Yale
University. In 1954, Druckman married Muriel Helen
Topaz. They have two children.

Druckman's musical interests have taken him
through a range of compositional methods. After
early work along serial lines, Druckman became interested in allowing certain freedoms in the performance of his scores. Subsequently, the incorporation
of theatrical devices became an important facet of
his music. What these scores all share in common
is the striking inventiveness and keen wit of the composer.

Jacob Druckman was interviewed on June 14,
1975, in his home in Manhattan. His lack of reserve
and formality proved to be as infectious and winning
as his humor.

Q: Could you tell us about your studies at Tanglewood with Aaron
Copland?

DRUCKMAN: I had never met Copland when I first went up to
Tanglewood, and I was a typical, smart-aleck graduate student,
figuring, "Well, he's OK for this Americana stuff, but how's he
going to talk to composers working in different idioms?" He was
teaching a class, and I watched him criticize other people's works.
He's an incredible man. He can put himself in someone else's
shoes, he can look at a work and talk about it within its own context and rationale, and criticize it that way. The man also has an
enormous curiosity. He's always fascinated with who's doing what,
who are the young composers arriving on the scene, what are the
new ideas.

Q: How did you first become involved with electronic music?

DRUCKMAN: You know, at this point it's hard to remember what
got me started with electronic music, even though I did start comparatively recently. The reason it's so hard to remember is because I was so turned around by my early experiences with it. I

154

kept running into realities and revelatory experiences that I never expected to find. Electronic music is a great debunker of the vanities that composers hold. Intellectual ideas crumble in the face of listening to the actualities of electronic music. It's completely unprejudiced. The machines have none of the preconceptions that composers and performers carry, and if you listen very honestly to what comes out of the machines, you'll find that very often it has very little to do with what you thought you were putting into it.

The most memorable revelation for me had to do with rhythmic complexities. In 1965 or '66, when I first started working with electronic music, I was also working on my Second String Quartet. I was very involved with Carter's Second String Quartet, and the use of complex rhythms. I thought it would be wonderful to be in an electronic music studio where one is not bound by the limitations of human performers. I thought that since I could get people to play six against seven, I could do much more complicated combinations with the machines, which is exactly what I set out to do. I listened to what the machines played back to me and discovered that I was not charmed or excited by it at all. I very quickly realized that what I was reacting to in Carter's music, and in my own music when I got into complex rhythms, was the sound of people playing complex rhythms. Not the arithmetic proportions, but the energy, the anxiety, the human effort needed to play complex rhythms. That effort is what I became fascinated with, and that's the turn the electronic music took. The early pieces were not terribly different from anybody else's, but as I kept going with electronic music, I was looking more and more for the sound of corporeal nuance, the sound of electrical energy coursing through flesh rather than wires.

Q: Your String Quartet Number Two has several passages in which the treatment of the musical materials strongly resembles certain treatments normally heard in electronic music. Were you trying at times to achieve such similar sonorites?

DRUCKMAN: Sure. There's no question but that it influenced my writing. That work was my big serial piece--or as close as I ever got to complete serial procedure. In its larger aspects, the macrocosmic organization, it is strongly serial. The note-to-note discipline is not that terribly tight, but the piece keeps referring to a given row and its derivatives. As I worked with the piece, I found other aspects of its organization to be much more important to me, and it was the last serial piece that I've done.

That was a very big year of change for me. I think it was largely due to the impact of the electronic music studio debunking ideas that I had cherished for quite a long time. Also, just working with the string quartet itself, which is a medium very close to me since I was a violinist. I wrote that piece not at the piano, but at the fiddle.

Q: Why did you finally move away from serialism?

DRUCKMAN: I don't know if "finally" is the best way of saying it. I think I was involved in it because it was at a time in the early sixties when intellectual organization seemed to be the vital concern of that moment in history. Also, not being a serialist on the East Coast of the United States in the sixties was like not being a Catholic in Rome in the thirteenth century. It was the respectable thing to do, at least once.

Q: Could you explain what is meant by "proportional notation" in a work like Incenters?

DRUCKMAN: That notation probably shouldn't be called "proportional." I don't remember who first made this observation, but traditional notation is proportional: a half note is twice as long as a quarter note, which is a given proportion. At some point or other, someone suggested we call it analog notation, since what we have is space on the page being analogous to the duration.

But what's more to the point is the physical experience of playing these rhythms. One can have music that's related to a pulse that's going by, which is one kind of relationship. Then you can have music that is felt in absolute time, so that a duration takes as long as it has to take because of its own inner necessities. For that, we have had varying conventions. It has existed in recitative since 1604. The French early Baroque nonmeasured keyboard works depend on inner necessities rather than a pulse. Analog notation leans on that kind of rhythm, as opposed to metered rhythm.

I still find it fascinating. This has not worn out for me. I don't especially like one kind of rhythm as opposed to another, but I love the idea of being able to move freely between them, which we can now do because of notation conventions.

Q: Does the use of analog notation in Incenters create an aleatoric element?

DRUCKMAN: It's aleatoric only in the sense that the actual coincidence of certain events is not given. I write very specifically which notes are to be played by which performers. The individual melodies, rhythms, and the harmonic content are controlled. But the actual simultaneity of certain events is not necessarily controlled. What happens in that piece is that a player or group of players is cast off playing repetitive phrases. Different groups change these repetitive phrases at different times. The exact moment of change is up to the sensibilities of the conductor. In the score, what I have notated is "about ten seconds" or "about eight seconds" for such sections. The actual duration of these sections can change from one performance to another.

Q: Why did you decide to give the conductor that leeway?

DRUCKMAN: What I'm doing with these sections in which the simultaneity is not exactly specified is simply an extension of what I was doing with adding analog notation for a given performer. Just as one man can make a decision about how long something should last before moving on to the next item, so can the conductor. The conductor can do this with a large group of people. I've done the same thing with the orchestra in Windows, a work I composed in 1972 for Bruno Maderna, who was a very skilled conductor in this kind of improvisatory performance. Using the orchestra as his instrument, he played so beautifully, and so brilliantly. Each performance was considerably different, depending on the emotional climate in the hall, or the temperature of the musicians' fervor, or of the audience.

In Windows, the conductor has the capability of casting off groups of instruments--or individual instruments--doing repetitive phrases and of changing some or all of these with a given signal. Some phrases will continue, some will change at dividing lines--I always think of them as the dark, leaded black lines in a stained glass window. These clearly marked divisions are called by the conductor, whereas the events that happen in between are not. These internal events are clearly specified, but again, the simultaneity within them is not. This procedure is rather like a bunch of geese being driven down a road by whatever the goose-equivalent of a shepherd is. You know what a bunch of geese sound like, and you know approximately what they're going to do, but you don't known which goose is going to be honking at which given point. So here they are moving down the road, doing a generalized kind of activity which is exactly specified in its overall form, although every detail is not. This kind of control allows the individual performer a different kind of expression from that which he would be able to use if everything were completely predetermined, completely designed rhythmically.

Q: What role does the quotation from Boris Gudanov play in Incenters?

DRUCKMAN: It's a quotation of a particular teetering harmony in the coronation scene from Boris Gudanov: two chords that are the quintessence, the epitome of a particular kind of ambiguity; an instability that makes for stability, if that makes any sense. They are two dominant sevenths which are traditionally the chords that must resolve somewhere. Mussorgsky found the only two dominant sevenths, the only possible combination in the whole system of twelve tones that would, in a sense, nullify each other. That note which should resolve up, when he changes to the next chord, becomes the note which should resolve down, and vice versa. And so there's a nervous, peculiar instability, which is symbolic of what the whole of Incenters is about; a very tenuous stability that can easily be upset. Hence the quotation. Also, peripherally, a homage to Mussorgsky, whom I admire greatly.

Q: Valentine has been recorded, but in view of its visual activities, do you think it suffers when simply heard?

DRUCKMAN: I think so. That's probably true of much of my later music--certainly the chamber works that have theatrical aspects, as Valentine clearly does.

Q: The comedy seems to be the first casualty when the visuals are lost.

DRUCKMAN, It's comic, but it's a black comedy, a kind of manic comedy. Animus III is on the same recording, and that suffers even more. There are sounds that are left out, places where the clarinetist has to speak, and mumble into his microphone.

Both of these pieces were done at about the same time, and they are two sides of the same coin. They both focus on the mindlessness, the driven quality of virtuosity. Some Freudian psychiatrist could probably make hay out of this, with all the years I spent practicing the violin! In Animus III, when it's done properly, there's a projection of complete insanity on the part of the performer, who starts as a completely dignified ultra-virtuoso, on top of his world and in control of everything. Then, as he begins to play, the whole environment deteriorates, he becomes more and more mindless, and at the end of Animus III, the whole thing comes down in a complete shambles.

Valentine is much the same kind of a piece. It's a little more gently presented; you laugh more than you cringe, but there's much the same view of virtuosity.

Q: What made you decide to incorporate theatrical elements in your music? Do you think that this technique has much of a future?

DRUCKMAN: I don't know. The movement seems to be losing some steam. At one point, there was great titillation as soon as anything theatrical happened onstage. The shock value is no longer there. In order to generate excitement we need really good theater.

My own reasons for having gotten into it in the first place,
I'm sure, are due to my early experiences in electronic music.
That exposure pushed me in the direction of things human, the actuality, the physicality of human beings--both in terms of the kind
of expression, and also the physical presence of a person in a theater. There's really nothing more horrible, more 1984-ish, than
being at a concert where there's nothing onstage except two loudspeakers.

Q: Do you prefer combining live performers with tape over strict
electronic composition?

DRUCKMAN: The only straight electronic work I've ever done was
for a Nonesuch record. It's a piece called Synapse, and it was
done as a prelude to Valentine. The only time I allow it to be
done as a concert piece is in relationship to Valentine. What we
do is make a point of the emptiness onstage. When it begins, the
houselights go down, and a light goes on an empty chair, a contrabass, and a microphone onstage, but there's no one there. The
electronic piece starts and, towards its end, the lights dim slowly
to complete black. When they come up, there is a contrabass player who has already begun to play very quietly but furiously, frenet-
ically, and we move into Valentine.

Q: Gerald Arpino has choreographed several of your works. Are
you happy with the way he handled them?

DRUCKMAN: I'm always delighted at Gerry's settings of my works.
He's a choreographer of great skill and panache and, while his setting may or may not always hew closely to my ideas of the piece
of music, his choreography is always fascinating. I think the closest he ever came to my way of thinking was with Valentine. That
was about as close to a real collaboration as we ever got.

Each of the pieces that Gerry Arpino did were written not
for the ballet, but for concert performance. The first one he did
even before we met. He had simply found a recording of Animus I.
I was living in Europe when he did it, and the first time I saw it
was in a ballet festival which took place in Vienna. That was the
first time I met him, and it was already the twelfth performance of
the piece. It was fascinating to see what he discovered in it, particularly because it was the second ballet done to that piece. José
Limon had also used it for a very different dance. It's amazing
how the moment of introduction for a choreographer colors how he
hears the work. When José Limon first heard Animus I, it was
done in a concert in Juilliard. I wrote the piece for Davis Schuman, a great trombone virtuoso whose playing, as a matter of fact,
is on the tape--not the trombone part, but the manipulated trombone amidst the electronic sounds. Davis died, tragically, before

he was able to play the piece. When it was first done at Juilliard, André Smith played the trombone, and both André and I decided to dedicate the performance of the piece to the memory of Davis Schuman. José Limon was at that performance, and José came up with a ballet based on that piece which had to do with death. He called it Macabre's Dance. Gerry Arpino did not come up with that kind of vision for Animus I.

On the other hand, Gerry Arpino's use of Animus III--it became a piece he called Solarwind--came out of a remark I made to him when I first played it for him. It was a self-deprecatory comment; I talked about a section of the piece being "Disneyland space music." And I remember Gerry's face lit up, and he smiled. I think this "space music" went into his mind, and shaped his conception of the work.

On Valentine we were very close. He picked up very quickly on what I was involved in when he expanded it into dance. As a matter of fact we got into almost a collaboration, because Gerry asked me if I couldn't extend the music. The concert version ends rather attenuatedly and softly, and Gerry wanted something a little more punchy and up. I added a section to the end, and then got actually involved in the choreography, in a sense. His Valentine is a pas de deux for a male and a female dancer with the solo bass player onstage. At the end of the ballet the dancers end up in some comical tangle on the floor, and I suggested to him that the bass player could very well do the same thing with the contrabass and could play the end of the piece lying down. Everything is horizontal at the end of the ballet of Valentine.

Q: How did Valentine come to be written?

DRUCKMAN: Bert Turetzky, the bass player from California, had asked me on several occasions to do a bass piece. In 1968, I was in Paris and was waiting to get into the Electronic Music Studio to begin working on Animus III. Another letter from Turetzky came while I still had a few weeks to wait and I decided, why not? We were living in Montmartre, a short walk to the Place Pigalle, where all the instrument rental places are. I rented a contrabass, took it up to my apartment, and started to work on the instrument. We had a typical French fireplace, with a mirror over the mantle, and as I was working, bent over that huge and grotesque female form, I kept seeing myself in the mirror and seeing how preposterous I looked. Hence the spirit of the piece.

Q: Have your activities as a teacher affected you as a composer?

DRUCKMAN: I have no idea. It's so much a part of my life that it's like asking if having black hair affects the way I compose. I don't know.

Q: Do you think that some theatrical elements may be used in your future works, or have you gotten a little tired of that?

DRUCKMAN: I'm hesitant to commit myself on pieces in advance. I'm not tired of it. As I said earlier, the surprise factor in theatricality has gone, and we really have to rethink things. I still adore theater, and I'm sure that one of these years I'll be up to my ears in opera. It would be wonderful to call on the forces of a huge opera company and all the magical things all of those people can do.

CATALOG OF COMPOSITIONS

1949	Duo for Violin and Piano	B&H
1950	Divertimento for clarinet, horn, violin, viola, cello, and harp	B&H
1952	Laude for baritone, flute, viola, and cello	B&H
1955	The Seven Deadly Sins for piano	B&H
1956	Concerto for Violin and Small Orchestra	NY Public Library
1958	Four Madrigals for SATB	Mercury
1962	Dark Upon the Harp for mezzo-soprano, two trumpets, horn, trombone, tuba, and percussion	Presser
1963	Antiphonies for two choruses	B&H
1964; 65	The Sound of Time for soprano and piano or orchestra	B&H
1966	String Quartet No. 2	MCA
1966	Animus I for trombone and electronic tape	MCA
1967	Sacred Service for tenor, chorus, and organ	B&H
1968	Animus II for mezzo-soprano, percussion, and electronic tape	MCA
1968; 72	Incenters for trumpet, horn, trombone, and chamber group or orchestra	MCA
1969	Valentine for contrabass	MCA
1969	Animus III for clarinet and electronic tape	B&H
1970	Orison for organ and electronic tape	B&H
1971	Synapse for electronic tape	B&H
1972	Windows for orchestra	MCA
1973	Delize Contente, Che L'Alme Beate After Francesco Cavalli (in memoriam, Bruno	

	Maderna) for woodwind quintet and electronic tape	B&H
1975	Lamia for soprano and orchestra	B&H
1976	Mirage for orchestra	B&H
1976	Other Voices for brass quintet	B&H
1977	Chiaroscuro for orchestra	B&H
1977	Animus IV for tenor, six instru-mentalists, and electronic tape	B&H
1978	Concerto for Viola and Orchestra	B&H
1979	Aureole for orchestra	B&H
1980	Bo for solo marimba, harp, bass clarinet, and three female voices	B&H
1980	Prism for orchestra	B&H

MORTON FELDMAN □

photo: Gene Bagnato

Morton Feldman was born on January 12, 1926, in New York City. He studied piano with Madame Maurina-Press, and went on to study composition with Wallingford Riegger and Stefan Wolpe. He currently is Edgard Varèse Professor at the State University of New York at Buffalo.

Interacting with New York's abstract expressionist painters, as well as such composers as John Cage, Earle Brown, and Christian Wolff, Feldman began writing music that would, in his words, "project sounds into time, free from a compositional rhetoric." In the early 1950s, he achieved these results through his invention of graphic notation, which permitted the performer freedoms in pitch and rhythm. From this method he went on to a more conventional form of notation, wherein pitch was determined but time values were only broadly fixed. Throughout his career, Feldman has also written traditionally notated scores. These pieces belong to the same sound world as his other works: They avoid systematic compositional methods and employ soft dynamics and subtle, undramatic gestures. Since the early 1970s, he has worked exclusively in conventional notation.

The authors interviewed Morton Feldman at his home in Buffalo on August 17, 1980. They were both somewhat apprehensive due to his initial reservations about granting an interview. However, their fears were instantly dispelled by his warmth and generosity. His good will and expansiveness informed everything he did: his conversation, his patience, his lack of reserve, and his cooking.

Q: We've read that earlier pieces of yours, such as Extensions 1 for violin and piano, employ the complete serialization of pitch, rhythm, dynamics, and even the succession of metronomic tempi. Is this accurate?

FELDMAN: That's wrong. It's the only piece where I ever used a kind of metronome modulation. I must admit that it was the only work I ever wrote where an idea from somebody else really influenced me. It was Milton Babbitt; the idea of the metronome changes came from his Composition for Four Instruments--which was written in the late forties, I believe. I use it now sometimes as a teaching suggestion for my students when their work is rhythmically somewhat boring, and they don't have the expertise for actually changing the rhythmic language of the piece--it looks funny to them if the piece immediately changes rhythmically.

Maybe the style of the piece suggested total serialization because it was out of the Webern atmosphere; very much so. But the piece didn't use any system at all.

Q: You've described your dislike of the sound of electronic music, likening it to "neon lights" and "plastic paint," saying that it's "too identifiable." Did you feel this way before or after the composition of your Intersection for magnetic tape in 1951? Would you characterize that piece as sounding like that?

FELDMAN: Have you ever tried to get a hold of that particular composition? I have a copy, but I've never wanted it realized by others. I'm sure they'll make it sound more interesting than the piece should sound.

I don't want to be political about it, but I loathe the sound of electronic music. I think it's perfectly fine as a teaching vehicle, if you don't have any money around for live performance. You know how certain pieces of Beethoven's are now played only on "Pops"? Well, electronic music started in universities; now it's in the high schools; pretty soon it'll be a device in kindergarten. You could spend a lot of time in a studio putting it all together. And you're very fortunate for having something to do. I really think you're very lucky to find something to do for an afternoon.

Q: Did you approach that piece as an obligation to investigate a new medium, or were you more excited about electronic music then than you are now?

FELDMAN: Let's put it this way: One of the best definitions of experimental music was given by John Cage. John says that experimental music is where the outcome cannot be foreseen. Very interesting observation. After my first adventure in electronic music, its outcome was foreseen.

Q: It's been suggested that works of yours that involve the decay of sounds were influenced by electronic works at that time, because of their emphasis on the decay of sound.

FELDMAN: Absolutely no connection.

Q: In the Columbia recording of your Piece for Four Pianos, you participated in the performance. Do you remember if you listened to the other three pianists? Or did you try not to think about what they were doing?

FELDMAN: It works better if you don't listen. I noticed that a
lot of people would listen and feel that they could come in at a
more effective time. But the spirit of the piece is not to make it
just something effective. You're just to listen to the sounds and
play it as naturally and as beautifully as you can within your own
references. If you're listening to the other performers, then the
piece tends also to become rhythmically conventional.

Q: What do musicians find most problematic about your music?

FELDMAN: When you play an instrument, you're not only playing
the instrument; the instrument is playing you. There's a role to
play. And the problem I have with the performer is that my sense
of the instrument is not that role-playing aspect. By role-playing
I mean the baggage one brings to performing by demonstrating how
good the instrumentalist is. They're not interpreting music; they're
interpreting the instrument, and then the music. When Heifetz
played Mozart, he was doing Mozart a favor. It was the violin he
was playing, and then Mozart.

Q: Of the three types of notation you've used--graph, free duration,
and precise notation--have you found that one invariably receives
the poorest performance?

FELDMAN: I think that my earlier, more unconventional notation
drew performers who were attracted to the performance freedom
inherent to the music. However, with my precise music, the performers are now more involved with me, which seems to annoy
them to death.

Q: Then performance problems for you have multiplied over the years?

FELDMAN: Recently, I went to a BBC studio recording of two
major works of mine. Luckily for the American conductor, a lot
of the performers for the BBC have continually played my music
under other conductors through the years. This conductor evidently looked at the score and thought that it was so simple, that he
came totally unprepared.

I don't even know if that's a serious problem now. The
question you ask would be legitimate for most, but not for me.
There's nothing wrong with your question. But half of my life was
spent being upset and concerned with this problem. And now I
think that if Milton Babbitt could say, "Who cares if they listen,"
my feeling is, "Who cares if they play it."

Everything that I'm going to say in this interview is not something that just came off the top of my head; it's something that I've been thinking about and living with for years and years and years. The problem now is that all these things are evasive subterfuges from sitting down and writing that piece of music. I don't think it's now a time for performance, anyway. I think it's now a time for work and reflection. I think it's time for a lot of young composers and a lot of not too young composers to perhaps also stop composing.

For me, a bad artist is an insane artist. And I think there are too many loonies writing music. And by loonies, I don't mean "kinky avant-garde." I mean people who work comfortably, don't worry, have no pressure. You know, they used to say that John Cage was a dangerous influence; and although he never at all said, "Anything goes," I would say that there is an intellectual atmosphere around in which considerably less "extreme" minds than John Cage feel that anything goes. And it shows in the music. It's bad music because it's delusionary.

Q: Are you implying that certain compositional styles are more pernicious than others?

FELDMAN: No. No, it's not a question of styles. What's compositional style? That's a dangerous subject to begin with altogether. The only style a composer is allowed is his own. If he doesn't have one, he should get out of music.

I don't even think that this is an elitist point of view. If somebody's causing a lot of trouble and confusion in his mental state as he's walking down the street, are you an elitist if perhaps you suggest to the family that this person should be put away? You know, there was a fad some years ago--it touched here, but it was very big in England--a very classy character: Laing. Familiar with Laing? "Three cheers for schizophrenia! They're the normal ones, and what is normal?" What's normal. I'll tell you what's normal. Perhaps twenty-four people are going to be interviewed in your book, right? What's normal would be if seventeen of them would stop writing music tomorrow. That's normal.

Q: Ten years ago, you declined a teaching position, saying that your idea of teaching wasn't what was happening in music departments. Is Buffalo a unique environment, or has there been a real change in academic attitudes toward music?

FELDMAN: I think it's almost accepted at major universities that when they bring in major people, those people are to teach the way they feel it's best to teach. And they establish a certain policy. But there is a problem in teaching composition. It reminds me of somebody I knew who was a damned good sculptor. At the time he didn't have too much money and he took a job teaching young people sculpture. He spent all his time in just teaching them how to hold a torch and how to take care of their materials.

The ideal student is the student who doesn't have to be taught. All you can do is be sort of an instrumental coach with important insights and suggestions. The problem that I find with teaching (and I would say that this probably holds true with any creative field) is that when a young composer has very little equipment, there is a fantastic vested interest in holding on to the little that he or she has. They learn two steps, and their concerns are in doing an exhibition dance with two steps.

Q: You've said that you use whichever notational style that a particular work calls for. But over the last ten years, your scores have been fully notated.

FELDMAN: I have to interrupt you here. A lot of people feel that they're not notated enough. I read a review of a score the other day: "Except for a few tenuto marks, not enough information is given for performance."

Q: Do you think you've been writing fully notated scores in recent years?

FELDMAN: Very few composers have the gift to write a notation where the piece really plays itself. Mahler had it. Maybe the expression helped. But if you're doing Haydn or Mozart: "Am I doing this too dry? Am I doing that a little too bright?" There are problems.

Q: Do musicians become indignant because they have to efface themselves in order to play your music?

FELDMAN: Everybody gets a little bit annoyed when they're involved with problem solving, especially when they don't know what the problem really is and they don't know if they've solved it.

Q: Have you just defined your situation as a composer? Trying to solve a problem without being sure what the problem is?

FELDMAN: You're absolutely right. I'm making a parallel to how I work. I'm involved with "problem solving," but I don't know what the problem is. In other words, a piece starts to develop, and problems arise. I don't begin with problems; if you begin with a problem, you'll solve it.

The piece is like an operation. Everything is going along OK, you're a good surgeon, and then problems happen. Pneumonia sets in, or you sew up the trumpet in the belly of the piece. All kinds of problems develop.

Q: In light of the range of problems that can arise, do you still feel that you'll use whichever notational style that might be necessary?

FELDMAN: No. Notation is an aspect of style. And I find that if you use a certain type of notation, it cannot help but develop into a certain style. And the style of my graph music was super for the time it was written. At the time I wrote it, I didn't know that it was going to be style. Now the question is, should I continually work in that area, that notational style, and perfect it and bring it into high style? Which, in a sense, was what the post-aleatoric period did with aleatoric music; they brought it into high style.

You have to understand that no matter what you're going to do, it always leads to style. But precise notation slows it down a little bit. Just enough. Like doing 55 on the highway. It slows it down. And I like that slowing down aspect. It's involved more with thought than ideas.

Q: Has this slowing down gone hand in hand with the increasing length of your pieces?

FELDMAN: I would say that the one who best answered something like this was Hemingway when he talked about the difference between typing and writing. I would say that the "chance" era was typing. Journalistic. Headlines. If you don't like the word "journalistic," then I would say prose.

I was talking to you about rugs before. What's interesting about a rug is that the whole rug culture was derived from the technical limitation of what kind of knots were being used. Or take a look at that Jackson Pollock drawing; it's absolutely elegant. And I'm not saying that there is anything wrong with it when I say that part of its elegance is part of the technique of how it was made. He splattered the ink on the page in the way that only he could do, and no one since could do with such an eye and with such elegance. But the technique of how he did it developed the look or the style of his work. That is what notation is to composition. How you notate determines more about the piece than any kind of system using this or that. Of course, if you're into a certain type of system, a certain type of tradition of how best to notate that system does develop; that's true enough.

All I'm really saying, in a long-winded way, is that notation, at least for me, determines the style of the piece.

Q: Did the time you spent away from precise notation affect your use of it when you returned to it?

FELDMAN: I wouldn't say that what I was doing was not precise. It was as precise as Pollock.

I never really "returned" to traditional notation. If you ever look at my list of works, I always alternated between one and the other.

Q: So you wouldn't think of the graph or free duration pieces as a hiatus?

FELDMAN: I saw it very, very differently. I saw it like somebody does a sculpture and then does a painting. For me it was very clear-cut that it was really another idiom with its own problems and its own solutions. One also didn't feed the other, or help the other.

But I did find things that I never expected. For example, I found that my most far-out notation repeated historical cliches in performance more than my precise notation. Precise notation is my handwriting. My imprecise notation was a kind of roving camera that caught up very familiar images like a historical mirror. I don't want the mirror of history in my work. I want it in my education, but I don't want it in my work.

Q: Your work Rothko Chapel seems a definite break with what you've earlier described as your compositional aim of creating a minimum of contrast.

FELDMAN: It was a piece written for an occasion, and I think it's one of those pieces which I'll never write again. I felt that I had to write something that I thought was appropriate. I enjoyed doing it.

There was a period--the Rothko Chapel, The Viola in My Life, a few other pieces--when I was thinking of Bob Rauschenberg's photo montages. At that time, I would use a tune just the way Bob would put a photo on a canvas. But I now feel that in music it doesn't work the same way.

Q: Throughout the '70s, your pieces have been getting longer and longer. Had you wanted to write lengthy pieces as far back as the '50s, but refrained from doing so because you thought you wouldn't be able to get them performed?

FELDMAN: No. There are two types of long pieces that annoy me: the epic--the padded, portentous piece--and the long process piece. I think my tendency now toward longer and longer pieces is actually a tendency away from a piece geared for performance. Psychologically it's not geared for performance. I also feel that my plunge into the longer and longer pieces had a lot to do with the change in my lifestyle.

The fact that I have more time to compose now means that I'm asking myself different questions. Also, what does any artist do when he doesn't have any problems? He looks for new ones. What began to interest me was what might happen in a very, very long piece in one movement. Stravinsky is the last great movement-form composer. Some things do become outmoded, for whatever reason; and I feel the movement form is outmoded.

So, as I go into that long piece, I come up against very interesting problems. And the problems are not necessarily the search for compositional solutions or devices for continuity. When you're working on a very long piece, you eventually have to ask the question: "Are there new forms?"

You also have to develop your own paraphernalia to hold it together, rather than maintain the conventional idea that what develops might hold a piece together. That's what I meant earlier by problem solving: To get through a big piece, you don't come with any kind of prearranged schema; you just find ways to survive in this big piece. And the most important survival kit is concentration.

Q: You mean your ability to concentrate on the materials you're working on?

FELDMAN: Just concentrate on not making the lazy move. For example, most composers are involved with the potential of the materials, and they milk it; and they milk it ingeniously. I'm involved in keeping the thing going, but not necessarily via its implications. So, if you're not going to be involved with the implication of your material, how do you keep it going?

Q: Do you see a piece like your recent String Quartet as a challenge to other composers to write pieces that run longer than one side of a record and still sustain interest and maintain musical invention?

FELDMAN: I can only attempt to answer that question indirectly. Someone like Elliott Carter, for example, would feel that the moment is not important; it's the overall construction of the piece. I agree with him on the overall construction of the piece--I wouldn't

agree with him on what he would think makes for this overall construction of the piece--but I feel that the moment, the rightness of
the moment, even though it might not make sense in terms of its
cause and effect, is very important. There's a remark of Giaco-
metti: He said he wants to make his sculpture so that if the tini-
est fragment was found, it would be complete in itself in such a
way that one almost might be able to reconstruct it.

The piece that I'm writing now is a piece that is involved
with fragments of material; just the presentation of fragments of
material. There's no implication of the material. But that's another
er story. I'm not interested in the aspect of completing, or satisfying a need to make what we think is that terrific, integrated piece
of music. I agree with Kafka: We already know everything. So
there's no need for me to finish the piece in terms of anyone's ex-
pectations, which include my own.

Q: You mean that there's no reason for you to put something in
an arch form because we know about arches already?

FELDMAN: Most concepts of form that one can articulate about
appear to be involved with a series of chronological insights that
succeed in only a relatively short work. Most musical forms are
really only "short stories" which begin, develop, and end.

With the violin concerto I wrote recently (it's only an hour
and a half), I wrote a "row for the moment." I spent seven hours
working on a twelve-tone row that I use only for three measures of
the piece. And then the piece goes on, and about ten pages later,
I felt that what I wanted was to have a little frame, and inside the
frame I wanted some beautiful symmetry. Symmetry isn't my bag,
but I needed some beautiful symmetry at that moment. I then quote
a row of Webern that is a prototype of perfect symmetry. (It's a
famous row.) I just quote it, like someone will quote a tune; but
I only quoted it for its symmetry. I also used it as a kind of
quasi-cadenza for the soloist. And then I just went on with the
piece.

Then I had another idea. All right, I'm not interested in
symmetry, so I quote Webern. I'm also not at all interested in
intervallic relationships. But I felt the piece needed some "intervallic logic." So I quote another row of Webern's. Actually, without that moment of symmetry, without that other moment of lucid
intervallic relationships, the piece would have lost a lot. In other
words, in writing a long piece, I would make curious moves but
only for the moment. Decisions that I would never think of, say,
in composing a twenty-minute composition. You want a piece to be
logical. Well, you're not going to sit down and have a ten-course
meal of logic; you're satisfied with just an hors d'oeuvre a little
logical hors d'oeuvre served to you by a famous waiter! You want
a piece to be beautiful. OK, give them a moment of beauty--how

much more do you need? So what happens in a long piece is that sooner or later you go through the whole parameter of possibilities, and everybody's going to get something out of it, I'm sure. The form of a long piece is more like a novel--there's plenty of time for everything.

In <u>Rothko Chapel</u>, I felt the piece needed a tune, so instead of writing a tune, I took a tune I wrote when I was 15. That's the photograph aspect. And even Webern is a photograph: an old, torn photograph of interval relationships; an old, brown, dirty photograph of symmetry!

Q: All we've been able to read about your studies with Stefan Wolpe was that the two of you argued all the time.

FELDMAN: I'm very sorry about that; Stefan was hurt when he read that. We talked a lot--that's about all I really meant.

Wolpe got a very bad deal. I would say that Wolpe's bad deal was very much like the relationship of Léger to the Cubists. They would say, "What the hell is he? Is he a Cubist, isn't he a Cubist?" And yet Léger was a fantastic painter, and since there are many more fantastic painters than there are composers, he had his day in court and he won his case. But if we had a whole bunch of intelligent people around, they would realize, "Oh, yeah, Wolpe, yeah, Léger, yeah! He has this special flavor, yeah, he doesn't have to be like...." Understand?

His string quartet's a very beautiful piece. He had this genius for writing beautiful music that wasn't beautiful--very hard to do. Like Léger.

Q: You've complained that in the last twenty-five years, there have been no composers who have really shook up anyone. Do you think that the music of Steve Reich or Philip Glass represents a new trend? Is it too popular with audiences to really shake them up?

FELDMAN: In some ways the message is a little shocking in the Reich phenomenon. And that's what makes it interesting. That's what I'm interested in; very strong alternatives. I'm already in my mid-fifties, I'm supposed to have a developed language, and if you think I can sit down and write a piece and not be worried about Steve Reich, John Cage, Pierre Boulez, and Xenakis, you're nuts. I worry about these people. I worry about strong alternatives. And sometimes, some people have something to worry about. Brahms had something to worry about with Wagner. It is a contest. And I don't know if most of your readers know this--I don't even know if the music lovers at large know it--but Wagner won;

Brahms lost. Of course, he didn't lose if you're lying on a blanket in Tanglewood and you hear the opening of his D Major Symphony. But he lost. He lost like Ted Kennedy lost, with everybody cheering.

Q: A not uncommon critical reaction to your music is, "It's a beautiful music that shows us no future." Does that comment mean anything to you? Are you concerned with the future of music in general, or of your music in particular? Do you believe that other composers will learn from you and that you'll thereby win, just as Wagner won?

FELDMAN: For any music's future, you don't go to the devices, you don't go to the procedures, you go to the attitude. And you do not find your own attitude; that's what you inherit. I'm not my own man. I'm a compilation of all the important people in my life. I once had a seven-hour conversation with Boulez; unknown to him, it affected my life. I admire his attitude. Varèse's attitude. Wolpe's attitude. Cage's attitude. I spent one afternoon with Beckett; it will be with me forever. Not his work; not his commitment; not his marvelous face, but his attitude.

CATALOG OF COMPOSITIONS

1947	Journey to the End of the Night for soprano, flute, clarinet, bass clarinet, and bassoon	CF Peters
1950	Illusions for piano	New Music
1950	Two Intermissions for piano	CF Peters
1950	Piece for Violin and Piano	CF Peters
1950	Projection 1 for cello	CF Peters
1951	Projection 2 for violin, cello, flute, trumpet, and piano	CF Peters
1951	Projection 3 for two pianos	CF Peters
1951	Projection 4 for violin and piano	CF Peters
1951	Projection 5 for three cellos, three flutes, trumpet, and two pianos	CF Peters
1951	Intersection 1 for large orchestra	CF Peters
1951	Structures for string quartet	CF Peters
1951	Four Songs to e.e. cummings for soprano, cello, and piano	CF Peters
1951	Film Music for Jackson Pollock	MS
1951	Intersection for magnetic tape	CF Peters
1951	Marginal Intersection for orchestra	CF Peters
1951	Intersection 2 for piano	CF Peters
1951	Extensions 1 for violin and piano	CF Peters
1952	Extensions 3 for piano	CF Peters
1952	Intermission 5 for piano	CF Peters

1952	Piano Piece	C F Peters
1953	Intersection 3 for piano	C F Peters
1953	Extensions 4 for three pianos	C F Peters
1953	Intermission 6 for one or two pianos	C F Peters
1953	Intersection 4 for cello	C F Peters
1953	Eleven Instruments for chamber ensemble	C F Peters
1954	Three Pieces for Piano	C F Peters
1954	Two Pieces for Two Pianos	C F Peters
1955	Piano Piece	C F Peters
1956	Piano Piece	C F Peters
1956	Piano Piece	C F Peters
1956	Three Pieces for String Quartet	C F Peters
1956	Two Pieces for Six Instruments	C F Peters
1957	Piece for Four Pianos	C F Peters
1957	Piano Three Hands	C F Peters
1957	Two Pianos	C F Peters
1958	Piano Four Hands	C F Peters
1958	Two Instruments for horn and cello	C F Peters
1958	Ixion for chamber ensemble or two pianos	C F Peters
1959	Last Pieces for piano	C F Peters
1959	Atlantis for chamber orchestra	C F Peters
1960	Durations 2 for cello and piano	C F Peters
1960	Durations 1 for violin, cello, alto flute, and piano	C F Peters
1960	The Swallows of Salangan for SATB and chamber ensemble	C F Peters
1961	Durations 3 for violin, tuba, and piano	C F Peters
1961	Durations 4 for violin, cello, and vibraphone	C F Peters
1961	... Out of "Last Pieces" for orchestra	C F Peters
1961	Two Pieces for Clarinet and String Quartet	C F Peters
1961	Durations 5 for violin, cello, horn, chimes, and piano/celesta	C F Peters
1961	Intervals for bass-baritone, cello, trombone, vibraphone, and percussion	C F Peters
1961	The Straits of Magellan for seven instruments	C F Peters
1962	For Franz Kline for soprano, violin, cello, horn, chimes, and piano	C F Peters
1962	Structures for orchestra	C F Peters
1962	The O'Hara Songs for bass-baritone, violin, viola, cello, chimes, and piano	C F Peters
1963	Piano Piece	C F Peters
1963	Vertical Thoughts 1 for two pianos	C F Peters
1963	Vertical Thoughts 2 for violin and piano	C F Peters
1963	Vertical Thoughts 3 for soprano and chamber ensemble	C F Peters
1963	Vertical Thoughts 4 for piano	C F Peters

1963	Vertical Thoughts 5 for soprano, violin, tuba, percussion, and celesta	CF Peters
1963	De Kooning for horn, percussion, piano, violin, and cello	CF Peters
1963	Christian Wolff in Cambridge for SATB	CF Peters
1963	Chorus and Instruments for SATB and seven players	CF Peters
1963	Rabbi Akiba for soprano and chamber ensemble	CF Peters
1964	Piano Piece	CF Peters
1964	The King of Denmark for percussion	CF Peters
1964	Numbers for chamber ensemble	CF Peters
1965	Four Instruments for violin, cello, chimes, and piano	CF Peters
1966	Two Pieces for Three Pianos	CF Peters
1967	Chorus and Instruments II for SATB, chimes, and tuba	CF Peters
1967	First Principles for chamber orchestra	CF Peters
1968	False Relationships and the Extended Ending for violin, cello, trombone, three pianos, and chimes	CF Peters
1969	Between Categories for two pianos, two chimes, two violins, and two cellos	CF Peters
1969	In Search of an Orchestration for orchestra	Universal
1969	On Time and the Instrumental Factor for orchestra	Universal
1970	The Viola In My Life (1) for solo viola with flute, violin, cello, piano, and percussion	Universal
1970	The Viola In My Life (2) for solo viola with flute, clarinet, violin, cello, piano, and percussion	Universal
1970	The Viola In My Life (3) for viola and piano	Universal
1971	The Viola In My Life (IV) for viola and orchestra	Universal
1971	I Met Heine in the Rue Furstemberg for mezzo-soprano and chamber ensemble	Universal
1971	Madame Press Died Last Week at Ninety for chamber ensemble	Universal
1971	Pianos and Voices for five pianos	Universal
1971	Three Clarinets, Cello, and Piano	Universal
1972	The Rothko Chapel for chorus, two voices, celesta, percussion, and viola	Universal
1972	Cello and Orchestra	Universal
1972	Chorus and Orchestra	Universal
1972	Chorus and Orchestra II for soprano, SSAATTBB, and orchestra	Universal
1972	Pianos and Voices II for five sopranos and five pianos	Universal
1972	Voice and Instruments for soprano and orchestra	Universal

1972	Voices and Instruments for chorus and chamber ensemble	Universal
1972	Voices and Instruments II for three high voices, flute, two cellos, and contrabass	Universal
1973	For Frank O'Hara for flute, clarinet, percussion, piano, violin, and cello	Universal
1973	String Quartet and Orchestra	Universal
1973	Voices and Cello for two high voices and cello	Universal
1974	Instruments for alto flute and piccolo, oboe and English horn, trombone, percussion, and cello	Universal
1974	Voice and Instruments II for voice, clarinet, cello, and contrabass	Universal
1975	Piano and Orchestra	Universal
1976	Orchestra	Universal
1976	Voice, Violin, and Piano	Universal
1976	Oboe and Orchestra	Universal
1976	Elemental Procedures for soprano, SATB, and orchestra	Universal
1977	Instruments 3 for flute, oboe, and percussion	Universal
1977	Neither opera in one act to an original text by Samuel Beckett	Universal
1977	Only for voice	Universal
1978	Flute and Orchestra	Universal
1978	Why Patterns? for violin, piano, and glockenspiel	Universal
1978	Spring of Chosroes for violin and piano	Universal
1979	Violin and Orchestra	Universal
1979	String Quartet	Universal
1980	Repertoire for violin, cello, and piano	Universal
1980	The Turfan Fragments for small orchestra	Universal
1980	Principal Sound for organ	Universal

ROSS LEE FINNEY □

photo: Gene Bagnato

Ross Lee Finney was born on December 23, 1906, in
Wells, Minnesota. He received his B.A. from Carle-
ton College in Northfield, Minnesota. Finney studied
composition with Nadia Boulanger, Alban Berg, and
Roger Sessions; Mario Davidovsky was Finney's in-
structor in the field of electronic music. Finney was
professor of composition and composer-in-residence
at the University of Michigan, where he is now Composer Emeritus. In 1930, he married Gretchen Ludke.
They have two sons.

Finney's early works were neo-classical and reflected his strong interest in American themes and
materials. By 1950, Finney began to utilize the serial techniques that have remained the basis of his music. In the early 1960s, he embarked upon a study
of electronic music, which resulted in the use of tape
in certain works. Finney's is a large body of work,
encompassing a wide range of means. But regardless
of whether the composition is solo or orchestral, early
or late in his career, all his music is characterized
by its rich chromaticism, logical structuring, and
warm and evocative expressiveness.

The authors talked with Ross Lee Finney on October 26, 1975, in the Manhattan home where the Fin-
neys reside some six months out of the year (the rest
of the time living in their home in Ann Arbor, Michigan). The man is as warm and expansive as his music; in fact, as is the case with his music, he will
unhesitatingly sing quotations from his favorite folk
songs to make his point during a conversation. Time
spent with Ross Lee Finney can be characterized only as instructive, invigorating, and delightful.

Q: Some of your recent compositions have utilized electronic
tape.

FINNEY: Yes, and in making electronic music I discovered several
facts very, very quickly. In the first place, when you reach my
age it's terribly hard work to stand on your feet in a laboratory
for the hours and hours that it takes. It's such an arduous undertaking that it just tired me out. The second thing, which is really
more important, is I felt that I had to make the electronic tape fit
my style of music, rather than, as young persons can do, adjust
my style to the electronic process. That just got to be too much
for me, and I decided that this better be left for somebody younger
than I.

Q: What did you feel was the value of electronic tape for you when you worked in that medium?

FINNEY: The electronic tape leads you to totally new concepts of time, to totally new concepts of density--managing density. It leads you--and I think this can sometimes be very unfortunate--to, shall we say, a disrespect for pitch. For me, pitch and the differences of pitch are very important, just like, I think, to a writer of my generation the nice nuances and differences between words are important--perhaps more important than they are to the younger person. There are just so many ways in which electronics contributes to a rethinking. I don't even have to mention such bizarre possibilities as wiring up your head so that you get various vibrations from your brain, and then translating these vibrations into a musical selective tape. Now this amuses me the least; I can't be very interested in these brain waves. But you're certainly shown the extent to which electronic tape can do all sorts of things.

I would feel differently if electronic tape was essentially a new kind of instrument that could be used solistically, or in chamber music, or with orchestra, and that was so potent in what it did that it brought in all kinds of new possibilities and practice. Perhaps what has to happen is just what happened when the organ began to be an instrument: you have a lot of music which isn't awfully good because it took some time before the organ began to be understood and used for its real value. I don't think there are many masterpieces that use the electronic tape all by itself, because somehow or other, I don't think composers have found how to make it human. But, for instance, the works with voice of Milton Babbitt, or the works of Mario Davidovsky, come as close to masterpieces in this idiom as you can come.

But that doesn't mean that it won't be done. A student of mine, Gerald Plain, who comes from Tennessee, writes electronic pieces. Of course, they're not pure electrically-generated sounds; they're all kinds of sounds--musique concrète. But they sound as if they had come from the mountains. They're "country" music essentially, although not popular country music.

Q: What does the electronic music laboratory which you started at the University of Michigan consist of?

FINNEY: It's very similar to the one at Columbia, and was established in the mid-sixties. During the past ten years, there have been enormous developments involving transistorizing and various circuitry which have changed it a lot.

As a matter of fact, Mario Davidovsky was my teacher. I had worked at the Columbia laboratory with Mario, and Milton Babbitt advised me about equipment. Afterwards, with the help of a university grant, I began setting up a laboratory at Michigan. I put George Wilson at the head of it, and he appointed technicians to work on it. It's grown now to a totally different setup. It is, essentially, like Columbia's.

Q: You studied with Alban Berg in the thirties. What motivated you to go to Europe and study with him?

FINNEY: This is a long story. I grew up in North Dakota and I worked my way through college by teaching cello and, believe it or not, the history of music. When I graduated, I got a job with a jazz orchestra on a ship and we played all through the Mediterranean. This was in 1927. When we got to France, I left the outfit and went to study with Nadia Boulanger. Now this is sort of funny because at that time I was really awfully ignorant. For instance, when I first hit New York, I got on the Times Square subway and went back and forth on the shuttle, and I didn't have sense enough to get off. Finally, I got off exactly where I had gotten on, and I didn't know what on earth was going on. I was awfully wet behind the ears. When I finally got out to where Nadia Boulanger was spending the summer, I asked for Boulanger. They sent me to every baker, every bakery in the place. I was shuttling around there until I finally found Nadia Boulanger; she took a look at me and dragged me in, made me take a bath, set me down to the table to have supper, and I got going.

I'm very indebted to Nadia Boulanger; for me at that time, she was a wonderful teacher because she was very sympathetic, very understanding of my limitations, and very understanding of my enthusiasm. Of course, I also learned a lot from her other students, such as Roy Harris and Aaron Copland. These people meant almost as much as studying with Boulanger. But Boulanger was the important one. Yet, by the end of the year, I just couldn't accept the idea of studying with a woman. Why is that so? I think, maybe, it is understandable, and it might even be understandable to a woman. Nadia Boulanger was very protective of her students. I don't know if it's quite right to say that she mothered her students, but she was extremely protective. And you've got to realize that I was in my late teens, and I just couldn't take it anymore--well, I didn't have any money to take it anymore. I don't think I ever minimized how wonderful she had been as a teacher; I was just a little rebellious. So when I went back the next time, I decided that I was going to do something else.

I went to Vienna to study with Egon Wellesz, but he was spending the winter in Egypt. Then somebody said, "But you know, there's a composer here by the name of Alban Berg." Well, I thought that would be funny because when I was a student in Paris in '27, they performed his chamber concerto, and the critics and everybody called it the "Sour Berg." But I can understand that, because it would take a long time for the French temperament to absorb that kind of a work. Alban Berg happened to live only a few

blocks from where I had gotten a room, so I went to study with
him. I think he was very different as a teacher, perhaps even as
an individual, than most people think. He was extremely warm--
"it comes from the heart, may it go to the heart." He just radi-
ated warmth and kindness. He was a wonderfully rambling kind of
teacher. At first, I didn't think he was a really good teacher; but
you know, he was a teacher that kept on reverberating in my mind
for fifteen years. Now this may be partly that having come from
North Dakota and Minnesota, it took a long time for me to absorb
the Viennese quality of culture. In the same way, I had felt completely out of place in Paris. Well, I didn't feel quite out of place
because on the left bank there were almost as many American students as there were Parisians. After all, being a student in Paris
in the twenties is something you don't ever regret or forget. But
Vienna was not like Paris. For instance, I remember when Alban Berg first looked at a work of mine (which, of course, has long
since been discarded). He tried to analyze the chromatic problems
involved in the work. This led him to point out that it was highly
chromatic, but not totally chromatic. He argued the virtues of a
more totally chromatic situation. So he advised that I get the Woodwind Quintet of Schoenberg and analyze every note of it. He showed
me how I might go about doing it, by using one color for the row
rightside up, and another color for the row upside down, and so on.
Everyday, I went to a cafe, got me a big beer, and had a really
good time analyzing the work. He never again mentioned the work.
Now this was rather typical of him. In other words, he would
throw out ideas to you, but he wasn't going to follow them up for
you. If you wanted to do it, fine; if you didn't want to do it, why,
he never came back to this. In other words, he wasn't essentially
a teacher; he was a person who gave you ideas, and it was your
business to pursue them.

　　He never talked about his own music. Once, however, he
said, "Well, wouldn't you like to go to rehearsals of the Lyric
Suite?" Of course I'd like to go to the rehearsals, so I bought a
score and he told me where these rehearsals were. So I would go
and listen to rehearsals. He didn't tell me anything about the work,
with one exception. I can't remember just how he said it--you
know, you reach the point when you're trying to remember something that far back where you don't know whether it was said or
you imagined it. I'm not sure, but I got the impression, somehow or other, that his quotation from Tristan und Isolde was not
for love, but was more psychoanalytical, more something in his
past that he couldn't forget. I don't quite know why I have that
impression. This has always led me to wonder what the relationship might have been between Alban Berg and Freud. My student
Donald Harris, who is writing a book on Berg, hasn't found any
connection. I don't think there was any; but of course, it was sort
of in the air, anyway.

　　Another thing that Berg did was to analyze the beginning of
Tristan und Isolde in order to show the total chromaticism and
point out the conflicts that arose from the punctuation, the cadences,

and so forth, that gave more emphasis to one pitch than to another. This came into conflict with my natural musical language, which I had grown up with out in the Dakotas; it was very sophisticated and didn't fit with me. So, at the end of that year, I was very confused and a little antagonistic--in fact, very antagonistic--to the whole twelve-tone thing. But he had made me understand it and analyze it in a very interesting way, and the result was that it increased in its impact. I can even go back over my music and see how during the thirties and forties it began to move until suddenly I found my own acceptance.

I should also point out that at the same time in Vienna, Hauer's music was being played a lot. His concept was a little different from Schoenberg's in that he was concerned with hexachords, which he called "tropes." I disliked his music, I must admit, but I think that, nevertheless, this concept of a symmetrical row that divides into two groups of six--into hexachords--has had an effect on me.

Q: What finally led you to decide to start writing serial music in the fifties?

FINNEY: It just happened. This seems inexplicable if you don't understand at least two things. As a student of Alban Berg, I was given a pretty good introduction to the technique; I knew the technique and had been thinking about it for a long time. So it wasn't a case of my suddenly saying, "Well, now I'm going to go into twelve-tone technique; I better get some books and read up on it." I never turned to books about it. Secondly, I was involved in the Second World War, and this was a devastating experience to me, as it was to a lot of people. I have such memories of the utter hopelessness of trying to express the feelings I had in the same way that I had done before the war. In other words, when I got back from this, I felt that I had to have more expressive stuff in my vocabulary. Then, in a certain work, I suddenly found myself writing twelve-tone technique. It wasn't a conscious effort; I never made big charts. And as a matter of fact, I don't even think that my style has changed too much, because I believe that twelve-tone technique concerns primarily the minutiae of a style, and that pitch polarity determines the large design. I don't find the two things in conflict. So my music remains neither fish nor fowl.

Q: Once you began writing music in the twelve-tone idiom, did you ever go back to writing non-serial music?

FINNEY: Yes, once. I made a cycle of songs of all of the Chamber Music of Joyce. I made no attempt whatsoever to use twelve-tone technique in that. But the songs have never been performed and I'm not very satisfied with them. They're good songs--they're kind of Irishy, banshee sort of things, which tap something in me.

Q: Earlier in your career, you would simply call your works symphonies, or sonatas, but more recently the titles have become much
more poetic: Landscapes Remembered, Spaces, Summer in Valley
City, to name just a few. Is this indicative of a major change in
attitude on your part?

FINNEY: Probably the answer is that I was a little lazy in the
matter of titles at that time. But titles really don't have much to
do with what the music is about. One work, for instance, which
I'm very fond of is my Third Piano Sonata. It's a "sonata," I suppose. I don't know what a sonata is, myself. I don't think that
there are two sonatas that are alike. Beethoven called all of his
Piano Sonatas, "sonatas," I don't find any two of them alike. So
it's just a convenience. To me, it isn't a matter of any great importance. But I've got to admit to you that even my First Symphony is not a symphonic form in the nineteenth-century sense. I
don't think I've ever been concerned about the classical form. I
was very, very concerned, and still am, about what used to be
called tonality--that is, the relationships of pitch levels and architecture, the way in which the composer can make a sense of space
through pitch. But that's another matter. I'm just as concerned
about that now, but in a slightly different way.

Landscapes Remembered belongs to a kind of kick that I'm
on right now. When you're close to seventy you have a right to
remember, and you suddenly find that there are periods that are
almost as vivid to you as the present. My childhood in North Dakota was really a very exciting one. Also, I'm very interested in
the process of memory. I remember being with Dallapiccola once
when we were talking about my interest in this, and he said, "Well!
What is there but memory?" Actually, this is right. After all,
what is there, because yesterday is already memory. When you
are working, you work in the present in such a tiny little area; it
becomes past so quickly that you're always working, in a sense, in
the past. But that's kind of dodging the point, isn't it?

One of the things that I got from Alban Berg is a strong interest in a variation form different from the old idea of variations
as a capsule that got repeated in exactly the same way. Alban Berg
used to talk about variational form as the sequence of happenings,
of musical events. One time, there might be a great distance between events, and another time much less--it was elastic. So this
interested me very much, and you find this in certain of my works.
I just had a premiere of a work which I call Variations on a Memory, and this I did in a very different way. The memory is of
something which my brother used to blow in my ear on his trumpet,
and the theme runs like a thread of memory through the work; the
whole work itself is always a comment on it. So it's a kind of
theme that is the length of the piece, and the embroidery-comment
on it, which varies. I'm very interested in these methods of shap-
ing.

Q: One element of your recent works which is particularly striking is your use of quotation. Could the current interest in Charles Ives have something to do with that?

FINNEY: No, not for me. I've known Charles Ives' music for a long time; I was very fortunate because when I taught at Smith I was a very good friend of John Kirkpatrick. So I knew the Concord Sonata as he was learning it for his New York performance. Even earlier than that, Radiana Pazmor came up to Smith and sang the Ives songs beautifully. So I was perfectly aware of the Ives "thing." However, I would be dishonest if I didn't admit that I don't admire everything that Ives wrote. I think Ives wrote some masterpieces. But there's a certain experimental faddishness that's come out of Ives that isn't of interest to me, although it may be of interest to others. Of course, any American musician who would belittle the importance of Ives' success would be nuts, because that success rubs off on him. Here at last is a composer that Americans take very seriously indeed.

But getting back to your question; I don't quote very many things. From my childhood on, I have always sung folk songs with guitar. My family sang all the time. I still, every now and then, get up with my guitar and sing a song. For instance, you know Landscapes Remembered; well, so much of it is based on

"O bury me not on the lone prairie"

To me, the openness of that, the intervallic quality, is very American. The jump of the octave.

"In Scarlet Town, where I was born,
There was a young maid dwelling,
Made all the boys come runnin' 'round
For love of Barbrie Ellen."

Look at the way that melody catapults over long intervals. So I usually quote things that are genuinely in my background. There's no fake here; I don't get out books on folk songs. There are a lot of folk songs that I don't sing. For instance, I have never sung Negro spirituals because I think I'd sing them badly, and I value them too highly to desecrate them with my Welsh voice. I don't know whether that answers your question.

I'm terribly interested in memory, and quotation has to do with it. What is the basis of memory? Why does one remember something, and what does memory do to continuity? This interests me. I mentioned this when we spoke about the idea of variation; that's one aspect of it. Well, there's another aspect, and it comes right out in Landscapes Remembered. Do you remember that that piece starts with a vibraphone chord? The vibraphone chord is F-G-A-B♭-C-D; that is one of the most basic hexachords that you can have in the twelve-tone technique. Its counterpart, the other

six notes, is B-C♯-D♯-E-F♯-G. So there is a parallel, a symmetrical hexachord, where you get the twelve notes that way. Now,
there's been all this talk about how twelve-tone techniques of this
century were suddenly discovered; but what is that hexachord? It's
B♭, F, C, G, D, A; it's the circle of fifths. Just how long has
the circle of fifths been around? Also, as a natural result of that
hexachord--F-G-A-B♭-C-D-- you have a pentatonic scale. In other
words, if you were to take F-G-B♭-C-D, what melodies belong to
that?

"Nearer my God to Thee ... "

So suddenly, in the hexachordal theory that has dominated my music, I find all kinds of roots back into my memory. I don't find
that it's restrictive.

Of course, there are lots more theoretical ways that I could
talk about it. For instance, Milton Babbitt talks about "source
sets." As I understand it, they are groups of notes that you find
reiterated on different levels. I call it an associative structure--
again, memory. In other words, you remember a certain note organization, and this comes out in many different places and on many
different levels. As I said, I find this very much related to memory, and I find that this is something that can be utilized in terms
of even my own personal, human memory.

Q: Do you think that the twentieth century is really an era of
"means" music, where the methods by which music is created tend
to overshadow what the ends are supposed to be?

FINNEY: I think there has been a little over-emphasis of--for want
of a better word--means. I think this has come about partly through
the fact that there has been such expansion in technology. It seemed
important to do a piece of music using nothing but electrically-generated sounds, regardless of whether or not it was music, whether
or not it was valuable. Obviously, this is simply a step along the
road, and I suspect that almost every generation, if it's been alive,
has gone through this. There have been times in art when the dictates of a social system or religion have frozen the thing, and the
artist never varied from that. Of course, this leads to a more
propagandistic art, or to a Christian art, or to an art that is rooted
in your mystic beliefs. So the frozen art situation, you might say,
was more expressive. But was it? In a time like our own where
there's such enormous change, there is great investigation for language, for the way of saying. I mentioned the fact that after the
Second World War I felt that my language was poverty-stricken; I
needed more ways to say things. So you are concerned with means.
Does that signify that you're going to be satisfied only with means?
I don't think so.

Nor can you say that there is one expressive thing. Nonsense. I remember Aaron Copland once telling an orchestra that he wanted them to play it differently. "Well," they said, "you've written 'espressivo.'" And he said, "I want my kind of 'espressivo.'" In other words, sure you're concerned with ends, but the ends are not always the same for different composers. One composer is much more emotional, another composer is much more reserved; so I don't really think that the situation is as severe as you said except for one thing. Why is this such a period of talk-talk-talk-talk-talk about music? My own feeling is we should play music just a little bit more, perform music a little bit more, and talk a little bit less about it. Obviously, I'm not maligning critics; a critic's job is to write about music. But composers? Why should composers talk all the time about music? That makes you feel that they're concerned only with the means. I just wish that composers would shut up a little bit, and become less theorists, and more composers. Actually, there are very great composers right here in this area and we should play their music, not talk about it.

Q: Can you tell us what you're currently working on?

FINNEY: Yes, I'm composing a new work for cello. After listening to my Variations on a Memory, I've decided I'm not going to write this new piece for cello and large orchestra. I have written a lot of works for large orchestra; if people want to play my music on a large orchestra, it's there. I don't feel like writing for the large orchestra--at least not in this work. I think I'm going to write it for cello and a group of instruments. Now don't ask me what it's going to be because I haven't reached that point. Very often, a work will have very tender roots in the work that just came before, especially if I've just heard it. There are two or three measures in the work I just heard that I love. The sound of them haunts me. After hearing it, I came back to my studio and immediately this began opening doors. I heard Variations on a Memory last Sunday, so it's just in the last two or three days that I've begun working on the cello work. Already I see that it's going to be for a smaller force. Perhaps it will involve mostly woodwinds and brass, but very, very solistically handled.

CATALOG OF COMPOSITIONS

1933	Piano Sonata in D Minor	Presser
1933; 52	Concerto No. 1 in E Minor for Violin and Orchestra	CF Peters
1935	String Quartet No. 1 in F Minor	B&H
1935	Poems by Archibald MacLeish for high voice and piano	American Music
1937	String Quartet No. 2 in D Minor	MS
1937	Bleheris for tenor and orchestra	CF Peters

1937	Viola Sonata No. 1	CF Peters
1938	Piano Trio No. 1	MS
1938	Three Seventeenth Century Lyrics for high voice and piano	Valley Music
1939	Pole Star for This Year for tenor, alto, SATB, and orchestra	MS
1939	Fantasy for piano	B&H
1940	Oh, Bury Me Not for TTBB or SSAA	Volkwein
1940	When the Curtains of Night for TTBB or SSAA	Volkwein
1940	Slow Piece for string orchestra	Valley Music
1940	String Quartet No. 3 in G Major	ACA
1941	Trail to Mexico for TTBB	Volkwein
1942	Piano Sonata No. 3 in E	Valley Music
1942	Symphony No. 1 (Communique, 1943)	CF Peters
1943	Hymn, Fuguing, and Holiday for orchestra	Carl Fischer
1945	Pilgrim Psalms for soli, SATB, and orchestra or organ	Carl Fischer
1945	Fiddle-Doodle-Ad for violin and piano	G Schirmer
1945	Piano Sonata No. 4	Mercury
1946	Words to be Spoken for canon a 4	Mercury
1946	Poor Richard for voice and piano	G Schirmer
1947	String Quartet No. 4 in A	SPAM
1947	Spherical Madrigals for SATB	CF Peters
1947	Nostalgic Waltzes for piano	Mercury
1948	Piano Quartet	MS
1948	String Quartet No. 5	MS
1948	Concerto No. 1 for Piano and Orchestra	CF Peters
1948	Three Love Songs for high voice and piano	Valley Music
1950	Cello Sonata No. 2 in C	Valley Music
1950	String Quartet No. 6 in E	CF Peters
1951	Violin Sonata No. 2	CF Peters
1951	Chamber Music for high voice and piano	MS
1952	Immortal Autumn for tenor and SATB	MS
1952	Variations on a Theme by Alban Berg for piano	CF Peters
1953	Piano Quintet No. 1	CF Peters
1953	Viola Sonata No. 2	CF Peters
1954	Piano Trio No. 2	Carl Fischer
1955	Violin Sonata No. 3	Valley Music
1955	The Express for high voice and piano	MS
1955	String Quartet No. 7	Valley Music
1956	Inventions (25 children's pieces for piano)	Summy-Birchard

1957	Chromatic Fantasy in E for cello	CF Peters
1957	Variations for Orchestra	CF Peters
1958	Fantasy in Two Movements for violin	CF Peters
1958	String Quintet	CF Peters
1959	Edge of Shadow for SATB, two pianos, and percussion	CF Peters
1959	Symphony No. 2	CF Peters
1960	String Quartet No. 8	Valley Music
1960	Symphony No. 3	CF Peters
1961	Piano Quintet No. 2	Galaxy
1961	Sonata quasi una Fantasia for piano	CF Peters
1962	Three Pieces for Strings, Winds, Percussion, and Tape Recorder	CF Peters
1962	Still Are New Worlds for narrator, SATB, orchestra, and tape recorder	CF Peters
1964	Divertissement for clarinet, violin, cello, and piano	Bowdoin
1965	Three Studies in Fours for percussion orchestra	CF Peters
1965	Concerto for Percussion and Orchestra	CF Peters
1965	The Nun's Priest's Tale for narrator, soli, SATB, folksong singer with electric guitar, and small orchestra	CF Peters
1966	The Martyr's Elegy for tenor, SATB, and orchestra	CF Peters
1967	Symphony Concertante	CF Peters
1967	Five Organ Fantasies	CF Peters
1968	Thirty-two Piano Games	CF Peters
1968	Concerto No. 2 for Piano and Orchestra	CF Peters
1969	The Remorseless Rush of Time for amplified voice, SATB, and thirteen instruments	CF Peters
1969	Summer in Valley City for concert band	CF Peters
1970	Twenty-four Inventions for piano	CF Peters
1970	Two Acts for Three Players for clarinet, piano, and percussion	CF Peters
1971	Landscapes Remembered for chamber orchestra	CF Peters
1971	Spaces for orchestra	CF Peters
1972	Symphony No. 4	CF Peters
1973	Concerto No. 2 for Violin and Orchestra	CF Peters
1973	Two Ballades for flutes and piano	CF Peters
1974	Tubes I for one to five trombones	CF Peters
1974	Concerto for Alto Saxophone and Wind Orchestra	CF Peters
1974	Seven Easy Percussion Pieces for four percussionists	CF Peters
1975	Variations on a Memory for chamber orchestra	CF Peters

1976	Narration for cello and fourteen instruments	CF Peters
1977	Concerto for Strings	CF Peters
1978	Skating Down the Sheyenne for band	CF Peters
1978	Waltz for Piano	CF Peters
1979	Earthrise for taped voice, contralto, tenor, SATB, and orchestra	CF Peters
1979	Quartet for Oboe, Cello, Piano, and Percussion	CF Peters
1980	Lost Whale Calf for piano	CF Peters
1980	Two Studies for saxophones and piano	CF Peters

photo: Gene Bagnato

Lukas Foss was born on August 15, 1922, in Berlin,
Germany. Foss came to America in 1937 and enrolled at the Curtis Institute in Philadelphia, where
his teachers included Randall Thompson and Fritz
Reiner. At Tanglewood he studied with Paul Hindemith. Foss received his LL.D. at the Los Angeles
Conservatory of Music. He has had an active career
as a teacher: He was Arnold Schoenberg's successor
as professor of composition at UCLA in 1953, and has
also taught at Tanglewood. Foss has been even bus-
ier as a pianist, first with the Boston Symphony Orchestra and later with the Improvisation Chamber Ensemble, which he formed at UCLA in 1957. He has
served as music director and conductor for the Buffalo Philharmonic and the Jerusalem Symphony Orchestra, and, presently, for the Brooklyn Philharmonia
and the Milwaukee Symphony Orchestra. In 1951,
Foss married Cornelia Brendel. They have two children.

Foss's early works were in a tonal idiom and
displayed a bias for both romanticism and neo-classicism; the major influences, the inescapable presences
of Stravinsky, Hindemith, and Copland. Foss's investigation into improvisation in the late 1950s led
him to avant-garde composition, where he has remained a major figure. After initial forays into serial techniques, he became increasingly involved in
chance procedures.

Lukas Foss was interviewed in his Manhattan studio on January 3, 1975. The following transcript cannot hope to represent the total range of Foss's wit,
articulateness, and charm. His is a winning personality, far better experienced than described. The
time spent with him was a pleasure that could not
be dampened even by the frequent telephone interruptions.

Q: Time Cycle juxtaposes four separate texts never before put in a
relationship with each other, and the music serves as a meditation
on, even a philosophical extension of the texts. Do you see yourself as a philosophical composer?

FOSS: Certainly not, no. I'm the son of a professor of philosophy,

This interview with Lukas Foss first appeared in the New York Arts
Journal, vol. 1, no. 2, September 1976.

so I know what it means to claim to be a philosopher. I am literary-minded, I like literature, and besides, I like voices. The voice
came with the word. For instance, the Greek word "music" meant
sounds with words.

Now, the problem is, we use words that were not meant to
go with music. Poems don't get better by being wedded to music.
Once we are aware of that, we realize that we're not doing the
poet a favor when we set him to music. I always have the feeling
that I owe the poet an apology. I feel that I should say to him,
"Look, I used you, which is not right. I have labeled your words
by setting them. I have interpreted them. They were meant to
fill the whole room with their own ambiguity, and I have pinned
them down by setting them. But accept my notes in place, as an
apology, as an homage." That is, I think, the correct attitude.
We should always have that in mind when we use something. We
should say, "Well, I'm sorry I used you, but, you see, the purpose is all right. It's for a good cause." That's the attitude that
I have in setting words.

But I became more and more weary of the idea of taking
somebody's words. In Time Cycle, I still did. Then I went to the
fragments of Archilochos. I used a marvellous translation published by the Oxford University Press. In that piece of music, every time you perform it you follow a different road map, which
juxtaposes different fragments. One Archilochos fragment is: "in
copulating one discovers that." That is all we have left of that
poem. This might, in one performance, find itself juxtaposed with
"kindness flows both ways." Or, in another one it might be "I've
worn out my dick"--in another one: "a measured motion governs
man." So you find that the poem shifts with every performance.
It might be, "kindness flows both ways, in copulating one discovers that." Or "I've worn out my dick, in copulating one discovers
that."

Q: So in this music--or in Paradigm--the performers are making
different poems.

FOSS: You're right, that was the next thing I was going to say.
In Paradigm I went one step further. I wanted to have different
words--not just different sentences but different words--juxtaposed
at different performances, and there I finally did the logical thing,
I wrote my own.

Q: In this way you seem to remove yourself from the responsibility
of writing music that will get at the inner meaning of the text, because the meaning will change at every performance. It takes you
away from writing something that might have to be more programmatic.

FOSS: Exactly. I really want to get away from mood music, because I think that painting a mood under a text is too arbitrary a procedure. I like the more abstract and functional way of going about it which I use in Paradigm, in which the words and syllables are cues, and in which the mood almost takes care of itself. The words are like tools. I may have to wrestle with this problem again because I've been commissioned for the bicentennial to do a large work for chorus and orchestra based on some American heritage idea.

Q: What are your feelings towards the pre-Time Cycle works?

FOSS: I was very much a traditionalist, for many years, and wrote music which I still love, and which now has to sort of live on its own merit. In other words, I'm not going to fight for it. My publisher always says, "Look, what about all these early children of yours, why don't you do something for them?" I said, "Well, I feel that if they're any good, they have to make it on their own. I'm going to help my younger children, because they're still fragile and close to my present way of thinking. I just hope that the older works will live." And it's true that I'm as fond of The Prairie, and the Song of Songs, and my fairy tale opera Griffelkin, as I am of any of my more recent works. But I am not going to promote them. The more recent works need my help. They have to be published and recorded, and also they present new and involved performance problems. So they should be helped along. Time Cycle was the transition piece between my earlier and my recent style.

There is a break. The break occurred about 1956. I was at UCLA. I was professor of composition, and I wanted to get my students away from the tyranny of the printed note. So I invented a form of non-jazz ensemble improvisation. It was meant to change my students; well, it changed me. At first these efforts were tonal, because at that time I was a tonal composer, and for a long time they sounded like music badly remembered, you might say. Then one day I asked myself what would improvised music sound like that is actually conceived that way, that would not possibly sound like music badly remembered, but actually capitalizes on the fact that it is spontaneous. And with this question I let in a whole Pandora's box of troubles, which eventually made me into a different kind of composer. I let in questions of chance control--in other words, aleatoric problems--at a time when the word "aleatoric" had not yet invaded the musical jargon.

So the break occurred in my music, but it wasn't from one moment to the next. When Time Cycle was first performed it included improvisations, chamber improvisations, between the set pieces. A rather dubious idea, one which I jokingly offered to my friend Leonard Bernstein, who was scheduled to do the premiere of Time Cycle. We didn't take the idea very seriously, but that night I got a call from the New York Philharmonic, engaging the Improvisation Ensemble to do just that, to appear like a commedia dell'arte group of clowns and improvise between the songs. This became rather famous, and I was stuck with this format for Time Cycle, so that I even had to bring my clowns to the Berlin Philharmonic for the European premiere. Now, finally, Time Cycle's being done without the improvisations, which is only correct since no one else really can improvise in a way that would be relevant to the style of the songs. No other group could possibly do it right, they would just spoil the composition.

Then the next piece, Echoi, is the one that really makes the final jump into that no man's land which I never meant to set foot on, and which I entered, you might say, against my will, through this experiment in improvisation--though Echoi is not an improvisation piece at all.

Q: Was it the freedom of working in improvisation that made you tired of the more rigorously structured, traditional music?

FOSS: No--improvisation is more rigorously structured. Freedom is a very misleading word, because first of all, when you make freedom available for a group, you have to have very rigid traffic controls so that you don't bump into each other. That is why it's really not so much a question of freedom. It's a question of a more experimental outlook. It's a question of treating music more like possibilities that you would like to unearth, discover, rather than to write the music you have always loved. The traditional composer, the conservative composer, is cultivating well-known territory. The experimental composer forgoes what he loves in favor of discovery, and hopes that he will love what he discovers. Schoenberg, for instance, loved classical music like no one else, and yet spent his lifetime in that no man's land of atonality, trying to do the thing that he loved in tonal music--which gives to his music a quality of failure, you might almost say. But that quality of failure gives it a kind of tragic grandeur that it wouldn't have if he weren't attempting the impossible. It's like Adam and Eve, you know, trying to make paradise on earth. It's bound to fail, but what an effort, what a grandiose effort.

This is really the tragedy of all inventors: They have to reconcile that new invention in terms of everything they were brought up with. So that very often it's the next person, in this case Webern, who reaped the rewards by being able to detach himself from the past more than the inventor; taking the invention for what it's worth and resigning oneself to the fact that this is not the paradise, it is the new no man's land, and let's see what we can do with the no man's land we now have. So therefore, Webern's music is maybe, on a smaller scale, more successful, although who am I to judge that? It's almost impossible to compare Schoenberg and Webern, they're so different.

Q: To get back to improvisation. You saw improvisation as a way

of stimulating composition. Do you still believe that? Have some
of your works grown directly out of improvisation?

FOSS: The improvisation workshop that I conducted at UCLA, and
that I took on tour through Europe and America, was a kind of running workshop for me. It became soon a form of "instant composition." At rehearsals I would say, "Why don't you do that, you
do that, you do this, and so forth, and then let's find out what happens." We'd tape it, and then we'd criticize it: "Let's see, well,
this is a good idea, that one is not so good." A piece got better
as we criticized each other and played it again, until it reached a
certain plateau where we were satisfied, and then it would get
worse. Then it became stale, so then we would discard it. This
gave me the idea of a form of instant composition, and anonymous
composition. We were the first people, I think, in the trend for
anonymity which is built into current musical expression but isn't
quite making it because no one wants to sacrifice his signature.
The signature has a way of hanging on, you know. Even if you
may have trouble finding the "R" on a Rauschenberg painting, somewhere it's hidden. Still, we can't deny that there is something in
the music of the sixties and seventies that is slightly impersonal
and anonymous, and my group was undoubtedly the first and last to
actually take the extreme step and discard our author's vanity.

Q: But you found that no matter how hard the ensemble worked at
a certain piece, it wouldn't be as satisfactory as one you could compose yourself?

FOSS: Right. The best example is probably the Non-Improvisation,
which is recorded, and which I called Non-Improvisation simply because the tasks were so clearly defined. I sat at the piano and
played something familiar--Bach's D Minor Concerto--and I am being obliterated by a fat cloud of sound which now and then allows
me to come through. Later this cloud deteriorates into glissandi
of various kinds. The whole thing becomes a strange dream piece,
not unlike my Baroque Variation Number Three, which is also a
Bach dream. Non-Improvisation isn't really an improvisation and
isn't really a kind of composition.

     Finally I tired of improvising because I found that I was play-
ing the music I knew. In other words, I was relying on routine,
on cliches, on things that I knew would work. You see, in ensemble improvisation you can't take certain chances you can take in
composition. You've got to make it work, you've got to be sure
that it will work. So what do you do? You play very soft, because you realize it's going to sound sensitive, that's safe, or you
play very loud,. it's going to be powerful, so that's safe. But mez-
zo-forte improvisation, that's much harder. If everyone plays very
low, you're going to get a sort of mood, a grumbling, if you play
very high, it's going to be like insects; there is unity of purpose.

But in the middle register, that's difficult. So improvisation became playing safe--as it most always is for jazz musicians also.

Q: This brings us right to <u>Paradigm</u>. In the fourth movement, you
point out how each kind of music--improvisation, aleatory, serial,
electronic--can degenerate into safeness, and you say, "Show me
dangerous music." Is <u>Paradigm</u> dangerous?

FOSS: I don't know if <u>Paradigm</u> has the answer, but it raises the
question--and there again you see, in order not to ruin somebody's
poetry, I simply took a lecture of mine, the very lecture from
which I am quoting as I get into this business of safeness, and I
set that to music. Yes, it takes more chances than improvisation,
I think; successful improvisation simply cannot afford to be dangerous. It has to rely on routine, it has to rely on tricks of the
trade.

Q: Would you say that there are other dangerous composers around
today?

FOSS: I think that every good piece of music takes a certain chance.
The nice thing, though, about dangerous music is that it doesn't do
anybody any harm.

Q: Harm in the sense of giving people what they've always heard,
and lulling them?

FOSS: No, no. It may do them harm intellectually, but it doesn't
kill, it doesn't wound. I think that's important to realize, that if
it did it would not be music. That's where I draw the line, and
where I think I'm right to draw the line. I don't know anymore
what music is. My definition of the word "music" changes every
year, with whatever I'm composing. Usually, what I once rele-
gated to the garbage can, I have since rescued from the garbage
can, and found out that that too can be music. Like Varèse taught
us that noise can be music. We stretch the word "music" all the
time. But I know, that when it comes to doing harm, that is the
scientist's or the technologist's domain. If I turn on the loudspeaker so loudly that it will hurt my hearing, it is technology that makes
me able to do that. I cannot sing or play so loud that it will hurt
my hearing. If I happen to know the formula that will make those
high sounds that are dangerous to one's nervous system, that will
force defecation, for instance--there is such a formula--well, I
have to be a technologist to know that formula and to apply it. I,
as a musician, would not know about it.

It's interesting that music cannot harm. Well, yes, you can

destroy a piano. But there is another reason why I am not interested in that. The kind of pieces that demolish a violin or a piano
were done some twelve years ago. The first one to demolish a
piano was Nam Jun Paik, I believe in Darmstadt or in Cologne. It
probably made some terrifying noises. Well, if you want to call
that music, you can do so, but it does harm to a musical instrument.
Nor does this thing bear repetition. Now that doesn't mean that it's
not music, if it doesn't bear repetition, but it means it isn't good
music, because good music is based on the idea that you can find
something new in it upon repeated listening. "Hey, I didn't hear
that," or, "Isn't that beautiful!" You get struck again, and deeper
the second time than the first. In fact, the first time that you hear
a Beethoven symphony, you cannot possibly grasp how good it is.
You have to hear it several times before you know what's in it.
Some music wears thin upon repeated hearing. Then we know that,
though it is music, it is not good music.

Q: There are pieces that use the sounds of war from news broadcasts. They're not doing harm, but they're exploiting harm.

FOSS: Well, that would come under the heading of background music, and background music is applied music, and is useful in order
to help the screen, or whatever, get a certain nonmusical message
across. That's not really a musical question then. It's a question
of whether these particular noises, suggestive of war, will help that
picture.

Q: No, without a picture.

FOSS: Oh, just by itself? It couldn't harm but it would be too
literal to be musically interesting. It's not very interesting to hear
something with all kinds of literal, nonmusical connotations. You
see, after all what we're doing is a form of stylization, like keeping something in the icebox so that it will live a little longer and
stay fresh. When you're too literal, it's going to be less fresh.
It's tied to the event and as the event becomes less important to
us, so becomes the sound that emanates. It's too tied to its non-
musical source.

But art as a weapon is not to be discounted. It's a beautiful
weapon precisely because it doesn't hurt and it does create a climate for peace. Because even violence, if given to us in the form
of art, in my opinion stimulates non-violence. Now this is a much
disputed point. The old Greeks would take exception with me immediately and would say, "Wait a moment, we have special scales
for war, we have special modes for peace, and therefore the ones
for war will stimulate war and the ones for peace will stimulate
peace." Well I would call that an old wives' tale.

Q: The whole idea of tragedy was to purge the audience of all these negative feelings.

FOSS: Exactly, and only art will do that. I would say that music first of all cannot really stimulate violent action because it is in itself a celebration. When you celebrate, you are not saying, "We're going to kill somebody." You are saying, "We're winning--we have won--let's celebrate!" You're already drinking your wine, and once you drink that wine of celebration, are you really going to go ahead and kill somebody? I would say no.

The words may be violence-inspiring, hate-filled. But you see, music isn't able to carry a hate message. It cannot do that. It can only arouse you, and if you arouse people then there is that notion of celebration. If you give them an unresolved dissonance, then you are seeking the resolution which is peace. Music is incapable of stimulating violence. The other arts can do it, but even when they do it what will happen is they will get into the field of propaganda, to be effective. And propaganda is a lie, and a lie is not art. Art is a mirror of truth. So the moment you use art for propaganda purposes, it's bad art, false art. So that even the other arts, I think, basically will wind up with a peace message as they show you violence.

Q: Earlier, you commented on certain electronic music as being too literal. In Ni Bruit Ni Vitesse you evoke certain electronic sounds from inside two pianos. Do you find that more satisfying than going to an actual electronic medium?

FOSS: I am not basically an electronic composer. The electronic medium is very useful. It's already proven its validity by challenging us non-electronic composers out of our complacency, and forcing us to reexamine what can be done with existing instruments and voices. I would say almost everything we do today is somewhat steeped and colored by the electronic climate. Certainly my music is. I now know that there are ways of starting or decaying a sound so manifold and so interesting, and all this I owe to electronic music. Sometimes I use electronic gimmickry in my pieces, although in that piece you mentioned, Ni Bruit Ni Vitesse, the point was: What can I get out of the insides of these pianos? And not the usual hammering sounds, which are bad for the piano--as you see, I don't like to harm instruments either--but beautiful, poetic sounds, remarkably electronic sounds, and I'm proud of the fact that they're all "done by hand." You know that charming Stravinsky story? When Stravinsky quoted a very high fee to a countess in Paris who commissioned a work from him, she said, "Well, isn't that rather steep?" and he said, "But Madame, it's all made by hand."

But there's also something else: When human beings make

these sounds by hand, they are actually more interesting than when machines make them. The machine is capable of an unbelievable array of sounds, unhampered by human frailty, and it's very use-ful to catalog these sounds. You get an enormous dictionary of sounds that way, and if I were an electronic composer I would cer-tainly work with these machines. As it is, I work with people who work with these machines. For instance, my friend Joel Chadabe has provided me sometimes with electronic sounds that were, so to say, "cooked to order."

Q: Chamber Music.

FOSS: Chamber Music, exactly, yes. It's a piece on which we're still working. MAP, for instance, started out with electronic tapes by Joel Chadabe, and one day I came to Joel and I said, "You know, these electronic tapes, they're no good for my purpose. They're too beautiful, they're like a beautiful gravy that makes everything sound alike. I prefer the imperfections of the human instrument, and I think that I want to rethink this whole piece so that the play-ers make their own tapes and then play against these tapes." As a result, MAP is a musical game now that is not done with elec-tronic sounds any more, although it uses tape.

I think, ultimately, electronic music will find its way to all background music purposes; the human being should be in the fore-ground. The human being and human performance is an element that cannot be replaced.

Q: There's an interesting quality in many of your works. Cave of the Winds has each instrument playing chords. Chamber Music re-quires the performer to imitate electronic sounds that are utterly unlike any instrumental sounds; he or she has to imitate the inim-itable. Baroque Variations is notable for its non-orchestral use of the orchestra, and Ni Bruit Ni Vitesse for its unusual tone colors. Do you see yourself as primarily a hunter of new sounds? Are new tone colors more important to you than new means of arranging your sounds?

FOSS: You see, just from the description you gave of these pieces, that it's not fishing for sounds, but ideas. In other words, fishing for meaning. The sounds are a means towards the meaning. If the Baroque Variations use Bach, it is not in order to get new sounds, but because the almost autobiographical idea of destroying my love for Bach is something that obsessed me at the time. I wrote three pieces that had something to do with Bach. We already mentioned two, the Baroque Variations and Non-Improvisation. There's a third one: the last movement of my Cello Concert, which uses Bach like a twelve-tone row--the Sarabande for cello. That was my particular obsession with my own past, you might say, and not just fishing for sounds. Because if I fished for sounds, then indeed electronics is the only way to go about it. But when you fish for meaning, then you have another problem. The multiphonic sounds on woodwinds have simply given me the possibility of extending the tasks of woodwind players, giving them something to dig into that is fresh and new for them, extending their technique on the instrument, and unearthing, at the same time, a whole climate of sounds that are both antique and pseudo-electronic. I mean, they sound like something out of Japanese court music, and at the same time they have these electronic connotations. They conjure up marvellous imagery. In other words, they make it possible for me to compose. You see, the difference with sound fishing and fishing for meaning is that the sound is just the raw material; then, composing means to make meaning with the sounds. Many composers stop with the sound fishing, and think that is what composing is about. That would be my principal argument against much existing electronic music, that it stops where composition begins.

All kinds of people might be more likely to hit on new sounds than composers. We really don't have any particular insight into sounds, but we know what to do with them. We work with them, like painters work with colors. But meaning is the important thing, because meaning is what communicates. Sounds don't communicate in themselves.

Q: This seems to bring us back to the beginning again. Are you something of a philosophical composer?

FOSS: Well, every artist is to that extent philosophical in that he has to communicate, but the philosopher would be able to tell me exactly what I want to communicate, and I don't know that. I am not my own connoisseur. The psychologist would be able to tell me why I want to communicate, why I have this need. I don't know why, and I don't know what. But somehow, something comes to pass when my music is being played--between me and the listener or the performer who listens--which I cannot even articulate in words, because if I could I would be able to write about it and maybe would have no need to compose. Something happens, something opens up to people. We still don't really know what Bach or Beethoven or Mozart convey to us. We can write metaphors about it, but finally you have to come to the music itself and listen to it. And when people listen together, even though everyone hears something different, in the light of his own life-experience, we experience the surprise that even though everyone hears something different we all also hear the same thing. That brings people together. When they say "Beethoven's Ninth," you know, to each it means something else, and still they talk about the same thing. Somehow, that is communication.

Q: What do you take into account when you compose? Do you consider how receptive an audience might be to some things, or do you feel that it is your position to make demands on them?

FOSS: I never really think of an audience as the people who buy tickets to a concert. I think of brothers and sisters, of people in the same boat, in the same trouble, who will be willing to follow me into my world, into my dilemma, into what I'm seeking. When something interests me, I take it for granted that it will interest somebody else, someone like me. Whether that's a big audience or a small audience has to do with the nature of my talent. If I'm a composer like Handel or Verdi--and I'm not--then I will reach a large audience, because they were "men of the people." They had this marvellous talent that almost no one else has, to be very simple and popular, and at the same time noble. Handel had this talent and Bach did not. Bach's music is much more introspect and thrives on complexity. One might say that the more you know about music, the more chance you have to really understand Bach. This is not true of Handel and Verdi. Complexity is one way of being deep. To be deep without being complex is very unusual. The greatest music is probably complex.

Q: So the given in your mind is that the audience is willing to try and understand what you do. You don't worry about not daring something for fear that they'll walk out on you; you have faith in them.

FOSS: I have faith in them, and besides I don't have the box office problem since I'm not the impresario that puts on the concerts.

Q: Have you ever cut anything out because you were afraid that it just wouldn't work with an audience?

FOSS: Never, never. When I make a cut, when I discard--and of course composing means constantly discarding--it's only because it doesn't satisfy me. It's because it's not as good as I can make it, because it's not as interesting. I keep saying to myself, "This is not why I'm here, to make this sound." Just now I'm at work on something and I'm just cutting out something I have been slaving over for two weeks. I feel, well, if I'm only winding up with that, why bother? This has been said before. Out with it.

Q: You've said that the symphony orchestra since Mahler is an anachronism.

FOSS: Well, you see, I conduct symphony orchestras all the time. In fact, I have two, Brooklyn and Jerusalem, and I commute to

Israel a lot. I do a lot of conducting, and my time is about evenly
spent between composing and conducting. I conduct because I love
to make love to the past. I think man has this need, and the need
to discover the future as well. The more my own composition is
busy with exploration and experimentation, the greater is my need
to keep my tie with the past which made me a musician in the first
place; my tie with Bach, Mozart, and Beethoven, and Wagner, and
Verdi, and Handel, and Schubert. So therefore I conduct, and therefore I find symphony orchestras are important. They are museums.
There's nothing wrong with a good museum. We need that, we need
that tie to the past. I think, in fact, that the people who have the
greatest impact on the future are people who have one big foot in
the past and one big foot in the future.

Q: You feel that the symphony orchestra is drained out for experimentation for the future?

FOSS: It's not really meant for experimentation. Occasionally, of
course, you can find something that is new and for symphony orchestra. But the symphony orchestra such as we know it--with its
particular setup of lots of strings, three or four flutes, three or
four oboes, three or four clarinets, and so forth--is, more or less,
a Viennese nineteenth-century thing, based on Haydn's eighteenth-
century idea, expanded by Beethoven, and further expanded by Mahler. And everything symphonic since Mahler really is, in a sense,
anachronistic. But the lovely thing about the arts is that anachronism is possible, a Benjamin Britten is possible today, and probably
more valid than many an avant-garde bandwagon-jumper.

Q: Does this mean that you now approach writing for orchestra
with a little trepidation?

FOSS: Perhaps, but I just notice that the best works are not really
written for symphony orchestra. I would say that our new music
roughly begins with Pierrot Lunaire of Schoenberg and Story of a
Soldier of Stravinsky. They are the new chamber music, and they
are mixed media, and you might say Pierrot Lunaire is psychedelic,
and you might say that Story of a Soldier is pop art forty years
ahead of schedule--and I said that to Stravinsky, and he smiled,
and didn't contradict, didn't disagree.

So there you are. Where are the great symphonies? The
Shostakovich symphonies are not bad, but the greatest achievements
since Mahler are probably to be found in the new chamber music,
combo music. I would say what's new about our music today is
the combo and electronic music. By the combo I mean really any
small group of highly skilled virtuosi, and that would include some
rock music and jazz. Those are the things that are new about the
last sixty years.

CATALOG OF COMPOSITIONS

1937	Sonata for Violin and Piano	MS
1938	Four Two-Part Inventions for Piano	Carl Fischer
1938	Grotesque Dance for piano	Carl Fischer
1938	Wanderer's Gemutsruhe for voice and piano	Southern
1938	Three Songs on Goethe Texts for voice and piano	MS
1939	Sonatina for Piano	MS
1940	Incidental Music for The Tempest	MS
1940	Four Preludes for Flute, Clarinet, and Bassoon	MS
1940	Where the Bee Sucks for voice and piano	Carl Fischer
1940	Set of Three Pieces for Two Pianos	G Schirmer
1940	Melodrama and Dramatic Song of Michel Angelo for voice and orchestra	MS
1941	We Sing cantata for children with piano and drums	MS
1941	Passacaglia for Piano	G Schirmer
1941	Duo for Cello and Piano	Hargail
1941	Two Pieces for Orchestra	MS
1942	Concerto No. 1 for Clarinet and Orchestra	G Schirmer
1942	Concerto No. 1 for Piano and Orchestra	G Schirmer
1944	Symphony No. 1 in G Major	G Schirmer
1944	Cool Prayers for chorus	G Schirmer
1944	The Prairie for soloists, chorus, and orchestra	G Schirmer
1944	Suite from The Prairie for orchestra	G Schirmer
1944; 58	Ode for orchestra	Carl Fischer
1944	The Heart Remembers ballet for orchestra or piano	MS
1944	Within These Walls ballet for orchestra or piano	MS
1944	Fantasy Rondo for Piano	Carl Fischer
1944	Dedication and Early Song for violin and piano	Hargail
1944	Composer's Holiday for violin and piano	Carl Fischer
1944	Gift of the Magi ballet for orchestra	Carl Fischer
1945	Pantomime for orchestra	Carl Fischer
1945	Song of Anguish for voice and orchestra	Carl Fischer
1945	Tell This Blood for chorus	MS
1946	Song of Songs for voice and orchestra	Carl Fischer
1947	String Quartet No. 1 in G	Carl Fischer
1948	Recordare for orchestra	Carl Fischer
1948	Capriccio for Cello and Piano	Carl Fischer
1948	Concerto for Oboe and Orchestra	Southern
1949	The Jumping Frog of Calaveras County opera in two acts	Carl Fischer

1949	Elegy for clarinet and orchestra	G Schirmer
1949; 53	Concerto No. 2 for Piano and Orchestra	Carl Fischer
1950	Prelude in D for Piano	Carl Fischer
1950	Behold--I Build a House for SATB and organ or piano	Presser
1951	Adon Olom for cantor (or tenor), SATB, and organ	G Schirmer
1952	A Parable of Death for narrator, tenor, SATB, and orchestra or chamber orchestra	Carl Fischer
1953	Scherzo Ricercato for Piano	Carl Fischer
1955	Griffelkin opera in three acts	Carl Fischer, Schott
1955	For Cornelia (Yates: For Anne Gregory) for voice and piano	MS
1956	Psalms for SATB and orchestra or two pianos	Carl Fischer
1958	Symphony of Chorales	Carl Fischer
1959	Introduction and Goodbyes opera in one act	Carl Fischer
1960; 61	Time Cycle for soprano and orchestra or chamber group	Carl Fischer
1960	Concerto for Improvising Instruments and Orchestra	MS
1963	Echoi for clarinet, cello, piano, and percussion	Carl Fischer, Schott
1964	Elytres for chamber orchestra	Carl Fischer, Schott
1965	Fragments of Archilochos for chorus and chamber ensemble	Carl Fischer, Schott
1966	For Twenty-Four Winds (Discrepancy or Stillscapes) for orchestra	Carl Fischer, Schott
1967	Etudes for Organ	Carl Fischer
1967	Cello Concert for cello and orchestra	Carl Fischer, Schott
1967	Non-Improvisation for four players	MS
1967	Baroque Variations for orchestra	Carl Fischer, Schott
1968	Paradigm for percussionist/conductor, electric guitar, and three other instruments capable of sustaining a sound	Carl Fischer
1969	GEOD for orchestra with optional voices	Carl Fischer
1972	Three Airs for Frank O'Hara's Angel for soprano, female chorus, and instruments; for soprano, flute, piano, and percussion	Salabert, G Schirmer
1972	Orpheus for violin, viola, or cello and orchestra	Salabert, G Schirmer
1972	Cave of the Winds for woodwind quintet	Salabert, G Schirmer

1972	Ni Bruit Ni Vitesse for two pianos and two percussionists	Salabert, G Schirmer
1973	MAP--A Musical Game for any four players	Carl Fischer
1973	Lamdeni for chorus and plucked and beaten sounds	Salabert, G Schirmer
1973	Fanfare for orchestra	Salabert, G Schirmer
1973	String Quartet No. 2 (Divertissement)	Salabert, G Schirmer
1974	Concerto for Solo Percussion and Orchestra or Chamber Orchestra	Salabert, G Schirmer
1975	String Quartet No. 3	Salabert, G Schirmer
1975; 78	Folk Song for orchestra	Salabert, G Schirmer
1976	American Cantata for tenor, chorus, and large or small orchestra	B&H
1976	Salomon Rossi Suite for orchestra	Salabert, G Schirmer
1977	Curriculum Vitae for accordion	Carl Fischer
1977	Music for Six for any six instruments	Carl Fischer
1978	Brass Quintet	Carl Fischer
1978	And Then the Rocks on the Mountain Begin to Shout for chorus	Carl Fischer
1978	Thirteen Ways of Looking at a Blackbird for voice, flute, piano, and percussion	Carl Fischer
1979	Quintets for Orchestra	Carl Fischer
1979	Round a Common Centre for piano quartet or quintet with or without voice	Carl Fischer
1980	Measure for Measure for tenor and chamber orchestra	Salabert, G Schirmer
1980	Curriculum Vitae with Time Bomb for accordion and percussion	Carl Fischer

photo: Gene Bagnato

Philip Glass was born on January 31, 1937, in Baltimore, Maryland. He received his A.B. from the
University of Chicago and his M.S. from Juilliard,
where he studied composition with Vincent Persichetti
and William Bergsma. He also studied privately with
Darius Milhaud, Nadia Boulanger, and Allah Rakha.
He has two children by his first marriage. In 1980,
he married Mary Burtyk.
Glass first composed works both in twelve-tone
and modern tonal idioms. When he was in Paris in
the mid-sixties, he worked on the notation, arrangement, and performance of a film score by Ravi Shankar. Indian music, particularly its use of additive
rhythmical structures, had a profound effect on his
own music. It led to his mature style, a music that
is based on, in his words, "repetitive structures with
very reduced pitch relationships, a steady eighth-note
beat, and a static dynamic level." He returned to
the United States in 1967, and shortly thereafter
formed the ensemble of musicians with whom he continues to perform today.
Philip Glass was interviewed at his Manhattan home
on November 13, 1980. Despite his having been be-
sieged by interviewers in the last few years, he responded to the authors with a good deal of interest
and enthusiasm. The authors found his directness
and lack of pretension equally appealing.

Q: You wrote a good deal of music in the late fifties and early sixties, especially for the Pittsburgh Public School System under the
Contemporary Music Project. How important would you say these
pieces are for you now? Do they seem completely remote to you?

GLASS: Yes. All together, I wrote maybe twenty pieces for that
project, and about fifty others when I was at Juilliard. So there
are some seventy to eighty pieces that I wrote between 1957 and
1965, and I don't think that any of those pieces interest me at all
at this point.

I was a very good student; I was an A+ student, and those
were A+ pieces--some of them were A-! I learned composition at
that time by imitating my teachers, and they loved it; it was a kind
of homage to them. At that point in my life, I had no music of my
own. I knew that I wouldn't find it by waiting for it to come, so I
did the best thing I could think of, which was to write music like
the people that I studied with--and I learned a lot from them in var-

ious ways. But the music that I ultimately wrote had nothing to
do with that; even at the time that I was writing them, I never felt
they were important. It was Vincent Persichetti, who was my composition teacher at Juilliard, who got me involved with publishing
them. In fact, in my last two years at Juilliard, as I was writing
pieces for him, some of them would go right to the publisher. That
was very flattering for someone of 23 or 24, and he meant it in a
good way. Little did I know that those pieces would be, if not em-
barrassing, certainly non-representative. If I could get those pieces
back from the publisher, I would. The best thing for me to say is
that those were written by somebody else. I don't think it's worth
anybody's time to bother with that music.

Q: It's been said that you consider Music in Fifths to be your own
personal tribute to Nadia Boulanger and her teachings. Is this true?

GLASS: Yes and no; that remark was kind of a joke. I didn't write
the piece for her in any way at all. You see, when I studied with
her, she started me right from the beginning with species counterpoint again, and of course the one thing you don't have, not just in
counterpoint but in harmony as well, is fifths of any kind, hidden
or otherwise. I spent three torturous years avoiding precisely that,
so when I wrote Music in Fifths, I couldn't help but remember that.

During the period that I studied with her, I didn't show her
any of my music; I wasn't interested in her comments on my music
at that point. When I first went to study with her, I showed her a
number of those earlier pieces that I did; I went there with a pile
of music, and she went through fifteen or twenty pieces, examining
them quickly but thoroughly, which was her way. She pointed to one
measure and said, "This was written by a composer." That was
the only nice thing that she said to me--for the whole time! She
agreed to have me study with her, but I never showed her any more
music. It was at about that time that I began to write the music
that I'm writing now, and I had too many problems with other musicians, let alone the person I was studying with. I was just terrified of the kind of remarks that I was sure she would make, so
I didn't show it to her. Even years later, when we did Einstein on
the Beach in Paris, I was terrified that I would see her in the first
row. She had that effect--and not just on me.

I didn't see her again after the time that I studied with her.
I suppose that I might have, or I could have. But it just occupied
too large a place in my mind for me to go back to her comfortably,
and so when I left, I left; I just left it behind and didn't look back,
very much the way I left a lot of other things--such as the pieces
we were just talking about.

Q: Do you consider her role as a teacher to be as separate from
you now as those early works?

GLASS: No; in fact, I don't think that I could be writing the music that I'm writing now if I hadn't studied with her--I'm sure of that. I didn't have the competence or confidence in my technique when I came to her that I had when I left. I just know that the music that I'm writing now couldn't have been written without the years that I spent with her.

People say, "Well, why should I study harmony and counterpoint when we don't do that anymore?" The funny thing is, I do do that, especially in the music I'm doing now, where a lot of the material is very fundamental, very basic material. In Einstein, the kind of cadential formula that runs through it, the I-$\overline{\text{VI}}$-IV$\flat$-$\overline{\text{V}}$-I progression that you hear in the Spaceship and the Knee Plays, the voicing and working out of that was done by somebody who knew very well how traditional harmony operated. I don't think that anyone who didn't have the training that I did could have written that. So even though my music seems so far away from her, it was only four or five years after studying with her that I began to find uses for the things that I had learned.

Another thing that was important was not just her teaching of technique, but that she understood style in a very profound way. Even after you succeeded in realizing a correct way to render an exercise, she might still say it was wrong. If you said, "Why? I followed the rules," she'd say, "Mozart wouldn't have done it that way," and then she'd show you how Mozart did it. After the rules became second nature to you, she went beyond the rules into style. That's when I began to understand that what she was really teaching was style. There are times when the supertonic resolves to the third, and times when it resolves to the tonic, depending on the voicing. Things like that, when you're on that level, go way beyond what you find in a harmony textbook. Most people can't teach that, because they don't know it. That's what she did know.

I don't want this to be a little eulogy for Nadia Boulanger, but I'm not the first composer to have acquired a serviceable and ready technique at her hands. An inescapable conclusion to studying with her was to acquire some real technique.

Q: Did you find a similar importance in your studies with Milhaud?

GLASS: Yes, but in quite a different way, because he approached music as a composer. I wrote a Violin Concerto that summer--I spent only one summer with him--and played it through on the piano. I remember him looking at the last movement of it for a while, and then with his finger he traced a line in the woodwind section and said, "You missed this line." He just traced a melody with his finger; that's something a composer would do. That he could hear and see things like that was very impressive.

You learn different things from composers; mainly, you learn tricks. From people like Boulanger you learn technique--it's not the same thing. There's a lot of things you can learn from composers if they're willing to teach it to you: tricks of the trade; ways of writing out a score so you can see the whole piece without turning the page, for example. Those are the kinds of things that I learned most from other composers, to the extent that they were willing to impart those things; sometimes they aren't.

Q: Earlier, you remarked to us that you had had problems with musicians. Could you elaborate on that?

GLASS: That was the time when I began writing in more or less the style I'm writing now, but let's define that very succinctly: I was writing in repetitive structures with very reduced pitch relationships, a steady eighth-note beat, and a static dynamic level. Those were things that appeared in the music in '65, with a whole new body of work. In a funny way, you can still describe the music today like that (you can also talk about all the ways it's different). But at the point where I was really working with repetitive structures and simple pitch relationships and approached other musicians with it, they actually became quite angry and wouldn't play it. That's when I realized that I would have to become the performer. I hadn't been a performer since I was fifteen, when I stopped playing the flute.

This was in '65, when I was 28, and I decided that I was going to go back to America. I made a long, roundabout trip out of it, and went back by way of India. But I went back knowing that I would have to become a performer of the music. I remember in Paris in '65, a young conductor asked me to write a piece, and I wrote him one of these repetitive pieces, and he actually became quite nasty about it. That was when I first realized what kind of reaction I was going to get with this music. And it's been true as recently as last year, when we did Dance at the Brooklyn Academy of Music. People threw eggs at us. Funny things still happen; even though you think, well, that can't happen anymore, very funny things can still happen.

But originally I was unprepared for that. It seemed to me that the music was so simple, so transparent, what was there to be angry about? Of course, that was precisely what there was to be angry about. I had, perhaps without intending it--although that's really hard to know--challenged so many precepts of the modernist tradition at that point. In fact, you could have almost defined my music in terms of polarities: If Stockhausen jumped all over the place, my music stayed in a very limited range; if his music changed pitches with every note, my music stayed the same; if he never repeated anything, I repeated all the time. I didn't go about inventing a language in those terms, but looking back on it, it looked as if I was dealing with polarities. In fact, I wasn't thinking about that at all. I was just trying to write some music, and it came out that

way--for a variety of reasons, partially having to do with my dis-
content with contemporary music at that time.

Q: In writing about your music, critics have employed several
terms: "hypnotic," "minimalist," "trance," "solid state." Do all
these terms help clarify what you're doing, or do you think they
tend to be misleading?

GLASS: I think they're almost all misleading, although lately I've
come to dislike "minimalist" less than I dislike other descriptions.
Insofar as "minimalist music" refers to a specific historical period, let's say from 1965 to 1975, the term is meaningful. But it's
rarely meant in a limited way.

When people talk about "hypnotic states" or "trance states"
or "druggy states" or "religious states," what they're really saying,
in a rather clumsy way, is that the music shares a non-ordinariness
with certain other experiences. But you can't say that everyone who
doesn't speak English speaks the same language.

For me, what sets the music apart is the fact that it's non-
narrative; and because it is non-narrative, we don't hear it within
the usual time frame of most musical experiences. As I look at
most other music, I see that it takes ordinary time, day-to-day
time--what I call colloquial time--as a model for its own musical
time. So you have story symphonies and story concertos--even the
modernist tradition continues that to a large extent. There's still
almost a compulsion with composers to deal with themes and the
treatment of themes. The theme becomes the focus of the listener's
attention, and then what happens to the theme happens to the listener via a certain psychological trick of identification. This obviously happens in the great concertos of the nineteenth century, with the
tortuous journey of the violin and so forth, with happy endings and
sad endings. It's almost on the level of "major keys are the happy
keys, and minor keys are the sad keys"; unfortunately, a lot of
people experience music in such a simplistic way.

When music doesn't deal with subjects and treatments, as in
my music, which is often a process where the musical material and
its evolution becomes part and parcel of the structure of the music,
then you don't have the psychological access to the music that I described earlier. That's why we don't hear the music as narrative
or as a model of colloquial time. What we're hearing then is music in another time system. Now, we have a lot of other experiences in our lives that take place in non-colloquial time systems.
Some of them happen to be drug experiences; some are religious
experiences; some are nature experiences. There are a wide variety
of them, and even within those experiences there are a wide variety of
them. They're not at all the same; what they share in common is that
they're non-ordinary experiences. So when people say to me
that music is druggy or trancey or this or that, I think they're
confused; they're confusing a variety of experiences that share in

common their difference from ordinary life, but which have vast differences between them. On the simplest level: This is music that, at least for me, requires a state of attentiveness, or provokes one; whereas, clearly there are drugged and hypnotic states that are various states of sleep. I mean, to use a term like "trance music"--I remember as a boy in Baltimore seeing people going to sleep during the symphony concerts. So apparently anything can put you to sleep. I couldn't have been more than seven or eight, and I remember that I was shocked to see people snoring away during a performance of Beethoven's Ninth Symphony; I couldn't believe that they were doing that. And of course, they're snoring away to this day. So, sometimes when I'm playing a concert and I see people nodding off, I don't feel so bad; it's a great tradition!

Q: In the notes for the recording of Parts One and Two of Music in Twelve Parts, you wrote that the listener should "discover another mode of listening--one in which neither memory nor anticipation ... have a place in sustaining the texture, quality, or reality of the musical experience." You wanted the listener "to perceive the music as a 'presence,' freed of dramatic structure, a pure medium of sound." Was Satyagraha composed with this same mode of listening in mind?

GLASS: Yes and no. A lot of the additive processes are in Satyagraha. In fact, like Einstein, Satyagraha is a structuralist piece. The seven scenes are cast as seven chaconnes--it's highly structuralist (or systemic, as the English like to say). However, I was highly aware of Satyagraha as a music-theater piece. Dating from the time I worked on Einstein, and then when I worked on Dance with Lucinda Childs, I began to think of my theater music as being in the theater. Satyagraha is a highly different piece in many ways from earlier works in that it's really a music-theater piece; I thought of myself as a theater composer when I wrote it. Einstein was a piece in which I kind of backed into the theater--although I had written theater music with the Mabou Mines for a number of years. I began working with the Mabou Mines in Paris, with a seminal group of people: Lee Breuer, Ruth Maleczech, David Warrilow, and Joanne Akalaitis. My early work grew out of my association with the theater; very static and repetitive pieces that I did for Beckett plays. So it's not as if I discovered the theater in 1975; rather, I saw myself as taking the lead and setting the tone of the work. Prior to then, with the Mabou Mines, I was writing music for them. Einstein, of course, was a collaborative piece with Bob Wilson; it was the kind of collaboration where we each wrote a piece and then put them together.

The main point about Satyagraha was that I saw it as a work existing in the theater, and I think that I began thinking about it rather differently. I planned when the finales would come, where the slow places would come; I thought of the overall theater-time in a different way than I had been thinking about time before.

Q: Does the non-ordinary time that you were discussing before still exist in Satyagraha?

GLASS: It exists within another framework, because here we're talking about dramatic time.

Q: But non-ordinary time can't be completely dramatic.

GLASS: No. But even Einstein works toward a finale; you can't miss it. I remember when I was talking about the last act, the Spaceship, with Bob, I said, "Look, Bob, I think I'm going to write a real finale; a real razzle-dazzle finale." I wanted to see how he felt about it, and he said, "Fine," he liked the idea. With Einstein, I decided that I would try to write a piece that left the audience standing, and I've almost never played that music without seeing everyone leave his seat; it's the strangest thing, almost biological. In fact, sometimes I've done concerts where I've played the Space-ship, and then as an encore played the last part of the Spaceship, and the same thing happens again.

Satyagraha was planned even more carefully than that. It's a three-act opera, and I planned a finale at the end of the first act, another big ending at the end of the second act, but with the third act being almost static, without any build at all, except for a slight one in the middle. So in planning it as a theater work, I inserted two intermissions, one in between each of the two acts. As I wrote the piece, I was thinking of the kind of music that people would have in their heads while they were waiting that twenty minutes before the next act. So I actually thought about all of these things.

On the other hand, you can't miss that the music is mine. It doesn't sound like "The Son of Einstein" at all; you don't expect this piece, but when you hear it, you know that I wrote it. It's a very big change in my music. But I can't say whether this change has come about because of this direct approach to theater music as drama or because of the gradual evolution of the music toward a richer harmonic language. It's also the first orchestrated piece I've done in eighteen years. For the first time, you hear my mu-sic in an orchestra--which was a big shock for a lot of people who knew my music.

Q: In writing Satyagraha, and now in accepting a commission for a third opera, have you gone back to the standard opera repertory hoping to learn something from it?

GLASS: No; I didn't hope to learn anything about music from those pieces. And I didn't. I don't mean that in a smug way. But there's not much for me to go on in the standard opera repertory, in light of the kind of music I'm writing and the way I'm thinking about opera, with the exception of learning how the voices or a chorus can be used as instruments. After all, my relationship to theater is not the tradition of literary theater; I'm not a composer who took a libretto like <u>Falstaff</u> and set it to music, and that's the way traditional operas were done. The tradition of theater that I feel a part of is the one that begins with the Living Theater: the Open Theater, the Performance Group, the Mabou Mines, Richard Foreman, Bob Wilson, Meredith Monk. They are the godparents of modern American non-literary theater, and my operatic work clearly relates to that tradition. It wouldn't make any sense for me to take an Albee play and set it to music. It would be just totally absurd; I wouldn't expect to do it, and no one would expect me to do it. On the other hand, working with the kind of people that I've mentioned is very natural for me, because that's the community of people I've grown up with: a non-literary theater. A lot of the ways in which that other kind of theater operates simply do not interest me at all. The operas that I've been involved in have been to a certain extent controversial and to a large extent successful (maybe because of their being controversial) because they represent a break in approach in my attitude toward opera as much as in the musical content itself. And there are a lot of sacred cows in the world of traditional opera; it's quite astonishing. Even with <u>Satyagraha</u> there were a number of people who said it wasn't a real opera because it didn't tell a real story.

Clearly, my idea of opera springs from a very recent past; one that, like a lot of American art, doesn't recognize a grandfather of tradition. We're mostly working pretty close to our shoes. This had led me to make choices that a European would never think of making--or even most American composers. We have a lot of American opera composers who are working from the literary tradition, from Menotti on. The real point about the operas that I'm working on is that they spring from this other tradition: a theater that comes from the worlds of painting and dance. And these are not ephemeral "downtown scenes"; these are things which have become an important part of American culture. You can see that as we export it and it comes back reinterpreted by the Europeans.

On the other hand, I found that there was a lot that I could learn about the theater by watching the standard opera repertory: how large a chorus it takes to fill up the City Opera House; how a 40-piece orchestra sounds; how 60-piece orchestra sounds; how off-stage things sound. I've been able to learn a lot of technical theater: how long it takes to bring a drop down; how long it takes to change a costume; how long you can leave singers on repeated A's without their going nuts. When I was doing the transition music for the scenes in <u>Satyagraha</u>, I had to think about how long it took to fly the drops, or how long it would take to bring the built pieces on for a particular scene. If I didn't think about all that, I would have created problems that were unsolvable, and a lot of rehearsal time would have been wasted.

I've learned a lot of technical things about the theater in the

last four or five years. Of course, I began working in the theater
without knowing any of that. But knowing it now meant that when
I did Satyagraha in Holland, it was working. There were problems
with the piece having to do with the amount of choral music that I
wrote: Again, one of the houses had a very short flyspace. So
being able to visualize spaces became very important to me; when
someone says, "This opera house has an opening of eleven meters,"
I know what that means. These are all parts of the craft of music
theater; they don't have much to do with Music in Twelve Parts, or
even with Einstein in a certain way, but they're things to work on
which have interested me.

Q: Then it really didn't matter if you went to see operas by Verdi
or Wagner or Mozart.

GLASS: No, it didn't. What mattered was the stagecraft involved.

        I saw a wide variety of things in New York last year; every-
thing from Wozzeck to The Barber of Seville--which, by the way,
was the best piece I saw last year, without any doubt. It turned
out to be a wonderful piece. I'd always liked Rossini, but my respect for him increased in hearing all this other opera. Some of
it was just so dull, so deadly.

Q: You were talking about "sacred cows" in opera before. Have
you found that there is a bureaucracy within the world of opera
which is disturbed by your attempts to contribute to it?

GLASS: I find it at every turn. The thing that's most surprising
for them is that these operas sell out every seat; neither Einstein
on the Beach nor Satyagraha has played to an empty seat. That of
course gets some people really angry, and I don't mean the opera
administration. In Holland, local composers took great issue with
the work and mounted a very public campaign against it, on radio
and in the newspapers. It was obvious to everyone that there were
a lot of hurt feelings involved; as far as I could tell, the issues
really didn't go beyond that. These were people who had seemed
pretty friendly up to that point; I was quite astonished by it. Had
the opera been less of a success, I think they would have liked it
better.

Q: How much of that was sheer chauvinism, as opposed to outrage
over your departure from their definitions of opera?

GLASS: There was a lot of that involved: I, an American, had
come in and gotten a rather elaborate production in their opera
house--although their operas are being done there, too. In fact,

an American opera house has yet to mount a piece of mine; we brought our production of Einstein on the Beach here. Satyagraha will be done at Art Park and maybe the Brooklyn Academy of Music, and neither is really an opera house. Art Park is a summer festival, and while BAM has a beautiful opera house, and Harvey Lichtenstein has got to be one of the most interesting and imaginative producers in New York, it's not an opera company. But those are the people who are doing my work in America. In Europe, Satyagraha will play in Stuttgart as well as the Netherlands, and there'll be other places. But there's a certain resentment about that; there's a lot of jingoism in Europe. Although if the work's good enough, you can get away with it; then you just ignore it and let people scream and rave. It doesn't make for a lot of friendly intercourse with European artists, but that's the way it goes.

Q: Did Satyagraha present unique compositional problems for you, insofar as it meant writing music that was not for your own ensemble?

GLASS: I made a very interesting and, as it turned out, successful choice. Over the last eighteen years, I've been writing for the ensemble, and I had formed a very clear sound image in my mind—one which had become, just through insistence, identified with my work. When I approached the orchestra, I decided to make it sound like the ensemble. So the questions that I asked myself when I was orchestrating Satyagraha were quite different from the ones that I asked when I was writing for orchestra eighteen years ago. At that time, I was asking myself, "How do I make an orchestra sound?" On a simpler level, what I was really saying was, "What do I give the bass players to do? What do I give the clarinetist to do?"—as if I had to find employment for them. With Satyagraha I asked myself a very different question: "How can I make the orchestra sound like my music?"

The answers came very readily. For one thing, there's almost no soloistic writing in the opera at all: You never hear a flute alone; you usually hear it with an oboe or an electric organ. The sounds you get are all the compound textures you might get with an electric organ. The basic sound of my ensemble is dominated by electric organ and reeds, and so what I had in terms of a sound image was a composite sound. An organ often imitates the sound of orchestral colors, such as a horn or oboe—and of course it never really sounds like them. But I used the orchestra to imitate the sound of the organ, which in turn is an imitation of the orchestra. I turned the trick back onto itself. There are also many places in the orchestra for Satyagraha where, if I don't find that the instruments are useful, I don't use them; they just sit and count. There are other places where I'm using everybody all the time. In a number of places, everyone is playing in unison as loud as he can, which is a very typical Phil Glass sound.

In a way, I was more secure with the wind writing than

anything else because I've been writing for winds for all these years; I wrote very difficult parts for them. The wind players actually had to take the music home and practice it. I wrote things that were typical of my music which they weren't used to playing. They learned the music, although there were some complaints at first--and at the end, too. There were even a few people who walked out of the pit and refused to play the music. Some people seemed to actually like the music toward the end--it's hard to tell. But in a sense, I didn't really solicit their good will in that way: I was trying to make the music sound like my music, and sometimes the wind players had a hard time.

Q: In terms of the circular breathing or other special techniques a wind player needs to know in order to perform your music?

GLASS: I've learned how to cover that. I had three wind players on each part: three flutes, three oboes, and three clarinets. I often divisi them and have them play triadically, but then I tend to double up the oboes, clarinets, and flutes; I've long known that when you have enough people playing, you don't hear people breathing. When they asked, "Where should I breathe?" I said, "Don't worry about that; play as much as you can, the breathing will cover itself." And for the most part, it did. If you get that much woodwind sound going, people don't say, "Hey, the oboist has stopped playing"; by the time they notice that, the oboist has started again. (With my own ensemble, I cover that up in recordings by double tracking a lot.) I had nine wind players in the pit to cover the kind of wind playing that I wanted, and I was kind of careful to do it in such a way that they would overlap their parts. There are some places where they're playing straight through a scene for fifteen minutes and they really have to take turns. Then, sometimes they'd work it out, saying, "I'll take these two measures, you do those two." Sometimes the conductor--Bruce Ferden--encouraged them to do that, sometimes he told them to do free phrasing or free breathing wherever it seemed appropriate.

The orchestration of Satyagraha is a very big sound: I have 51 people in the pit--that's just about all you can fit into many a European pit anyway. I left out the brass because there was no place for them in the music. At the outset of the piece, the head of the opera asked me, "Well, what about the brass players? What should I do with them?" I said, "Send them home." He wasn't too happy about that, so I said, "Look, I'll tell you what: I'll write another piece for brass that they can do in another part of town at the same time." He took that suggestion rather badly; he thought I was pulling his leg, which I was to an extent. But had he taken me up on it, I would have done it. As it was, he just kind of shook his head and walked away, and that was the last that we talked about the orchestra. He had to pay the brass players anyway, and of course they were delighted. But it's all right; they're going to play in the next opera. They'll do double time then!

My point was that I had these people--the chorus, the singers, the orchestra--and it was my intention to bend them to the music and make it sound the way I wanted it to, rather than in the way
Sessions or someone else might have done it.   I wasn't interested
in discovering things in the instruments that may or may not be
there; those things don't interest me at all.   I got through the whole
opera without one pizzicato; I use mutes only in the last act, and
they could be used or not.   There are almost no tricks of that kind
at all.   I didn't look at the orchestra as a virtuoso instrument;
what I tried to do was, in a certain sense, make the orchestra disappear into the music.   At a certain point, I wanted you to forget
that you were hearing the orchestra.   I didn't want the orchestra
to do anything that drew attention to itself apart from the music--
which is not at all a common idea in contemporary music.   In fact,
I don't know any other orchestrator working now who would so frankly say that that's what he's doing.   Most composers feel compelled
to trot out a few tricks: a few fluttertongues, or something with
the back of the bow.   We've known all that for years; people have
been doing it since 1914 or 1915, and before.   But the same bag of
tricks still gets trotted out: glissandi and so forth--"ooh, ah, look
what he figured out; did you know that the French horn could do
that?"   Who cares?   Yet there's a whole tradition of contemporary
orchestral practice which is about precisely that.   I find it so boring; it seems to me that we've been hearing that music for 65 years.
In themselves, those things have no value whatsoever, no content at
all.   So I didn't look at the orchestra as a virtuoso instrument.
But the odd thing is that the piece is quite hard to play anyway.

Q: Do you foresee writing more and more music that is not for
your ensemble?

GLASS: That really comes down to what's interesting for me to do,
and the money involved and who'll do it.   I've been writing music
that's played for so long now, that I don't think I would consider
writing a piece that I didn't know was going to be played.   I don't
even start writing until I know when the piece is going to be played
and how much I'm going to be paid; it's a very practical enterprise
for me at this point.   The Stuttgart Opera has asked me for a new
opera and that's the next one I'll do, the Akhenaton one, which'll
be in '83.   But I've decided not to do more than one opera every
three years; that's as much as I should do.   I've talked to another
opera company about another opera in '85, so I can sort of stagger
those down the road and do other pieces in between.

Operas are paid pieces; you get paid when you write them,
and you get paid when people play them.   They're real good in that
way.   Opera is the only vein of gold that I've found in the music
business.   I'm just sorry that I didn't find out about it sooner!

Q: Could you see yourself writing a string quartet?

GLASS: I've written five string quartets; in fact, one of the first pieces I wrote which I wrote in the style that you would recognize as mine was a string quartet. If I wrote another one now, it would be my sixth quartet. (The second, third, and fourth were played; the first wasn't, and neither was the fifth--which is probably the only good one.) I was asked to write a quartet by a string quartet in Holland, I forget which one. I said I was interested in doing one, provided I had the time. We talked about the money right away, straightened that out; it was a businesslike discussion about when the piece would be ready and when they could do it. The difficulty was that I wasn't sure I had the time to do it. I'm working on Akhenaton now, and I've got to get into the music by this summer in order to deliver a score by the following fall, fourteen months after I start. Right now I'm working on the content of the opera; there are a lot of problems that I have to figure out. Again, there's the problem of language; again, the problem of structuring the piece sequentially but not narratively. Most importantly, I have to find out who I think Akhenaton was. I'm just not sure I have time to do a string quartet now. But I've had ideas for a string quartet, as well as for symphonies.

For me, the ensemble is still the main vehicle for the music. It's the best showcase for the music; it's the one that I control most directly, the one where I can appear as a performer. All those things are important to me. I really think of my music now as branching into three directions. One is the ensemble music, which has been the main thrust of it for the last twelve years. Second is the operas, which we can see leaping forward into the future. The third is the solo pieces I've been writing over the years; I also do solo concerts. I'm not so terribly interested in other people playing my music. The idea of a string quartet interests me, but I find that it doesn't have high priority for me right now, because of the other works that I'm doing. Right now I'm experiencing myself as a theater composer, after years of being a chamber music composer--because, for me, the ensemble was chamber music; amplified chamber music without strings. So it's more likely that the music that I write for other people will be in this genre.

Q: Will you continue to withhold your scores from publication?

GLASS: Publishers still haven't been able to interest me in what they can do. They promise me that they'll take 30 percent of everything that they make; beyond that, they won't promise anything. I formed a publishing company five years ago, and most of my income is from publishing. Publishing means print rights; mechanical rights, which is records; synchronization rights, which is movies and video; and performance rights, which is when anyone uses your music--a dance, for example. Those are the main areas of publishing, and I get income from all of those areas now. I belong to the proper societies, I've incorporated the company in New York

State, and I get checks from Europe, England--from the people who
use my work. Mike Oldfield put some of my music on one of his
records, and I got a lot of money. I didn't do anything, just gave
him mechanical license; that was $2\frac{1}{2}$ cents per record, and he sold
300,000 records. How's that? That was more money than I got
for writing the whole piece. If a TV station uses some work of
mine on a non-exclusive basis, they have to pay for that.

In Europe, if a theater piece is done, the theater must pay
the composer 8 percent of the box office. That's how composers
in Europe are able to live. They've worked that out because they're
anxious for their artists to be able to live like human beings. In
this country, we just don't give a shit, we don't care. We're interested in sports and television, and that's about it. To hell with
composers, they're beatniks, right? If they don't want to teach
school, then fuck 'em. We don't do anything for them at all. In
Europe there are ways that a composer's income can be assured
from the use of his work. So when a work of mine is done, even
when I'm not involved with it, I'm still paid as a publisher. Therefore, when a big publisher comes to me and says that they'll publish a work of mine, I see money flying away. The rentals on the
performance of an opera can be 800 dollars per performance, and
companies will often do ten performances in a year. If someone
takes 30 percent of that, it turns out to be real money.

Let's go over the things that I mentioned. The performance
rights I'm interested in restricting for my own use. As long as I
have a performing ensemble, I'm not interested in competing with
another group that's playing my music. The best way for me to
insure the viability of the ensemble is for it to be the only ensemble that can play my music; that's all I've got. That's the case
for performing rights, except for the operas. The print rights I'm
not interested in doing for the same reason. The synchronization
rights I can deal with directly through my own publishing company
and through collection agencies. The mechanical rights I can also
deal with directly with the record companies. So there seems to
be no place for a publisher right now, unless they were really willing to say, "Look, we're going to relieve you of all your financial
cares and woes." Then we could talk turkey. But they're not interested in that; they never have been. That's not the kind of relationship they have with composers; no matter what they say, their
relationship in the past has always been exploitative.

Q: You are virtually the only major composer today who has written
nothing for percussion, with the possible exception of $1 + 1$. Would
it be fair to say that you've gone out of your way to avoid it?

GLASS: Sure, yes. Very early I discovered that if I suppressed
the percussionist as a person in the group, it made everyone else
in the group become the percussionist. In other words, they became even more aware of the rhythmic value of what they were

doing; they also began to see the melodic contour of their part in
its rhythmic nature. Sometimes, just for fun in the studio I added
a drummer, and the sound became flabby. There may be another
way of approaching percussion, and maybe in another piece I'll do
that. I usually like to contradict myself; if I do something long
enough, after a while I'll do the opposite. So obviously it's only a
question of time before I write some stuff for percussion. But the
initial reason why I didn't was because the ensemble was the percussionist. We shared that role amongst ourselves, and it brought
a tightness to the music that I'm sure we otherwise wouldn't have
had. People begin to lean on a drummer; they rely on it, and it
makes the music less sharp for me.

It's just like me to solve a problem with a solution that's
so strange that it creates a whole bunch of aftereffects for the music. The decision to deal with percussion this way then informed
a lot of the character of the music. An early decision like that
often leads to unexpected results--and decisions in other areas as
well, whether it's timbre or pitch relationships. I've thought that
it's those limitations that have often given the music its distinctive-
ness.

Q: Has electronic music ever interested you at all; either other
people's works or the possibility of your using the medium yourself?

GLASS: Almost no interest whatsoever. We were talking about the
orchestra and the funny sounds it can make; this is almost on the
level of funny sounds for me. The real issue for me has always
been the language of music and not effects and "chinoiserie." I
haven't been drawn to music that's done that. Even when traditional composers have wandered into those areas, those are the pieces
that interest me the least. The Bartók music where he gets into
the night music stuff--rustlings and funny sounds in the dark--that
I've always found less interesting. For me, that was always music that was programmatic and on the surface; that's the way I've
related to it. Other people have found a great deal in that kind of
thing, but I found nothing in it. In my own music, I find almost
no need for it. I just don't think in those terms at all; I'm not
attracted to it.

Q: None of the composers we've spoken to have followed the developments in rock music with the interest and respect that you
have for it.

GLASS: The most important and vital new music scene today, for
me, has been in the clubs. The New Wave scene is basically another form of non-commercial music. Rhys Chatham was music director at The Kitchen, and I was an advisor there and talked with him

a lot about the programming. Two or three years ago, he told me that bands were requesting to play at The Kitchen. So I went to hear them, and I was very impressed with the music. I thought it was really interesting and lively, and much better than most of the experimental music that I had heard. This was a genre of music that was developing right under our feet, and which had no place to go. It was a form of pop music, but it wasn't commercial; their way of thinking about music was more like that of the avant-garde experimentalists. These were people who didn't have a hope of getting a record label, and even if they did, couldn't sell more than a couple of thousand records at the most. In an economic sense, they were more radical than most of the people that were on the CRI label. So I was looking at the music that way, and wondering, "Hey, who are these guys? Why are they doing this weird music and living these weird lives when they aren't making a lot of money?" I had been taught that you did pop music for money, but these people were obviously doing pop music and they weren't doing it for money. There were other values, another sensibility involved that was much more challenging and risky and innovative than what I was hearing coming out of the schools or from people that were imitating me.

So I began going around and listening to a lot of bands and I became friendly with a number of people that played in them. I enjoyed the music and found that in a certain way, they also identified with my music: the stripped-down quality and repetitiveness were things that I often heard in their music. I often found these people at my concerts, and then I would go to their concerts; someone like David Byrne has exchanged concert tickets with me many times. In a certain way, I have more of a real dialogue with these people than with the people in the so-called New Music scene. I've probably spent more time talking with these musicians than with the people who are in your book. (I doubt whether I've talked with anyone in the book at all.) We talk about things like recording techniques, recording contracts, publishing, who are the good promoters, who are the bad promoters, who makes good cases for traveling (we have a lot of instruments in common, different kinds of electric organs): things that are in the day-to-day life of a musician, the practical things. We rarely talk about music, but neither do most composers. I've probably talked about it more with you than I will with other composers.

I find their approach to their music serious, lively, risky; these guys are doing all the things that artists are supposed to be doing. It's a hand-to-mouth trip. I don't know any of them that are doing it for the money. If they thought they were, they'd be crazy; even the successful ones aren't making that much money. It's not about money. You're more likely to find people in the straight music world who are interested in money. This is almost an art rock trip, but it's not that arty either; it's something more committed than than, and it's very serious.

Q: We'd like to talk to you about the impact your music has on audiences, particularly young audiences. Recently, you played with your ensemble at a rock club in New York, and the entire audience stood clustered about the stage for 75 minutes in dead silence-- which is not the way that they would listen to a rock group. And this was not a crowd of your fans; a lot of these people had never heard your music before. Why does the music evoke this kind of response?

GLASS: I don't know. It's strange. It's clear that, apart from all the more or less theoretical things that we've touched upon in this talk, and apart from the ideas that are contained in the content of the music, the music has a very visceral effect. On some level, the music depends on and aims at a very visceral reaction. I think there's sufficient intellectual content in the music; someone could go through a score like Einstein and find a lot there just on the level of analysis. But I don't think that that's what the response of the audience is about--then again, I think that may have been true of someone like Wagner too. I don't know if I want to divide music into the head trips and the body trips, but if you were to talk in this way, this music is a very physical experience. It's disarming for many people too, partly because of the amplification, but mainly because of the directness of it. It's very hard to evade the point of the music; you have to just downright not like it--and plenty of people respond like that too. But to respond to it at all is to have to take it on its own terms.

What I see that's nice about the response of the kids is that the cerebration--is that a real verb?--that goes into the music on my part actually translates into highly emotive stuff that people get bowled over by. Some of these things I just think of in my head, and they come out in the musical content in that way. I mentioned before that I've never seen an audience still seated after hearing the Spaceship of Einstein. I play with the same people all the time: Michael Riesman has been with me for six or seven years now, Richard Peck and Kurt Munkacsi for ten, Jon Gibson for twelve years, Iris Hiskey for five or six years, and Jack Kripl--he was one of the first people I played with in Paris in 1965; I lost track of him and then he came back to play with me last year to replace Dickie Landry, who began a solo career. And after a concert where we've played the Spaceship, we've talked about why that happens. I think it's the chords. Sometimes I think it's those changes; there's something about that that seems to work that way.

The trouble is that a lot of the content of the music that has a direct, biological effect is what we know least about music--at least in our Western tradition. We know that there are Asian and Central Asian traditions where the response mechanisms of music were once known. We hear of music that was used medicinally, to cure headaches, create paralysis, or calm hysteria. I don't know anything about that music itself, but I've read about it, I've heard about it. I'm sure that it existed; even on a crude level, we can see that it's happening in a lot of Western music. It's not hard to imagine a science of music which took advantage of and directly induced psychological/biological states. It may even be a practice that's still current in parts of the world, but politics being what they are, those places are hard to get to these days. It's a Sufi tradition, so you might find that kind of thing in parts of Iran or northern Afghanistan; parts of Russia, too. It's not likely that we're going to go there, though. I think those things were always somewhat secret to begin with, too. So for our purposes, I think those things are lost.

I remember that once I gave a talk about music in that way, and someone came up to me afterward and said that he knew about that tradition and that it was in fact still alive. He was non-Western, but not from one of those parts of the world. He rattled off the name of some book about it, which I'd never heard of. I didn't pursue it; I figured that part of being a Westerner is being dumb in that way--it's part of my heritage!

Q: Could you tell us about the Akhenaton opera that you're working on now? Did you have an interest in Velikovsky's writings like your interest in Gandhi?

GLASS: I was reading Velikovsky for the fun of it--I think that's a good way to read Velikovsy! I'm not a scientist; I don't care what Carl Sagan thinks about Velikovsky, that doesn't matter to me at all. But I like Velikovsky because his mind was so lively; he asked so many questions, he turned over so many stones in looking for things. That's how I came across the Akhenaton story. He was an 18th Dynasty Pharaoh who lived in the fourteenth century B.C. What appealed to me about Akhenaton was that I saw that it could fit in with the other two characters, Einstein and Gandhi. Like those people, he was a composite character. Gandhi was both a politician and perhaps a saint; Einstein was a scientist and perhaps a poet. Akhenaton was another religious person who worked as a law giver--more as a law giver than as a revolutionary, which was what Gandhi tried to be. Like them, he was a composite person who changed the world that he lived in; the world was a different place after he left. Again, he was a person who had controversy attending everything he did. He seems to me to be almost a brother to them. In fact, the Stuttgart Opera is treating the three subjects as a trilogy. They'll present them that way, which'll be fun. They're doing Satyagraha in '81, Akhenaton in '83, and they'll do all three operas in '85--that's their intention. Leave it to the Germans, huh?

CATALOG OF COMPOSITIONS

1965   Music for Woodwind Quartet and Two
        Actresses   MS

1965	Music for Small Ensemble	MS
1965	Incidental Music for Play	Dunvagen
1965	String Quartet	Dunvagen
1967	600 Lines for ensemble (two electric organs, woodwinds, voice)	Dunvagen
1967	Trio for Violin, Cello, and Piano	Dunvagen
1967	Strung Out for (amplified) violin	Dunvagen
1967	Two Down for two soprano saxophones	Dunvagen
1968	Music in the Shape of a Square for two flutes	Dunvagen
1968	Solo for Jon Gibson for soprano saxophone	Dunvagen
1968	In Again Out Again for two pianos or electric keyboards	Dunvagen
1968	How Now for ensemble or solo keyboard	Dunvagen
1969	1 + 1 for solo performer and amplified table top	Dunvagen
1969	Two Pages for ensemble or solo keyboard	Dunvagen
1969	Music for Eight Parts for ensemble	Dunvagen
1969	Music in Fifths for ensemble	Dunvagen
1969	Music in Contrary Motion for ensemble or solo organ	Dunvagen
1969	Music in Similar Motion for ensemble	Dunvagen
1970	Incidental Music for The Red Horse Animation	Dunvagen
1970	Music with Changing Parts for ensemble	Dunvagen
1972	Music for Voices	Dunvagen
1973	Incidental Music for The Saint and the Football Players	Dunvagen
1974	Incidental Music for The Lost Ones	Dunvagen
1974	Music in Twelve Parts for ensemble	Dunvagen
1975	Another Look at Harmony, Parts 1 and 2 for ensemble	Dunvagen
1975	Incidental Music for Cascando--Another Look at Harmony, Part 3 for solo cello, solo voice, and solo organ	Dunvagen
1975	Einstein on the Beach with Robert Wilson, opera in four acts for ensemble, solo voice, chorus, solo violin, actors, and dancers	Dunvagen
1976	Film Music for Mark DiSuvero, Sculptor	Dunvagen
1977	Another Look at Harmony, Part 4 for chorus and electric organ	Dunvagen
1977	Incidental Music for Modern Love Waltz	Dunvagen
1977	Modern Love Waltz for piano	CF Peters*
1978	Fourth Series, Part 1 for organ	Dunvagen

*By arrangement with Dunvagen Music

1978	Music for a Performance/Reading by C. deJong--Fourth Series, Part 2 for flute and harmonica	Dunvagen
1979	Dance Nos. 1-5 for ensemble (Nos. 2 and 4 also for organ)--Fourth Series, Part 3	Dunvagen
1979	Film Music for Geometry of a Circle	Dunvagen
1979	Incidental Music for Mercier and Camier	Dunvagen
1979	Satyagraha opera in three acts for six soloists, chorus, and orchestra	Dunvagen
1980	Music/Theater No. 1 A Madrigal Opera for solo violin, solo viola, and six voices	Dunvagen
1980	Incidental Music for Dead End Kids	Dunvagen

photo: Gene Bagnato

Lejaren Hiller was born on February 23, 1924, in
New York City. He studied composition with Harvey
Officer and oboe with Joseph Marx. At Princeton he
received his B. A., M. A., and Ph. D. in chemistry,
and studied theory and composition with Milton Babbitt and Roger Sessions. He received his M. Mus.
from the University of Illinois in 1958, where he
founded the Experimental Music Studio. Hiller is
currently Slee Professor of Composition at the State
University of New York at Buffalo. In 1945, he married Elizabeth Halsey. They have two children.

In 1957, Hiller collaborated with Leonard Isaacson
on the Illiac Suite, the first significant use of a computer in composition. Over the years, he has remained at the forefront of this area of music. But
his energetic and inquisitive mind and his considerable
musical talent have carried him into a wide range of
compositional methods and media: electronic music,
indeterminacy, serialism, theatricality, tonality.
All of his works display his distinctive profile: a
special blend of wit, intellect, and imagination.

The authors interviewed Lejaren Hiller in their
Buffalo motel room on May 25, 1980. They quickly
discovered that the humor and informality that characterize many of his works are very much his own
qualities as well. Even more unusual and impressive
was his generosity: He loaned and gave them tapes
and documents which greatly facilitated their work on
Hiller and on other composers as well.

Q: We'd like to start with your studies at Princeton with Roger
Sessions and Milton Babbitt.

HILLER: I went to Princeton because I saw a college catalog one
day and it sounded nice; my choice was as random as that. At that
time, I was interested in chemistry, but had also started some music studies; I'd been taking private lessons in New York City with
Harvey Officer, learning harmony, counterpoint, and piano. By
the time I had graduated from high school, I had written a few simple things like a graduation march for our class. (I recently discovered in an old envelope two short orchestral pieces from around
1939 I had thought I had long since lost or destroyed.)

So I just dropped into the music department office at Princeton, and Milton Babbitt happened to be standing there. I said I
wanted to study music. He said, "Well, sure, we'll take you on;

we'll put you in my sophomore class in strict counterpoint." So it was with Milton that I did my first actual formal studying. This was species counterpoint. He was a thorough teacher in this subject and I've never regretted that.

It was a very small department in those days. Sessions and Babbitt took care of most of the theory and composition teaching. I studied basics with Milton, and then moved into Roger Sessions' classes in elementary composition and analysis. I was very definitely interested in pursuing this, even though I was majoring in chemistry. When Sessions quit Princeton in '45 and went to Berkeley, I was studying fugue with him and he urged me to come along-- or, possibly, to study with another composer. He suggested people like Darius Milhaud or Křenek. He liked the idea of people switching to different teachers; he even offered to try and put me with Schoenberg. However, by then I was very much involved with the graduate program in chemistry and was about to become a research assistant in a newly formed "Textile Research Institute," starting work in cellulose chemistry that eventually led to my doctoral dissertation.

Q: So it wasn't a particular interest in the style of composition of Babbitt or Sessions that brought you to them.

HILLER: I was too innocent to know about such things. Neither Sessions nor Babbitt stressed modernism in their teaching, at least not at the level I was at. Almost everything I was told about dealt with Mozart or Beethoven; for example, the models for composition exercises were the Beethoven piano sonatas. There was very little talk about contemporary music in class; Sessions did not discuss twelve-tone music and all that. Of course, twelve-tone wasn't popular in those days, as you know; neo-classicism was the going thing.

As far as Babbitt's music is concerned, I heard some piano music in one concert, but that's about all. You've got to realize that he was a very young person then; I'm not even sure his style was entirely formed.

Q: Then you're self-taught in the area of serial techniques?

HILLER: Oh, yes, entirely. Once I had quit studying with Sessions, I didn't have any other teachers except Hubert Kessler at the University of Illinois years later, and that was primarily Schenker analysis--things of that sort--plus about a year of polishing up compositional techniques. So essentially, I was self-taught from 1945 on.

Q: One unusual aspect of your career is the amount of time you spent away from music. After graduating from Princeton, you worked for DuPont for five years, and then taught chemistry at the University of Illinois for another six years. You didn't work professionally in music until you began teaching it at Illinois in 1958. Had you wanted to change over to music prior to that point?

HILLER: Yes, indeed, I did; the desire grew and grew and grew, so to speak. But it was not as easy to do as you might think. It got to be very frustrating, because by the middle fifties I'd turned out quite a bit of music, but all as an avocation and none of it had ever been performed.

I became upset about the whole situation because music became more and more a compelling interest. Also, I became aware of the fact that if you're not inside the field professionally, you are simply written off as non-existent: "Who's this chemist writing music? We don't want to be bothered with him."

So until I wrote the famous Illiac Suite--which was the door that opened lots of things--I had never had a complete piece of music played at a concert, even though I was over thirty years old. I was writing in a complete vacuum, and of course after a while that got to be a situation which was more and more unpleasant because it was so frustrating. The only person who was at all sympathetic was Milton Babbitt. I would see him now and then socially in New York, but in all fairness to him, I guess he could hardly take me seriously until something really happened to excite his interest. Once I did the computer music, his attitude changed in terms of really wanting to give me a push professionally. Maybe all this sounds worse than it really was because I should remind you that chemical research had been my first choice for a career and it was one from which I derived much satisfaction. I had published a number of research articles and a chemistry textbook, and had some patents, including one rather important basic one dealing with the dyeing of acrylic fibers like "Orlon."

Q: Was it difficult to switch from teaching chemistry to teaching music at the same university?

HILLER: Well, it was astonishing to people that I made such a switch.

I wrote the Illiac Suite and that hit the headlines--quite literally. All of a sudden I went from a nobody to somebody who was actually on the front page of many newspapers--usually in the most absurd kind of news article, but nevertheless, it drew attention to me.

I mentioned to Frederick Wall, who was not only the dean of the graduate school at Illinois but also the man who had hired me to work for him when I left DuPont in 1952, that I was frustrated with teaching chemistry and was thinking of leaving. He said, "Well, you shouldn't do that; what would you like to do?" I said, "I'd really like to start an electronic music studio, or something of that sort." So he called up the director of the school of music, and they discussed my idea for a while, and then invited me to come over to the music department and do just that.

They did this during the summer because they anticipated that there would be serious opposition to me in the music department. So I was sort of brought in by the back door, because I don't think I ever would have gotten the job if it had gone through conventional channels; some people had already become livid with rage over Illiac Suite. One of my few supporters out there in those days was Ben Johnston.

I started by teaching musical acoustics, and used this as a way also to introduce electronic music into the curriculum. I did in fact teach musical acoustics of the traditional sort; how instruments behave, and so forth. But also I started the studio in an attic across the street from the music building. As you probably know already, it was the second electronic music studio to get started in this country.

I had forgotten to mention earlier that yet another aspect of my technical background came into use here. I had had, among other things, a number of courses in electrical engineering and electronics at Princeton, and of course nothing could have served my needs better than this in 1958 in getting the studio started.

You might be amused to know that one day back then the editor of American Men of Science called me up from Arizona and said, "Mr. Hiller, what are we going to do with you? You were in physical science, and you can't go into music! How am I going to list you in my book?" I said, "Well, you can call me an information theory specialist," and he said, "OK."

Q: Was it your decision to approach John Cage and initiate all the work that eventually became HPSCHD?

HILLER: No, it was John's. I was sitting around one day and the phone rang. It was John, and he said, "I'd like to do some computer music with you. Is there any chance I could come to Illinois?" (He was down in Cincinnati.) I said, "Well, I don't know. Let me look around and see what I can do." After talking to various people at Illinois, I was able to get him appointed as an associate Member of the Center for Advanced Study at Illinois. I had been one of these a year or so previously. This Center, which had some faculty and a number of outsiders in it, was modeled after the one at Princeton (but much more modestly). You could get salary for a year or so without having regular teaching duties, doing instead whatever research you wanted. So one way or another we worked it out, and John became an Associate Member for 1967-1968. Later on, they renewed his appointment for the following year.

When he came he brought with him two basic projects which he wanted to work on with me and with computers. One eventually became HPSCHD. The other was something to do with computer sound synthesis and modification of thunder sounds; he had an idea for a piece about thunder and had gotten some tapes of real thunder that had been recorded in various places. Somehow we never got around to that piece, and it's never been done so far as I know.

All HPSCHD was initially was a commission for a piece for solo harpsichord by Antoinette Vischer. She had commissioned a number of contemporary composers for new harpsichord pieces; I think Luciano Berio and Duke Ellington, for example, also wrote pieces for her. John and I sat in a trailer on the back of our property, and the ideas got more and more grandiose; the modest commission grew into that mammoth piece.

Our first project was simply to see if we could program the I Ching oracle; we did that and got it working. Then he spoke about the idea of doing something with Mozart. He said, "It's not only Satie who's one of my favorite composers, but also Mozart"--which most people don't realize. I guess he likes the clarity of these composers. So we decided to make the work a kind of homage to Mozart, as you well know. The idea of the Mozart dice-game came rather late. I don't remember just how it happened; I think I thought that one up because it too was a chance piece. We located the score and programmed how to make the solos from it. I don't remember either how the idea came about to substitute other composers in the solos with the I Ching; we were probably out there in the trailer telling anecdotes or something like that and it just happened. I really don't remember.

We got all the programming done by the summer of '68, when I left to come to Buffalo; into September, I was frantically on the telephone, still having assistants running tapes off every day. During that second year, John stayed on at Illinois and did all the preparations for the premiere, such as getting the parts copied and tapes edited. I went out there in December to help him prepare the collage for the Nonesuch record. We got the tape background done, and later he recorded the three solos. We put all this on a tape and Nonesuch had the disc all done before the performance, which is sort of amusing. As for the computer printout for twirling the knobs which went with the record, I think I thought that one up--again, I don't really remember. Anyway, I ran that material off here in Buffalo.

HPSCHD was truly a collaboration, which was not the original idea at all. I had planned to get Cage started, perhaps locate a programming assistant for him and let him proceed on his own. I was busy programming both Avalanche and Algorithms I. But I got more and more intrigued with the project, so that when the day arrived when Cage proposed an authentic collaboration, I found it impossible to turn down. Cage told me it's the only time he's really collaborated in that way; when he composed Double Music with Lou Harrison, it was all done by long-distance telephone. I was more used to collaborating because of the earlier computer pieces, such as the Computer Cantata with Robert Baker or the Illiac Suite with Leonard Isaacson.

Q: You've collaborated in the making of pieces far more than most other composers have. A lot of these pieces involved computer programming. Is that a factor which necessitated collaboration?

HILLER: No, not at all; it was convenience. Isaacson was a chemist like me. We just got talking about the idea of programming counterpoint, and he was interested in it as an abstract project in computer programming. He was a super programmer. Robert Baker, who worked on the Computer Cantata with me, was then a graduate student in music composition; a very bright young composer, who wrote "straight" music as well. He did this programming as part of his doctoral dissertation. That's how a lot of the collaborations came about--also some of the research articles on information theory and music theory that I've published. Ravi Kumra, who worked with me on Algorithms II, was a graduate student in computer science. He sought me out, came all the way from India; he had done a project in programming strict counterpoint at the Indian Institute of Technology in New Delhi.

I've noticed that a fair number of the younger composers take to programming very rapidly. In fact, the computer department at Illinois used to hire them away from me because they had more money for programming than I did. I should point out also that, having been in science, I was used to collaboration; there it's the norm, you see. I don't find it ego-threatening, like I suppose many composers do.

An analogous situation would be some of the theater pieces where I've worked with playwrights on original scripts. A good example is Avalanche. Frank Parman is a close friend, and the two of us actually assembled Avalanche in stages; I thought about the music, he thought about the text, and back and forth it went. So collaboration has nothing to do with computers, per se.

Q: So in the future you might collaborate with someone on a piece which has nothing to do with computers.

HILLER: Oh, sure, sure.

Q: In the mid-sixties, you said: "My objective in composing music by means of computer programming is not the immediate realization of an aesthetic unity, but the providing and evaluating of techniques whereby this goal can eventually be realized."

HILLER: Well, I've changed my ideas somewhat. I think that was a correct approach, and still is, as with some of my newer computer music for which I provide rather elaborate documentation of what I do. For me and for the relatively few other people who are interested in composing with computers rather than in synthesizing sounds with them, the interest has been in process as well as in end product. It's just like the way one reads articles about serial methodology, which explain how one does what one does. Otherwise, the result, the music itself, may not make a lot of sense, at least initially.

Nowadays I think that my computer pieces possess more expressive content than I would have first guessed. In other words, I hear in the pieces more of a reflection of my general approach to music than I would have supposed at the beginning. I don't find even the Illiac Suite that far disjunct from the other things I do. I suppose that my programming contains biases that are subjective. Other people have made this comment; they say, "Well, that's all very well; the programs you've written suit you, but they don't necessarily suit me." That's one of the reasons why it's been hard to convince people that this is a legitimate way to compose. It's much more difficult to generalize a whole method of composition than it is to create sounds as with MUSIC V. The practical value is not quite so easy to demonstrate.

Anyway, I've come to change from that older point of view. Certainly HPSCHD reflects both Cage and myself very accurately and in many ways: not just the computer element, of course, but the theatrical element, the whimsy, the things of this sort. Also, I've used computer methods for more recent pieces which seem very much personalized. Persiflage, for example, seems like mainstream Hiller to me. I also went back some years ago and re-labeled the Illiac Suite "String Quartet Number 4" in order to incorporate it within a set of what are now seven quartets. I don't consider it that peculiar, even though I wouldn't write in a style like that at my desk.

Q: How much closer then have we actually come to this goal of realizing genuine aesthetic unities?

HILLER: I think that's the main problem that's going to have to be faced during the next decade or two. It's taken longer than I would have guessed. Of course, I myself have contributed only part of my composing time to writing computer music. I get involved with many other kinds of projects. Right now, I'm finishing Algorithms III--

finally, after much delay. I now have one movement of it done,
and I'm working on the remaining ones. I hope to finish up that
whole cycle, then review the whole situation as far as I'm concerned and probably publish some sort of monograph on all my
computer music to date. I have much of this already written up
as so-called technical reports, but of course all the material in
these reports would have to be boiled down. With the new kinds
of programming techniques now coming in, I think that the approach
I've taken over the years would probably have to be modified, primarily in terms of a more general approach.

I tend in my work to take a very practical approach: A
harp has certain constraints that have to be dealt with--you can do
this, but you can't do that. Or a certain kind of melodic line is
specified to have such-and-such properties. I think a certain kind
of more advanced algebra could handle a lot of these things in a
context that isn't quite as literal as the one I tend to use. But
I've always worked in a very practical way--get pieces out, get
them performed, and see what's wrong with them (so to speak)--
rather than try to develop such a general algebra that I would spend
a lifetime making work and have nothing much to show for it in the
concert hall. There's where you learn whether what you did worked
or didn't work: Can you hear what you programmed? That's really what it boils down to. If yes, then perhaps it has some use; no,
then you've gone off into a dead end. That's been part of the learning experience for me.

So I hope now that I will get this project cleaned up; that's
my number-one priority at the moment, as a matter of fact. And
then publish a substantial how-I-did-it type of report that would be
generally available. One of the reasons why I haven't written many
articles lately is that I've been collecting all this material to pack
into one volume. In there I hope to do some reflecting on what,
if anything, I've achieved aesthetically. Clearly, I'm hedging my
answer to your question in the time being.

Q: It's curious that you're so involved with computer music, and
yet have written only a few pieces for solo tape. Do you prefer
combining tape with live performers?

HILLER: So it seems. But I have a large, new solo tape piece
called Electronic Sonata. It's a whopper.

For the bicentennial, I was commissioned by a group called
BHAM in St. Louis. On the night of July 3rd, and the start of the
4th, we set up the whole downtown of St. Louis as an electronic environment; many, many streets with loudspeakers in them. It made
HPSCHD look like chamber music! It covered some twelve or fifteen city blocks; the main area of downtown St. Louis, all cordoned
off by the police. We must have had twenty or thirty thousand peo-
ple--something of that sort. It was like a huge rock concert. The

sounds bounced off the architecture and cascaded through these streets--it was very nice. All sorts of people were invited to contribute to this environment; bringing laser beam shows, ultrasonic environments, little mini-Moog set-ups in foyers of business buildings and so on and on. It was a big carnival atmosphere.

That big "outdoor piece," which was for 46 channels of tape (if I remember rightly), was called Midnight Carnival, and ran about four or five hours. Out of the so-called "core tape," I extracted a more practical piece which I call Electronic Sonata; that's the "indoor piece." It's a four-channel composition (or reduced to two for practical situations), runs 53 minutes, and is pure tape.

Electronic Sonata has been "performed"--if you want to call it that--a number of times. It's a mixture of concrete sounds and computer-generated sounds. In it, I also did something that's rather seldom done in computer sound: I used analog-to-digital conversion. That is, I put concrete sounds into the computer, altered and transformed them in various ways, and then brought them back out again. One of the things that has disappointed me so far about computer sound processing has been the very limited use of input of sounds into computers. That's one of the things which I'm particularly interested in doing more with here in Buffalo. It's perfectly practical technically, and it's obvious you can do a great deal with voices, concrete sounds, and all the rest with computer algorithms.

Q: Several of your pieces from the mid-sixties--Computer Cantata, Seven Electronic Studies, the Fifth String Quartet, HPSCHD--utilize microtonal scales. Had your work with electronics led you to microtonality, or had you been interested in composing that way for a while?

HILLER: Some of both, I would say. It was obvious to me that there was no earthly reason to stick to the tempered scale once you were into electronic music. We did not have a keyboard unit at Illinois back in 1958, which I now think was a blessing, considering all the junk "composed" today with keyboard-controlled synthesizers. This occurred to me even with my earliest tape piece, Blue is the Antecedent of It, and especially in my Seven Electronic Studies, which you just mentioned. I was also interested in microtonalities just from the point of view of musical acoustics. And I was very much fascinated with Harry Partch's work. Don't forget that he was at Illinois at that very same period. In fact, Harry became a pretty good friend of ours. One of the major roles in Revelation in the Courthouse Park, the leader of the chorus, was written for my wife because he liked her work as an actress. Of course, I got to know his theories and was intrigued with the instruments--who wouldn't be? A lot of things converged to make this an interest of mine.

One of the first things I bought for the studio at Illionis was a frequency counter, and I began tuning things very tightly. It was amazing what it did to my ear, in terms of hearing differences between, say, a pure fifth and a tempered fifth, or hearing partials and overtones. I became intrigued with a lot of these details which you normally don't think much about when you're dealing with an instrumental ensemble. The so-called "gestalts" of the sounds begin to unravel for me a great deal, even in a distressing way occasionally.

Q: Do you find it more satisfactory to compose microtonally for tape or for traditional instruments?

HILLER: Well, the Fifth Quartet's been my lame duck; only the Concord Quartet has tackled it. My Sixth Quartet, which is much more recent, has had many more performances. But the Fifth has been a hard one to mount because performers look at those quarter-tones and groan in despair. It's too bad, because one has favorites among one's own pieces, and the Fifth Quartet's one of mine. So most of my microtonal music has been for tape for practical reasons.

Q: You've written several theatrical pieces. Do you see any distinction between them and opera?

HILLER: No, not really. People have asked me, "Why don't you write an opera?" In fact, I got a letter just the other day requesting me to compose one. For some reason, I've gotten close, but never around to doing it. I think it's because, largely through my wife, I've been more involved in other types of theatrical environments--spoken theater in particular. I started out writing incidental music for well-known plays by Ibsen, Strindberg, Pirandello, Aristophanes. That's how I learned ordinary theatrical know-how. I think that was very valuable, because when you have a given script, and you have to set a scene that the director wants to last $2\frac{1}{2}$ minutes, for example, you can't just ramble on and on musically. It's got to fit. It also has to express the mood of the text and, above all, not overwhelm it.

I moved on to original scripts with my early electronic pieces, and then more and more into multi-media. Actually, getting back to the question of opera, I've not written much vocal music; Five Appalachian Ballads is one example, Jesse James another. The Computer Cantata happened because Helen Hamm was an excellent singer and was willing to do it for me. I've composed a lot of songs in my theater music; The Birds is full of songs. So there's a fair amount of song literature, but it's usually embedded in something else.

But I've never dealt with something that's straight opera. I came close to it with a recent piece called Ponteach. Although now it's a melodrama for speaker and piano about Ponteach, the Indian chief, originally I planned it as a chamber opera. By the way, the Gregg Smith Singers recently recorded my Portfolio for CRI; it's a piece for up to ten performers of any sort, and up to eight channels of tape. Since its scoring is indeterminate, it's a practical piece, all sorts of groups have performed it: an old music instrument group, solo cello, ten instrumentalists, and singers too.

Q: In thinking about pieces of yours from the mid-sixties and on, like HPSCHD, Avalanche, or even the Quartetto Miniaturo and its four simultaneous movements which ends your Fifth Quartet, one is automatically reminded of Charles Ives. But Jesse James also suggests Ives, and that was written in 1950, well before the real Ives renaissance began. There are really two questions: Had you known Ives' music thirty years ago, and does it have much of an appeal for you now?

HILLER: The answer in both instances is yes, although I didn't know much about Ives thirty years ago; how could I find the material? The very first Ives I heard was over station WNYC in New York, when I was in high school. They played six songs that were on an ancient disc that New Music Edition put out. But the songs caught my ear immediately, particularly Charlie Rutledge. That was the very first piece of his I ever heard, and I thought, "Boy, that's pretty good stuff." I liked it right away. (I think it was perhaps the same week, over the same station, that I first heard a piece of Varèse--Density 21.5--and that also impressed me.) This was long before I knew much of anything about sophisticated music; I was struggling to learn who Beethoven was. I started in pop music, basically.

Kirkpatrick's first recording of the Concord Sonata came out around then; I listened to that, and it didn't make too much sense. Then I heard a violin sonata, under what circumstances I don't remember. Later I was running a little concert series in Virginia, and a pianist named Paul Moor brought a program that, for the hills of Virginia, was provocative--to put it mildly: things like the Aaron Copland Piano Variations, the Bartók Out of Doors Suite. He also included the Hawthorne movement of the Concord Sonata. That was about 1950, thereabouts. So I had a smattering of an introduction to his music, and I liked it--but I didn't know quite why.

Over the years, like everyone else, I got to know more and more of his music. I continue to be intrigued by it. Thus, for example, I just taught a course this semester on Ives, along with the people like Varèse, Antheil, and Ruggles. So I'm very sympathetic to it. I recognize, like a lot of people, some of Ives' problems of adjustment and why he stopped composing because his small-town nostalgia no longer fitted the twenties. But I think he is an amazing composer. Certainly, you're not the first ones to comment on the idea that my music has Ivesian things in it; that's been quite common in reviews--at least in ones that don't tear me to pieces! Ives and Cage are often mentioned as composers I resemble, at least in general if not necessarily in detail. But I don't think it has been conscious as such; it just came naturally.

Q: Your music moves freely from serial organization to chance methods to computer techniques, even using all three in a single piece.

HILLER: And tonality too--which is very old-fashioned!

Q: Do you find combining these approaches difficult, or do you think there's much more common ground among them than has been traditionally suggested?

HILLER: My general approach is empirical and eclectic. Of course, I don't mean that in the pejorative sense. I just assume that everything and anything can go into a piece if it is appropriate. So, for example, I'll write tonal music if I want to; I'll even insert key signatures if it is useful, something which some people regard as provocative. Naturally, I'm not interested in reviving tonality, or neo-classicism, Lord knows. But I will use tonal elements when I think they're appropriate and embed them in a more general structure.

While I'm on the subject of using traditional materials like tonality, I must emphasize that I'm not reacting against more modern compositional techniques, like some other composers are. Some say that everything that's going on today is wicked and destructive and therefore we should go back to our old moorings. Obviously, I don't feel that way at all. Nor do I particularly like the idea of becoming either overly dogmatic or overly simplistic--the kind of mini-aesthetic which is very popular in Europe, for example, at the present time. Taking a tiny tune and them elaborating upon it ad nauseam; there's a redundancy which gets on my nerves after a while.

But I certainly use tonal methods, serial methods, of course, chance methods, charts, mathematical formulas like Fibonacci series, eye music--you name it. And all of this with or without computers and electronics. But again I say that I try all of them in what you might call a total matrix of possibilities.

In the mid-'50s, with regard to concepts of musical structure, I certainly was helped a great deal by being introduced to the Schenker theory of hierarchy in music. That clarified a lot of muddled thinking on my part. It permitted me to see beyond the tonal context of prolongation of the tonic chord, and made me aware of generative grammars (in terms of language structures) and eventually of information theory. I could see that the question of moving from order to disorder, back and forth, was really what a composer deals with. When you talk about such things as Leonard Meyer's theories of musical affect, you are really talking about order and disorder in the most broad and general sense: A person becomes more disturbed when the number of possibilities increase; disorder increases and you build tension, and then resolutions come when one arrives at more organized, more static situations. This is what causes the ebb and flow of drama in a piece. So I think that any element that can cause this to happen is fine.

I have another fetish, namely, that I don't like to repeat myself any more than I can help. I try to make each piece a new point of departure. So there's very little repetition of structure or gesture or expression to my music; each piece is different. Once I've done a project, I tend to drop it and go on with something else if I possibly can. Through all this variety, I nevertheless think there remains the thread of a given composer's profile--mine-- which makes the music clearly identifiable and not just bland, mainstream "modern music." For example, two of my most recent pieces are for folk instruments. One is for a "devil's fiddle," which I bought in a souvenir shop in Poland. Diabelskie Skrzypce is the name of both the piece and the instrument. It's a stick of wood upon which is mounted a little drum that looks like a tambourine with jingles, and it had three wires running down it. I replaced these three wires with cello strings, because the wires were made of copper, believe it or not, which you cannot tune. I put a bridge on the instrument, so you can play the fiddle just as if you were playing on the G, D, and A strings of a cello. It has a very different sound from a cello, much smaller. Then I wrote the composition for that instrument and harpsichord. My most recent piece is for piccolo and berimbau, a Brazilian percussion instrument made out of a piece of bamboo, a coconut shell, and a single iron wire that's rapped. This is a far cry from computer music, you see. (I'm not going to build up a large inventory of pieces for unusual instruments, however, because you get into a trap: You can't easily get them performed.)

One attitude these recent pieces reflect is what I might call my residential or geographic aesthetic. When I'm living in a place I tend to respond to it and write a piece that says something about it. So, in a general sense, Diabelskie Skrzypce is about the year in Poland, and An Apotheosis of Archaeopterix (the piccolo and berimbau work) obviously has to do with Brazil. I wrote a piece called Malta for tuba and tape in response to living in Malta. Ponteach is about the Mohawk and Illinois Indians, hence the Great Lake region; I also wrote a piece called Spoon River, Illinois, when I lived in Urbana.

Q: Has your eclecticism annoyed some of your colleagues who would feel tied to one approach more than another?

HILLER: I don't know. I suppose so, but people don't talk to me about it too often. Anyway, it wouldn't make any difference. I'm independent, and write the way I want to regardless of what is supposed to be proper and respectable. When my Suite for Two Pianos and Tape was played in New York, one composer came up to me afterwards at the reception. I was near the table, gnawing on a shrimp, and he picked up a shrimp, bit off half of it, and said, "People shouldn't write retrograde pieces on a tonal basis!" (The waltz in the Suite runs front and back.) "Only serialists can do this," he said, and stalked off.

Q: You've published a great many articles, but they're almost all technical pieces. Have you wanted to write more aesthetic or polemical articles?

HILLER: Polemical pieces, no, not particularly. And writing about general aesthetics seems like an awful lot of work. My general attitudes are being expressed to you right now--the kinds of things I've been talking about. I've written synopses and analyses of all of the pieces I've written, but they're rather brief. They're kind of blown-up program notes, to save me from writing such notes over and over again.

As you say, in writing I've concentrated rather narrowly on technical things, because that seemed the most necessary thing to do. I don't particularly like writing articles about the state of music in general; lots of people can do that better, perhaps. Writing articles takes time away from composing, so I decided to limit myself pretty much to research documentation. Get the facts down as accurately as possible. Describe what I did, how I did it. Let others worry about why I did it. One record magazine wrote that I was motivated by a hatred of humanity. Is that what you mean by polemical writing? If so, you can have it.

Q: Do you find that teaching takes away too much of your time that could go to composition?

HILLER: No. I can't say that I've been overworked either here or at Illinois. I have, by and large, taught the more advanced courses, which has been nice. I did my duty as a young professor in elementary courses of chemistry; we had huge classes. But I haven't taught much elementary counterpoint or theory. I enjoy teaching and working with students, and the teaching load isn't that heavy.

Q: The academic environment must be important to a lot of your music in terms of getting at the technical equipment.

HILLER: That has been a big advantage, of course. This is lessening now that one can buy a computer of one's own if one wants to. It's also one of the main reasons why I've stayed in America more than I might have otherwise. We're far ahead in computer music, compared to Europe, although not so much so in conventional tape music. Although I didn't do it, I think Europe would have had distinct advantages as a place to settle in. The musical environment there is more productive for a composer in many ways, such as publication, performances, and income. For example, the publishing situations are like night and day; in this country it's terrible. In Europe, a composer's work is assiduously promoted, compared to here, where it can just sit on a shelf.

I get as many performances in Europe, on the average, as I do here. This comes occasionally through publishers that represent me over there, like Universal, but primarily from just being frequently on the scene. As you have seen, I've lived in Europe a good deal, and know the situation in some ways really better than here. I'm rather unusual among American composers in this way. Mort Feldman's another example; I think he also does much better abroad than he does here.

Q: Could you tell us what you're working on currently, besides completing Algorithms III?

HILLER: I just finished my Seventh String Quartet; it's going to be premiered here at "June in Buffalo" by the Kronos Quartet, who commissioned it from me. They're coming along as a group rather like the Concord; they devote a lot of time to contemporary music, and they're very, very good. That's just finished, and the Algorithms III is the number one project coming up.

A pianist here, Yvar Mikhashoff, who does quite a bit of my music, keeps after me for a new piano piece. So I am sketching a piece that will be laid out on a big sheet of lucite. You can see through the score, so you can see what's on the back as well as the front. You can also turn it ninety degrees to obtain different versions. It's going to be called Quadrature because you get eight variants depending on which edge you set it on. Since you can read the background as well as the foreground and since the background will be backwards relative to the foreground, the possibility of forward and retrograde material being played simultaneously arises.

CATALOG OF COMPOSITIONS

1946; 68	Piano Sonata No. 1	MS
1947	Piano Sonata No. 2	MS
1947	Trio for Violin, Cello, and Piano	MS
1948; 73	Seven Artifacts for piano	MS

1949	String Quartet No. 1	MS
1949	Concerto for Piano and Orchestra	MS
1949	Violin Sonata No. 1	MS
1949	Children's Suite for piano	MS
1950	Piano Sonata No. 3	MS
1950	Jesse James for vocal quartet and piano	MS
1950	Piano Sonata No. 4	MS
1951	Suite for Small Orchestra	MS
1951	String Quartet No. 2	MS
1951	Fantasy for Three Pianos	MS
1953	Symphony No. 1	MS
1953	String Quartet No. 3	MS
1954	Twelve-Tone Variations for Piano	Presser
1955	Violin Sonata No. 2; Cello Sonata	MS
1956	Two Theater Pieces for piano	MS
1957	String Quartet No. 4, Illiac Suite (Co-composer: Leonard Isaacson)	Presser
1957	Incidental Music for A Dream Play	MS
1958	Incidental Music for The Birds	MS
1958	Scherzo for Piano	Presser
1958	Five Appalachian Ballads for voice and guitar or harpsichord	Waterloo
1959	Divertimento for Chamber Ensemble	Presser
1959	Incidental Music for Blue is the Antecedent of It	MS
1960	Cuthbert Bound--Chamber Music for Four Actors and Tape	MS
1960	Symphony No. 2	Presser
1961	Piano Sonata No. 5	MS
1961	Time of the Heathen suite for chamber orchestra	MS
1961	Nightmare Music for monaural tape	MS
1962	String Quartet No. 5	Presser
1962	Amplification for tape and theater band	MS
1962	Incidental Music for Man with the Oboe	MS
1962	Spoon River, Illinois for Narrators and Instrumental Sextet	MS
1963	Seven Electronic Studies for two-channel tape	MS
1963	Computer Cantata for soprano, tape, and chamber ensemble (Co-composer: Robert Baker)	Presser
1964	Machine Music for piano, percussion, and tape	Presser
1966	A Triptych for Hieronymous for actors, dancers, projections, tape, and orchestra	Presser
1966	Suite for Two Pianos and Tape	Presser
1968	An Avalanche for Pitchman, Prima Donna, Player Piano, Percussionist, and Pre-recorded Playback	Presser
1968	HPSCHD for 1 to 7 Harpsichords and 1 to 51 Tapes (Co-composer: John Cage)	CF Peters

1968	Algorithms I, Versions 1 to 4, for nine instruments and tape	Presser
1968	Computer Music for percussion and tape (Co-composer: G. Allan O'Connor)	Presser
1969	Three Rituals for two percussion, film, and light	MS
1970	Violin Sonata No. 3	Presser
1971	A Cenotaph for two pianos	MS
1972	Piano Sonata No. 6	MS
1972	Algorithms II, Versions 1 to 4, for nine instruments and tape (Co-composer: Ravi Kumra)	Presser
1972	String Quartet No. 6	Presser
1974	Six Easy Pieces for violin and piano	MS
1974	A Portfolio for Diverse Performers and Tapes	MS
1975	Malta for tuba and tape	Presser
1975	A Preview of Coming Attractions for orchestra	Presser
1976	Electronic Sonata for four-channel tape	ACA
1976	Midnight Carnival for a principal tape and an indeterminate number of subsidiary tapes and other events	ACA
1977	Persiflage for flute, oboe, and percussion	Waterloo
1977	Ponteach for narrator and piano	MS
1978	Diabelskie Skrzypce for stringed instrument and harpsichord	MS
1979	An Apotheosis for Archaeopterix for piccolo and berimbau	MS
1979	String Quartet No. 7	MS
1980	Two Dances for Zygmunt Krause for clarinet, trombone, cello, and piano	MS

BEN JOHNSTON □

photo: Gene Bagnato

BEN JOHNSTON

Ben Johnston was born on March 15, 1926, in Macon,
Georgia. He graduated from the College of William
and Mary (A. B., Fine Arts), the Cincinnati Conservatory of Music (M. Mus., Composition), and Mills
College (M. A., Composition). He names Darius Milhaud, Harry Partch, Burrill Phillips, Robert Palmer,
and John Cage as his principal composition teachers.
He is currently professor of theory and composition
at the University of Illinois. In 1950, he married
Betty Ruth Hall. They have three children.

Johnston's early compositions demonstrate a facility for both serial and tonal techniques. In more
recent years, he has also composed works utilizing
chance methods. His most significant achievement,
however, has been in the area of microtonality, where
he has been at the forefront in realizing new and more
appropriate organizational methods, establishing scales,
and perfecting performance techniques.

The authors spoke with Ben Johnston on February
3, 1980, at the Manhattan home of his long-time friend,
Wilford Leach. A shy, soft-spoken man, Johnston
prefers to place himself in the background when discussing his music and direct the listener's attention
to both his collaborators and the music itself. But
any conversation with Johnston, however brief, must
leave one with a strong impression of his warmth and
wit.

Q: We'd like to start with your student days with Harry Partch
and Darius Milhaud.

JOHNSTON: I had been at the Cincinnati Conservatory for a year,
which was the first musical school training that I'd had. I was not
particularly satisfied with it; I got a rather desultory kind of compositional training there. So I was looking around to see what to
do, and somebody showed me Harry Partch's book. I wrote to him
through the publisher--which was the University of Wisconsin Press
at that time--and they sent the letter to him in California, where
he was living. He wrote back to me, telling me how to get started
on doing the sort of thing he was, with all sorts of dire warnings.
And it sounded impossible! So I said, "Could I come out there and
work in your studio?"--not knowing that he was living on somebody's ranch in a smithy. He said, "Yes. It's a little bit primitive, but if you can manage to get some way to live from month
to month, it'll be all right to do that."

My wife and I went out there, and I worked with him for six

250

months. Then he got ill, and had to move into the city and close
up shop. So he got me into Mills College by introducing me to
Agnes Albert, who was on the Board of Directors of Mills. She
spoke to Milhaud, and I got in at the last minute. This was in
1951. I worked with Milhaud, and I think it did me a great deal
of good. If you know how to mine the gold that's there, a teacher
like that is very good. If you don't, you can find it absolutely
blank, because he was not a systematic teacher. Milhaud was a
sort of intuitive, systemless improviser as a teacher.

Q: Did Milhaud cast any light on composing microtonally?

JOHNSTON: Not really. He was interested that I was doing it, and
he asked me some questions about it, but he didn't have anything to
offer in that way.

  I found it eventually very useful. The manner in which I
compose is different from the way Harry Partch composed, although
it's based on the same kind of tuning: an extended just intonation.
This is very suitable to polytonal ideas, while not so easily suitable
to atonal and serial ideas. It's not completely incompatible, but it
is very difficult to amalgamate those two approaches. The first
works that I did were an attempt to do that. I had studied atonal
technique at Cincinnati with Mary Leighton.

Q: What kind of teacher was Harry Partch?

JOHNSTON: Harry Partch would say he was not my teacher, that
he didn't want me to say that he was, and that he never let anybody say that. But I say it anyway because, of course, it's true.
He had me as an apprentice in his studio; I had to run and fetch,
I was his "gofer." I helped him record. I tuned all the instruments and learned that way. He would answer any questions I had,
which was all that Milhaud did. You had to ask good questions, or
else you got no answers. He was always willing to do that, and I
don't see why that isn't a teacher.

  I hadn't heard any of Harry Partch's music before I went
there. Gate 5 recordings were still in the future then. There
were only limited 78 rpm releases that didn't really give a very
good picture of his work anyway. They were available only through
him personally, and I hadn't even heard those. So I didn't know
what he was doing, really. I could only go by his descriptions of
it in the book, which intrigued me very much. Especially the hobo
pieces--which were the best.

  I was impressed, but I wasn't drawn to move in that direction. It was too foreign to me. I'd had no experiences like that
in my life.

Partch was difficult, very difficult. He was a very lonely and cantankerous individual. Like a lot of people who'd been loners for forty years, he was difficult to get along with. But we managed, and got along pretty well.

I got him to the University of Illinois during the fifties to do some works. We did The Bewitched first, then later Revelation in the Courthouse Park. And the Illini Union Student Activities group supported Water! Water!, which was not a composition Partch ever pushed; he didn't like it terribly well.

Q: Under what circumstances did you come to study with John Cage?

JOHNSTON: In 1951, the first year I was at the University of Illinois, someone from the theater department asked me to write a score for a production they were going to premiere during a festival of contemporary arts. Burrill Phillips, with whom I studied later, had recommended me. So the director came to me and said, "I don't know any of your music, and neither does anyone else here. I need someone's evaluation of it, so I've asked the playwright to find somebody in New York." The playwright, Arthur Gregor, turned it over to John Cage, who looked at the stuff and said, "Oh, yes, this is interesting; you should get this man to do it." And that was that.

Then Cage came for a lecture during the festival. He did one of the lectures he subsequently published in Silence, the one on I Ching. And it created a furor; people were outraged, and got up and walked out. Afterwards, I went out to speak with Cage. We ended up at my apartment, drinking coffee, and he suggested that I come and work with him during the summer in New York. So we agreed that I would do that. But this was my first year of teaching, and I didn't have time to do all the preparation that he wanted me to do for that. When I arrived, and he discovered that I hadn't done any of the things that he had asked me to do, he set me to work splicing tape for Williams Mix. So I sat there splicing tape for the thing the entire time I was there. That's all that amounted to.

That's very typical of him; he was utterly realistic about things like that. He would prescribe for people: He would give them things to do that were calculated to bring about a recognition of whatever it was he thought they ought to see.

The real teaching that I got from him wasn't until 1959. I got a Guggenheim--it was a lot of work to pull that off. I'd proposed to begin composing microtonally, and I wanted to go to the Columbia-Princeton studios and work there. (They were then within a year of opening, and said they would accept me.) But I found that it was not suitable. I would have had to use a synthesizer, and Milton

Babbitt wouldn't let anybody at it at that point. He was very nice, but that was that. I would be able to learn something about electronic music there, but I couldn't really do what I wanted to do. And I saw Cage socially, and he asked how it was going. I mentioned this, and he said, "I could have told you that wouldn't work. You should be working with Maxfield. But if you go to Maxfield's studio now, and they discover it, you'll be booted out of Columbia, because they don't respect each other. You're in a bind." I said, "Well, what can I do so I won't waste my time?" and he said, "Why don't you come up and work with me once a month?" I said, "All right, I'll get busy with all those preparations," and he said, "Oh, that won't be necessary now!"

He was living in Stony Point, and so I would drive up there once a month. It was really very valuable. He didn't stop me from doing what I was doing; he simply criticized--and very perceptively--what I was doing. I'd just written my first string quartet, Nine Variations, which is a twelve-tone work, and he criticized that very usefully; I made revisions on his suggestions. I was writing another piece which I never really got off the ground. It was for a jazz ensemble--I'm sure he didn't like it. Nevertheless, he was very good with criticisms about it. He didn't try to push me in the direction of his work.

He did a premiere at Circle in the Square Theatre of Theatre Piece, and he wanted my personal reactions and criticisms of this. So I gave him a long critique of the whole thing--which I didn't think was very successful--and he was very pleased about that. I suppose that was our most in-depth exchange, because he was very concerned about that. From then on we talked about a great many things, not always just composition.

Q: Perspectives of New Music published a very intelligent and valuable defense of John Cage which you had written. You clearly understand Cage's ideas, and recognize what his accomplishments are. But what would you say is the value of his work for your own compositions?

JOHNSTON: Other than just general encouragement, and the kind of criticism you could get from any intelligent artist, there wasn't any usefulness as far as microtonality is concerned. But that's not the only kind of thing that I've been doing. I was doing a lot of indeterminate works. They really are just typewritten sets of instructions--recipes, I call them. For that sort of thing, he was enormously valuable. He gave me a real perspective on how you may proceed if you want to leave a large area of the decision-making process to either the performer or some agency of chance. What do you do, how do you participate in the composition in that way? That's the way I look at it, as participating in the composition. It's like a collaboration, an incognito collaboration where you never meet the other person.

Q: You met Partch at the beginning of the 1950s, and later in the decade you helped him prepare productions of his works, yet your own microtonal compositions aren't until the 1960s. Can you explain why there was this long gestation period?

JOHNSTON: There are three reasons. First, I simply didn't know what to do with his compositional methods. Wilford Leach asked me to write the music for a production that he did at the University of Virginia called The Wooden Bird, when I was out there working with Partch in California. I didn't want to take off time from anything that had to do with working with him, to write music for something like that. Besides, I had to send tapes. I couldn't just send the music, and I had no way of getting it performed. So the only thing I could do was to try to use Partch's instruments. I asked Partch's permission to do this, and he said, "Of course, but are you ready to tackle something like that?" I said, "Frankly, no, but I don't know what else I can do except let him down, and I'd hate to do that." Then Partch said, "Well, let me work on it with you." So actually we collaborated on that, and Partch wrote more than half the music. So I did that, but that was a very special kind of thing, and not really typical of any of us--Leach included!

Working with Milhaud made me realize how much I had to learn just about composing. I had had really very poor teaching up until then. All Milhaud could do was set me on a certain track and expect me to work it out for myself. Which is what I did, and it took me about ten years to do that. I tried to go back and digest all the stuff I had learned about twelve-tone music. I really didn't get involved with that until late in the fifties. The first completely twelve-tone work I wrote was my first string quartet, which wasn't done until 1959. So I was a long time even getting that really cooking. Meanwhile, I had written a lot of things, but I was really, I think, just learning how to compose. That was one of the reasons. A big one.

The second one is an obvious one: it was very difficult to digest everything that I learned from Partch. I had no instruments to work with; I couldn't decide on how to approach the problem, and that held me up. Finally, when I did decide, I made a decision that turned out to be wrong: I thought that electronics would be the answer. So I went after that and found out it wouldn't work. Well, I turned around immediately and started going after instrumental things, and I realized I would have a bad problem with all the wind instruments: What are they going to do? I tackled that first and discovered that it was too hard for me; I had too little cooperation from wind players, and I gave it up after a couple of small pieces. These later proved to have been successful when I had decent people to work on them. But I didn't know that then, so I had to give them up. I started to work with strings, but I also had no cooperation from those people. The Walden Quartet, who did my first string quartet, wouldn't attempt anything of the kind; they were very adamant about that.

My Sonata for Microtonal Piano was a way of getting into this. It took me five years to write it, because I had to train myself. I retuned the piano for that. Then Salvatore Martirano introduced me to the Composers Quartet, and they got interested in doing a quartet of mine which I had written for the LaSalle Quartet, who never did it.

The third reason: There was a kind of psychological moment for getting into this, which was really indefinable--it had a lot to do with the other two reasons. But I had a sort of sense of timing about it which I can't explain, that somehow the moment hadn't arrived. When I felt that it had, I got to work on it.

Q: Had you been afraid that perhaps only a true rebel like Partch could ever really compose that way?

JOHNSTON: No. I knew there was no sense in my trying to build instruments; I just don't have any of the right talents. Why should I get involved in that when I wouldn't do it well? Same thing with electronics; I'm not good at that, and I didn't really want to do it, either. So those looked like dead issues to me, and really are not directions that I believe in for the future. I do think there will be new instruments; I do think they will be electronic. (They already exist, but only in a half-assed way.) It'll be a long time before we really have them, but when we do, we'll have incredible resources.

Q: The problem of finding capable performers led you to the Sonata for Microtonal Piano?

JOHNSTON: Once you've got the tuning, nobody has to worry about it by ear. Nobody but the composer! That was what took five years: to get the tuning in my head. I didn't want to write music strictly computatively. That's not to my taste. I don't think anyone does that. I don't think Xenakis does, notwithstanding the public image he might have. He knows what that's going to sound like, approximately--probably very accurately.

Q: Could you be more specific about the problems of using the electronic medium for microtonal composition?

JOHNSTON: It was too hard. Honestly, every note had to be sculpted if you wanted to do what I was doing. All the mechanical aids that make up a synthesizer had only just been invented. There was just this huge monster of a synthesizer, and it was the only one. It would have been hard to handle because the pitch was set for equal temperament. You could do something about that, but it was a great deal of work. In the studio, it would have been fantastically hard to do that. Somebody with a natural facility for doing that sort of thing would probably have been able to pull off something, but I'm not that person. And while I don't think Stockhausen is either, Stockhausen had the advantage of the European method of working, which is with a Tonmeister. That was not set up here, and never has been in this country. So there was not that possibility, either.

With John Cage's support, I had put in for a Fulbright to France to work in the Studio de Récherches with Pierre Schaeffer. I was accepted by Schaeffer, but I never got to the final stages of the Fulbright Committee because I decided to stay at Illinois. It was a question of leaving and giving up the job, or staying and trying to keep it. It was a good job, and in a place where there was some commitment to contemporary music, which was unusual at that time. So I decided it was unwise, and I didn't do it. But that would have been another thing, one which would have put me in still a different direction that would have been equally hard to work out.

Q: The area's opened up now, though.

JOHNSTON: Oh, yes, one could do it now; it wouldn't be all that hard.

Q: But you still haven't used it.

JOHNSTON: I just don't like the idiom that much. Also, I believe that there's no solution to the problem other than to learn what you're doing by ear. I've worked that way, and now I'm convinced about it--it works. I'm not frightened of it anymore. It works long distance; I can send pieces to people with instructions and get the right result.

Q: In "Tonality Regained," you talk about using the computer "not only as an instrument but also as a decision-maker in the compositional process," meaning not just deriving microtonal scales with the computer, but using it as an onstage performer.

JOHNSTON: Never have done it yet, and I don't know that I ever will get to that. But yes, of course, it's workable. The person who took over that idea is Salvatore Martirano, who probably will be doing that--and with microtones too (although I don't know in just exactly what way; his interests in the area are quite different from mine). His instrument, the SalMar Construction, is the only real-time performing computer I've seen that honest-to-God works.

He's learned a lot of electronics, and knows how to do this. That's very difficult for me, although I think I possibly could, with maximum effort, have gotten something like that off the ground. Provided I was collaborating--it needs to be a team research.

Q: You've mentioned collaboration several times. You once said that you were tired of having an autocratic relationship with the performer, that you'd prefer having more of a collaboration.

JOHNSTON: I had a lot of talks with Claire Richards about the Sonata for Microtonal Piano as it progressed, about what I should try to do, and in what way to do it. (She, of course, premiered the work.) That's a conventional piece, one which is highly controlled from a compositional point of view, and even there I was highly pleased to be working with her on that. I haven't worked that way with string quartets; those are pieces I cook up myself. But I haven't had a string quartet right at hand. I've had to work long distance. With choreographers, in most cases, I work very closely. And with Wilford Leach, it's a very close collaboration. And I do like that. I've also written a lot of pieces where it's just a recipe, the performer is really doing most of it. The performer makes most of the conventional decisions, the ones you think of the composer as usually making. A lot of the others I've made--but that's the influence of Cage.

Q: In "Three Attacks on a Problem," you describe intellection in the process of composition as a "nozzle," a "focussing mechanism," saying that "Without it what comes out is weak and diffuse." Does this actually contradict something like your recipe pieces, or is that recipe the intellection, the nozzle?

JOHNSTON: If it's well made, it is. Chance has to operate on something, and when you select what it's going to operate on, there you have made the composition. And it can be just as signed and identifiable as anything else, because chance may not operate on anything you didn't give it to operate on, and you've given it these things. You can even have other people select those things, but you've biased it in a certain way, and what they select is sure to turn out within a certain ambience. When John Cage collaborated with Lejaren Hiller on HPSCHD, he refused to let Hiller use a random-number generator to produce the chance results. He wanted a program written that would produce exactly the same result as consulting the I Ching. This is because he had studied the effect of that particular method, and he didn't want the other method.

It's operating at several removes from the material--a little bit like scientists using mechanical hands to manipulate radioactive materials. You can't handle these things yourself, but you do it. I've been interested in that process, the process of manipulating the thing at some remove. And, lately, even the audience--trying to write pieces that will involve the audience; set it up so that when the audience gets involved, they will do so in certain ways. That's been only partly successful. I'm interested in that problem, though.

Q: How do you try to use the audience?

JOHNSTON: Set up a situation that will force the audience to perceive certain things, and that will get their reactions to those things, whatever they are.

Q: Are they more or less hostile than musicians to being manipulated?

JOHNSTON: They're less tractable, of course. They never agreed to do it!

I read such a piece which sets the audience up. What it's really about is paranoia in modern socio-political situations. It sets up a situation where the audience is triggered to this by the subject matter under discussion, and is then subjected to the same techniques. They're made to be frightened, to feel, you know, "What's going on?" This piece is called "The Age of Surveillance." It's a mean piece, but it's about something mean.

Q: A lot of your works are for voice, yet you've commented on how hard it is to project English, saying that with dramatic works you've always had to involve some element of parody. Could you explain what you find troublesome about writing for voice?

JOHNSTON: You go to the opera and you can't understand the words; it's that simple. You go to a lieder recital, and you've got to have the text in front of you to know what they're saying--even if it's your language. This is partly the method of singing, it's partly the nature of the accompaniment, it's partly the acoustics of the hall--it's all kinds of things.

The acoustics of the hall are the easiest thing to tackle if you really want to get at the problem: You just do it by amplifying the voice. Then you have to accept the sound of an amplified voice. In Carmilla--which I did with Leach--we did it with a total amplification of everything, using a mixer as in a rock concert. The whole purpose there was to focus full attention on the meaning of the text. I composed the vocal lines with the greatest care to get across every nuance--and with good singers, you can. I've been very pleased with that; it really works.

I left the whole orchestration to the ensemble; it does change from performance to performance--not greatly, but it does. We took the best of the realizations and wrote it down--that's more or less what's on the recording--so we could send it out and have it done elsewhere. Which it has been. Yet La Mama continues to develop the piece; everytime they do it, they do it differently. But always with the same aim. You have to understand what that aim is. But you've got a lot to go on, there are a lot of other elements in the piece that do remain fixed: the text, the slides, the film-- everything that you can use as a guide.

But the principal thing there is that everything has to be balanced so that there's a transparency against which the words come out very clearly. One reviewer--New York has good theater reviewers but terrible music reviewers, unbelievably unperceptive-- really got that, and centered her comments on the fact that it was the only musical she'd ever been to where it was no effort to under-stand the words.

Q: Part of the difficulty in grasping a sung language is simply the fact that the voice is behaving in a manner unlike the one with which we normally communicate.

JOHNSTON: That's part of it. A lot of it has to do with the voice production, and trying to fill a large hall. After all, you don't have that problem with Renaissance madrigals, but you do with Baroque music. The reason is Baroque music was projected to a large audi-torium, and Renaissance music was chamber music. So you really have that problem entering with the invention of the large musical auditorium and opera house--and it begins to disappear when you introduce amplification. The vocal technique problem begins to dis-appear too. Take the Experimental Vocal Techniques Ensemble, or Joan LaBarbara--many of their techniques are not audible beyond the first seats without amplification. It's the nature of the voice; you just can't project some of those sounds easily in the usual way. And I'm very much interested in those developments, too; they open up the voice to a whole new set of possibilities. Now you can get all these tiny sounds and take them out into the hall.

I also use text in the conventional way, where I'm not great-ly concerned with people getting the words. The text then is the reason for the vocal line. If you do get to know the text--maybe by having it close at hand--you can see the relationship, and it does deepen your appreciation of the piece. But you can understand the piece anyway. That's the way all lieder operate.

Q: The voice would seem to be one of the most amenable instru-ments for just intonation.

JOHNSTON: Yes, it is. There's the whole tradition of Renaissance and Medieval music--which immediately interested me very much. I was very much aware of that, and I used it in a piece for the Swingle Singers. Working with people like that, I can get the equivalent. And, once again, they're using mikes. They're bringing back the small hall, in effect; they can do the sort of thing you can do only in a small room, but in a large one, because they're using mikes.

I did an experimental vocal piece, an improvised piece called Visions and Spells, for the New Verbal Workshop. It uses experimental vocal techniques, and was very successful. I participated in that, using my voice. I've also done a piece for Phil Larson which has three and a half octaves of male vocal range. That's the Two Sonnets of Shakespeare. It's an incredible sound that he gets: It's from low D below the bass clef to A above the treble clef; thorough, full use of that entire range, all over it, all the time.

Q: Is it true that the St. Louis Symphony Orchestra was a lot of trouble for you when they premiered your Quintet for Groups?

JOHNSTON: We had a lot of trouble with the strings. The just intonation wasn't the problem, however. The problem was the kind of semi-graphic stuff that you find in a lot of scores, where they're meant to play contours. As in Penderecki, or numerous other people; nothing at all unusual in contemporary music--in fact, it's become a cliché. But I had some of that in there. Being the only massed group in the orchestra, the string section was being used as a mass--some of the time an inchoate mass, some of the time a highly differentiated mass. The differentiated part was what we used to soothe them after they got so upset about the rest of it.

One of the percussion players decided to show off because he thought that the piece had humorous potential. He nearly got fired as a result of that. There were efforts to disrupt from those two quarters. One of the harpists refused to retune the instrument, and was finally compelled to. The extra percussion parts were not filled in by percussionists but by sixth-stand violists, and so forth. They were totally inadequately prepared. The orchestra pianist was used, and the part was too hard for him.

There were all kinds of bad things like that. They gave me extra rehearsals, but I couldn't do anything because these people were not capable. They were nice, well-meaning people who didn't know what they were doing. There was not much we could do except fake, which is what we agreed to do. We faked our way through it, and we got by. These were things that were beyond the control of the conductor, Eleazar de Carvalho. He let me know right away what the problems were going to be, and he was right in every case. We had no trouble with the brass, no trouble with the woodwinds-- it was the rest of the orchestra.

Q: Has Chinese or Indian music played much of a part in your own microtonal composition?

JOHNSTON: Not Chinese; I don't know enough about it. Indian music, yes, not because I ever studied it, but because I've just always liked it and been very much interested in it. I've felt a very close affinity to a lot of the things about it. So, yes, there was a big influence from that, mainly from just listening to records-- and, when I could, sitting down and talking to Indian musicians. I never set myself down to learn it as a student, but I know it as best as you can from the periphery. I've read Alain Daniélou's writings about it. His books really gave me some insight into what was going on tonally in Indian music. (They don't think about it that way, but I think it is a valid description of what they are doing.)

Q: Have the quarter-tone compositions of people like Alois Hàba or Hans Barth been at all useful to you, or did you find that to be just traditional music only with more steps between the notes?

JOHNSTON: That's the way it struck me. Hàba's music I liked maybe a little better than the others. Barth I never have heard to this day. I only heard Ivan Wyschnegradsky recently, and I liked what I heard. But it played no part because my own point of view is pretty well formed by now.

Hàba I found just a little too traditional nineteenth-century, with twentieth-century trappings. I didn't find that awfully attractive, and I don't think it would have influenced me. I've gradually come to an appreciation of it; I like it better than I liked it at first, but still it's not anything that I felt excited about.

I didn't like Carrillo very much. I found it the type of music that just didn't interest me a lot. His use of microtones seemed to me coloristic, and little else--kind of an extension of Impressionistic attitudes. I like some of the Impressionistic attitudes, but not those. It didn't interest me as music--the ideas, somewhat. I've just not particularly been drawn to that.

The Netherlands group, around Adriaan Fokker, interested me somewhat more so. A lot of Badings' music is really impressive. It was some years before I heard those things; they weren't available on records, and I didn't have the chance to go there. I knew about it, but I didn't know it. Fokker's writings were available in German and Dutch, but not in English--until recently. So all of that's been slow getting to me.

Q: If you don't mind being put in the position of a prognosticator,

we'd like your response to a two-part question: First, will some
significant mechanical revision of traditional instruments have to
take place for the eventual performance of microtonal music, and,
second, will just intonation itself ever come into the mainstream
of composition?

JOHNSTON: It never really left. The only system of composition
which really disregarded just intonation as a basis of choice was
atonal serialism. And I submit that it really hasn't proved itself,
even after all this time. It doesn't work with the public very well;
it doesn't even work with the musicians very well. So notwithstanding the contribution that it's made, it's not going to be the new
mainstream--ever.

That means that what we've been doing was simply a compromised form of just-intonation thinking. Well, I'm for getting
rid of the compromise. We don't need it anymore. We never
needed it at all anyway, except for keyboards. And with electronics, the keyboard is no longer the standard of musical thought. We
aren't thinking just in terms of a gamut of pitches, laid out linear-
ly; we're thinking of the world of sound. This is because we can
deal directly with that if we want to. We don't all the time, but
we can.

I think that instruments will be modified--they already are
being modified. I think there'll probably be a direct type of evolution right through what already is. I don't think we're going to hit
any sharp breaks. I think there will be more and more electronic
aids to instruments. You may find in the future that a lot of the
difficult stuff will be assisted electronically. For example, it will
be possible to keep the intonation within certain limits electronically,
and then the player will make all the rest of the adjustments.

Q: Then you don't feel like a voice in the wilderness, composing
in this way?

JOHNSTON: Not really, no.

Q: The people who compose tonally today, using equal tempera-
ment--are they wasting their time?

JOHNSTON: They're not wasting their time, but it's like anything
that you do in a halfway: If you don't really throw yourself into it,
you're just sort of doing it. That's the criticism I have of that. I
think that's why, largely speaking, twentieth-century tonal music
doesn't have a lot to offer--and it doesn't. This is because there's
only so much you can do, working that way.

The kind of equal temperament that we have now was not

really established until during Beethoven's life. It was that late.
Now up to that point, there were I don't know how many varieties.
That was pretty lively. So this other situation has existed then for
not quite two hundred years--plenty of time to exhaust it completely, and that's what's happened. We have something that's really
tired, and the reason that it's tired is because it was too restricted. It wasn't a wide-open field; it was an artificially closed field.
I'm just reopening it, that's all. I think, in effect, that that's what
has to happen.

Q: Randall Shinn has commented that, for you, microtonality works
best "in tree-structure morphology, rather than serial or indeterminate morphology."

JOHNSTON: All of these different morphologies are not incompatible. The rubric under which they all can be made to make sense
together is statistics. It would appear that the most basic work is
being done by people like Xenakis, in dealing directly with that area.
But the way in which they're dealing with that area is only one way.
Xenakis is interested in setting the average behavior, which will
then be determined by a formula of distribution. That's one way to
use statistics. The indeterminacy principle has found its way into
all sorts of areas.

But you can also have various degrees of organization, and
ratio organization is probably the most precise of those. Being the
most precise, it can trigger in the mind the highest degree of success for prediction. If interval scale activity is all you can manage, then prediction will be less accurate. If it's merely greater
and less, then still less accuracy will result. So if you present a
person with an organized sound object, and it is organized only to
one of those degrees, his ability to remember it intelligibly will
diminish as the organization gets less precise. Prediction and
memory are two of the basic factors in understanding music.

I feel that ratio organization had fallen into partial disuse
over a period of time as a result of this artificial situation produced by the introduction of equal temperament. So I was setting
about to free that situation up and allow those things to come back
into play. In my article, "Rational Structure in Music," I pointed
out that the kind of complexity that's simply dealing with large numbers doesn't interest me so very much. The kind that's dealing
with subtleties of relationship does. Now for that, you need the
highest form of organization you can get. If what you're trying to
do is delineate fine differences between the way one thing relates
to another, then you want the most precise measurements you can
have. And you want the mind to pick up on every little thing, every nuance. That's what interests me. This business of getting
average behavior is interesting, but I don't want to spend my time
working with that.

Q: What made you decide on "Amazing Grace" as the theme for the variations of your Fourth String Quartet?

JOHNSTON: This'll read like a nineteenth-century program note! This was a few years after I had converted to Roman Catholicism, and I was very intense about that. I remember going to church, and some woman got up and sang that song. She did it not very well, and the accompaniment was abysmally bad. And I thought what a durable tune it was; it could stand up under that. It stands up under Patti Page, Tennessee Ernie Ford, and all the rest of them, and still maintains its integrity--it's sort of unassailable! That interested me; I just remember registering that. Then I was trying to write a string quartet because the Fine Arts Quartet had asked me to. I wasn't getting anywhere with it, and I found that that was on my mind, so I decided to write a set of variations on that. So I did.

Q: Have you found your career as a teacher conflicting with your work as a composer?

JOHNSTON: More and more I do want more time to compose. As soon as I can economically manage it, I will get out of teaching. The two things are beginning to get in each other's way; that's only because now I have a lot more demand for the music. And that's good, I'm glad of it.

I remember an interview with Elliott Carter, about his then new style of writing--his use of metrical modulation. He said that for years he had been wanting to get into investigating that area, and that he had finally decided that a career doing something he only halfway wanted to do wasn't worth it. He would rather gamble the loss of all the musical support that he had--from performers and audience alike--on the chance of successfully using the thing that he found most interesting: the thing he wanted to investigate, even though he knew it would make his music essentially--he didn't use the word, I don't think--an elitist kind of thing. So he went ahead and did that. He had the option to because he was not in need of making a financial success as a composer. (Actually, he did in the long run, but he didn't know that he would.)

I made a very similar decision--and that's part of that third reason for delaying my microtonal composition, which I mentioned earlier. I had to establish myself as a composer, as any kind of a composer, before I could attract the attention of the performers who were good enough to play the sort of thing that I wanted to ask them to do. That would have been true for Elliott Carter; he did establish a firm footing as a serious, respected composer in a neo-classic idiom. I did the equivalent. It was within a university ambience, it was comparatively restricted, but I got the respect of such people. I knew I had a secure job, it finally reached tenure, and I wasn't going to lose out if I was dabbling around in an area that most people thought was kooky. It was a question of that sort of gamble. I was willing to spend five years on one piece, and turn out maybe two or three pieces per year, maximum.

As it seems, I've turned out more music than I had a right to expect I would, given the methods that I finally ended up using. But I don't produce a lot, even so, compared to some of my friends. I don't find that this has inhibited me. There's one thing that it has done: It's at a premium for me that each piece count for something. I just can't throw off something which is one of a series because each one is too important; there are not that many of them. I'm not sure that I always live up to that level, either. It hurts more if I have a piece that people think is a potboiler.

CATALOG OF COMPOSITIONS

1949	Etude for Piano	MS
1949	somewhere i have never traveled for tenor and piano	MS
1950	Le Gout de Néant for baritone and piano	MS
1951	A Nocturalle upon St. Lucie's Daye for baritone and piano	MS
1951	Concerto for Brass for brass ensemble and tympani	MS
1951	Incidental Music for The Wooden Bird (Co-composer: Harry Partch)	MS
1952	Incidental Music for Fire	MS
1952	Dirge for percussion ensemble	MS
1953	Satires for piano	MS
1953	Celebration for piano	Orchesis
1953	Portrait for piano	MS
1954	Variations for piano	MS
1954; 58	Incidental Music for The Zodiac of Memphis Street (Trapdoors of the Moon)	MS
1955	Night for baritone, women's chorus, and chamber ensemble	MS
1955	St. Joan ballet for piano	MS
1955	Three Chinese Lyrics for soprano and two violins	MS
1956	Two Dances for piano ("Of Burden" and "Of Mercy")	MS
1956	Incidental Music for Ring Round the Moon	MS
1958	St. Joan suite for piano	MS
1958	Septet for wind quintet, cello, and contrabass	Smith
1959	Aubade for piano	MS
1959	Nine Variations for string quartet	Apogee
1959	Gambit for Dancers and Orchestra	ACA
1959	Ludes for Twelve Instruments	MS

1960	Sonata for Two for violin and cello	Smith
1960	Passacaglia and Epilogue from St. Joan for orchestra	MS
1960	Ivesberg Revisited for jazz band	MS
1960	Newcastle Troppo for jazz band	MS
1960	Five Fragments for alto, oboe, bassoon, and cello	Smith
1961	Incidental Music for The Taming of the Shrew	MS
1962	Knocking Piece for two percussionists and grand piano	Smith
1962	A Sea Dirge for mezzo-soprano, flute, oboe, and violin	Smith
1963	Duo for flute and string bass	Marx
1964	Of Vanity for SATB and two percussionists	MS
1964	String Quartet No. 2	CPE
1965	Sonata for Microtonal Piano/Grindlemusic	Smith
1965	Gertrude, or Would She Be Pleased to Receive It? opera	MS
1966	Prayer for boys' choir, SSA	Smith
1966	Lament for flute, trumpet, trombone, viola, cello, and bass	MS
1966	Quintet for Groups for orchestra	MS
1967	Ci-Gît Satie for SSAATTBB, bass, and drums	Smith
1967; 72	One Man for trombone and percussion	Media
1969	Film Music for Museum Piece	MS
1969	Auto Mobile sound environment	MS
1969; 78	Five Do-It-Yourself Pieces	Media
1969	Knocking Piece Collage for tape	MS
1970	Carmilla opera	MS
1971	Rose for SATB	Smith
1972	Mass for SATB, eight trombones, and rhythm section	Fostco
1973	I'm Goin' Away for SATB	MS
1973	String Quartet No. 3	MS
1973	String Quartet No. 4	Galaxy
1974	Three Songs of Innocence for soprano, flute, alto flute, oboe, English horn, clarinet, bass clarinet, viola, and string bass	MS
1975	In Memory, Harry Partch, 1975 for soprano, computer tape, tape, string quartet, eight percussionists, and slide show	MS
1976	Vigil	MS
1976	Visions and Spells	MS
1977	Since Adam for STB or SAB	MS
1977	12 Psalms for SAB and STB	MS
1978	Suite for Microtonal Piano	MS
1978	Strata for tape	MS
1978	Two Sonnets of Shakespeare for bass-	

	baritone/countertenor and chamber ensemble	Smith
1978	Duo for two violins	Smith
1979	String Quartet No. 5	MS
1979	Diversion for eleven instruments	MS
1980	String Quartet No. 6	MS
1980	Sonnets of Desolation for SSAATTBB	Lingua
1980	Twelve Partials for flute and microtonal piano	MS

BARBARA KOLB ☐

photo: Gene Bagnato

Barbara Kolb was born on February 10, 1939, in
Hartford, Connecticut. She received her B. M. and
M. M. degrees from the Hartt College of Music of the
University of Hartford, where she studied with Arnold
Franchetti. At Tanglewood, her teachers were Lukas
Foss and Gunther Schuller.

With her exploration of what she has called "positive staticism," Kolb has created a sound world that
is increasingly her own. It is a world displaying an
impressionist's feeling for color and mood, in which
serial, aleatoric, and electronic techniques are utilized sparingly and in a highly personal manner.

The authors talked with Barbara Kolb in her Manhattan apartment on July 27, 1975. She was an entertaining and amiable hostess, and although the attention she gave the authors drew noisy protests from
her cat, the interview was conducted smoothly and in
a relaxed manner.

Q: Could you tell us something about the structure of your work
Solitaire?

KOLB: The idea is that if you have an expanse of time from A to
E--which amounts to approximately thirteen minutes and thirty seconds on the record--what you really have is a form of modulation
in which you begin in the area of A and end up in the area of A
flat. (A flat is the key in which the original version of the Chopin
prelude is played.) But you never really hear this modulation as
a modulation because there is no nineteenth- or eighteenth-century
technique in which one modulates. Instead, there is a gradual change
of pitches over a slow period of time, which culminates in A flat.
I approached this through different speeds: I made each letter,
whether capitalized or lower case, represent one and one-half minutes in duration. Then, as the piece progressed, I gradually changed
the pitch area from A to A flat, beginning slowly at first and then
progressing more rapidly towards the end. As a result, once I
start bringing in the Prelude in A Flat Major of Chopin, one begins to feel it as a whole. I eliminate the pitch area of A, because it would disturb the Prelude itself. In order to create a
harmonic progression which is smooth, I employ certain enharmon-
ic relationships. For example, if I use a D flat (enharmonically
C sharp) within the framework of A, it becomes a major third relationship to A, and a perfect fourth relationship to A flat; so it's
not so dissonant after all.

According to the instructions I've provided for this piece,

one must always proceed consecutively. One can go from capital letter to capital letter, or from lower case to lower case, or from capital letter to lower case. But, for instance, you can't go from "B" to "E." That would make no sense because harmonically they're too far away from each other. If one follows the instructions properly, one will find that although there are consecutive progressions horizontally, each consecutive progression will not reproduce any given letter twice. Just as when an entire version of Solitaire (three sequences juxtaposed) is completed, there will be no vertical reproductions. So the piece is primarily a horizontal piece which progresses, harmonically, more in a horizontal way than in a vertical way. Yet, somehow, it progresses very slowly in a vertical way as well, because everything works closely together.

Q: Why the Chopin quotation?

KOLB: It's very hard to say how one thinks of an idea for a piece at the beginning. First of all, I was living in Rome, and that is already a fantasy world. Secondly, I was working on a particular stylistic approach to writing which was a little different from the one I had been working on prior to going to Rome. I was working with letters, sections, and superimpositions of different speeds. Also, I had been influenced literally by trobar clus, which is Provençal poetic form of the eleventh century. I had a friend in Rome who explained this form to me; it was very intricate and yet very carefully worked out.

One day, I was just fooling around with letters and decided that I wanted to write a rather rhapsodic piano piece. I thought I would like to write a quote piece; it seemed to me that a very sentimental, rather rhapsodic, sensual type of piece with tape would be rather fun to do. (It's an idea that probably came to me after a bottle of wine!) In any case, I thought of Chopin because he's so rich harmonically, and because he's someone I've always very much respected. It seemed to me that one of his preludes would probably be a very good piece to use. So, for a period of seven to ten days I drove everybody at the American Academy crazy: I played all of the Chopin preludes at least five hours a day. In a kind of superficial way, I analyzed the harmonies of each in an attempt to figure out which harmonies would be best suited for me. I decided on the A Flat Major Prelude because it was highly chromatic and very nebulous in its progression from one area to another, and because it had also a very beautiful melody. I felt that the melody was so rich in its intervallic relationships that it would probably be a good leitmotif to have in my piece.

Q: Does the use of quotation interest you on a more regular basis?

KOLB: Yes, but in a different way. I don't use my quotation in the way that, for example, Lukas Foss uses it in his Baroque Variations. There, he uses the quotation verbatim and then does what he wants with it. In Solitaire, my use of quotation is less verbatim, simply because the nature of the piece is more nebulous than the nature of the Baroque Variations.

Q: In Chansons Bas, you set six Mallarmé poems. How did you come to select those particular poems?

KOLB: Well, that's a very interesting story. I was still a student, and one day I was having lunch with my old professor--this would have been around 1961. His name is Arnold Franchetti, and he has a beautiful house, with a pond and a patio, and cute little wild animals running around--all with Italian names, I might add. So we were having lunch on his patio one day, and he said, "Barbara, why don't you write some songs?" I said, "Well, why? You're not my teacher anymore, why are you telling me what to do?" He said, "No, no, I don't mean it that way. I have some songs that I was going to set, but I've decided that I don't want to do that now; I want to do something else. But it might be a good study for you to set some songs in another language--they're in French. Why don't you do it, they're lovely poems." So he translated them for me, and he thought if I used a very delicate setting I would probably be able to use them very well. At that time I was still very young and vulnerable, and I thought, "What an honor! that my teacher should give me poems that he himself was going to use!" So that's how I selected the Mallarmé poems.

Q: Do you now feel far removed from such earlier works as Solitaire and Trobar Clus?

KOLB: I would say that, in essence, those works have given me a basis for the works that I am now writing. Like a number of people, I like the works I am doing now better than those I did before. I regard Trobar Clus and Solitaire as works that I like very much and of which I am proud. I don't have any desire to change them, so that must mean something. However, they were works written just after my student years, and I didn't feel quite sure of myself at that time. Now, I feel a little more secure.

Those works presented a basis for a certain concept of writing which I relate more to technical aspects in film than in music. I came across this purely by accident. Since I've been dealing with the juxtaposition of various tempi, I found that if, for instance, you take fifteen seconds of the quarter note equalling seventy-two, and then combine it with fifteen seconds of the quarter equalling sixty, and then the quarter equalling eighty-four, what you have is six bars against five bars against seven bars. When you create fifteen seconds of a particular tempo, you must be sure that the metrical marking is right on; otherwise, the simultaneities will not occur. Everything is rigidly controlled. When the three are combined, you find that you've lost all sense of time. So if you relate that, just from a technical point of view, to your subject matter, then you find that you have something similar to what Antonioni or Buñuel is doing, where they will take something of normal action, then slow it down and combine it with something going at another speed: It becomes a whole different subject matter. Something is taken out of context and put into another context. Both thought processes have been changed, so that the combination creates an entirely different reaction for the viewer. Aurally, that happens in music. If you all of a sudden lose your sense of timing by hearing something juxtaposed with one thing and then another, it's a whole different subject matter, depending on what it's combined with. This technique is, I think, very closely related to certain aspects of film in that respect.

Q: How do works like Solitaire and Trobar Clus relate to your more recent works? Have you made any radical stylistic departures?

KOLB: Actually, Solitaire and Trobar Clus, as I said before, have been the basis for certain things I've been doing recently. I've almost completed a piece for two pianos which will be performed in New York in January. For that piece, I use tape in which I incorporate the mandolin, guitar, marimba, and vibraphone. Then I wrote a guitar piece in which I used humming voices at the end, which, oddly enough, was influenced by a recording I heard of the Paul Winter Consort. So it's a combination of things that I'm constantly being influenced by, and right now I'm being very influenced by jazz, although I don't write jazz. There are just so many sophisticated people around that it's very hard not to be influenced by what is considered commercial, but which isn't really commercial at all.

Q: Could you tell us something about Soundings?

KOLB: Soundings was written after Solitaire, between '71 and '72, and was first performed as a chamber piece by the Chamber Music Society in 1972. That piece was really a direct outgrowth--a combination--of Solitaire and Trobar Clus. But it's more impressionistic. As a matter of fact, it sounds like La Mer because the opening in the strings is a group of sextuplets going at sixty, and then something comes in at seventy-two, and then something else comes in at eighty-four, so you get a feeling of a very sensuous meandering around of parts intermingling with one another. Actually, it's more tonal than the other two pieces--in an impressionistic sense, which produces this quasi-Debussyan effect. I also use a row, but it's basically a whole tone scale row.

That's about all I can say about Soundings, other than that it evokes a certain imagery concerning the sea.

Q: How did it happen that Soundings will be given its New York premiere by Pierre Boulez and the New York Philharmonic?

KOLB: One day, the phone rang, and a woman's voice said, "Hello, is this Barbara Kolb, the composer?" I said "Yes." "Well, Mr. Boulez would like to speak with you." Boulez then proceeded to ask me how many conductors were necessary in Soundings. I said two, and that more or less ended the conversation. Then, about a month later, I was having a telephone conversation with Louise Varèse, who commented, "I understand Boulez is doing a piece of yours with the New York Philharmonic." I said, "Isn't that interesting, Louise, that you should be eighty-four years old and you should find that out before I do." That's how it happened.

So I don't know. I have no idea who recommended my music. I have no idea how he got to know about that score. But he did call, he did ask my publishers to send various pieces to his studio, and then he selected Soundings.

Q: How did Three Place Settings come about?

KOLB: In 1968, I knew I was going to have a piece done on the Creative Associates Concert, the Lukas Foss series in New York. I didn't have anything that I really liked, so I decided that I wanted to write something that was a little bit different, and for some strange reason I decided to write about food. Two of the poems are by two people I know, and the third--event, I should say--is simply a recipe taken out of a 1936 wine cookbook. So that's how these three pieces came about.

Q: How strictly did you outline the narrator's part in the score of Three Place Settings?

KOLB: The vocal line of the narration is not notated, as such, in traditional notation. In some cases there is a combined use of both traditional notation and proportional notation; however, there's always a bar line of some kind. For example, after a certain word, there might be a single cymbal crash, abruptly. Or the vocal line might say, "emphatically," and there will be some kind of indication of the type of voice he should use. If there are many inflections of speech and various gestures that appear on the recording, it's because Julius Eastman is so terrific. And I have to admit that that recording was made at three o'clock in the morning, and anybody who can be that enthusiastic at three o'clock in the morning should be given tremendous applause.

Q: Are there theatrical elements included in a performance of this work?

KOLB: Well, the poetry is supposed to be witty. Some people don't think it's so witty, but I suppose everybody has a different sense of humor, and not everybody can enjoy the same kinds of things. But the idea is that the settings should be in a subdued atmosphere, and the four instruments should be in a kind of combo situation, in that they're like a little accompaniment in a Lower East Side Village bar, or something like that. But it's not terribly theatrical in that a painting is not lowered from the ceiling, and balloons are not exploded in the background. It's not meant to be that kind of piece.

Q: What are your feelings toward utilizing tape in your compositions?

KOLB: The first time I used tape was in Solitaire, and I used it only because I had to; it is totally impractical to put three pianos on the stage. Furthermore, one may not get the same type of playing from those three pianists; it would probably not come out as well as I would like it. Then, there's the whole idea of "solitaire" meaning that you play a game with yourself. And it's a difficult game, because you're continually playing against three different tempi. The whole piece sounds more like a reverie with a kind of manipulated tape sound in the background, emerging and disappearing. I felt that the tape was necessary for this, but as I state in the notes, it's meant more as a collage, not as an electronic device at all. I've not been terribly interested in electronic devices. Although I find it very fascinating, I know that it would require a considerable amount of time to study, and I'm not so sure if I want to write exactly that type of music. I don't know yet; I'm too busy just writing notes.

Q: Do you think there are problems inherent in the electronic medium which make you hesitant about composing in it?

KOLB: I think so. It's a sound world which is, certainly, very valid, and something I respect. But I'm not particularly happy with the end result at this point. Part of it has to do with not having learned the technique. But for the moment, I would just prefer not to be writing what is considered electronic music, or even musique concrète, for that matter.

With regard to my other works using tape, I do, on occasion, use manipulated sounds; I use filtering devices and echo devices--a few basic techniques which are not too complex--but always with the use of the actual instrument involved.

Q: There's a special static quality to several of your works--Tro-bar Clus in particular. Is this something which you have deliberate-ly tried to create?

KOLB: It's something in which I've just gotten involved. Soundings has it quite a bit, but I think Soundings is a more sophisticated and more intricately worked-out piece of music. It's just something that I, personally, like. Maybe, in some strange way, it's the in-fluence of jazz; it's a certain type of repetition of sounds with very slow changing harmonies and rhythms that kind of weld together, rather than being kept separate, to create different characters. In-stead of having one rhythm in the foreground and the other in the background, they're either both in the foreground or they're both in the background. No one event is necessarily more important than another. Yet it's not the same kind of staticism as you find in the music of Steve Reich or La Monte Young; I think their aesthetic is entirely different.

Q: Earlier, you mentioned that Soundings utilizes a row. How prominently do serial procedures figure when you compose?

KOLB: If I do use a row, I'm fairly loose with the row. I will often change vertical structures. Horizontally, I normally don't have to make changes, but very often I find that I do change cer-tain vertical structures purely because I prefer another sound. I do it arbitrarily, and that, of course, enrages strict serial com-posers. That's why I'm very hesitant about saying that certain de-vices that I use are serial, because they're always with reserva-tions.

Q: Are there certain composers or certain works that have influ-enced the way you write music?

KOLB: I think less specific works and perhaps more stylistic ap-proaches of certain composers have. At this point, really, there are so many people who have influenced me, and who are still in-fluencing me. It's very hard to say that any one person is influ-encing me at this point. It's mostly the fact that there's a multi-tude of stylistic approaches to composing music these days, and so many composers are using all of them. You know, using certain serial techniques, tonal techniques, aleatoric techniques, all in one piece. It's a tremendous revelation for the young composer today. One doesn't have to write a formalized composition anymore, in specifically one style, to represent something valid.

I can't really name any one composer who's influencing me. I admire Takemitsu very much. I like the way he uses color most of all. He, too, has been very much influenced by the Impressionistic period; I think Debussy is the foremost composer who has influenced him. When he's asked which composers have influenced him the most, Debussy is one of the names he mentions.

Q: In evaluating your formal musical education, have you found that you had to "unlearn" much of what you were taught?

KOLB: Compositionally, yes. I went to a very good school for basic theory. But I was also majoring in performance at that time. My bachelor's degree is with a major in clarinet, and my master's degree is with a major in composition. So I had things that I had to make up.

It was very informative for me, but I did have to unlearn a great deal once I left Connecticut, because of the rigidity of my private teacher. He didn't believe in a lot of things which I subsequently learned to believe in very strongly. So that took me two or three years. But by living in New York, one is aware of and exposed to a lot of new music, whereas in other places, one is not necessarily exposed to that. So I unlearned very rapidly.

Q: Did you find it very difficult to get recorded?

KOLB: It's, of course, an awful lot of money to record any piece, but when the recording companies know that they're not going to make any money from the music they're recording, then it gets even more difficult to get recorded. The two recordings that I have--one on Desto and one on Vox--were under the Ford Foundation. That folded, roughly, in 1972. Something went wrong, and they no longer gave money for that. But that's supposedly coming back, and there's a project concerning the Rockefeller Foundation that's coming back, so more contemporary music will probably be forthcoming within the next year or two, particularly concerning the bicentennial.

As far as my CRI recording goes, that has to do with an Institute of Arts and Letters award, which I received in 1973. The recording is affiliated with the award.

Q: Do you see yourself writing a work for orchestra in the near future?

KOLB: I'm really very anxious to spend time writing an orchestral piece, because I think I'm ready to do that now. I think I have enough technique to be able to write an orchestral piece, although I don't feel comfortable in large forms. It's not just the size of the orchestra; it's that as the amount of players grows, the structure of the composition should also become larger, and I don't know if I think along those lines.

I think it's very easy to separate those composers who are more comfortable in chamber music, and those who are more comfortable in orchestral music. I believe a man like Aaron Copland, for example, is definitely an orchestral composer. He's stronger in his orchestral music than he is in his chamber music, because his mind, somehow, thinks along those large lines. My mind does not think along those lines, so therefore I feel more comfortable with chamber music. Beginning in September, I'll be living in Rome, and I hope to be able to write an orchestral piece this year --depending on what commissions I get, and what direct responsibilities I have to fulfill. A composer can get away just so long without writing an orchestral piece.

Of course, it also depends upon one's stylistic approach, I feel more comfortable writing counterpoint, oddly enough, than I do in writing harmony, or vertical structures in general. Among composers, I find this to be more uncommon than common; counterpoint usually gives composers more difficulty than vertical structure. The intricacy of a line is sometimes more clearly audible in a smaller ensemble than it is in a large orchestra. Therefore, the chamber ensemble is more suited to my personal style. Take Bartók as an example. In his six string quartets the technique is condensed and intricately worked out; and yet, his most popular piece is probably the Concerto for Orchestra, which has nothing, really, of the involvement of line, the intermingling of lines, present in the string quartets. Perhaps he, too, felt more comfortable in the chamber medium.

CATALOG OF COMPOSITIONS

1962	Three Songs for baritone and piano	B&H
1963	Tell Me That Dream for voice and piano	B&H
1964	Rebuttal for two clarinets	CF Peters
1965	Chansons Bas for lyric soprano, harp, and percussion	Carl Fischer
1967	Figments for flute and piano	Carl Fischer
1968	Three Place Settings for narrator, clarinet, violin, contrabass, and percussion	Carl Fischer
1969	Crosswinds for alto saxophone and wind ensemble	B&H
1970	Trobar Clus for chamber orchestra	B&H
1971	Solitaire for piano and tape	CF Peters
1971	Toccata for harpsichord and tape	CF Peters
1972	Soundings for chamber orchestra and tape	B&H
1975; 78	Soundings for orchestra	B&H

1975	Looking for Claudio for guitar and tape	B&H
1975	Spring River Flowers Moon Night for two pianos and tape	B&H
1976	Appello for piano	B&H
1976; 77	Homage to Keith Jarrett and Gary Burton for flute and vibraphone	B&H
1977	Musique Pour Un Vernissage for flute, violin, viola, and guitar	B&H
1979	Grisaille for orchestra	B&H
1979	Songs Before an Adieu for soprano, flute and alto flute, and guitar	B&H
1979	Chromatic Fantasy for narrator and six instruments	B&H
1980	Related Characters for trumpet and piano	B&H
1980	Three Lullabies for guitar	B&H
1980	Poem for a cappella chorus	B&H

Conlon and Yoko Nancarrow

photo: Don Gillespie

Conlon Nancarrow was born on October 27, 1912, in Texarkana, Arkansas. He studied music at the Cincinnati College-Conservatory of Music, and with Roger Sessions in Boston. In 1937, he went to Spain as a member of the Abraham Lincoln Brigade to fight against the fascist Franco government. Nancarrow returned to the United States in 1939 and moved to Mexico City the following year. He has resided there ever since, and is now a Mexican citizen. In 1972, he married Yoko Sugiura. They have one son, Mako.

In the 1930s and early 1940s, Nancarrow established himself with pieces for solo piano, chamber groupings, and orchestra. But since 1949, he has written exclusively for the player piano, punching the paper rolls on his own machine. Some of his earlier pieces in this medium reflect Nancarrow's interest in jazz, blues, and Spanish music. However, as he further explored the possibilities available to him with the player piano, his compositions became increasingly sophisticated and complex. His Studies for Player Piano are a unique and continually expanding body of work, unprecedented in both their sound and their extraordinary temporal relationships.

The authors spoke with Conlon Nancarrow in his studio in Mexico City on July 12, 1980. Their attempts to clarify conflicting historical data, when combined with Nancarrow's terse, non-ruminative answers, resulted in asking eleven times the usual number of questions for an interview. His brevity does not stem from any sort of hostility or reserve. Rather, it reflects his lingering amazement that people are sufficiently interested in his music to spend time discussing it. It was very special to meet Conlon Nancarrow and experience his lively sense of humor, his total lack of pretension, and his openness and warm cordiality.

Q: Is it true that the most important musical experience of your early life was your first exposure to The Rite of Spring?

NANCARROW: Well, it was a total revelation. At that time I'd heard practically no contemporary music, and suddenly The Rite of Spring was thrown at me, and it just bowled me over. This was when I was in Cincinnati. I heard it at a concert there, and it just opened up a new world to me.

Q: Was that piece in the back of your mind when you were writing some of your early works?

NANCARROW: It's always been in the back of my mind. It's one of my favorite pieces of music, and Stravinsky is one of my favorite composers. Not only The Rite of Spring, but The History of a Soldier, Les Noces, and several others. He's my favorite composer. He and Bach.

Q: Do you admire his twelve-tone work as well?

NANCARROW: Not so much. I'm not a great twelve-tone addict; I don't like it too much. But he went into twelve-tone work and it still sounds like Stravinsky, which is something unique.

Q: Was playing jazz trumpet a hiatus between your formal musical studies at Cincinnati and at Boston?

NANCARROW: I didn't have any formal musical studies. I had a few months of just nothingness at Cincinnati.

Q: It was after that that you started playing jazz?

NANCARROW: Oh, no. I played it before, during, and afterwards.

Q: Would you characterize performing jazz as your real musical education?

NANCARROW: Well, probably, I suppose. My real musical education I just got by myself. The only formal studies that I did that were important were the studies I had in strict counterpoint with Roger Sessions. That was the only formal training I ever had. And they were rigid! I'd do this strict counterpoint exercise, and then I'd take a piece of my music and say to him, "What do you think of this?" "Very interesting; where's your counterpoint exercise?"

Q: Could you tell us about your studies with Nicolas Slonimsky?

NANCARROW: Well, with him it wasn't really studying. I went to see him a few times, showed him a few pieces of music, and he commented on them. It wasn't studying because he didn't teach; he was just saying, "Well, this is good, this is bad."

Q: Did he expose you to the music of Ives, Ruggles, or Varèse?

NANCARROW: No, he didn't expose me to anything. This "study-ing" didn't go on for very long. I finally got to be friendly with him, and I would go to his house for dinner, and the studying sort of drifted off into the background.

Q: And Walter Piston?

NANCARROW: He was a little similar to Slonimsky, in the sense of "Well, OK, let's see this ... OK, fine." He was kind of vague. You know, I was never a great admirer of his music, but I was an admirer of his musicianship and his character. In the early thirties I was a "rabid radical," you might say. We organized this concert in Boston Symphony Hall: a Lenin Memorial Concert! I don't know how we ever got in there, but we got it. We played this concert with, I don't know, all kinds of serious pieces of music, although the main thing was the political point. And Piston came, appearing as a pianist in his Sonata for Oboe and Piano. You know, he was a professor at Harvard at that time, and after that they told him, "If you ever do this again, you're going to get fired." Now, I ad-mired him for this gesture--he was far from a radical. He thought he'd just see what they'd say about his participating. He found out.

Q: In 1938, New Music Edition published your Toccata, Prelude for Piano, and Blues. Had you composed a great deal of music prior to these?

NANCARROW: Odds and ends, more or less in the same period, for a few years. They're lost now, and I don't even remember what they were.

Q: Was that music basically in the same style as the pieces that were published?

NANCARROW: More or less, yes.

Q: Do you remember why you chose those three pieces to be pub-lished? Did you feel that they were your best efforts at that point?

NANCARROW: I didn't choose them; Slonimsky chose them. I went to Spain, and had left pieces with him, and he picked those and sent them to be published. I have no idea why he did that. I suppose he figured, well, maybe they're worth sending in.

Q: Have you ever heard them performed?

NANCARROW: Oh, no. A couple of years ago, Charles Amirkhanian said to me, "Oh, that <u>Toccata</u> for violin and piano--why don't you make a roll of the piano part? When I go to one of these festivals, I'll take it and get a violinist to play along with it." So I did, and I sent him a tape of it. He took it to this festival in Berlin and got a violinist to play with the tape of the roll. But I haven't heard it. I just got the tape of the performance from him recently, but I don't have a tape machine, so I haven't heard it.

Q: You haven't heard your Prelude or <u>Blues</u> for piano?

NANCARROW: No, but those are nothing pieces.

Q: Do these early works, or the Sonatina for Piano or the Septet, have any interest for you now? Could you see yourself revising them?

NANCARROW: Oh, I wouldn't dream of it, no. I don't even have the score of the Septet; I don't know what happened to that. I have the Sonatina. In the early days, I punched that out on a roll because I'd never heard it. They're going to put out that roll on the new record from Arch.

Q: Then you don't want to suppress or disown these early works?

NANCARROW: Oh, no, I'm delighted if anyone wants to play them.

Q: Could you see yourself now composing music for chamber ensembles like those?

NANCARROW: Wouldn't dream of it. I'm so tied up now with the player piano. I'd have to start thinking again: Does the hand reach there? can it go here? The whole thing. No, no. You know, when I do these things for player piano, I just write music; and the notes go here, there, wherever. I don't have to think about anything else. I used to, when I was writing for instruments. It's a real luxury not to have to think about all that.

Q: In Mexico, you composed your Trio for Piano, Clarinet, and Bassoon. When did you write that?

NANCARROW: Probably '42, '43.

Q: Before you began your work with the player piano?

NANCARROW: Oh, yes, much before.

Q: Do you have the score of the Trio here?

NANCARROW: It's probably somewhere, but I've never found it.

Q: Aaron Copland was writing very warmly about your New Music publications in Modern Music in 1938, and in 1940 you were contributing articles to Modern Music. Was he behind your getting those writing assignments?

NANCARROW: I don't know whether it was that way or the reverse. Minna Ledermann was the editor of Modern Music, and I don't know whether she gave those scores to Copland, or Copland gave them to her.

Q: Was this at the time you were living in Mexico?

NANCARROW: No, no, it was before I came here.

Q: One of the pieces you wrote was a review of somebody's book about music in Mexico.

NANCARROW: Oh, yes, this book on nationalism in music. That I wrote here.

Q: Going to Spain to fight Franco meant putting a halt to your compositional career. In that regard alone, was your decision to go a difficult one for you to make?

NANCARROW: Look, at that time what you call my "compositional career" was no big deal. So it wasn't any great sacrifice.

Q: Did you anticipate the problems that you encountered upon returning to the United States?

NANCARROW: No, I couldn't imagine it. I thought it would be just the opposite. But it happened.

Q: We've heard a lot of conflicting stories; could you tell us precisely what did happen to you after you got back?

NANCARROW: When I got back, I wasn't anxious to stay in the States, and I wanted to get a passport--I didn't know to where. And I couldn't get a passport. They just refused, because I was an "undesirable" something--I forget the word; I don't even remember what they said. But in any case, they just said no. They said, "You'll never get a passport again." After I became a Mexican citizen, they changed that; they could not refuse any American citizen a passport. But that was too late then.

Q: So you could go only to countries where you could enter without a passport.

NANCARROW: I had only the choice of Canada or Mexico, and I wouldn't have dreamed of going to Canada--it just didn't appeal to me.

Q: When did you first read Henry Cowell's book New Musical Resources?

NANCARROW: I got it in the States, I guess when I came back from Spain. So I probably read it in '39 or '40.

Q: Was it important for you?

NANCARROW: Oh, very.

Q: As a revelation of ideas, or a confirmation of your own ideas?

NANCARROW: Well, a little of both. From the time I started composing, I'd always had this thing of working with temporal matters, rhythm and so forth, and this thing sort of grew. By the time I saw Cowell's book, it was just a big push ahead.

Q: Does the book specifically refer to player pianos?

NANCARROW: Oh, yes, yes. In fact, someone--I forget who--

pointed out that Cowell always talked about these things, polyrhythms
and so forth, but neither he nor Ives ever dabbled in player pianos,
which would have been the ideal way of doing that. It surprises me
that he never did.

Q: Probably because it's too much work.

NANCARROW: No, I don't think that would have stopped him. I
don't know why he didn't.

Q: Cowell had tapes of a lot of your music. At the Lincoln Center Library in New York, their tapes of your first nineteen Studies
are from his collection. Did you know him at all?

NANCARROW: I met him once. He asked me for those tapes and
I sent them, and I never heard a word from him again. And the
same thing happened to me again with Lejaren Hiller. You know,
I got tired of sending people tapes! I mean, I'd like them to at
least say thank you, or something. But that's not important.

Q: Was reading or meeting Cowell an influence in your interest in
world music?

NANCARROW: Oh, no, I'd already been into that a long time. My
introduction to non-Western music was a long time ago, in Boston.
Did you ever hear of the Shankar Ballet? In the thirties, he was
touring the world with this Indian dance group. (Incidentally, he
was the brother of Ravi Shankar.) He had this group, and the music was a little Westernized, to make it palatable or whatever, but
it opened a whole new world of things to me. From that time on,
I got interested in all kinds of non-occidental music--first Indian,
then African, and then Balinese and a whole series of things. Performances practically didn't exist, apart from records and tapes.
Little by little, I got a collection of those things. I've got an
enormous collection of records of Indian music--but you have no
idea of the trouble it was to get them.

Q: When you began working on the First Study in the late 1940s,
did you expect that you would wind up devoting your entire compositional life to the player piano?

NANCARROW: I really didn't even think of it; I just started doing
it. And I got more and more involved, and deeper and deeper, until finally there I was--stuck!

Q: Study No. 1 was published in New Music, and the Lincoln Center Library has the scores of Studies Nos. 2 and 3. Did you decide to stop attempting to promote your music after those pieces, or had you never been attempting to promote it at all?

NANCARROW: No, at the beginning I wasn't trying; I didn't care.

Q: How important to you is the dissemination of your music?

NANCARROW: I don't know, really. Up until the time I got married and had a family, I really wasn't interested in whether it was disseminated or not; I was just working and happy. When I finally got a family, I decided, well, I'm going to have to leave them something, so I began getting interested in maybe promoting it a little.

Q: What steps did you take to do that?

NANCARROW: Cooperating with people who wanted to do something about it.

You said that 2 and 3 are in the Library?

Q: Yes.

NANCARROW: How did they get there?

Q: That's what we wanted to ask you! They're photostats of your manuscript. In fact, the third study that the Library has is not the "Boogie-Woogie Suite," but the one you abandoned.

NANCARROW: Oh, I know why 2 is there. That's one of the ones Merce Cunningham used. You know, I sent these tapes to Cage, and I sent a score because Cunningham did a book on dance or something, and he wanted the score of No. 2, and he published the score. But 3, the one that I discarded--I don't know how that got there.

Q: Do you remember what it was about that third Study that made you choose to discard it rather than revise it?

NANCARROW: That original No. 3 was one that should have gone into the eventual 3, in that it's sort of in this "boogie-woogie" style. But I used to have another piano here which had another time relationship; it had to be played very fast. I finally gave it up because that piano didn't work the way I liked. So I got this other one. But I couldn't play that particular piece on this piano unless I adjusted the whole time thing down to where everything else in the Suite wouldn't work. So I just dropped it.

Q: Did it subsequently become the basis for another Study?

NANCARROW: Oh, no, no. It was a nothing thing, anyhow.

Q: Do you still have the roll for that Study?

NANCARROW: Yes.

Q: James Tenney has written that you've probably withdrawn No. 13 from the set. Is that true?

NANCARROW: Not exactly "withdrawn." I originally wrote the Studies from 13 to 19 as a series called "Seven Canonic Studies." No. 13 was sort of an introduction to that. But I didn't withdraw it, it's there; it's part of that series. Arch has that, and they're going to issue it.

Q: In an article written in 1955, Elliott Carter recognized the importance of your contribution to rhythmic procedures in American music. Did you know him at that time?

NANCARROW: Oh, yes, at one time he was an old friend, although I didn't see him very often. I met him when I came back from Spain. I saw him several times and we were quite friendly.

Q: How long were you in the United States between your return from Spain and your move to Mexico? Was it a short period of time?

NANCARROW: Fairly; less than a year.

Q: And that's when you met Carter?

NANCARROW: Yes, and Copland and Minna Ledermann and these other people.

Q: What year did you come to Mexico?

NANCARROW: 1940.

Q: Before, you were talking about Slonimsky giving your scores to New Music in 1938. Do you remember the circumstances of New Music's publication of your Study No. 1 in 1951?

NANCARROW: Oh, that's curious. Apparently, Elliott Carter sent this to New Music, and five years later, I heard about it. They never sent me a copy of it; I didn't even know about it! Let's see, how did I find out? I guess Carter wrote me about it, and I said, "Well, how about letting me have a score or something?"

Q: So you had not prepared that score for New Music; Carter had had only your manuscript?

NANCARROW: Yes. Those early things were fairly easy to put into conventional notation, so it could be copied out by a good copyist. I don't know what they'd do with some of the later ones.

Q: After Study No. 12, references to jazz and Spanish music pretty much disappear from your work. Did you deliberately choose to exclude these styles?

NANCARROW: No, I just did what I wanted to do. It had nothing to do with excluding or including.

Q: We were wondering if, because you were working in a new medium with all its unexplored possibilities, you found it useful at first to maintain your ties with styles of music that were familiar to you.

NANCARROW: Possibly. I don't know. I really don't know.

Q: Did you find that, the more you worked in it, the medium opened up so much that it was constricting to keep using these older styles and sounds?

NANCARROW: I've had an obsession with the player piano from way back, for many reasons. But after I got into it, it began developing, and my own experience with it changed all kinds of perspectives.

Q: How far back does your involvement with the player piano go?

NANCARROW: We had a player piano in the house when I was a child, and I was fascinated by this thing that would play all of these fantastic things by itself. And so from then I had this way in the back of my mind--I wasn't thinking of composing at that age, of course, but it fascinated me.

Q: Was your family at all musical?

NANCARROW: All of them were tone-deaf. But they were great music lovers. This was way back in the early days of recordings --I remember my father had these corny John McCormick songs: "Mother Machree" and all that. Oh, they were great music lovers!

Q: Have you been able to perfect a method of preparing the player piano?

NANCARROW: I was thinking of doing it and never got around to it. I did a couple of things for prepared player piano, but the problem is that the preparation can be done only in a grand; when you put all these things between the strings of an upright, they just fall down. A grand is horizontal; you put it there and it stays. I had a small player grand, but I had so much trouble keeping that thing working, it was so complicated, that I finally gave it up. I was very interested in doing something for prepared player piano. There's only one piece I did--30--and it's not a very good piece anyhow.

Q: Don't Studies Nos. 28 and 29 involve preparation as well?

NANCARROW: No. I started on those, and they were supposed to be for prepared player piano, but--and I frequently do this--I started and left them, and finally I got to 30 and finished that, and by the time I got back to 28 and 29, the player grand was gone, so I just left them as pieces for piano without preparation.

Q: Would Study No. 30 suffer if we were to hear it without the preparation?

NANCARROW: It would be completely meaningless. Even with the preparation it's no big deal, as I told you. But without that, no, it's meaningless.

Q: Certain musical parameters are defined purely timbrally, and without the preparation they don't exist?

NANCARROW: Yes, they're just lost, totally.

Q: Is Study No. 30 withdrawn, then?

NANCARROW: No; before I got rid of the player grand I made a recording of it. In fact, Arch has a tape of it and they're going to put it out.

Q: Is it true that you were present in New York in the late forties for one of the first performances of Cage's Sonatas and Interludes for prepared piano?

NANCARROW: Yes.

Q: Had you known Cage at that time?

NANCARROW: No. Again, I think it was Minna Ledermann who sent me there. Cage doesn't remember that I was there, but I was, and it made quite an impression on me.

Q: So then there would be an association between your having heard that and your own work in preparing the player piano.

NANCARROW: Yes, of course.

Q: Are Studies Nos. 38 and 39 completed?

NANCARROW: They're completed. No. 39 was a commission from the European Broadcasting System. It was just played this year. In fact, I just got some information from them saying, "Oh, it was a big success." I don't know what they mean by a big success!

Q: How did that commission come about?

NANCARROW: Well, somehow they'd gotten hold of a tape of some of my pieces--I don't even know how they got it--and played it. Apparently, it was successful. (In fact, my father-in-law in Tokyo heard it on the Tokyo radio!) And so they wrote me and commissioned me to do a piece for them. And I did it.

Q: Was that the first commission you received since moving to Mexico?

NANCARROW: Yes--since ever!

Q: Have you received any more commissions?

NANCARROW: No.

Q: Could you tell us about Study No. 39?

NANCARROW: No. 39 is two pieces for one piano. There's one piece for one piano, and a second piece for the same piano. And, of course, you can't hear them together without doing it in a recording, putting the two pieces together. They're two separate, autonomous pieces: A is A, B is B, and C is A plus B, played on the same piano. So it has to be combined on the recording.

Q: Is there any particular reason why, with Study No. 39, you wanted the C section on the same piano, instead of using both of your pianos, as Studies Nos. 40 and 41 do?

NANCARROW: I just wanted it that way. No. 40 has no C, B is A combined with itself, but using two pianos; it's a contrast between two pianos. No. 39 combines one piano with itself.

Q: We understand that a certain temporal discrepancy occurs in the pieces that combine two pianos. Have you been able to overcome this problem?

NANCARROW: On the contrary, I've given up two pianos because of that problem. I'm going back to one piano; too many problems with this non-synchronization, even with 39 and synchronizing the two parts on the recording of the one piano: I was with the guy who recorded it, we went to a studio and we kept fooling around and fooling around, but it never did come out the way I wanted it to; only an approximation.

I would like to have two synchronized pianos, but I don't. There's just too many problems involved with trying to synchronize two pianos. They both have a paper roll, and in the period of a minute, there's an enormous discrepancy from a little slippage of paper.

Q: So no two performances of Studies Nos. 40 or 41 could ever be exactly the same.

NANCARROW: No, never.

Q: Is it important to you that what's happening vertically always be the same in those pieces?

NANCARROW: Well, that's the way I would like it.

Q: Would it be possible if you put the two pianos on tape to manipulate the tape for a greater synchronization?

NANCARROW: A real technician in the field could do it. But I certainly can't.

Q: Earlier, you remarked that you wouldn't want to write music just for live performers. But since you don't want to write for two player pianos anymore, have you considered combining the player piano with live performers, in chamber music, art songs, or even a concerto with orchestra?

NANCARROW: Oh, it's too complicated. The thing of a concerto for player piano with orchestra: This player piano's just going along, doing what it wants to do. It's a real problem of synchronizing. As a matter of fact, someone here once suggested I write a concerto for player piano. No, it's just too complicated. I'm happy with my work, and now I'm getting back to one player piano-- where I started.

Q: A lot of pieces have been written for live performers and tape, and with sufficient rehearsal, musicians can play in synch.

NANCARROW: I don't know, I haven't heard these things for many years. I remember years ago hearing this piece for tape and orchestra--Ussachevsky, I think. Well, what it was: The tape played, it stopped, then the orchestra played, it stopped, then the tape played.

So what's the point? Really, what it would amount to with player
piano would be the same thing.

Q: You wouldn't be interested in writing, say, an art song for one
vocalist and player piano, or a piano quartet for player piano and
string trio?

NANCARROW: Well, I'm not a string-instrument addict. No, it
doesn't appeal to me very much.

Q: Have you ever written vocal music?

NANCARROW: No, that's one thing I never wrote. I've written for
orchestra, string quartets, and various things, but never vocal, no.
I don't know anything about it!

Q: When you compose for player piano, do you try to avoid writing
something that a live pianist could realize?

NANCARROW: Oh, no, not at all; I just write a piece of music.
It just happens that a lot of them are unplayable. I don't have any
obsession of making things unplayable. A few of my pieces could
be played quite easily--a few! In fact, Study No. 26, "Canon-1/1,"
you could play that with organ, orchestra, or any way.

Q: Did you select the scores that appear in Peter Garland's book?

NANCARROW: He had some scores, and I told him to put whatever
he wanted into it. Basically, he selected them. But he asked me
if those selections were all right.

Q: Is it true that around 1960, you stopped composing and devoted
your time to preparing scores of all the Studies, for almost five
years?

NANCARROW: Yes. I don't know for exactly how long.

Q: Why did you come to that decision?

NANCARROW: Well, in the first place, I didn't feel like composing.
So I passed the time studying Chinese and writing scores.

Q: Did anything in particular prompt you to return to composition?

NANCARROW: No, I just felt like composing again.

Q: Would it be unfair to describe that time as a block?

NANCARROW: I don't know; I have no idea. You can describe it as a block if you want to.

Q: Have you kept abreast of musical developments in both the United States and Europe in the years that you've been in Mexico?

NANCARROW: I did for a while, but for so many years I've been really out of touch with everything. When I first moved to Mexico, I subscribed to all kinds of things: Perspectives of New Music, Journal of Music Theory, The Musical Quarterly. I had an enormous collection. But for about almost ten years I haven't subscribed to anything; the mails got so bad I didn't get anything! So I just stopped subscribing to them.

I was sort of keeping up with things, what people were doing, but for the last ten years, I've had no idea what anyone is doing.

Q: Has this been an advantage to you in your composition?

NANCARROW: Well, it's not an advantage or a disadvantage; it's just a fact. You do what you do.

Q: Over the years, had you found that what other people were doing was not useful to you in your work?

NANCARROW: Yes; it was unrelated, really.

Q: Do you have any ties with the music scene here in Mexico?

NANCARROW: No, almost none.

Q: Are you surprised at the recent interest in your music, after working in isolation for so many years?

NANCARROW: A little.

Q: Are you disappointed that there wasn't more interest all the way along?

NANCARROW: Not really. I didn't care very much--then. As I told you, I've got a family now, so I'm interested in cultivating that interest.

Q: Has your current desire to cultivate that interest altered your approach to composition at all?

NANCARROW: No, I don't think so.

Q: Could you see yourself traveling to the United States in the next few years, in connection with this growing interest?

NANCARROW: Not really. Why would I go there? To give lectures? Look, I'm still not sure that I can even go to the U.S. They refused me a visa fifteen years ago--that's after I became a Mexican citizen.

Q: Did they give you any reasons?

NANCARROW: I was an "undesirable alien" then. I was an alien. As long as I was still an American citizen, they couldn't keep me out. In fact, I went back to New York--I think it was in '48--to get this punching machine. I was still an American, so they couldn't keep me out. After I became a Mexican citizen: "undesirable alien."

Q: What would be the problem with sending someone out with your piano rolls so the Studies could be performed in concert?

NANCARROW: On what piano?

Q: Is that the problem, the type of player piano that would be used?

NANCARROW: Yes, basically. Look, my pianos here, while not prepared, have a certain sound; it's a preparation, but not a Cage-preparation. One of them has a harpsichord type of sound, and the other a percussive sound. And apart from that, there's all kinds of adjustments that I've made for these things to sound a certain way.

I think the best reproductions of my music are on the Arch records, which are really top quality. If those are played in a place with top fidelity equipment, it's almost as good as live. So what more do I want?

Q: There would be an audience to hear the music performed on player piano.

NANCARROW: Oh, of course. You remember what Cage once said about electronic music, when it was just beginning to come in? He said that you have to have some theater. In other words, people don't go to an auditorium to hear a recording.

In fact, I remember, years ago, Quintanar gave a concert of what he called "live electronic music." Live. Electronic music is recorded, it's all on tape. You know what he did? He had this whole stage like a Hollywood set of equipment and everything, and for this concert he went around supposedly turning knobs and pushing buttons. That was his performance--the music was already there on tape. It was what Cage said, years ago: You have to put on a performance. (Cage is good at putting on performances!)

Q: Are you afraid that something would happen to the piano rolls in your absence, and therefore don't want them out of your hands?

NANCARROW: Well, partly that, but that's not really the main thing. It just wouldn't work, I don't think. Besides, if they're ever played, I'd like to be there to see how they're played.

Q: If the travel difficulties could be smoothed over, and you were approached to come to the United States with some of your piano rolls for performance, would you come?

NANCARROW: You mean to play them on other pianos? Who knows how long I'd have to take to get those pianos the way I wanted them. No, it's too complicated. I'm telling you, a good recording with good reproduction equipment is the best way to hear them. The Arch recordings are really top quality.

Q: The Columbia and New World recordings are not as good?

NANCARROW: No, those are terrible.

Q: Do you still have just one copy of each piano roll, or have you taken steps to make additional copies?

NANCARROW: No; just one copy.

Q: Punching a roll is very time-consuming, but once one has been punched, can it be reproduced more easily, or does the same process have to be repeated?

NANCARROW: Repeated. In the old days, when they made commercial rolls, they had very complicated machines: They made a master roll and then turned out copies. I don't think they even have that anymore. They might; I haven't even thought about that at this point. I just make a roll to play the piece.

Q: Could you tell us what you're working on now?

NANCARROW: I'm now on a series of what I call "didactic studies." I took a very early, simple piece--Study No. 2--and decided I would keep the complete harmonic and melodic structure and change all the rhythmic structure; as a didactic study for people to listen to. Unfortunately, most people identify a piece by the harmonic and melodic structure. (Of course, I don't know, if you put "The Blue Danube" waltz in a march, maybe they'd notice.)

These are very subtle changes in rhythm. I'm doing a whole series of pieces using this same piece, melodically and harmonically, but at different rhythmical bases, different rhythmical relationships.

Q: You describe the ostinato in Study No. 27 as "the ticking of the ontological clock." Is that the closest you've ever come to writing music with extra-musical associations?

NANCARROW: Well, the "ontological clock" is not programmatic. As a matter of fact, that idea came to me after I'd written it; I thought, OK, this is what it is, the ticking of the ontological clock. But I wasn't thinking of that when I wrote the piece.

Q: Would it be accurate to say that your primary interest in composition is tempo?

NANCARROW: Yes, of course. A sort of subdivision of tempo is rhythm and combinations of rhythm; polyrhythms or whatever. The other things, harmony and melody, I use only as a crutch for tempo or rhythm, that's all.

Q: Can you now perceive tempo relationships that years ago you wouldn't have been able to hear?

NANCARROW: Yes, probably. I hadn't thought of that, but I guess so, quite a bit. I do a thing, at whatever tempo relationship, and I hear it; then from there I go to something else, and I hear that-- yes, I suppose it's been a whole series of developments.

Q: Can you really hear such subtle differences as 60 to 61?

NANCARROW: Look, I can't say; since I know what's on paper, I hear it. But whether anyone else can hear it, I don't know.

Q: Which paper do you work at first when you compose, the roll or the score?

NANCARROW: First the paper that it's punched on. Afterwards, I make the score. I sort of make a primitive score first, but only for my own use in punching. Then I draw it out on the roll and punch it. The process of punching is sort of like editing: I make little changes here and there when I'm punching it. Then I make a legible score that people can read. The only time I ever re-vised something after punching it was No. 27. I repunched it be-cause it was too slow. My piano can go from zero speed to a fairly fast speed. Usually I calculate the middle tempo of what I'm writing. Then after I finish, I put it on: OK, a little less, a little more, it's just what I want. That time, I miscalculated very badly, and even up at maximum speed it was too slow. So I repunched, because I sort of liked the piece and I wanted to get it right. It was a proportion thing, a percentage thing, and you have no idea of the work that was.

Q: Do you find it constricting that there's only a certain length of time that a piano roll can cover in one piece?

NANCARROW: Not really. My time span is short anyhow. My attention span!

Q: In light of the brevity of your early instrumental scores, it would seem that the restriction on time with the player piano was congenial to your temperament.

NANCARROW: That's right; that's my personality. It's never been a problem.

Q: Do you see a general direction to your entire series of Studies? Is there a culminating point, a plateau that they could reach, or could they keep extending for however long you keep at it?

NANCARROW: I don't know; I hadn't even thought of that. As a matter of fact, at one time I was thinking of using three player pianos to do certain things. Well, since I've given up even two, I guess I'm regressing! I'm going back to one player piano, maybe I'll go back to one melodic line!

CATALOG OF COMPOSITIONS

1930	Sarabande and Scherzo for Oboe, Bassoon, and Piano	ACA
1935	Toccata for violin and piano	New Music
1935	Prelude for Piano	New Music
1935	Blues for Piano	New Music
1940	Septet	MS
1941	Sonatina for Piano	NY Public Library
1942	Trio for Clarinet, Bassoon, and Piano	MS
1943	Suite for Orchestra	MS
1945	String Quartet	MS
*	Study No. 1 for Player Piano	New Music
	Study No. 2 for Player Piano	NY Public Library
	Study No. 3 for Player Piano	MS
	Study No. 4 for Player Piano	MS
	Study No. 5 for Player Piano	MS
	Study No. 6 for Player Piano	MS
	Study No. 7 for Player Piano	MS
	Study No. 8 for Player Piano	Soundings, Fall 1977
	Study No. 9 for Player Piano	MS
	Study No. 10 for Player Piano	MS
	Study No. 11 for Player Piano	MS
	Study No. 12 for Player Piano	MS
	Study No. 13 for Player Piano	MS
	Study No. 14 for Player Piano	MS
	Study No. 15 for Player Piano	Soundings, Summer-Fall 1976

*Note: The composer has chosen not to date the Studies.

Study No. 16 for Player Piano	MS
Study No. 17 for Player Piano	MS
Study No. 18 for Player Piano	MS
Study No. 19 for Player Piano	Soundings, Fall 1977
Study No. 20 for Player Piano	Soundings, Fall 1980
Study No. 21 for Player Piano	Soundings, July-October 1973
Study No. 22 for Player Piano	MS
Study No. 23 for Player Piano	Soundings, Fall 1977
Study No. 24 for Player Piano	Soundings, Spring 1973
Study No. 25 for Player Piano	Soundings, Summer 1975
Study No. 26 for Player Piano	MS
Study No. 27 for Player Piano	Soundings, Fall 1977
Study No. 28 for Player Piano	MS
Study No. 29 for Player Piano	MS
Study No. 30 for Prepared Player Piano	MS
Study No. 31 for Player Piano	Soundings, Fall 1977
Study No. 32 for Player Piano	Soundings, Summer-Fall 1976
Study No. 33 for Player Piano	MS
Study No. 34 for Player Piano	MS
Study No. 35 for Player Piano	Soundings, Fall 1977
Study No. 36 for Player Piano	Soundings, Fall 1977
Study No. 37 for Player Piano	MS
Study No. 38 for Player Piano	MS
Study No. 39 for Two Player Pianos	MS
Study No. 40 for Two Player Pianos	Soundings, Fall 1977
Study No. 41 for Two Player Pianos	Soundings, Fall 1980

STEVE REICH ☐

photo: Gene Bagnato

Steve Reich was born on October 3, 1936, in New
York City. He studied composition privately with
Hall Overton; at Juilliard with William Bergsma and
Vincent Persichetti; and at Mills College (where he
received his M.A.) with Luciano Berio and Darius
Milhaud. He has two children: one by his first mar-
riage, and a second son by his present wife, Beryl
Korot, whom he married in 1976.

In the mid-1960s, Reich began exploring the musical effects of repeated patterns that incorporate
gradual changes over an extended period of time.
His investigation of such music has grown increasingly ramified and complex over the years, partially due
to his studies in the 1970s of non-Western music:
African drumming, the Balinese gamelan, and Hebrew
cantillation. In 1966, Reich formed his own ensemble
of musicians that has similarly grown over the years
into the group with which he performs throughout the
United States, Canada, and Europe.

Steve Reich was interviewed at his Manhattan
home on April 13, 1980. A courteous host, he was
direct and efficient without seeming remote or overly
businesslike.

Q: You've said that electronic music simply can't reach an audience
emotionally, the way instrumental music can. What, then, is your
attitude toward your early tape pieces?

REICH: My early tape pieces use speech as their only sound source.
They don't use electronic sounds, and I'll tell you a funny story
which answers your question.

My ensemble gave a concert in 1967 at the Park Place Gal-
lery. It was the first concert of live phase music, and for that
reason was very important to me. We played a four-piano version
of Piano Phase, which I thought went very well, and we played Reed
Phase, which was Jon Gibson playing soprano saxophone against
tape, and I also played the taped speech piece Come Out. After
the concert, a man came up to me and said, "I just loved Come
Out." I said, "Mmm?" He said, "It was so human."

Now I know what he meant: It was the human voice, and
there were words which he could understand, and they gradually
became more abstract. The source of that music, the sounds which
he heard, was the human voice, and the human voice is a very rich
sound source, acoustically speaking. I don't like the way electronic

music sounds. "Electronic music" meaning electronically generated music, where the origin of the sound is an oscillator, however complexly manipulated after it leaves the oscillator. That's my taste. What can one say on the level of acoustics? Quite a bit.

Take a person playing the violin. You say, "I want you to just draw the bow across the A string, no vibrato. Just play it 'like a machine.'" When you hear it, with your ear, you say, "That's perfect, a perfect tone." You put a microphone on it, and you put the microphone into an oscilloscope, and what do you see? All kinds of dancing irregularities. You take an oscillator and tune it to A and put it into the oscilloscope; you see an absolutely steady state wave form. You don't have that microvariation. If you have a program built in to make microvariations, then it follows the dictates of that, even if it's a random program. It doesn't come out sounding the same as the live instrument. Now, throw the oscilloscope out, blindfold yourself, and in five seconds your ear, your mind, and your heart react to those things. In other words, there is an acoustical basis, you can discuss it; there is an intellectual basis, it's not irrational. But you don't need those things. You can work with your own sensory apparatus. There is an effect, and the effect gets to people.

That's the reason I've generally moved away from electric organs. Now, my most recent piece, the Variations for Winds, Strings, and Keyboards, uses electric organs. The important thing to note is that they're sandwiched inside the sounds of flute, oboe, piano, and strings. They give the acoustical sound a kind of buzz, a kind of raspy timbre that I think is very effective; it also gives the piece a continuity, binding the various orchestral elements together. So I don't have any theory that will override my ear in a particular case. The final arbiter to me is what sounds right; what makes good musical sense in my ear, and in the ears of others.

Q: Any other comments about electronic pieces themselves?

REICH: Where's the masterpiece? Electronic music is not new; it goes back to the late forties. Outside of perhaps Stockhausen's Gesang der Jünglinge, Pousseur's Trois visages de Liège, Lucier's I Am Sitting in a Room, and whatever qualities some of my early tape speech pieces may have, where are the great works of electronic music?

Q: There are the Varèse pieces, Déserts and Poème Electronique.

REICH: There is a small body of work. But I don't know if those are Varèse's greatest works. I don't know if you can really compare them with Octandre and Ionisation.

Q: In 1970, you wrote: "The pulse and the concept of clear tonal center will re-emerge as basic sources of new music." Do you still believe this? Why do you think it will happen, or has begun to happen?

REICH: I think that it's happened in ways that I both could and couldn't foresee at the time. But first let me say that I'm not interested in making predictions anymore, although in fact several of them have come true. That's an activity which I'd rather not participate in anymore.

But to answer your question: The pulse, the way I use it, probably would apply mostly to the music that I make, and to music of other composers who write similarly to the way I do, of which there are now quite a few. Outside of that, there are other composers writing what is called New Classicism, or New Romanticism. While they don't work with a pulse in the sense of an absolutely steady beat, the way I work, they do work with much more of a regular rhythmic profile than the music of Boulez, Berio, Stockhausen, Cage. And certainly with a much clearer tonal center. There are also younger composers working close to rock and roll. I didn't foresee that these styles would be on the horizon then, but they are certainly playing a role now; and so, given a certain leeway, I would say that that prediction has in fact definitely come true.

Q: When you said that, were you thinking that more people were going to compose the same way you were composing?

REICH: No, although as you know many people are. Actually, when I wrote that, in 1970, I was thinking that we were at the end of a period of dominance of a non-rhythmic atonality that had come out of Vienna at the turn of the century; that this had run its course. It was in its third generation, which was an academic watering-down of the first generation (Schoenberg, Webern, and Berg) and the second generation (Stockhausen, Berio, and Boulez). Those who followed them in this country were already to me somewhat questionable because they seemed to be in the wrong place to be doing this kind of music; and their students just seemed to be insupportable.

Q: How do you mean in the wrong place?

REICH: Pierrot Lunaire was last year presented brilliantly at the 92nd Street Y with the cabaret songs that Schoenberg wrote as a young man. And in fact, Pierrot Lunaire can be heard as a kind of apotheosis of Kurt Weill (whom Schoenberg hated--which is too bad for Schoenberg, because they were both great composers). Pierrot is obviously a Germanic piece of music; more particularly, it

is the product of a very refined, humorous, big-city Berlin-Vienna
kind of attitude, endemic to 1910, 1920. Bartók's music and its
national sources have been remarked on many times.

All music that we know and love, for whatever reason--and
certainly Bach, Stravinsky, and Bartók are at the top of this list--
is clearly, "hearably" from a certain time and place. Since the
roots of the Second Viennese School were obviously where and when
they were, for an American in the 1950s, '60s, or '70s to take this
over lock, stock, and barrel is a little artificial. The sounds that
surrounded America from 1950 through 1980--jazz and rock and roll
--cannot be ignored. They can be refined, filtered, rejected, or
accepted in part, but they can't be ignored, or you're an ostrich;
you're ill-informed. To ape another culture of another time has
to have a certain sterility as a result. It's like taking a plant that
grows in another very different environment; you have to build a
hothouse, a miniature tropical environment, to keep it alive. That's
what museums are for, and that's why it's important to have orchestras that play the music that they do; I'm all for that. But in
terms of living composers, I don't think that you can pretend you
are someone who is completely divorced from this time and place.
And that's been very much how I've dealt with non-Western music;
I avoid sounding like it, because I think that would be absurd.

Q: One always hears about your studies of non-Western music--the
Balinese gamelan and African drumming. But considering such recent works of yours as the Variations for Winds, Strings, and Keyboards, the Octet and the Music for a Large Ensemble, have you
found that your more traditional studies with men like Milhaud,
Berio, and Persichetti are more of a resource than you had first
found them?

REICH: Yes. But I wouldn't limit it just to them. At the age
of fourteen, I first heard Bach, Stravinsky, and bebop--Charlie
Parker and Miles Davis. That nexus of tastes--Baroque music,
Stravinsky, and jazz--stayed with me ever since. That spoke to
something that was waiting to be spoken to inside of me, and since
then I've followed that path.

I spent part of July 1979 looking over Schoenberg's Studies
in Structural Harmony, which is a very fine book. The harmony
textbook that I used with Hall Overton--who was a very important
teacher for me before I went to Juilliard--was the Hindemith harmony book, which was just exercises. What interested me in the
Schoenberg book was his layout of the relationships between the tonic and dominant, subdominant, etc., and their various relative
minors. It's something that you know, but he displays it in a way
that makes it very clear, covering all the keys. It's a gestalt,
you take in the whole tonal system at a glance.

There's another study I made then of even more importance.

I had been drawn to a certain chord form; a series of fifths in both hands. This is the opening chord form of the second movement of the Second Piano Concerto by Béla Bartók. This kind of a chord structure--three fifths in the left hand and three fifths in the right-- I found in a song I wrote for Hall Overton in 1957. It's also Violin Phase: you've got C♯, F♯, G♯ in one hand, you take the F♯ down an octave, there's three fifths; in the right hand, you have A, B, E, you bring the B up over the E, and you've got the same chord form; three fifths and three fifths.

What I began to notice is, here's a chord form that I'm drawn to intuitively; I don't think about it, I just go to it. I knew that Bartók had used this, and I just zeroed in on that one page of his. I tried to analyze it in traditional terms, how he was moving it, at what distances he kept these groups of fifths. And I began to think, "Well, how would I move those same chords which I have kept static?" I'd move them rather differently than he did. I'd move them by suspension, one note at a time. So I wrote actually a whole movement--that was rejected--which was the first move- ment of the Variations. I had conceived of it all in strings. And this really had some dissonant parts, because if you move each in- dividual voice a semitone down you can end up with a tritone be- tween the tenor and bass. So it's functional harmony; it's going somewhere, creating dissonance to get to a point. I tried it out in strings, and it didn't sound very good. I dropped it, but kept the basic idea of suspensions, moving one note at a time. I started inverting the chord; keeping all of the notes in the middle register. (The bass I assigned to the occasional brass.) Keeping that invert- ed series of string fifths in the middle register creates a quite dif- ferent effect: They're less dissonant.

Several reviewers who don't listen and didn't read my notes very carefully said that the Variations goes from C Minor into B and back to C Minor. No way. It gradually goes through several keys between five sharps and three flats. Sometimes, with different notes in the bass, it goes through two or three modes in the same key. Harmonically speaking, for me, it is a very developed piece. I don't think anybody heard the piece as derivative of Bartók, but if you listen to just the string part, there is an influence there. I don't think I would have written it that way if I hadn't taken the time off to study that page of Bartók's.

I even went through a ground bass piece of Purcell at that time; studying various ideas that appeal to me, but that I hadn't looked at recently. I think it's very healthy for people like myself, who have spent a great deal of time with non-Western sources, to re-look at those parts of Western sources that meant a great deal to them. As a music history student one is obliged to look at al- most everything that precedes you as an academic assignment. In the course of doing that, one discovers certain periods or compos- ers that one loves; that gives you the energy later to go back and explore their techniques.

Q: A lot of the newspapers have created an image of you as a composer who stands outside the Western tradition of music. Do you see much of that? Does it bother you when you read that?

REICH: I'm obviously a Western composer, and so naturally I like to be understood as one. It's quite erroneous to think that I'm involved in some pursuit which has nothing to do with or is a complete break from Western tradition. Specifically, the way to connect my music to the Western tradition is not to look at what comes immediately behind me chronologically, the series of post-Webern compositions. Though if you want to do that, then look at Webern himself. Look at the number of notes on a page, think of the reduction involved in what he was doing, and the organization that went on in serial music. Actually, there's a great similarity between that and my early pieces, like Piano Phase: the severity and clarity of the organization. A very different kind of sound, but a very pared-down, severely organized kind of music. (That's changed considerably in time.)

More importantly, there are resemblances with Baroque and earlier music, and these are becoming increasingly clear recently. Particularity in procedure. My music is canonic; "phase" is merely a word for a new canonic procedure. Augmentation arises in the Middle Ages, and is an absolutely Western technique. These two techniques, in their various forms, are essential to what I do. And there is a certain resemblance, particularly in the Octet, to Stravinsky's music. I learned about the modes from studying Bartók. The non-Western influences are there, but they're there in a lot of composers: Debussy and Boulez, besides all the very obvious composers that I haven't mentioned.

As for the newspapers, I try not to get too involved in reviews. (Though like everyone else, I do.) Fortunately, I get mostly good reviews. I would say that there are two factors that determine whether music will survive or not. One is the reception by musicians themselves. If a number of musicians are attracted by a piece over a period of time, then it will survive; they're the ones who are going to decide whether to play it or not. The other factor is the naive, popular reaction of the concert-going public, and the less they are involved in musical politics, the better. We played a concert once at a prep school, and a kid came up to me afterwards and said, "Gee, I just loved that piece with the two pianos!" I said, "How old are you?" and he said, "Twelve." (He was a very bright twelve-year-old!) There's a pleasure I get from a naive reaction, and sometimes this can be a very telling musical reaction.

Q: Recent works of yours, such as the Octet and the Music for a Large Ensemble, were commissioned and premiered by groups other than your own musicians. What's been the effect of writing for other performers?

REICH: The effect of doing that has convinced me that I want to be able to do it with my own ensemble first. The Netherlands Wind Ensemble premiered the Music for a Large Ensemble. The experience of working with them was very positive; the musicians were very good, they're young, and they are interested in my music. The difficulty was, they had five rehearsals--which is quite generous, vis-a-vis the way things are usually done. But it can't compare with ten or twelve rehearsals over six months, with people who've played most of my music--which is what I would have done, and later actually did, with my own ensemble.

It's not only a question of the quality of performance. As I'm writing a piece, and I carry it through from inception to performance, I revise it; I'm a composer who changes a lot. I don't so much change notes and rhythms as a result of rehearsals; I change instrumentation, and I also reject either entire pieces or parts of pieces. Music for a Large Ensemble had five sections; the third section--in six flats--was always a drag, the tempo would go down in rehearsal. If that happens in several rehearsals with my musicians, then there's something wrong with the writing, because the musicians are good and know my idiom--so it's me. I didn't get far enough in the New York rehearsal procedure to really get clear about that. So when I went to Holland, the piece hadn't gone through the revision that would have happened if it had gone through complete rehearsals and then performance in New York City.

I came back from the world premiere in Holland very unsatisfied. After several rehearsals here with my ensemble, I took out the third section; I added violas and then changed notes in the soprano saxophones and violins; and the tempo went from about 176-184 to about 212, which lightened the piece up. (That happens to a lot of my pieces.) So there was nothing at all that the Dutch did wrong; they were as generous as they know how to be, and I hold nothing against them. But I learned something from the experience. I would prefer a sponsor to commission a piece and then have us come over and play it for them as well; since we go to Europe fairly regularly anyway, that's not a difficulty. If it's an orchestra piece, then I'm in another position, and I might have to do what I did at Carnegie Hall with the San Francisco Symphony commission, which is to do a chamber version first. I can't, as some composers can, hear fine distinctions of orchestration in my head. I depend in the finished piece on a minutely worked-out musical sound. Every detail means a great deal to me, and since I cannot project that in my imagination, I must hear it. So I'm committed to doing a first performance, or preview performance, with my own ensemble--possibly with the addition of guest artists if the instrumentation demands that.

Q: Do you have any interest in writing music for more traditional ensembles, such as a string quartet or art songs or opera?

REICH: In general, yes, I do. I already have; I believe the Octet is a step in that direction: string quartet, two pianos, two flutes, and two clarinets is simply not a combination that's difficult to find. The difficulties in playing it--of which there are several--are difficulties that classically trained Western musicians can solve, and are used to solving; there's no basically new technique, such as phasing was, that has to be accomplished. The Variations for Winds, Strings, and Keyboards is even simpler. If they are willing to get the electric organs and the amplification for the woodwinds, it is very easy for orchestras to do. I don't think there's any point to writing an orchestra piece that can't be done, or doesn't sound good.

Some of the combinations you mentioned are more appealing than others. The most appealing is string quartet, though I have no string quartet in mind at the moment. We were talking about Bartók before, and I spent quite a bit of time as a music student listening to his Third, Fourth, and Fifth; the little Beethoven that I really do enjoy is particularly Opus 132. If I were to write for that kind of combination, it would be more interesting if it were a sextet of two violins, two violas, and two cellos, giving me three pairs to work with. But it's not what's on my mind at the moment.

As for songs with piano, that raises a greater difficulty. Again, if it were two voices and two pianos, I'd say sure, because I'm really drawn to working with canonic structures. Canonic structures can be very different; in the Octet, the two violins are playing canons, but because of the length of their lines, it is almost an harmonic accompaniment to the pianos, which are also canonic.

As for opera, I have no interest in it at the moment. It has not been a form that I was attracted to at any point in my life --with the exception of The Rake's Progress, which I was introduced to by Professor William Austin at Cornell University at the age of seventeen and which I still love. But if someone had played me my Variations for Winds, Strings, and Keyboards five years ago, and said, "You're going to write this in five years," I'd have said, "You're crazy." So I've learned to say, "I don't know." I'm doing things now that I wouldn't have predicted. I think it's very boring to have manifestoes; I think it's more interesting to be a composer and a music student all your life, which I am.

Q: Could you see yourself setting text?

REICH: I'm thinking about it right now in terms of Hebraic text. It might start out being a transcription of the Book of Jonah exactly as it is chanted in the synagogue on Yom Kippur. I've recorded one cantor here in New York, and I'll record another who sings in a very simple, almost Sephardic, i.e., Oriental, style. I'm choosing Western cantors, because Oriental Jewish cantillation is like

Oriental music and can't be played on Western instruments. I was in Jerusalem in 1977, and recorded the first five verses of Bereshith, or Genesis, chanted by older Jewish men who were born in Baghdad, Yemen, Kurdistan, and India, and they sound like people from Baghdad, Yemen, Kurdistan, and India. The structure of the chant is always the same, and that's the part that interested me. (My background Judaically is Reform, and therefore I didn't learn very much. Because of my lack of education in Torah, I had more or less no interest in things Jewish the first 35 years of my life. I only began to study Hebrew when I was 37.)

I might transcribe the Book of Jonah. Not for performance by another male voice--I think that that would probably be a poorer version of what's done in the synagogue--but for female voice and/or solo instruments: clarinet, violin, and voice. We'll see what happens. It may be that I'll feel that it's better in its original form. I reject a lot of things, and I may reject this. But it's on my mind to try it. Perhaps settings of some of the Psalms in the original Hebrew would be easier since the oral tradition for singing Psalms has been lost in the Western Jewish tradition and would leave me free to compose the melody.

Q: Several works of yours from the late sixties and early seventies have just been published by Universal. Will they take on your more recent pieces as well?

REICH: Yes, they want to take on everything. The question is, when do I want to publish them. The attitude that I have toward publishing is that since I work as a performer in my own ensemble, when a piece is new it means a considerable number of performances and possibly recording, so I'm not anxious to have it published right away and give away half of my copyright royalty. That's my feeling in general. But Universal published some pieces we still do because I'd like other musicians to do these pieces. I never wrote music as a kind of private property for my ensemble, as a cult object which was not open to musicians in general. Quite the contrary, it was music which I wrote for performers who were interested in playing it, and there was no one else to do it. My policy over the years was to give scores to anybody who approached me and impressed me as being serious about really wanting to do it well.

A composer can't make money from selling printed music; the only money one can make is from performance royalties. You can hardly do that at all in America, because most performances of chamber works happen in universities, museums, or other locations where they're not even policed by BMI or ASCAP. But in Europe, all performances are chalked up.

I am obviously a Western composer, and so naturally I want to make my contribution in a form that's meaningful and serious

vis-à-vis Western tradition, which is in notated form.   I spent a
long time with the scores recently published by Universal, not because they're so long--they're very short--but because the original
ink manuscripts were written for my players, after a year or two
of doing the pieces from rough pencil scores.   The scores always
came after the world premiere, and still often do.   Therefore, they
were kind of skeletal, particularly with the early pieces that need
verbal explanation, such as the phase pieces: How many repeats
do you have for each bar in Piano Phase?   Two hundred or three?
So I wrote down the limits we've discovered in performance, and
they're in the score.   I keep the limits very wide, but they do define the limits of duration, so it's clear that you're not there to do
Vexations overnight, nor are you going to zip through it in five minutes; something in the middle.   This is derived from years and
years of playing the pieces, and seeing that they really go a certain way.   We never thought about how long they went; we didn't
think about how long Drumming was.   That was left entirely to the
musicians in my ensemble, but after we performed it many times
we realized that it can last from an hour and ten minutes to an
hour and twenty minutes.

The resulting patterns in Violin Phase were another thing.
Two or three violinists are playing at the same time, or two or
three channels of tape.   One violinist chooses patterns that he
hears resulting from that mix of the other voices, and plays them.
Now, which ones does he choose?   The score includes what I chose,
what Paul Zukofsky chose, and what Shem Guibbory chose.   In the
original manuscript, I wrote the violin parts out, and underneath
them I wrote the sum, what they all add up to, and below that,
ordered down, the various resulting patterns.   It's a shorthand.
But if you were a violinist and went into a music store, it'd be
Greek; you wouldn't know what it means.

The sixties led some composers to believe that notation was
going to change drastically; that has not come to pass.   So I spent
a great deal of time with these scores making them as conventional
as possible; taking the resulting patterns and writing them out one
after the other, so a musician could open up the music and read it.

My more recent pieces reflect a continued movement towards
traditional notation.   Outside of a couple of extra repeats per bar,
the Octet is notated conventionally.   The Variations has no repeated
bar markings whatsoever; you read it from beginning to end.

Q: Your music has a much wider audience than that of probably
any other contemporary composer, particularly among young people.
Certain facets of your music--the incessant beat, the repeated pat-
terns--have an affinity with rock music.   Do you see any parallels?
Do you have any interest in rock?

REICH: No, but I had a tremendous interest in jazz when I was younger. When I was fourteen, as I told you, I first heard jazz, and I started studying snare drum with Roland Kohloff, who is now tympanist with the New York Philharmonic. When I went to Cornell University as a philosophy major, I would play dances on the weekends. I played with musicians who listened to Miles Davis and Charlie Parker--that was the model. I was sixteen when I went to Cornell, and I thought I was too old to be a composer (although I secretly wanted to be one). When I was seventeen, I took a general music history course with Professor William Austin. He became a very important person in my life because he was the first to encourage me to become a composer. After graduating from Cornell I studied privately with Hall Overton. In 1958 I went to Juilliard, and throughout that time I was listening to jazz, particularly John Coltrane. While at Mills College I was listening to Coltrane again at the Jazz Workshop in San Francisco. John Coltrane's music between 1961 and 1964 made a tremendous impression on me. You can hear it.

So there was the effect of jazz at a formative period in my life, along with whatever it is in me physiologically that drew me to studying drums in the first place. There's obviously something in me that precedes all these influences, that drew me to rhythmic music. That's been continuously reflected in my own music. Therefore, I think that it's quite understandable that especially in comparison with other kinds of contemporary "serious music," the kind of music I compose and perform would attract people who listen to jazz or rock and roll or other forms of popular music. But I never really went through a rock-and-roll period. When I was fourteen, rock and roll was Bill Haley and Fats Domino, and I preferred Charlie Parker and Miles Davis. Perhaps they all have their places, but that was my choice.

My music has a beat, and perhaps you can even dance to it, so in that sense it's closer to jazz or rock and roll than is the music of Boulez, Stockhausen, Berio, Carter, Cage, and Crumb. I understand that. And I would add that most of the music we know and love has always stayed in touch with popular, folk, and dance sources whether it's Bach, Bartók, and Stravinsky, or Ives, Gershwin, and Copland. So if my music can appeal to serious musicians and to those who listen to jazz or rock and roll as well, I think that's genuinely a good situation which I welcome.

CATALOG OF COMPOSITIONS

1963	Film Music for The Plastic Haircut	MS
1964	Music for 3 or More Pianos or Piano and Tape	MS
1965	Film Music for Oh Dem Watermelons	MS
1965	It's Gonna Rain for tape	MS
1966	Come Out for tape	MS

1966	Melodica for tape	MS
1966	Reed Phase for soprano saxophone and tape	MS
1967	Piano Phase for two pianos or two marimbas	Universal
1967	Slow Motion Sound for tape	MS
1967	My Name Is for three or more tape recorders, performers, and audience	MS
1967	Violin Phase for violin and pre-recorded tape or four violins	Universal
1968	Pendulum Music for three or more microphones, amplifiers, and loud-speakers	Universal
1969	Pulse Music for phase shifting pulse gate	MS
1969	Four Log Drums for phase shifting pulse gate and log drums	MS
1970	Four Organs for four electric organs and maracas	Universal
1970	Phase Patterns for four electric organs	Universal
1971	Drumming for eight small tuned drums, three marimbas, three glockenspiels, two female voices, whistling, and piccolo	MS
1972	Clapping Music for two performers	Universal
1973	Six Pianos for six pianos	MS
1973	Music for Mallet Instruments, Voices, and Organ for four marimbas, two glockenspiels, metallophone, three female voices, and electric organ	MS
1973	Music for Pieces of Wood for five pairs of tuned claves	Universal
1976	Music for Eighteen Musicians	MS
1978	Music for a Large Ensemble	MS
1979	Octet for two pianos, string quartet, two clarinets/bass clarinet/flute/piccolo	MS
1979	Variations for Winds, Strings, and Key-boards for chamber orchestra or or-chestra	MS
1980	My Name Is--Ensemble Portrait (Octet) for tape	MS

ROGER REYNOLDS □

photo: Gene Bagnato

Roger Reynolds was born on July 18, 1934, in De-
troit, Michigan. At the University of Michigan, he received an undergraduate degree in engineering physics
and master's degrees in literature and music composition. His principal music teachers were Ross Lee
Finney and Roberto Gerhard. While studying music
at Ann Arbor, Reynolds was one of the founding members of the legendary ONCE Group. He is currently
a faculty member of the University of California at
San Diego where he helped found a computer facility,
the Center for Music Experiment and Related Research,
in 1979. In 1964, he married Karen Jeanne Hill.
They have one daughter.

Reynolds moves with remarkable assurance and
success through a wide range of compositional styles
and media, including theatricality, improvisation,
film and slide projections, and electronics. He also
has both the ear and the imagination for investigating
new timbral possibilities; along with his use of theatricality, these developments have resulted in the innovative notation used in many of his scores. Although a strong organizational sense underlies all his
diverse musical activities, it has never compromised
his unmistakable flair for the dramatic.

The authors spoke with Roger Reynolds during one
of his frequent trips through New York City on June
9, 1980. As with the Ralph Shapey interview, the
only convenient meeting ground was the judge's cham-
bers of the Fordham Law School courtroom. Reynolds
proved to be a relaxed and articulate interviewee.
Their only regret is that they didn't run the tape recorder throughout all their time together--his conversation proved equally fascinating after the interview,
touching on such topics as the music scene in California, films, his meeting with Conlon Nancarrow,
and the music of the Doors and the Beatles.

Q: You graduated from the University of Michigan with a degree
in engineering physics, but apparently were unhappy in this field
and decided to major in music. Did you return to the University
of Michigan specifically to study composition with Ross Lee Finney?

REYNOLDS: No. I didn't have studying composition in mind because I had no experience with composition; and there was certainly no indication that there was any reason to study it at that
point. I graduated from engineering school, went to work in the

missile industry in California, found it was not rewarding (as I had anticipated it would not be), and began to practice piano at a local church. When the number of hours I was putting in on the piano exceeded the number of hours I was working, I thought that some imbalance was arising that needed correction. So I decided to go back to the University and study music formally.

I had had a rather limited period of formal musical study. Actually, my involvement began when I was fifteen, at which time I started to study piano as a result of hearing a Horowitz record that quite overwhelmed me. When I went back to the University, I decided that the only practical goal at that stage (I had already gone through a five-year engineering program) was to be a small, liberal arts college piano teacher; that's what my thought was. So I practiced very hard and came, gradually, to the alarming realization that all of my fellow pianists at school spent virtually every moment of their time working on music that had been written, let's say, before 1910. Having come through engineering and being very much aware of contemporary practices and the need to be involved with them, this seemed an anomaly. It became more and more disturbing to me, in the abstract, probably because there was a lot of pressure on me to justify why, after just six months, I had left a lucrative engineering job which took five years to prepare for. There hovered about my life at that time these kinds of moral overtones that led me to examine why I was doing what I was doing. So I thought, what better way to find out something about contemporary music and how it's written than to take a course in composition? It happened that Ross Lee Finney taught a course at Michigan which was "composition for non-composers." (That class in fact produced quite a number of remarkable results.) It was filled with people from law school, engineering, and so on. He ran it with a younger composer as a teaching assistant. (In fact, the composer who was assisting then was Henry Onderdonk, who wrote a substantial article about Ross in Perspectives of New Music.) You had to write a piece; it didn't matter whether you even knew how to notate, you had to write a piece--I produced a string trio. At the end of the semester, these pieces were all performed and Finney reacted. His responses were coruscating, sometimes beyond belief in the degree to which they shattered a person. He tied into my little trio and reduced it to dust, rapidly and effectively.

After the class, however, he said to me, "You know, the opening gesture was actually very good, but you didn't understand its implications. If you're going to be in school this summer, I'm teaching and I'd be glad to meet with you about composing." So I thought, "Well, it can't be any worse than it already has been"-- however, it was. That summer was one of the most miserable periods of my life, because the harder I tried, the less everything I brought in met with his standards. Clearly, I was using my brain instead of my ear, because that's what I had to work with then, that's the way I had been trained; I had lots of involvements with system but not enough with listening to what the implications were in the sounds that I wrote.

At the point in September when I was just about ready to throw in the towel, one day he said, "Marvelous." So there was a reprieve, and I went on and worked with him intensively, which was an extraordinary good fortune because he's, of course, a great teacher in every way that one can imagine. Even though most of his students were doctoral candidates, I had the privilege of working with him as an undergraduate; sitting in on the composition seminar that at that time was a very strong group of people, including Crumb, Ashley, Van Solkema, Humel ....

I could go on about Finney indefinitely. Also about Roberto Gerhard.

Q: Did you study with Roberto Gerhard at both Michigan and Tanglewood?

REYNOLDS: Yes. That was a second facet of my good fortune, the way that those two men complemented one another: Finney with a kind of indomitable pragmatism who said bluntly and effectively the things that mattered to him--gesture, tonal function, putting your ideas down very clearly on paper, practicality in performer demands, and so on; whereas Gerhard was hermetic, extraordinarily intellectual and abstract, also highly emotional in his human interactions. Not that Ross is not, but Roberto was more so because he had much less experience in dealing with young people; he'd never taught at all before that time in his life, and he was in his sixties then. It later became known to me that he had a serious heart ailment at that time. But no one knew that then. And he gave of himself in the most astonishing way. I remember one particular lesson in which I was reaching for the meaning of what he was saying, and I paused out of the real awe that I had for him--he was almost saintly, an extraordinary man humanely, intellectually, musically--and he looked at me, smiled, and said, "Think of me as a lemon; squeeze."

To have studied with two such extraordinarily moral and musical teachers had an enormous impact. It allowed me to dream of moving forward in spite of my very late start: I didn't actually compose anything until I was twenty-five.

Q: Could you tell us about your role in the ONCE Group, and what importance it had for your development as a composer?

REYNOLDS: At the beginning, it consisted primarily of Bob Ashley, Gordon Mumma, and me. (There were, of course, others involved.) I was the fledgling in the group; Gordon and Bob had been active musically for a long time, and they had more or less separated themselves from the University; I was still in it.

What it provided for me was, first of all, a set of alternate ideals that were perhaps not looked on with great favor by the University. I dealt with these people on a daily basis; I saw their force, their integrity, in doing things that were considered very experimental at that time--and indeed were. We had a marvelous balance in ONCE which, I think, is what kept it going as long as it did. When I left, the balance was attenuated. The more mainstream instrumental and vocal values disappeared. Gordon kept up the electronic aspects while Bob tended to concentrate on the theatrical. When Gordon left, it went even more towards theater.

I think it gave me two or three particularly important things. One was the knowledge that you can do virtually anything if you have enough energy and capable friends. We found ways to get what we wanted to happen, whether it was dealing with the Unitarian Church, or the VFW, or the band director at the University; if you had a large enough array of reasonable arguments and energy, you could get things to happen. We did ONCE on a minuscule budget, yet we invited people from Paris, from New York, from California, and really put on a remarkable series. So the first thing was you can do what you want if you are willing to work hard enough and if your ideas are well founded.

Another, of course, was the flexibility of various media--the knowledge that very diverse values could work in easy conjunction. My first experiences with theater were there; The Emperor of Ice Cream was written for that festival. Tape, electronics, the use of music with visuals which Mumma was doing then with artist Milton Cohen, of the art department--a range of possibilities were planted immediately as a result of the vivacity and variety of people and ideals that were a part of the ONCE Group.

Q: How important has your science background been for your involvement with electronics in composition?

REYNOLDS: The most fundamental impact that the engineering education had was in making me less anxious in the presence of machines. I'm not afraid of them, as many musicians are.

I didn't actually use engineering or an interest in machines very directly until quite recently. Primarily, that was because I was not sufficiently impressed with the quality of sound that they produced. I've used tape a good deal, and electronics for amplification, but I've never had any interest at all in analog synthesis, none. I never used analog transformation except in very minor ways, modifying concrète recorded sounds.

The main thing is that the uses of science in art have always been natural notions to me, that when you need it, you use it. Several years ago, it came time for me to make a decision about whether or not to go into computer music. It was awkward in that it meant, essentially, going back to the sandbox when you're already professionally skilled--and it's not at all comfortable to play with sand and blocks again! But there, the engineering background certainly has been very useful. Before that time, I don't think it had much impact except in whatever influence it had on my thinking, planning systematically.

Q: In the 1960s, you spent a long time in Japan. Did your stay there have a greater effect on your music than the time you've spent in other countries?

REYNOLDS: Oh, indeed; certainly, for several reasons.

In Europe, I had a marginal existence. I didn't attend a single music festival in the four years that we lived in Europe; there wasn't any money. We were barely keeping alive. I had decided after leaving Michigan that the thing I had to do, because of my late start, was to establish a basic repertoire of pieces. So I proceeded to write the pieces that I thought necessary, just to learn what I could learn, without any regard for whether there was a chance of their being performed. So most of the time I spent in Europe was very isolated, and at an absolutely minimal subsistence level.

When I went to Japan, I was much better funded and could live decently. Also, of course, the values that were offered by Japanese society were strikingly different from those in Europe. I was learning the language and felt much closer to the sources of Japanese ideas and culture than I had to those in Europe. Strangely--and I don't really know what reason there might be for this-- many of my Japanese colleagues said after I arrived that they thought that the music I had written before I came--Quick Are the Mouths of Earth, Ambages, Blind Men to a degree (although I'm not sure how many heard that)--was very Japanese. I don't know what they meant by that. Maybe Quick because it has long periods of sustained sounds that are static, without much melodic movement; textural exploration, an interest in the moment as opposed to the evolution of things.

There was certainly an immediate and very intense interaction between myself and a number of Japanese composers. And also in my experience with Bunraku--the puppet theater always has been the thing that had the largest impact on me, more than Noh, certainly more than Kabuki--and some of the traditional instruments, particularly the shakuhachi, which I had an opportunity to hear just a few weeks after being there, in a little tatami room--it was an extraordinary experience that was arranged by Toshi Ichiyanagi.

Q: You have a book coming out soon on Japanese music.

REYNOLDS: Yes. It's a complex task, and in fact I'm going to

Japan at the end of this week to do what I hope will be the final editing on some translations of writings by Takemitsu, Takahashi, and Yuasa. I think people will find them surprising. It's not a set of essays that you would expect if you were to tap three prominent American composers. They are all previously published writings, and their concerns, the things they choose to write about, are far wider in scope than I think you would find here. They are, of course, concerned to a considerable degree with the contrast between Japanese tradition and the requirements of what you might call the international market, and that intrigues me: the roots of their energies, the roots of the current energies of Japan. The primary article, the largest, is by Takemitsu, called "Mirror of Tree, Mirror of Grass." The image that he draws is between the existence in the West of major individual sources which moved music--such as a Beethoven--and, in Southeast Asia, a music which is anonymous, a social phenomenon that doesn't derive from a single person; if you cut out half of its practitioners, it continues without change. He sees Japan, strangely enough, as being separate from both of those traditions.

Perhaps, again as a result of the work with the ONCE Group, I've always felt that part of the responsibility of any creative person was to contribute, in some way, to the flow of information experienced within one's discipline. I think that these Japanese are important composers and thinkers, and I think that it could be of real value for the West to have access to their current thoughts. As you know, Japan produces an enormous number of coffee table books on the arts and of scholarly works on medicine, electronics, perhaps sociology. But the amount of information that we have about current intellectual or aesthetic thought there amounts to virtually nothing.

Q: In 1966, you did a great deal of research in how time is perceived. One result was <u>Blind Men,</u> which utilizes three different approaches to time perception. What has been the effect of <u>Blind Men</u>'s experimentation on your own use of time in subsequent compositions?

REYNOLDS: I have always felt that Cage was accurate when he pointed to time as the most fundamental aspect of music, and the articulation of time as being the thing which, presuming an appropriate set of sounds, was most important in making an impact on an audience. It's certainly the basis of the architecture; there can be no doubt about that. And, perhaps partly because my father was an architect, that's always been the primary way in which I have looked at music, as a kind of architectural problem.

However, in reading about the perception of time, it became clear that borrowing ideas from architecture, the idea of symmetry, for example--symmetrical forms such as certainly were important in much of the history of Western music--was absolute nonsense.

You couldn't experience symmetry temporally, as you could visually. Those kinds of things led me to try to change my approach with Blind Men.

Before that time, I had used almost exclusively a rather complex organization of time on the basis of ratios, where the movements and then the phrases or sections--right down to the individual event in each piece--were all controlled by a set of simple, whole-number ratios. I found that that produced something which sounded orderly, but did not produce the thing that sounded experientially as I wanted it. And so I thought that it was necessary to break out of that and do something that allows for those moments when you want a more flexible experience to enter into the music.

I liked much of what happened in Blind Men. If you look at the score, the materials look chaotic and almost unmanageably disassociated. But as an actual experience it doesn't have that effect; my flexible intentions come through. And that's because I was very careful about the nature of the functions: expository material is controlled in a certain way; material which links is controlled in another way; material which allows reflection, in a third way. So those ideas carried over into other pieces, certainly in Threshold, and Again, and in I/O.

Subsequently, though, I again got dissatisfied. It seemed to me that the lack of certain traditional architectural supports--let's say, of tonal function--in contemporary music meant that some other means of establishing an undercurrent of growth, or of dissipation, was important. And I got to using--and still do, primarily--geometric series to control the proportional underpinnings of almost all of the work that I have done since the early seventies. This has to do with groupings of events that tend either to accumulate length or to become shorter; not in a regular, arithmetic (or additive) way, but in an irregular way. So the formal effect is of acceleration or ritard: accumulations that one hears cresting, almost wavelike. That sensation has been important to me recently.

At this point, in fact, I'm looking for another approach. I feel comfortable with the geometrical series, but now they seem a bit too easy. So I'm searching for other ways of organizing time.

Q: In your 1968 essay, "It(')s Time," you spoke of the primary "importance of changing and enlarging ... the individual listener's responses" toward the temporal aspect of music. Have you come any closer to achieving significant change in this respect?

REYNOLDS: It's very hard to impose different outlooks on audiences without being able to reach them through a fundamental alteration of the context within which music is heard. I've tried that in a number of ways.

I think that the most experimental activities of mine in the past five years have been a series of pieces called Voicespace, for quadraphonic tape. One of the things that I have tried to impose as a requirement in those pieces is complete darkness or a carefully constrained visual experience. The excuse for that is that one is distracted by contradictory visual cues, and it's difficult to give yourself to the auditory illusions that the sounds are trying to simulate.

Another benefit is that if you do close your eyes, you of course are separated from other means of gauging the passage of time. I've found that the most vivid and interesting temporal experiences have happened with those pieces; pieces in which you're sitting in a dark, very quiet room, and your sense of what it is that's significant becomes entirely auditory. I usually present Voicespace as a kind of lecture-demonstration, and I specifically ask people to close their eyes. Of course, not everyone does; but when you do, and you're free to be in an auditory realm, more can happen.

People tend to feel that music needs to delimit time by some kind of tactus in order to make it sensible, and that they need to know what the "dimensions" are. But if you remove some of the standard trappings of musical discourse (as in these pieces; much of the sound is vocal and only relatively pitched), you can get away from some of the feeling of compulsion that Western listeners have about trying to control their perception of time.

The truth is that it's no longer a terribly central thing to me to try to create fresh temporal experiences. I think that there are, clearly, a number of composers who are working with vast-- perhaps far too vast--temporal canvases, trying to create that sense of openness.

I have in mind a project that may be realized at IRCAM within the next couple of years, which would have a quite different approach to the use of temporal experience. It would involve extremely intense auditory and visual events coming in a perfectly controlled environment--that is, absolutely silent and totally black-- over extremely wide temporal intervals. I'm interested in what would happen as a result of such stimuli, partly because of curiosity regarding the analogs between auditory and visual afterimages that I got involved with in doing I/O (and then never actually had a chance to carry out fully because of the need for special conditions; IRCAM has such an auditorium, where it would be possible to have complete silence and total blackness). I'd like to deal with unpredictable, though structured, extremely intense, individual auditory events coming, as it were, out of "nowhere."

Q: You've written several multimedia works that use slide projections. Do you think these works suffer when one experiences only a recording of them?

REYNOLDS: The first time that I had to face that was in recording

Ping for commercial release. It wasn't serious there because I was able to augment the density of events; the recorded version is considerably more musically or auditorily dense than one that I would have done improvisatorily within the media context.

I try to write the music so that it holds up by itself. I like Compass, for example, and feel that it works well without the slides. In my works that include them, the slides are there for the purpose of guiding or assisting the listener, in view of the fact that he or she is going to have a limited amount of experience with the piece, especially its textual dimensions. I tend not to set texts so that they can be readily understood, and it seems a minimal courtesy to provide an audience with the words, but in a way that doesn't force them to use flashlights and squint at programs.

In the case of Ping, the slides have an architecture of their own; their sequence has its own form. In Compass, the purpose of the slides is to play upon what I feel will be a listener's natural tendency to develop images out of the very symbolic flow of the music. I feel that the music is rather dreamy in much of its meanderings, and it seems to me that one's tendency is going to be to have images. I hope it is; that's what Borges is after in the poem. The Uelsmann montages are meant to suggest a world for those images, but not actually to augment or replace what's happening auditorily.

Q: Isn't there the problem that the images could distract from the music?

REYNOLDS: I've never used them in a situation that I thought allowed that. In the case of Compass, it's quite clear in the score that the slides are supposed to appear and disappear periodically, but rather briefly; they evoke imagery, rather than serve as something which you are supposed to study and retain. In the case of Ping, the solution to that potential problem was to insist that each element should interfere with every other. The projection of an image on film, the projection of words on slides, were made onto separate planes, and the music also ran non-synchronously with the projections, although the overall relationships were broadly ordered. I planned that one would necessarily have to redirect one's attention.

It is certainly possible that visual images could detract from the perception of the sound, of its organization and substance, but I don't think I've been in a situation where I allowed that to happen.

Q: Do you have to relinquish a certain amount of artistic control in collaborating with someone for the images?

REYNOLDS: I've never really collaborated with anybody until this

year, when I did a media piece with filmmaker and video artist Ed
Emshwiller. In that instance, we approached the task through a
series of meetings. It was clear from the beginning that we didn't
want to coordinate the visual and the auditory; we approached it
through alternation. There was an auditory introduction, then images faded in, then the sound came in again and the images went
out, and only at one point did we actually put them together, and
the coordination of that was very carefully worked out. That was
an area during which there was, so to speak, an overload situation;
so, again, there wasn't the problem of relinquishing.

I think it's a major problem. In fact, I gave a paper at
that unfortunate intermedia festival in New York last January; it's
called "Modes, not Media, Matter." The idea is that too much attention has been paid to technical gimmickry, and not enough to
thinking about what the visual modality involves, what factors are
common to the two and how they might be profitably coordinated.
I've been doing a lot of thinking about that. It is not easy to combine input to several modalities effectively; they often do interfere
with one another. That is why I think that most "media" work, the
great majority of it, is sensationalism, not fully developed art.
This may have been one of the hidden messages in Gerhard's teaching. He always said that working in composition meant working
with the total person; every aspect of emotion and intellect and energy had to go into each composition, or it wasn't a composition--
only an exercise.

Q: In 1974, you revised The Emperor of Ice Cream. What prompted those revisions, and how extensive were they?

REYNOLDS: They weren't terribly extensive. That piece was written in '61 and '62, and it was put together more rapidly than I
would have liked, ideally. It was done for a group of singers that
I knew existed at the University, and for the Bob James jazz trio.
(Bob, of course, now has a big name in many contexts, but at that
time he was winning college jazz festivals.) I really wrote it for a
jazz trio. It turned out that, in that trio, the pianist and the percussionist were very reliable and of very high quality, but the bass
player read music a lot less well, and was less technically agile.
Thus, the bass part was rather sketchy. The primary thing I did
in the revision was to enlarge the bass part.

I also increased the flexibility of the work's timing. The
original piece was premised on a book--I've forgotten at this point
what book it was--that gave lists of the average duration of common
English phonemes. I had gone through and analyzed Wallace Stevens' text on that basis. I tried to create a vocal style that almost
never uses melisma (in fact, it occurs at only two points in the
piece), and always involves the precise proportions that the original
phonemes have in Stevens' text. The scale changes, of course, so
that different lines move at different temporal rates, but within that,

the pauses and lengths and so on are all exactly as this book said they ought to be, according to the rules of English pronunciation.

When I listened to this work carefully again, I realized that a lot more flexibility would be in order. I would say that this is another tendency of all my work: to rather rigorously use systems in creating the materials, but to be quite open to the notion that after the materials are there, it may be that the exigencies of performance require changes. Generally, those changes would be of a temporal nature: articulation, how much of a pause, how long one should hold a note, and so on.

Q: In their instrumentation, " ... from behind the unreasoning mask" and " ... the serpent-snapping eye" are very similar pieces. Then there's the further connection of the Melville references, which seems to be a deliberate attempt to refer one piece to the other. What deeper relationships, if any, exist between the two pieces?

REYNOLDS: Of course, " ... from behind the unreasoning mask" also relates to an earlier text for a choral-orchestral piece called Masks, that was done in 1965. I always liked that image, as Melville presents it--that is, the idea of masks, what is real and what is illusory. I don't remember exactly why I fixed on that phrase, but that chapter of Moby-Dick--"The Quarter-Deck"--is a very compelling one, an interesting and tumultuous one. When I sat down to do " ... from behind the unreasoning mask", I had in mind (metaphorically, of course) that the mask represented unreasoning authority, and that players would attempt to deal with that authority in various ways. Authority was vested in the quadraphonic tape; very aggressive transients continue to come and the players react to them in a variety of ways, depending on the section.

But those transients are all organized according to geometrically expanding and contracting temporal series, so each series of transients either ritards or accelerates through the course of the entire piece (with the exception of the six very clangorous events which are equally timed). While planning the work, I dealt with those series, moving them around in temporal relationships to one another, until I got an overlap, a coordination between them, that pleased me. Then the structure of the piece really was an explication of the relationships between these series, a series of trombone attacks, a series of wood attacks, metallic percussion, and so on.

Some time later, I wanted to do a piece for a colleague, Ed Harkins, who is a most remarkable trumpet player. It occurred to me that it would be interesting to make a set, to make a pair of works out of the same geometric series. Normally, I don't ever repeat anything--at least consciously; each piece represents some new kind of task. But in this, it seemed that an interesting thing might be to take the same architectural elements and force them to behave differently. So I looked for an image (just to be pedantic) in the same chapter; I went through and just looked for striking phrases. One was " ... the serpent-snapping eye"; I still have no idea what it actually means, but it's implication is clear. It comes from a section when Melville is describing Ahab's effort, essentially, to seduce the crew into his own altered state of consciousness. I thought that since the earlier piece was about reacting to an active and external form of authority, then one might conceive of another inner form of authority, which was submission--joining with or going with--and that this also had something to do with drugs, with being high in a variety of ways. So that's where the image came from. The "eye" suggested a mandala, a center which radiates symmetrically, which may see or be seen into.

What I did was to take those geometric series that tend, as I said, to converge, and instead of having them end, I had them temporarily reverse and return. So in " ... from behind the unreasoning mask" the tendency is to arrive abruptly at a termination; whereas in " ... the serpent-snapping eye", it's always wave-like; you take a long time to get into something, it crests, and then it reverses itself and drops away. So the piece is about radiant centers, whereas " ... from behind the unreasoning mask" is about delimited temporal intervals. I liked very much the idea that the ensemble in " ... from behind the unreasoning mask" involves problems of tension, of accuracy, of submission to the tape's authority and reaction to it; whereas in " ... the serpent-snapping eye", it's a flow; one goes with something that one hears developing on the tape, and the question of absolute synchrony between the tape and the instruments never arises. Of course, it does in the middle section between the three instrumentalists, because there they have to emulate the tape, to be authoritative in their own way.

There are a number of connections, then: The works are the same length, one tape is entirely concrète and the other is entirely synthesized; both works are concerned with an ambiguity between the taped materials and the live materials. And I would say that in " ... the serpent-snapping eye" there occurs, certainly, the most intriguing ambiguity that I ever managed, partly because of the spatial drifting of the synthesized components, and partly because of their extraordinary consonance and richness. The synthesized materials are based on acoustic properties of the instruments that are playing live, and you get a lot of very strange experiences in a live performance--a sort of aquatic divestiture, events are vivid but one cannot always identify their sources.

Q: Is there any other kind of connection between these two works and your other works that make use of a Melville text?

REYNOLDS: No. There are several reasons for using Melville; one is that he's defenseless because his copyrights have run out. And I've gotten into unpleasant situations over getting text permissions.

Also, of course, his language is so marvelously rich in allusion--it tolerates all kinds of things. So he's an ideal collaborator.

Q: Did you have any difficulty in getting Samuel Beckett's permission for Ping or A Merciful Coincidence?

REYNOLDS: Strangely, I had no trouble at all getting his permission. I've had difficulty with Grove Press, but not with Beckett.

The same with Borges. When I wrote Borges about the text for Compass, he proposed an alternate translation. I had to write back and argue at some length why it was that I couldn't accept the translation that he had commissioned for his collected English works. And he acquiesced there too. So it may be messy, but it is usually not impossible.

Q: There's a curious similarity in the program notes for Fiery, Wind and for " ... from behind the unreasoning mask". In Fiery Wind you utilize what you call "a metaphysical image: the existence in human affairs of an undefined force, disinterested but catalytic." " ... from behind the unreasoning mask" tries "to evoke a kind of 'Unreasoning' monolithic authority." One thinks in turn of works like Ping, Blind Men, Compass, Voicespace, and especially The Emperor of Ice Cream. Throughout all of these works, there seems to be a fixation on human frailty and death. Have you been deliberately trying to deal with these issues, is it something you find in your work only in retrospect, or are we reading too much into the music?

REYNOLDS: I wouldn't include death as a concern, although you can certainly do so if you wish.

In fact, it has annoyed me that I seem to be unable, generally speaking, to write light-hearted or brief pieces. I feel often that I am very light-hearted as a person, but when I sit down to write music it doesn't seem to come out that way.

My favorite story about that concerns the writing of Ambages, the flute piece that I did when my wife Karen was attending a workshop in Switzerland, taught by Marcel Moyse. I went along and she said, "Why don't you write a little flute piece while you're here, something like Syrinx--something that could be played, that's really very simple and short." I thought that was a splendid idea; then I came out with this monstrous, complex piece. I really don't understand why it needs to be that way.

Another anecdote--this is the best I can do, I think, in answer to your question. I got an award from the National Institute of Arts and Letters in 1971. I don't know if you know how those things are run, but everyone sits in rows up on the Institute stage, and whoever it is that is running the ceremony stands up and reads citations and then you walk up and get your award. I remember knowing that I was next, so as he began to read I rose and started forward. And I heard him saying something about "a troubled world of conflicting emotions," and I thought, "He must be talking about somebody else; I'm out of order." So I went back to my seat. Then he finished and announced my name, and I thought, "That was me?" And I walked forward and created a certain disruption in the ceremony by having to read the inscription and verify whether that was actually what I had heard. Such a perspective would never have occurred to me.

Of course serious human questions matter to me. I've never had any direct involvement in political matters--again, not on principle--because I believe that the greatest contribution that human beings can make to their time is to do their best at whatever it is that they do; if we all did that, things would be far better. So certainly I tend to have always some subject in mind when I write a piece. It is by no means always textually based; it is often metaphoric. The more powerful those generative images are, the more archetypical, the more likelihood there is that the resulting music will in some sense find a resonance in the listener.

So I wouldn't include "death" as a concern, but I certainly would questions of authority, the dilemmas of individuals and masses of people in the face of varying kinds of authority.

Q: What are you currently working on?

REYNOLDS: The main project is to finish a work which is for computer-processed voice and live singer; it's the fourth in a series of these pieces entitled Voicespace. The text is again by Borges, a poem called "The Palace." It concerns an enormous structure located in an unknown society on an unknown landscape. It's one of the few poems of Borges, I feel, that contains within poetical form the kind of visionary and remarkably exhaustive imagery that is in some of his earlier stories.

I read it--as I do when I'm going to work with a text, I've been reading it over a period of several years--and felt that there were two kinds of personas in the text. I began to call them the voice of active authority and the voice of reflective authority. The one was an actor in the course of events who described in a very direct way what it was that was there; the other was one who was in a position to be, to a degree, separated, standing apart from the course of events. So I worked with vocalist Philip Larson, settling upon two voices--his normal voice for active authority, and a special sort of old man's voice, with complex sonic characteristics, for the voice of reflective authority. And then we worked at recording them, over a period of about a year, rehearsing and recording these lines, and then went to Stanford and recorded them at CCRMA's digital recording studio, repeating takes again and again until just the right inflection was obtained. Then I edited the resulting sound files with their digital editing programs, and processed them so that they took on the characteristics of a space that could not physically exist, but which one can certainly experience auditorily.

This space, for example, has the characteristic that the decay time for its reverberation is about fifty seconds. When a single word has been spoken with some force, it will last a long time. And the elements retained are the pitch and spectral characteristics of the primary vowel in the word that has been reverberated, that has stimulated the reverberation program. I had Larson give the text a very spacious treatment which allowed vowels to overlap and beat against one another--to create what is a rather orchestral effect. Then I refined this imaginary, this programmed room by filtering spectral emphasis so that it has two states that are mathematically exact obverses of one another: One selectively reverberates low frequencies very intensively; the other, with equal intensity, certain high frequencies. Then, when the active authority voice speaks, it speaks with an omniscience and resonance which is quite chilling. (The people at Stanford jokingly referred to it as the voice of The Force. We proposed approaching the National Science Foundation over the phone with this voice--they couldn't possibly have refused.) The reflective authority is resonated in the opposite way, so that a sonic halo shimmers above the words. Spoken words become a harmonic and orchestral fabric which he sings against.

He sings in a pseudo-language that I have derived from the actual text. It's a very demanding work, sung, successively, in chest and falsetto registers--the vocalist has to have a very wide range. The part goes from low D up to F on the treble clef; the chest voice maybe from B flat, below middle C, up to F or F sharp, the top of the treble clef in falsetto. The vocabulary has forty-four words: Twenty-two of them are sung in falsetto, and have a vowel-consonant-vowel structure, and twenty-two are for the chest register, and are consonant-vowel-consonant. They're employed in such a way that their articulation allows very rapid ornamentation to take place alternating between chest voice and falsetto. So he can do some rapid and very precise ornaments which are quite extraordinary. I don't know of any other music, so far, that's allowed vocal ornament to be quite so specific. The reason it can be so clearly articulated is that it's switching registers; the vocal track is reconfigured very rapidly and my "language" provides all the consonants I need in order to articulate each of these grace notes. This work, then, combines a tape and a series of live vocal sections; their proportions are logarithmically related. The live sections accumulate length and the taped sections have the same proportions, exactly the same timings, but are out of order. It's about seventeen minutes long.

Another piece that is in process, not quite completed yet, is a work that was written for TASHI. Unfortunately, TASHI's personnel instability has hindered its progress. Shadowed Narrative is based on a group of four sentences from García Márquez's The Autumn of the Patriarch. That novel's most extraordinary feature is the degree to which time and perspective and voice are incessantly and marvelously altered so that from moment to moment, inside of one sentence--and the sentences are very long--the century, the time of day, the person speaking, and so on, whether it's a character or a narrator, will change without notice, yet, somehow, gracefully. In a sense, it is not so unlike The Tale of Genji, the original novel by Lady Murasaki. One of the things that led me to an interest in it was this unaccountability--we don't really know who's saying what or when or why.

I use four sentences that increase in length. I read them, read them and read them and read them and read them and read them until I came to a way of reading them that had a narrative flow that I liked. Then I timed that and made that the temporal structure of the piece. Then I went through and wrote four lines: There's a violin solo at the beginning, then a clarinet solo, then cello, and then finally the piano. What happens, essentially, is that each instrumentalist plays an individual and highly idiosyncratic solo, while the other three players shadow; they play so softly that it's almost impossible to tell what they're playing. They shadow the narrator in the most mimimal way possible. Then in the last movement, when the piano comes in, some of the earlier solos become again parts of the material, but played very, very softly, so that you have multiple layers of implication. There's very little direct relationship to the text; rather, I was seeking the sort of changes of perspective and narrative that García Márquez achieves as the underpinning of the piece.

That might be another way of getting time organized; that is, at least the way I do it in this work.

CATALOG OF COMPOSITIONS

1959	Epigram and Evolution for piano	CF Peters
1960	Acquaintances for flute, contrabass, and piano	CF Peters
1960	Sky for soprano, alto flute, bassoon, and harp	MS
1961	Four Etudes for Flute Quartet	CF Peters
1961	Continuum for viola and cello	MS
1961	Wedge for chamber ensemble	CF Peters
1961	Mosaic for flute and piano	CF Peters
1961	String Quartet No. 2	CF Peters
1962; 74	The Emperor of Ice Cream for eight voices, contrabass, piano, and percussion	CF Peters

1963	A Portrait of Vanzetti for male speaker, instrumental ensemble, and tape	MS
1964	Fantasy for Pianist	CF Peters
1964	Graffiti for orchestra	CF Peters
1965	Quick Are the Mouths of Earth for chamber ensemble	CF Peters
1965	Gathering for woodwind quintet	CF Peters
1965	Ambages for flute	CF Peters
1965	Masks for SSAATTBB and orchestra	CF Peters
1966	Blind Men for twenty-four voices and chamber ensemble	CF Peters
1967	Threshold for orchestra	CF Peters
1968	... between ... for orchestra and electronics	CF Peters
1968	Ping for flute, piano, percussion, electronics, tape, slides, and film	CF Peters
1969	Traces for solo piano, flute, cello, electronics, and tape	CF Peters
1970	I/O: A Ritual for 23 Performers for nine female vocalists, nine male mimes, two flutes, clarinet, two technicians/performers, electronics, and projections	CF Peters
1971	Again for two sopranos, two flutes, two trombones, two contrabasses, two percussionists, and four-channel tape	CF Peters
1974	Compass for tenor, bass, cello, contrabass, four-channel tape, and projections	CF Peters
1974	Phantom Panel for four-channel tape	MS
1975	" ... from behind the unreasoning mask" for trombone, percussionist and assistant, and four-channel tape	CF Peters
1975	Still (Voicespace I) for four-channel tape	MS
1975	The Promises of Darkness for chamber ensemble	CF Peters
1976	A Merciful Coincidence (Voicespace II) for four-channel tape	MS
1977	Only Now, and Again for twenty-three winds, piano, and percussion	CF Peters
1978	Fiery Wind for orchestra	CF Peters
1979	Less Than Two for two pianos, two percussionists, and four-channel computer-generated sound	CF Peters
1979	" ... the serpent-snapping eye" for trumpet, piano, percussion, and four-channel computer-generated sound	CF Peters
1980	Eclipse (Voicespace III) for four-channel tape	MS
1980	Incidental Music for The Tempest	MS
1980	The Palace (Voicespace IV) for baritone, four-channel tape, and lighting	CF Peters

GEORGE ROCHBERG □

photo: Gene Bagnato

George Rochberg was born on July 5, 1919, in Paterson, New Jersey. He studied under Hans Weisse,
George Szell, and Leopold Mannes at the Mannes
School of Music, and with Rosario Scalero and Gian-
Carlo Menotti at the Curtis Institute of Music, where
he received a B. Mus.   He has also received a B. A.
from Montclair State Teachers' College and an M. A.
from the University of Pennsylvania.   He is presently
on the faculty of the University of Pennsylvania.   In
1941, he married Gene Rosenfeld.   They have one
son (deceased) and one daughter.
    In the 1950s, Rochberg established himself as an
important composer of serial music.   In 1963, however, he composed his last twelve-tone work.   The
next several years could be characterized as a transition period for Rochberg; during this time, he composed several collage pieces which contained literal
quotations of other composers as well as gestures
evocative of various styles of music.   His most recent works are more homogeneous stylistically and
reveal a renewed preoccupation with tonality.
    The authors interviewed George Rochberg at his
home in Newton Square, Pennsylvania, on March 16,
1980.   At first somewhat cautious as he sized up the
nature of the project, Rochberg soon relaxed and appeared to enjoy the opportunity to respond to their
questions.   After completing the interview, they remained with the Rochbergs for some time, engaging
in a wide range of conversation and enjoying their
gracious hospitality.

Q: In your 1963 essay, "The New Image of Music," you describe
the importance of what you call "spatialization" in music.   Is this
concept still important to you?

ROCHBERG: I'm not particularly interested in it for myself any
longer--which is not to say that it may not continue to have validity
for other composers.   In the past, whenever I wrote about music,
I did so to try to clarify and crystallize my thoughts about what
seemed to me to be an important issue or question or problem.
At the time that I wrote that particular essay, it wasn't so much
that I was directly involved in spatialization myself (although I'd
made some forays in that direction) as that it seemed to me to
be a very special and distinct characteristic of a good deal of contemporary music in the period from 1960 to 1965, the period that
saw the apex of the whole efflorescence of new music.

Spatialization is probably still valid for certain composers. I would guess, for example, that the minimalist music of composers like Steve Reich tends very much toward a kind of spatialization, the kind in which texture and surface is all important. Even though it's internally active, such music lacks a line, i.e., it is not making any significant progression from one point to a later point, but is rather concentrating on sound configurations for their own sake.

If the idea of spatialization still has any value, then that value lies in trying to grasp one of the essential characteristics and tendencies of the music of the sixties. It was the acoustical or sonic aspect of the philosophic or psychological impulse that was driving composers toward spatial realization. Frankly, I think that enough radical changes have taken place in the seventies so that what we're talking about has, by now, become ancient history.

Q: In your own music, spatialization would refer to pieces such as Apocalyptica and Black Sounds?

ROCHBERG: I would also apply it, in a limited way, to the Music for the Magic Theater, in its use of phrases that seem to hang in the air. Sometimes, even though the music seems to be moving-- there's obvious motion, of course--the psychological state itself is one of suspension. I think it would be a very serious mistake to narrow the term so it refers only to the physical sound; there's always a psychological, a psychic condition of stasis inherent in spatialization.

Q: But you now feel rather removed from that kind of composition?

ROCHBERG: Very much so. It's a peculiar characteristic of our generation to find words for certain newly perceived phenomena, and then to think that we've invented them. What do we mean by "spatialization"? The sound is static; it doesn't seem to move; it's hanging there in the air. I can think of any number of pieces from the classical repertoire--obviously slow movements--which are already on the edge, bordering on what we've come to call "spatialization." One of the most beautiful of such pieces is the slow movement of the Schubert String Quintet. It doesn't have the same kind of effect upon the psyche as the more recent spatial music; but I think there is a curious kinship, a remote, yet real relationship.

I suppose we could go still further and suggest that the idea of spatialization derives from a very real urge to slow down the tempo of this frantic civilization of ours. It has deeper impulses than simply what you find in music. But the fact that it surfaced in music in this way indicates it has significance in some wider sense.

But if you were to ask me to name a half dozen works that are ideal realizations of this impulse, I don't think I could. Perhaps a couple of pieces of Varèse, perhaps some Webern; and that's about it.

Q: Do you see Ralph Shapey in this tradition?

ROCHBERG: Not really. I find his music very restless.

In the ideal sense, spatial music is the precise opposite of the old classical tendency of music to realize itself through multiple statements, development, and motion from a common center--going through all these adventures and finally crystallizing itself, making its final statement of assertion of its own nature.

One of the problems I have with the notion of spatialization in music is that it doesn't permit any specific form; which is another way of saying that it allows you to do anything you want. That can be very dangerous and often results in shapelessness. A lack of shape is tantamount to putting a curtain between the music and the listener. I believe that we have a very powerful need built into us which has nothing necessarily to do with music but, nevertheless, operates in music all the same: a need for clarity, for logic in the progression of ideas--whether they're musical, verbal, symbolic, or pictorial. If this need is not satisfied, then something in us balks. This could explain why a lot of contemporary music has simply gone by the boards; it hasn't crossed over into those receptors. I seem to be involved in a long, running argument of both a personal and public nature about this very question with friends and colleagues. And it goes without saying I'm well aware that not everybody agrees with my views on this issue which I see as central to the aesthetics of modernism.

Q: You mentioned the Music for the Magic Theater before. Do you think that there's an ideal listener for a collage piece of that sort? Is it problematic if a listener brings a flood of ideas and memories to the quotations of Mozart and Mahler? Would you prefer a listener who was not deeply familiar with that music, one who just would know that something new was going on musically?

ROCHBERG: Of course, you always want the ideal listener who knows what you're dealing with. When Brahms was writing his chamber music, there was a very select audience of Viennese cognoscenti--let's say, some two hundred and fifty people--who, almost without exception, knew every chamber piece Brahms had ever produced. So naturally there was an incredible knowledge, excitement, anticipation--an electric quality in the air--at the premiere of a new Brahms work. When they heard this new piece, they were in a position to say, "This doesn't stand up to Opus 25," or "This piece is better, except that its scherzo is not as good as the scherzo in the other piece," etc. This is the kind of listener you want, always. I'm not against the great unwashed, but an audience that has no consciously developed experience to bring to the listening of any kind of music can derive very little from their first experience of a new piece. I can still remember the first time I heard the Mahler Tenth: It seemed like an enormous, chaotic piece to me. The first time around I couldn't hear the piece as he had composed it, as he had had it in his head. That took a while to approach. We delude ourselves if we assume that even very competent, educated, experienced listeners hear new pieces with absolute clarity. Many people make this wrong assumption. If it's not true for the experienced listener, how can it possibly be true for the unexperienced listener? But give me the experienced listener every time. If there's an audience in which there are at least five people who know the Mozart K.287 and the Mahler Ninth, and even some of the references to Webern and Varèse that are in Music for the Magic Theater, they're going to get a lot more out of it. Which is not to say that they're going to like it. That's another kind of distinction; knowing something about what you're perceiving doesn't mean that you are going to like it automatically. But at least you're in a better position to deal with it.

When you're dealing with enthusiastic ignorance--and worse, casual indifference--it's a pretty sad situation. It used to bother me a good deal. I'm more philosophical about it now. When I was young, I was an elitist, but I gave it up because I thought it was too hard, too unyielding a position, and as a result I became egalitarian in my outlook. I'm once again totally elitist in my view. I'm not convinced a culture exists on the basis of the widest possible number of people; it exists only because of the support and enthusiasm of those who know what they're dealing with--however small the number. This takes us back to Brahms and his audience. What if there were only two hundred and fifty people in the whole city of Vienna who understood Brahms? That would be enough. You don't need two hundred and fifty million. We delude ourselves with statistics; we're told more money is earned at the box office of all opera performances and orchestra concerts annually than at all the football or baseball games, etc. That may comfort some people, but it means nothing to me. It says nothing important. You can't measure a culture by the number of people who attend an event. You measure it in terms of what these people bring to the event, not only what they get from it--that's where they really meet the composer; they can deal with what he has to say.

Q: One last question about Music for the Magic Theater: Do you prefer the full-orchestra version to the chamber version?

ROCHBERG: I like the orchestra version much better than the chamber version. The orchestra version gives the Mahler quotations truer size; it also points up more clearly some of the chamber characteristics of the work. It's impossible to get the five solo players that comprise the string quintet in the chamber version to produce as much sound, sheer physical weight and intensity, as even a small string orchestra can. It invariably enlarges the context in which the musical ideas and their constant juxtapositions take place.

Q: You reworked music from the slow movement of Electrikaleidoscope into your Piano Quintet. Did you feel that the music had more possibilities than had been explored in the earlier piece? Were you unhappy with what you had done with it in Electrikaleidoscope?

ROCHBERG: No. I think borrowing is one of the essential traditions of music, an ancient one. And if you're a borrower, as I am, then I see nothing to prevent borrowing from oneself. I was looking for a theme for a variation movement I wanted to include in the Piano Quintet, and I'd always loved that particular section that serves as a coda for the slow movement of Electrikaleidoscope. It's seven bars long, and something in me said, "It's perfect. It's just right for what I want," so I simply lifted it out of context and gave it another kind of shape and function. That's not at all uncommon for me, and I know that it's not uncommon for a number of other composers living today. Either consciously or unconsciously, we borrow from ourselves. I prefer to do it consciously.

Q: Two of the movements of Electrikaleidoscope have a strong rock sound to them. Have you followed rock music at all closely? Does it have a real attraction for you?

ROCHBERG: To be perfectly candid, I hate it; I absolutely hate it. At the time I wrote Electrikaleidoscope, it did interest me briefly, but basically I find the whole character of rock worse than vulgar. It's a purely commercial product; it has all sorts of cultural implications which I don't care for and don't agree with. But I'm a realist; it's here, and it represents something very real and present in the culture-at-large--not good, but something real nevertheless. Milan Kundera, the Czech writer, describes it as "music without thought." It's the very essence of mindlessness.

When I was fifteen I began playing in dance bands and I continued until I was about twenty or twenty-one. (My real interest in jazz suddenly diminished at the age of nineteen, but I kept it up because I needed the money.) But I always loved playing the blues. I played in every "low dive" in northern New Jersey, and I particularly loved those times when there was practically nobody in the place--we'd be a trio, maybe a quartet--and we'd just take off and play the blues for an hour at a time. It's only in recent years that I've understood my early passion for the blues: It is the great contribution of jazz to the art of variation. After Beethoven and Brahms, there are one or two efforts that Mahler makes, and the occasional effort in the direction of producing a variation movement that Bartók, Stravinsky, or Schoenberg makes. The obsession, the passion, the love that classical and romantic composers had for variation is one of the clues to their whole view of form and shape. If you go through all the piano sonatas of Haydn, Mozart, and Beethoven, all the violin and piano sonatas of Mozart and Beethoven, I don't know how many variation movements you could cull. Probably many hundreds at least. I have always loved the whole idea of variation; and, of course, this is the principal form and interest of jazz itself.

Q: People frequently have difficulty with your collage pieces; because of the variety of material in them, listeners can be puzzled as to how they're supposed to react to the music. Had you anticipated this when you first began writing these works? Is there basically one way to approach these pieces?

ROCHBERG: That's hard for me to say. I never have any prejudices one way or the other when I write a piece about how one should listen to it. Some people have apparently enjoyed the collage pieces very much; they seem to understand what's involved and respond to this purposeful friction of different styles, and even different historical periods--particularly in Music for the Magic Theater. Some people are very much put off by it. I wouldn't dream of telling them how they should respond, or whether they're right or wrong. I wouldn't want to prejudice a listener or an audience in any particular pre-set direction. It's really none of my business.

I don't write for audiences per se. When I say that, I don't mean that I have disdain for audiences; I don't. I've come to the conclusion that somewhat different audiences attend chamber music concerts, orchestral concerts, and opera performances. I think chamber music audiences have a greater knowledge of what it is they've come to hear; there's a greater degree of intensity, of direct relationship to the music as well as the quality of performance. Opera audiences seem to have even more of it--or certainly as much. It's the big middle, the orchestral audiences, that can be pretty vapid. Still, most music lovers strike me as quite intelligent and often very sensitive. As I like to tell my students, they're easily as intelligent as any group of composers you might assemble. They know just as much about life, certainly as much about the problems of reality, and sometimes as much about music--except that they don't compose it. You cannot start out with the adversary notion that the audience is made up totally of ignoramuses and you've got to educate them. This idea is and was so much a part of the attitude of apologists for contemporary music: We have to condition audiences to accept contemporary music. We don't have to do a thing. It either lives or passes into oblivion. You cannot force-feed people; you cannot impose taste; you cannot set up false psychological conditions or circumstances to satisfy self-serving ends. Nor have you the right to demand of audiences that they spend a lifetime listening to or studying a handful of pieces because you say they're good. They don't have time. The only way to test that is to put yourself in their position, and you can see immediately how you would react yourself. It's the zealotry and fanaticism of the old-style contemporary-music apologist who doesn't understand that things either happen or they don't happen. There are no guarantees in the dynamics of culture.

There are two traditions, and depending upon how you view the situation, you can argue on one side or the other. There have been numerous works that were accepted immediately. The London Symphonies of Haydn are an excellent case in point. Haydn's reputation in Europe, the very reputation that was the basis for bringing him to London, did not arise after he died. It happened while he was still very much alive. The London Symphonies are absolutely beauties; they still are among the best things he ever produced, and as good, in their way, as anything anyone else produced afterwards. Are we to think less of them because they were immediately successful? On the other hand, there are cases of out-and-out rejection of certain works, a very painful experience for the composer involved. The example of Bartók's Bluebeard's Castle comes to mind. But then eventually some of these are accepted. The curious thing is that Schoenberg is still not wholeheartedly accepted into the repertoire. Webern has a certain relationship to the repertoire, but we can't say that Webern is accepted warmly either. But Berg is now established in the opera repertoire. This is obviously not a simple issue. I do resent, quite frankly, for impersonal as well as personal reasons, the notion, still abroad today, that if the piece is successful, then it can't be good.

It serves no purpose to believe that you have to make art which is so difficult of perception that even the most sympathetic listener is not persuaded. I've always felt a keen responsibility to know what my colleagues were doing. All artists literally eat the environment. I have had the experience where in several instances I have not cared for particular works, but when I saw that there seemed to be obvious enthusiasm for them, I'd say to myself, "There must be something here; maybe you missed it the first time around. Let's find out." I'd start working away at the score, studying it closely; if there was a recording, I'd get the record, listen to it. But invariably, first reactions are the most telling; just as when you're writing, first ideas are usually your best ideas. I have to confess that I've come to the point where I've given up the game of trying to comprehend the incomprehensible.

Q: Are you referring now mostly to serial works?

ROCHBERG: Not necessarily. Although I suppose that the majority of pieces that I have in mind are serial in part or in whole. But serialism by itself is not the problem. This is another myth.

To call something "serial," and then go on to say that that deprives
it of the possibility of its being appealing or attractive, the possibility of its being real music, is simply not true at all.   There
are any number of pieces which I have enjoyed and still believe in
as music.   The important thing is that I'm talking about music.
Not the method or aesthetic or point of view from which it was
composed.   Ultimately, that shouldn't concern us.   Naturally, if
you're a musicologist, theorist, or composer, then you want to
find out about these things; that's a professional concern.   Nevertheless, even as a professional, the only way you're going to become seriously interested in such matters is if the music appeals
to you.   Frankly, I think too much time has already been spent
with considerations that are not music--the mechanics of method,
etc.

I'm either a pessimistic optimist or an optimistic pessimist--
which is not important.   I've always felt that the truth emerges,
reality finally reveals itself.   My chief concern is that composers
write music that can live side by side with the music of the past.
Incidentally, there is another serious and present danger in our
culture.   I personally deplore "new music" concerts.   I think it's
a form of ghetto-ization, a form of cultural segregation.   How do
we know whether or not a new piece of music has any quality unless we put it in the context of other pieces that do have quality?
How do we find out if the composer of a new piece of music can
begin to approach the stature of a good composer of the past--I'm
not even talking about the greatest composers.   I think it is necessary to proceed by comparison.   We have to accept the fact that
we are involved in an on-going tradition and continuity.   We can't
claim that the things of the past no longer have a connection, a
relation to us, that their values do not obtain any more.   I find
that an impossible point of view.   If you deny the past, you philosophically deny your own future.   If you are ready to erase everything that preceded you, then you are erasable by your own standards.   It should work the other way: Here is an existing body of
continuous tradition that has been painstakingly built up by serious,
hardworking, disciplined artists, over generations.   What can you
do?   You can at least strive to add another wing to that building;
add something of value, however small, to it.   But if you come
along with a demolition ball just to make room for your own little
shack, you've destroyed, not built.

Q: In your own music, have you now ruled out the option of em-
ploying serial techniques?

ROCHBERG: I'm not especially interested in the continued use of
serial ideas.   In my Fourth, Fifth, and Sixth Quartets, there are
a number of movements that are heavily atonal; that is to say,
they're freely chromatic.   I suppose, if one cared to look very
closely, one might find collections of twelve notes, or significant
collections of partial twelve-note rows, and so on.   But I wouldn't

make a conscious effort to employ such devices which are, quite
frankly, played out for me.

On the other hand, there are a couple of places in those
quartets where I consciously used ways of working that I would
never have been comfortable with had I not written serial music.
For example, in the first movement of Number Four, there's a
brief passage--perhaps five or six measures--which, when it returns just before the end of the movement, is totally inverted. All
the intervallic relationships are retained, but the harmony changes.
I suppose this is something that one could do without ever having
written twelve-tone music, but composers who use serial devices
are in the habit of thinking of such possibilities.

Q: Do you think that you've reached a point now where your compositions will be unified stylistically, as, for example, your Violin
Concerto is, or do you think that you'll continue to write works
such as your Third String Quartet, which employs a wide range of
styles?

ROCHBERG: I suppose that sometimes certain things with which
you've occupied yourself intensely do lose a certain interest; perhaps you exhaust them. I must admit that I have recently been
wrestling with the whole question of direct juxtaposition of atonal
movements and tonal movements. Not that I intend to give it up.
If I find that that is precisely the emotional gesture I need, then
of course I'll use it. But I don't ever want to feel trapped into
doing everything the same way. I prefer, for example, Picasso's
way to Rothko's way.

The Violin Concerto was not part of a conscious program to
achieve a homogeneous style. It was simply the result of dealing
with the ideas I had in the ways they required of me. They had to
assume their own lives, their own characteristics. On the other
hand, the three quartets are different again. They've been followed
in turn by four other works: One of them is heavily tonal, but not
in the classic or romantic sense; another is freely chromatic; another one is heavily atonal; and the dissonance quotient of the last one
exceeds the dissonance quotient of the one just before it. Those two
pieces are, within themselves, very homogeneous, stylistically. I
suppose that if you never heard any of the music that preceded those
last two pieces, you would assume that that's the way I write.

My Octet is the first piece in which I've consciously tried
to find some way to fuse the absolutely tonal and the absolutely
atonal. But, I must add, without using either one of them literally. It seemed to me that it was no longer enough for my purpose
to continue bobbing back and forth between one extreme and another. The mental effort to accomplish that is greater than I can describe; and it is precisely that which makes me admire Picasso's
flexibility so much.

Part of the desire to fuse the two has to do with the fact
that I began to feel that there must be another way in which to use
the atonal, but framed differently; that is, give the atonal the force
and the direction of the tonal, without necessarily introducing the
tonal in its more traditional sense. The new Octet is such an attempt.

Since we're talking about this kind of juxtaposition, it's worth
mentioning that one of the curious notions I've run into is a tendency to believe that writing tonal music is easier than writing atonal
music. It's quite the reverse; writing atonal music is easier.
Writing good tonal music that can stand up with the best is the
hardest thing I know, because it's the kind of music which is totally exposed; there are no obscuring factors to mask the paucity
of ideas or cloud the presence of ideas, whichever is the case.
Tonal music depends on the process of thought, of musical thinking.
In the end it comes down to the question: Can you write a good
tune? Tonal music is not as simplistic as stringing triads together.
We can't talk about Mozart, Haydn, Beethoven, Schubert, or Schumann without talking about the power of melodic thought. In a sense,
it's easier to write atonal music because you don't have to write
melodies--although, in truth, there's nothing to prevent you from
doing so.

Q: In the 1960s, you wrote about electronic music that it "lacked
passion." The medium itself has grown quite a bit since then, and
many more composers have been taking it in all sorts of directions.
Do you still feel the same way about electronic music today? Has
it gotten any passion over the years?

ROCHBERG: Not that I've heard. It has no "voice." A violin has
a voice; an oboe has a voice; a piano has voices; electronic music
is spiritless, sterile, as sound. It has no voice. It lacks the
warmth which makes passion possible.

Q: Do you mean that because its possibilities are so broad, it has
no distinct profile?

ROCHBERG: In the early days there was a lot of talk about the
infinitude of possibilities in the electronic medium; but no such thing
as an "infinitude of possibilities" exists. We realize that, in reality, possibilities are very limited. This can be applied to any
area of human systems. Once you cross the threshold of the limit
on any side of a situation, the situation is no longer the same as
the one you started with. New conditions pertain.

Back in the forties and fifties, everyone was excited about
this "infinitude of possibilities." It's understandable because some
composers wanted very much to make a music which is truly repre-

sentative of a technological age, which speaks in the voice of the
twentieth century.   As I look back now, I think that the enthusiasm
was not supported by the facts of either life or music.   It is possible, perhaps, someday someone with a special intelligence and a
real musical gift will make something of it; but I have very strong
doubts.   In any case, I'm still in love with the sound of the human
voice and the sound of instruments that evoke responses in me as
a human being and as a musician.

It is important to recognize the limits of the medium itself.
It's a serious mistake to believe that electronic means have created
a separate branch of music.   Probably the greatest composer of
electronic music was virtually the first one--Varèse.   There have
been no powerhouses like him since.   There have been a few sophisticated, slick people, but nobody who felt the raw, percussive
power inherent in it.   The first time I heard Déserts, with the
electronic interpolations, I was deeply moved.   Those wild, roar-
ing electronic interpolations made a real impact.

Q: You knew Luigi Dallapiccola for many years.

ROCHBERG: Yes.   That was a very happy association.   When I
was in Italy in 1950, I played my Second Piano Sonata for him.   (It
has no existence any longer; it's one of the works that I've put away
in boxes in the attic.)   I was a young composer then and what he
said to me made a lasting impression: "You know, if I were a
music critic, I could tell you right away what I think of your work.
But since I'm only a poor composer, would you please come back
tomorrow and play it for me again?"   He was dead serious.   So I
came back the next day and played it for him again.   When I finished, he said, "Ultimo lavoro."   I wish I could agree with him
now!

At Tanglewood in 1952, I played the first eight of my Twelve
Bagatelles for him--my first twelve-tone piece--and he liked them
very much.   Naturally, I was very encouraged by his reaction and,
subsequently, when they were published, I dedicated them to him.
A curious assumption grew out of the dedication--namely, that I
had studied with Dallapiccola.   We were colleagues; I was never
his student.   In fact, his Quaderno Musicale Di Annalibera, a set
of short piano pieces, was composed after my Bagatelles.   I like
to think that he was so enamored of them, so charmed by what I
had done, that he was prompted to write his own set of short pieces.

We saw each other infrequently over the years.   In 1963--un-
fortunately, it was the last time we saw each other--we were both
in Israel for a conference of musicians and composers.   They took
us on tours, and we spent many hours on buses.   By that time in
my work, I had reached a point where I was dissatisfied with twelve-
tone methodology and knew that something else had to happen where
my music was concerned.   I said to him during one of our conver-

sations, "What's going to happen after twelve-tone?" And he replied, "Nothing. We're here. This is our language. I see no
reason for even questioning it." (This was the sum and substance
of his response.) I didn't press him because I didn't have any
answer myself. I had come to feel very disturbed by the extremely narrow confines of what he called "our language." Two years
later, I wrote Contra Mortem et Tempus and Music for the Magic
Theater. That was the great watershed for me; that was the new
starting point: 1963 was the year of my last twelve-tone pieces.

Q: Do you think that your approach to composition will eventually
become more and more common among future composers?

ROCHBERG: There are signs in that direction, but I don't have
the sense that what I'm doing will necessarily become part of the
repertoire of means that most composers will use. I think it will
happen only to those who have, perhaps, as I have, a certain kind
of proclivity for the past, a necessity to re-discover and embrace
it. You can't do it if you don't, because you've got to know and
love that old stuff, you've got to have a real affinity for it. Not
every composer does.

When I think of contemporary music, I'm not overly optimistic, for a lot of reasons. One is purely external: There is less
and less contemporary music being programmed by performers outside the university circuit these days. This is very dispiriting,
very discouraging. That's the external side of it, and it's very
depressing.

But something still more serious disturbs me: Young composers don't seem to have any vitality of mind or psyche. Still,
I don't want to make this a total indictment.

Q: That's right; your students may read this.

ROCHBERG: I don't know how many times I've asked students in
the past, "Why does your music sound like you're already eighty
years old? Tired, fatigued, so depressed, so down. Why?"
They're already old in certain ways. The music that emerges
lacks the drama and power of thought necessary to awaken the
listener to its life. There is more sheer vitality per square measure in the Beethoven Seventh Symphony than in any number of pieces
by major composers of our time. I'm not talking about decibel
levels; I'm talking about the spirit of the thing that carries you,
the excitement of the way it happens. It bothers me very much;
more than I can say. It's inherent in the politics of our time, the
social disturbances, the fear of nuclear war, the economic dis-
tress. You simply have to cut through the malaise and say something which has strength and say it in a clear voice. I'm not talk-

ing about the cheap optimism of a Norman Vincent Peale; I'm talking about a real grasp of what it is to be alive. Can anyone in
his right mind say that Mahler was a composer who gives one "positive" thoughts? Far from it; the man was in anguish, and we share
his anguish empathetically. But look at the energy with which he
presents himself. This is what I mean. Granted, the world we
live in is distressing. But a composer must deal with it in a way
which engages and takes the audience with him. In the end it has
much less to do with the kinds of devices we use to make music
with than the spirit that goes into the making of that music.

Q: At the Stratford Festival, in the summer of 1960, you remarked:
"We are not competing with the classicists. We live under an entirely different kind of cultural system; we have different problems
from those which faced Beethoven, and so our problems must be
our own. Therefore, in solving them, there is no question at all
in our minds of attempting to compete with Mozart, Haydn, or Beethoven." Do you think that, in spite of this cultural difference, we
are in competition with Mozart and Beethoven?

ROCHBERG: Quite the contrary. I have an intense, constant, living relationship to the past, but I have never felt in competition
with those giants. That would require some sort of combination of
all the worst forms of mania known to the psycho-pathologists. And
it's not even a question of being humble.

   If we could be half as good as they were, that would be something tremendous. That's certainly not a competitive view. For
me that's the key to understanding their heritage in our time, and
our own culture in our time.

Q: Half as good in their idiom or in our own?

ROCHBERG: In our own way, whether we borrow from them or
not. But "half as good" in convincing performers and audiences
that this is a music that deserves to live. An artist who claims
that he's not interested in the future of his work is deluding himself. A large component of being an artist is ego, however you
deal with it. One of the consequences of having a large ego is
that you want to be remembered. As Faulkner said, "Kilroy was
here." Every one of us identifies with Faulkner's "Kilroy," and
we want that writ large as possible.

   On the other hand, I don't believe in the Norman Mailer syn-
drome, that you live your life as a celebrity. Success as an artist has nothing to do with having your picture on the cover of Time
magazine. If you're going to produce lasting work, then you must
do your work apart from the world. If our work has passion and
force and energy and authenticity, if people are convinced by it,
then we've done our job and the culture will go on.

Q: Could you give us a progress report on The Confidence Man?

ROCHBERG: My wife and I are in the last stages of polishing the libretto. I must say, she produced a remarkable piece of work. Once we get the thing to the point where I feel comfortable with what we have, then I'll start writing the music.

Q: Now that you're writing an opera, do you find yourself thinking back to the time when you studied with Menotti?

ROCHBERG: Oddly enough we never talked about opera. It may have been a mistake not to have questioned him about that at the time, but, hard as it may be to believe, I wasn't the least interested in opera at that point. I saw myself as evolving chiefly into a composer of instrumental music. Songs, yes, but I never thought of opera. Still, in the back of my head, there was at least the hope that I might some day get to it.

Q: Have you experienced a negative reaction from performers, colleagues, or critics because of your break with serial composition? Did any of them ever suggest that you dropped it because the going got too tough for you?

ROCHBERG: There have been all kinds of reactions. Some performers were very interested. Some composers were very upset. Some critics were baffled. Some angry. Some seemed to welcome my efforts to reestablish tonal music.

A singularly curious situation arose in the case of my Ricordanza, which I wrote for Michael Rudiakov. I sent the score to him, and he called me up and said, "It's very beautiful, George, but I don't know what to think." So I said to him, "What can I say? If you want to play it, play it; if you don't want to play it, then don't play it. But how can you say, 'It's beautiful but you don't know what to think'?" I found that very strange.

It's been this kind of response, from one side of the spectrum to the other: positive to negative, and all the shades in between. It came back to me through a student of mind that a colleague remarked after hearing my Violin Concerto, "Rochberg has sold out." To what, he didn't say.

I certainly didn't set out to create controversy. Jake Druckman was at the first performance of Electrikaleidoscope; afterwards, we went to a party--the players were there, along with other composers--and Jake said, "Here we are, knocking our brains out, trying to be shocking and controversial, and George does it without even trying." There have been all these interesting shades of response, and all the while I'm thinking, "I'm just trying to write music." I want to write things that I can live with. I would like to be able to look back on these things later and say, "Yes. I made my contribution. I still believe in these works; I think that they're valid. I think that they're good as music. They have nothing to do with all of the politics and aesthetic battles; they have outlasted that whole business." I think that's the way it has to be. Whether I'll be that fortunate, I don't know. But certainly, that's the way all real works turn out: They rise above the time from which they emerged, whether they were received well or not when they came into being.

It's a very strange situation to be the center of controversy when you had no intention of creating it in the first place. I certainly have no intention of maintaining it. I'm doing what I think is necessary, and I would hope that whatever controversy there is about it will eventually fade away, and the music will be discussed as music in terms of its intrinsic values, or lack of them. That's all that matters.

There's too much irrelevant publicity and talk these days. None of it is about the thing itself, but the ephemera and trivia which surround it. I get the impression that people like to be deluded; they seem to enjoy illusions. But if you're a composer, you have to train yourself in the discipline of certain realities, and those realities that arise when one confronts existence itself and those which arise in the process of trying to make art.

All these things that I've told you are part of what the work has produced. But sometimes, it all seems very remote, as though it's all happening to somebody else. In that sense, it really doesn't matter. In the end only the work and working matter.

CATALOG OF COMPOSITIONS

1941	Variations on an Original Theme for piano	MS
1946; 79	Duo for Oboe and Bassoon	Presser
1946	Songs of Solomon for voice and piano	G Schirmer, Presser
1947; 80	Trio for Clarinet, Horn, and Piano	Presser
1948; 77	Symphony No. 1	Presser
1949	Night Music for orchestra	Presser
1949	Capriccio for Two Pianos	MS
1952	String Quartet No. 1	Presser
1952	Twelve Bagatelles for piano	Presser
1953	Chamber Symphony for Nine Instruments	Presser
1954	David, the Psalmist for tenor and orchestra	Presser

1954	Cantio Sacra for small orchestra	MS
1954	Three Psalms for mixed chorus	Presser
1955; 59	Duo Concertante for violin and cello	Presser
1955	Serenata d'Estate for six instruments	Leeds
1956	Symphony No. 2	Presser
1956	Sonata-Fantasia for piano	Presser
1958	Cheltenham Concerto for small orchestra	Suvini Zerboni, Presser
1958	Dialogues for clarinet and piano	Presser
1959; 62	La Bocca della Verita for oboe (or violin) and piano	Impero
1959	Arioso for piano	Presser
1959	Bartokiana for piano	Presser
1960	Time-Span (I) for orchestra	MS
1961	String Quartet No. 2 (with soprano)	Presser
1962	Time-Span (II) for orchestra	Leeds
1962	Blake Songs for soprano and chamber ensemble	Leeds
1963	Trio for Violin, Cello, and Piano	Presser
1964	Apocalyptica for band and percussion	Presser
1965	Zodiac for orchestra	Presser
1965	Black Sounds for winds, piano, and percussion	Presser
1965	Contra Mortem et Tempus for flute, clarinet, violin, and piano	Presser
1965; 69	Music for the Magic Theater for fifteen players; for small orchestra	Presser
1965	Incidental Music for The Alchemist	Presser
1966	Nach Bach for harpsichord or piano	Presser
1967	Passions According to the Twentieth Century for soloists (singers and speakers), chorus, and instruments	Presser
1968	Fanfares for wind ensemble	Presser
1968	Tableaux for soprano, two actors' voices, small men's chorus, and twelve players	Presser
1969	Symphony No. 3 for soloists, double chorus, chamber chorus, and large orchestra	Presser
1969	Prelude for Piano	Presser
1969	Book of Songs for voice and piano	MS
1969	3 Cantes Flamencos for high baritone	MS
1969	Eleven Songs for Voice and Piano	Presser
1969	Two Songs from Tableaux for Voice and Piano	Presser
1970	Fifty Caprice Variations for violin	Galaxy

1970	Sacred Song of Reconciliation (Mizmor l'Piyus) for bass-baritone and chamber orchestra	Presser
1970	Songs in Praise of Krishna for voice and piano	Presser
1971	Fantasies for voice and piano	Presser
1971	Carnival Music for piano	Presser
1972	String Quartet No. 3	Galaxy
1972	Electrikaleidoscope for amplified ensemble of flute, clarinet, cello, piano, and electric piano	Presser
1972	Ricordanza (Soliloquy) for cello and piano	Presser
1973	Ukiyo-e (Pictures of the Floating World) for harp	Presser
1973	Behold, My Servant for mixed chorus	Presser
1973	Imago Mundi for orchestra	Presser
1974	Phaedra for mezzo-soprano and orchestra	Presser
1974	Concerto for Violin and Orchestra	Presser
1975	Transcendental Variations for string orchestra	Galaxy
1975	Piano Quintet	Presser
1976	Symphony No. 4	Presser
1976	Partita-Variations for piano	Presser
1977	Songs of Inanna and Dumuzi for alto and piano	Presser
1977	String Quartet No. 4	Presser
1978	String Quartet No. 5	Presser
1978	String Quartet No. 6	Presser
1979	Slow Fires of Autumn, Ukiyo-e II for flute and harp	Presser
1979	Book of Contrapuntal Pieces for keyboard instruments	Presser
1979	Sonata for Viola and Piano	Presser
1979	String Quartet No. 7 (with baritone)	Presser
1980	Octet (a grand fantasy)	Presser

photo: Gene Bagnato

Roger Sessions was born on December 28, 1896, in Brooklyn, New York. At fourteen he entered Harvard, where he received his A.B., and after graduating, attended Yale where he received his Mus.B. under Horatio Parker. Sessions also studied with and worked under Ernest Bloch at the Cleveland Institute of Music. He has taught at the University of California at Berkeley, Juilliard, and Princeton University. He resides with his wife, the former Elizabeth Franck, in Princeton, New Jersey. They have two children.

Sessions' early compositions display a marked affinity for a Straussian, post-Romantic idiom. His later, neo-classical compositions also have elements of this highly chromatic and expressive style. By the late forties, Sessions was exploring serial techniques. These methods were and have remained subservient to his broader musical conceptions. He has steadily cultivated, through consummate craftsmanship and profound emotional intensity, a personal idiom most conveniently described as atonal chromaticism.

The authors spoke with Roger Sessions on the evening of November 19, 1975, in his New York City hotel room, just after his composition class at Juilliard. Perhaps most winning was the grace and courtesy with which he treated them. Woven throughout his warm reminiscences and his eloquent expression of musical convictions was a very singular quality which tends to elude the printed transcript: his gentle sense of humor.

Q: Your teachers included Horatio Parker and, of course, Ernest Bloch. How did you respond to each?

SESSIONS: I went to Ernest Bloch because I had problems which I didn't know how to solve. Studying with him was a very rich experience. Horatio Parker was a good musician, but he was a somewhat disillusioned and lonely man. I did not study privately with him. I later felt I had gotten to the point where I needed the advice of somebody really first class, and Bloch was the only person in this country whom I felt I could trust to give it to me, and straight from the shoulder too. The first time I met Bloch, he treated me rather roughly. I didn't mind it, because that was what I was there for. But a couple of years later, when I was his assistant in Cleveland, he was in my studio and read an account I had written about our first meeting. In it, I said that meeting

Bloch marked the first time that I had come in contact with a really tough musician. His face fell, and he said, "You make it sound as if I didn't like your music." I said, "You gave me no reason to think that you did like it." He said, "Of course I did. But I wouldn't treat an American student that way anymore." I said, "Why? That's what I came to you for. It wasn't particularly important whether you liked my music or not. You gave me something I needed." Again he said, "Well, I'd never treat an American student that way." I said, "Why not? You ought to." He said, "You were the only one that I had who knew how to take it."

I know what he meant. One thing a teacher has to do is to see that a young man or woman develops his or her own self-confidence, and as a teacher I try to do that. But I demand a lot of them just the same. When I taught in California I was told that I demanded more of my students than anybody else on the faculty. I doubt if that's true; the University of California is a big place.

Q: As a composer, how do you regard your extensive teaching career?

SESSIONS: I'm a teacher as a _composer_; I don't consider myself a teacher at all. It's nice having gifted and interested young people around one. I'm giving them advice when they need it, pointing out problems when I feel that they have them, and encouraging them to find the solutions themselves.

Q: Do you feel that teaching uses up the time that you could have applied to composing?

SESSIONS: Of course it does, but I did it because I had to earn a living. At first I started by giving private lessons, and I discovered that the interested students found it most difficult to pay me, while the ones who had the most money were the most lax about paying. Later, I accepted an offer to teach at what's now Douglass College, and that gave me something that I could depend on. A couple of months later, I was asked to go to Princeton. Before these teaching jobs I had spent eight years in Europe--six in Italy and two in Germany. If somebody had told me, just before I landed in New York, that when I came back from eight years of living in Europe I would be teaching at a university within three years, I would have tossed him overboard or jumped overboard myself, because it was the last thing in the world that I wanted to do. But wherever I've taught, I've always had the chance to do everything my own way. At that time, having composers at universities was something new, and so I could plan things as I wanted, both in Berkeley and in Princeton.

Q: One of your most famous students--Milton Babbitt--told us that during the thirties you didn't have much regard for the music of either Schoenberg or Webern. But later on you became a strong admirer of Schoenberg. Why this change in attitude?

SESSIONS: He exaggerates it a little bit. I always knew some of Schoenberg's music very well, but I was not at all sure that Schoenberg's system, which I didn't fully understand at that time, could fit my needs. I came to it fairly slowly. When I lived in California, I had some very good talks with Schoenberg and found out that our ideas were not very far apart. Soon afterwards, I found myself in favor of it. Then, in Italy, I got to know Luigi Dallapiccola very well; he was also using the twelve-tone system. I said to him one day, "You know, I'm fifty-five years old now and I don't see myself learning a new technique at this age." He understood perfectly well.

It's important to remember that Schoenberg wasn't at all dogmatic about the use of twelve-tone technique. In fact, at one time I told Schoenberg that I thought that he had been misunderstood very much. I especially felt that his twelve-tone system had been misunderstood because it had been over-publicized and somewhat turned into a system of rules and formulas. He looked glum for a minute and said, "Yes, you're quite right; I have to admit that it's partly my fault." Then he suddenly grew more animated and said, "But it's much more the fault of some of my disciples!" Of course, I understood that very well; I always felt much closer to Schoenberg than to Webern, because Webern was, or seemed to be, very dogmatic about it, and that's quite contrary to my own nature. This is a technique that one comes to by one's self or one does not. When I actually came to it, I used it very freely--as I still do--because I was writing my own music and not Schoenberg's music at all.

I had a student--now a distinguished composer--who, because of some of the things that I had told him, suspected me of trying to lure him into it. I wasn't trying to do that at all; I was giving him purely practical advice about his work. So without saying a word, I took the first of my twelve-tone pieces to him. It was a big solo violin sonata, which is a funny thing to begin with; but I had just found myself slipping into it almost unconsciously. (I had toyed with it before on my own, but only as exercises for my own enlightenment.) Anyway, this young man said, "Well, well! One-two-three-four-five-six-seven-eight-nine-ten-eleven-twelve!" I still didn't say anything. Then he sat down and read the first movement of the sonata and said, "But it's still your music." I said, "Of course it's still my music. I wouldn't have any business doing it if it weren't my music." That's the way I think it should be.

Q: Besides teaching when you returned from Europe, you also started the Copland-Sessions concerts.

SESSIONS: It was really Aaron Copland who started them. I was still living in Italy at the time, and I guess Aaron wanted some moral support. So I did what I could during the time I was in the United States. But then it became a little cumbersome and I found that I had less and less to contribute; so it's my fault, really, that these concerts were given up. I told him to get somebody else.

Q: Were the audiences at the time of the Copland-Sessions concerts more receptive to contemporary music than today's audiences are?

SESSIONS: Oh, I don't think so; I think, in general, less. It was a small audience, even though I suppose the music wasn't as difficult as it is now.

Around that time, there was this whole movement for being "American." I don't think that's the way to make American music. I think the way to make American music is to forget about being "American," and let the composers write the music which is genuinely their own. They were, I felt, often merely creating an "image," adapting themselves to a sort of European image of America which is not the whole reality at all. I don't like "images." We still think too much in terms of images and too little in terms of the real facts of the situation--the clothes people wear instead of the people themselves.

Q: It would seem that your music has been given a label--"severely intellectual"--which does not do justice to its profoundly expressive qualities.

SESSIONS: Well, of course, it depends upon whom you talk to. In the last few years, I've felt that people are beginning to catch on to what my music is really like. When it's performed outside of New York, or abroad, the image is quite a different one. For instance, when my music is played in England, I get quite different kinds of comments from those I get in certain quarters here. The musical world is a complicated place, and it's a much bigger place than a lot of people realize.

Q: Do you take audience accessibility into account when you compose?

SESSIONS: I don't think that any composer who really has something of his own to say ever does--how can he? If I do not like something that I do, it seems awful to me, and I have to work at it until it's the way I want it. The only way to communicate is to communicate from conviction; if you have no real conviction, then you don't communicate very much. Of course, some people may like such music and be willing to listen to it, and one can get a certain following that way. Once, a friend of mine and I agreed that we would rather have a few people love our music than have lots of people simply like it. It's the people who <u>love</u> it, not the number of votes one gets, that matters and provides a much greater satisfaction. All I ask is that my public does not wither away.

Q: Earlier, you mentioned your friendship with Luigi Dallapiccola; from what we've read, it seems there was a special kinship between the two of you.

SESSIONS: We hit it off very, very well, from the first time I met him. I had just come to Florence and a friend of mine from California, an Italian friend, told me that I must meet Dallapiccola. On the first evening we were there, my friend telephoned him and we arranged to meet that same night. We had a very good time. He was a marvelous human being. We agreed about most things-- I always felt very close to him as a musician. Two or three years after I was in Italy for the first time, I wrote the <u>Idyll of Theocritus</u> and dedicated it to him, because I was very much moved by the way he used the Italian language in his music. I was inspired to do in English something in <u>my</u> way similar to his treatment of the Italian language. That's why I dedicated it to him, really; in gratitude, as well as in admiration and affection.

Q: Dallapiccola once said of your Fourth Symphony: "I was struck by its so very singular 'divergent' process: as the emotion increases, the sonorous means which are used become less and less." Does this apply to other works of yours?

SESSIONS: Well, I'm not sure if that could be applied to all my music, but I think I know what he means with that work. The last movement is very important (not all of my friends understand that) and it is very simple. But then, I never did ask him what he meant by that!

We were having a very good time together one night, talking about Robert Schumann, who was not very popular at that moment. We discussed one work of his after another, and I said, "I love his symphonies." Dallapiccola said, "Yes, I do too. Of course, I'm not sure if they're symphonies." So I said, "What's a symphony?" and he laughed and said, "You're right." Later on in the evening we were talking about my Fourth Symphony, and I told him that I wasn't sure whether I should have called it a symphony or not. I told him why: Originally, it was to be three separate pieces. Then I realized that I always wanted these three pieces to go together, and that a symphony could be something in which the three different

movements weren't based so much on a difference in tempo, but
on a difference in expression. (I called the three movements "Bur-
lesque," "Elegy," and "Pastorale."). Dallapiccola said, "But of
course it's a symphony!" But I was still a little bewildered.

We always had a very good time discussing everything under
the sun. We went through the whole of music literature, with few
exceptions. I don't think we discussed Brahms much, because he
didn't really like Brahms. Of course, I do love certain works of
Brahms very much. When I was very young, you either were for
Wagner or for Brahms. For instance, the idea prevalent in the
'teens was that Wagner was wonderful with the orchestra and that
Brahms simply was not. This was nonsense. As a matter of fact,
around that time I read an interview with Maurice Ravel in which
he was talking about Cesar Franck, who was supposed to be a good
orchestrator. (God knows why; I think that was certainly one of
his weaknesses.) But Ravel said, "Of course, Brahms was a far
greater man, even by his tremendous gift as an orchestrator."
Coming from Ravel, that puzzled me and I thought, "Wait a minute, yes, that's really true; it does sound wonderful on the orchestra."

Q: In light of your talks with Dallapiccola on the symphony, do
you have any general, a priori structural conceptions of what a
symphony is?

SESSIONS: No. As far as I'm concerned, the symphony is an orchestral piece with big contrasting elements in it; that's the most
convenient title to give these things. A few years ago, a good friend
of mine, a European composer--(not Dallapiccola, but somebody
else who had written symphonies)--told me that his publisher had
refused to publish any more symphonies, and he said, "So I just
call them something else."

Q: Do you consider yourself to be primarily an orchestral composer?

SESSIONS: No. I've written more orchestral music than anything
else mainly because that's what I've been asked to write. But I
love to write for the voice. I've written two operas, a big cantata,
choruses, and the Idyll of Theocritus, which is a monstrous problem because it's a very difficult forty-five minute piece for one singer. But that's the way it had to be. I had been interested in that
Theocritus poem for years. I had read about it when I was in college, in 1913 or '14. There was a piece by Charles Martin Loeffler called A Pagan Poem. It was based on a poem by Virgil, and
the review I had read stated that this poem wasn't nearly as good
as a similar poem written by Theocritus. But I couldn't find the
Theocritus. I even bought a copy in Greek and tried to read it,

but my Greek wasn't good enough, and I needed to have some explanations. Later on, when I knew it better, I did read it in Greek. Then, I ran across an English translation which had come out in the 1870s. This was a pretty little poem, but in its Victorian way it took all the juice out of the original--at the big moment, the lovers simply sit on a couch and hold hands! After returning from Europe in 1952, I was preparing to fly to California from New York. I decided to buy something to read on the flight, and at a nearby book stand I found a collection of Greek poetry. I looked in it and I saw that the poem was in the collection, translated by a man I had known quite well when I had lived in Italy. I took it on the plane and was bowled over by it. I thought, "I've got to set some of this to music!" and I finally decided that the only thing to do was to set the whole thing.

Q: When setting a text to music, do you feel a special responsibility towards the author, in terms of what you can or cannot do?

SESSIONS: I wouldn't exactly put it that way. I read the text over, and it begins to set itself to music--in vocal terms. I'm very apt to make notes in the margins, to draw a little staff and put a few notes here and there. Little by little, it takes shape. But, in the first place, I think that in setting a text to music--and this I try to make very clear to my students--one certainly has a responsibility to the text, not so much for the sake of the text as for the sake of the music. If the music and the text fit, then the music will take shape; if they don't, then the music won't take shape properly, and the accents will come in the wrong place.

I felt this very much when my opera Montezuma was performed in German in Berlin. Naturally, I think operas should be translated, but this wasn't too good a translation. Let me give you an example. In the opera there is a young man who causes the catastrophe by a very violent act: He suddenly stages a massacre while Cortez is away. When Cortez comes back, he finds that the Spaniards are cooped-up in a castle in the middle of town, vastly outnumbered and surrounded, unable to escape. He lays this young man out for bringing this about, and the young man tries to justify himself by, in effect, quoting Machiavelli. He argues that when a ruler doesn't have hereditary authority, he has to assert his authority by violence. The phrase this man says to Cortez is, "You're not the offspring of a crowned king, nor even the son of a Pope!" He's referring to Cesare Borgia, who was the son of a Pope. But in the German translation--and I think it could have been done well if someone had tried hard--it became "a Pope's SON!" After all, everybody's somebody's son--or daughter--but it's the Pope that's important, not the son. That's the kind of thing I mean. The rhythm of the text has to go into the blood and bones of the music.

Q: Is there going to be an American performance of <u>Montezuma</u> in the near future?

SESSIONS: <u>Montezuma</u> is being done in Boston in March, by Sarah Caldwell. As a matter of fact, a week from tonight the vocal coach is coming to spend the evening with me and we'll go over it. The singers know their parts already and everything is very much underway. The piece is very expensive simply because it requires a lot of rehearsal and because it has a large cast.

This was a project that Antonio Borgese, who was another very good Italian friend of mine, suggested to me forty years ago. I didn't finish it until a little over ten years ago. He took six years to produce the text, and then there were all sorts of things that had to be done to it.

Q: In the early 1960s, you became one of the co-directors of the Columbia-Princeton Electronic Music Center.

SESSIONS: I haven't done very much there. Milton Babbitt, a former student of mine, was very much interested in this, but it hasn't particularly attracted me. I gave it my moral support; I was full professor at Princeton, and that gave it a certain weight and helped it to get started.

Q: Why haven't you used electronic means in composing?

SESSIONS: I think that some of the people who have been most interested in this are not so interested anymore. Mechanical reproduction is all very well until you get used to it. The minute you become aware that it is a mechanical reproduction, it becomes dead. I learned this years ago not only with records but with movies. I listened to certain works over and over again on a record until I realized that I knew exactly what was going to happen, and could hear it ahead of time--this made me angry. I didn't want to listen to the damn thing any more. I think that this is a problem with electronic music. Someday, I think, it might be one of the instruments. After all, the organ is a mechanical instrument also, and it must have sounded terrible when it was first invented. They used it in the circuses in Rome, the gladitorial combats, and it made a terrific noise which you could hear for miles away. Then, little by little--it took fifteen hundred years or so--it became more and more refined. I don't think that the electronic medium is going to take quite that long. If it becomes an instrument that can be used directly by a performer, then that would be a different matter.

I don't find that there's any comparison between an electronic performance and a live performance. I talked this over with friends of mine who are experienced with it, and, generally, they agreed. I don't fully agree with Milton Babbitt. Once, we were together on a panel and he said that in the electronic medium he had control of everything. Of course that's true, but the only thing he hasn't got control of is the machine itself. But I don't see any reason to think that the time won't come when it can be really played-on. So far, the electronic pieces which have impressed me most--including Babbitt's own--have been things in which live performers have been involved too. But perhaps that only means that I haven't been particularly interested in that medium myself. I very often felt that if I had an orchestra, I could write the same music for it, and it would sound much better. For years, a lot of the electronic music consisted of a bunch of clichés which, as sounds, were rather amusing for a while. But we knew exactly what they were, and everyone got bored with them.

Q: Do you think that electronic music has affected non-electronic music in terms of revealing new or different dimensions of sound?

SESSIONS: I wonder; I don't know. I think that this happens almost inevitably. The trouble is that there's too much interest in sound as pure sound. Sound, in itself, means nothing; a sound is only effective if it's in the right place, in the right context. In itself, a sound is just a sound; it can be a new sound, but it's not new very long--it's only new the first time you hear it. If it becomes a cliché--as I was speaking of--it becomes a bore; it gets to be an old sound very quickly. But when these things are really in a place where they work strongly, that's when they become significant themselves, and remain always fresh.

Q: What are you currently working on?

SESSIONS: I'm working on another big orchestral piece--that's all I will say.

Q: Will this be your Ninth?

SESSIONS: I suppose so. Why not?

CATALOG OF COMPOSITIONS

| 1923 | Incidental Music for The Black Maskers | EB Marks |
| 1923 | Suite from The Black Maskers for orchestra | EB Marks |

1925	Incidental Music for Turandot	MS
1926	Three Chorale Preludes for Organ	EB Marks
1927	Symphony No. 1 in E Minor	EB Marks
1929	Pastorale for flute	MS
1930	On the Beach at Fontana for soprano and piano	EB Marks
1930	Piano Sonata No. 1	G Schirmer
1935	Concerto for Violin and Orchestra in B Minor	EB Marks
1935	Scherzino and March for piano	Carl Fischer
1936	String Quartet No. 1 in E Minor	EB Marks
1938	Chorale for Organ	HW Gray
1938	Three Dirges for orchestra	MS
1939	Two Children's Pieces for piano ("Waltz for Brenda" and "Little Piece")	EB Marks
1940	From My Diary for piano	EB Marks
1942	Duo for Violin and Piano	EB Marks
1944	Turn O Libertad for SATB and piano four-hands or orchestra	EB Marks
1946	Symphony No. 2	G Schirmer
1946	Piano Sonata No. 2	EB Marks
1947	The Trial of Lucullus opera in one act	EB Marks
1951	String Quartet No. 2	EB Marks
1953	Sonata for Solo Violin	EB Marks
1954	Idyll of Theocritus for soprano and orchestra	EB Marks
1955	Mass for unison male chorus and organ	EB Marks
1956	Concerto for Piano and Orchestra	EB Marks
1957	Symphony No. 3	EB Marks
1958	String Quintet	EB Marks
1958	Symphony No. 4	EB Marks
1960	Divertimento for Orchestra	Merion
1962	Montezuma opera in three acts	EB Marks
1963	Psalm 140 for soprano and orchestra or organ	EB Marks
1964	Symphony No. 5	EB Marks
1965	Piano Sonata No. 3	EB Marks
1966	Symphony No. 6	Merion
1966	Six Pieces for Cello	EB Marks
1967	Symphony No. 7	Merion
1968	Symphony No. 8	EB Marks
1970	When Lilacs Last in the Dooryard Bloom'd for soprano, contralto, bass, chorus, and orchestra	Merion
1970	Rhapsody for orchestra	Merion
1970	Double Concerto for Violin, Cello, and Orchestra	Merion
1971	Canons for string quartet	Tempo, No. 98
1972	Concertino for Chamber Orchestra	EB Marks
1972	Three Choruses on Biblical Texts for chorus and chamber orchestra	Merion
1975	Five Pieces for Piano	Merion
1978	Waltz for Piano	Merion; CF Peters
1979	Symphony No. 9	Merion

photo: Gene Bagnato

Ralph Shapey was born on March 12, 1921, in Philadelphia, Pennsylvania. He studied violin with Em-
manuel Zetlin and composition with Stefan Wolpe. He
is currently both professor of music at the University
of Chicago and Music Director of the Contemporary
Chamber Players of the University of Chicago. In
1957, he married Vera Shapiro. They have one son.

Shapey's intention as a composer has long been
to write a music that exists "as an object in Time
and Space." He achieves this quality through his
statement of distinctive musical materials that are
set forth, juxtaposed, reiterated, and overlapped
rather than traditionally developed and varied. Although Shapey relies in part on serial technique, his
unique pieces generate an energy and urgency that
make them immediately identifiable as his.

Ralph Shapey was interviewed in the judge's cham-
bers of the Fordham Law School courtroom on February 18, 1980. The authors had heard stories about
his bluntness and his colorful vocabulary, and he proceeded to live up to his reputation in every respect.
Less well known are his kindness and wit; they were
treated to both of these qualities as well, and so
think back on their time with Ralph Shapey with warmth
and respect.

Q: We'd like to start with your studies with Stefan Wolpe.

SHAPEY: In about 1938, he came to the States, to Philadelphia,
where I was studying at the time. We were all in a class, and
he gave us a hearing and writing test. I had already studied theory,
harmony, counterpoint, and I was dabbling in composition. I'd been
doing it for years, and knew a little more than just pot luck. He
was playing the piano and hit a high note, and I yelled out, "Christ!
that piano's out of tune!" He said, "Write it down! Write it down!"
and the next thing I knew, he's hovering over my shoulder. He'd
given us a harmony exam, and as I was doing it he grabbed it off
the desk, looked at it and yelled: "Why don't you prepare?" I
said, "Who the hell said I had to prepare? I don't want to prepare." He said, "Oh. I see you after class!"

So we talked, and I told him what I was doing. He said,
"All right, bring something in next week and show it to me." I
brought in a piece I had just finished, and he said, "OK, you'll
study composition. You don't need the class, you know that stuff,
obviously." That's how it happened.

Q: Had you been familiar with his music?

SHAPEY: No. I didn't know anything about him. He was a complete stranger to me.

Q: How long did you continue to study with him?

SHAPEY: Well, that was in 1938, and in 1942 I went into the army for three years. Then I came back and moved to New York and resumed studies. By the time I wrote my Second String Quartet, 1948-49, it wasn't formal studies. We had become quasi-friends. If I wrote something, I'd say, "Hey, Stefan, I want you to look at something," and he'd come over, or I'd go to his place. Or he'd call me and say, "Ralph, come on over, I have something to show you that I'm writing." It was that sort of friend/student relationship for many years.

Q: What would you say the results were of studying with Wolpe?

SHAPEY: I don't know. One can't answer a question like that. It's like when someone on a seminar will ask, "Who influenced your music?" or "What influences your music?" I finally came up with the thought that everything does: the past, the present, hopefully the future, what I ate this morning, whether I had a good night's sleep the night before, a good lover, or what have you.

It's like the question about "technique" at these forums and seminars. Somebody always brings up that particular question. What the hell are they talking about? What is technique? Do they mean the technique that you learn in a book, or from some teacher that stands up on a platform, or that you can learn by yourself? Real technique is imagination.

Yes, I studied with Stefan. The influence? Well, I don't write Wolpe music, everybody knows that. I'm really completely different from Wolpe. But somehow, by a kind of osmosis, it was an influence, like everything is an influence.

Whatever it is you're learning, you first learn fundamentals (hopefully), then you learn to think. I tell my students: "If I can teach you how to think, then I've taught you everything possible. You're here because we think you have talent as a composer. That, you've proven. The next step is to teach you how to think, as a composer. Then the rest is up to you." The influence that a teacher has is peripheral, a guidance. I'm not trying to evade the question, I just find it an extremely difficult question to answer.

Q: Your 1957 piece Ontogeny has been described as marking a

break from your earlier approach to your concept of "it is," "the graven image." Would you agree with that description?

SHAPEY: I don't think there's a break. The "it is" business that you're talking about was clearly formulated at that time, but I was always interested in "it." I had never formulated it that clearly for myself. But historically, somebody else will do a better job than I.

I find a constant line throughout my music. Looking backwards, I was always struggling with that formulation. The whole idea of the graven image has always been pertinent to me. I have always tried to make my music so sculpted that you could hold it in your hand--you feel as though it's a piece of sculpture. I was very pleased and flattered when Eric Salzman heard my piece Discourse, and then in his review talked about "sculpted forms." I called him up and asked, "Hey, Eric, did we ever talk about this?" He said, "No, we never discussed it." "So where did you get it from?" He said, "From the music." I said, "Oh, boy! I did it! I did it!" That was a marvelous moment: Here was a critic who wrote about my music in the terms that I was trying to write; I had not formulated it publicly; but he heard it in the music.

Around the time that you're asking about, I spent one whole year asking myself, "What is it that made the old masters so great? Is it just genius? Or talent? Or is there something else that they knew and had that we don't." It was at that moment I got fed up with all twentieth-century music: "It's a pile of shit, a mess! You can't differentiate one from another!" Then I thought, "Hell, in Beethoven's day, in Mozart's day, there were hundreds of composers, but only the geniuses survived." What was it that was special? After all, in that day, everybody could write a sonata-allegro form. Exposition was nothing; everyone had the craftsmanship to do that. But it was the development section that showed the genius of a Mozart or a Beethoven against all the hundreds around them.

So I went back, but in a different kind of analysis. (This was not the kind of book analysis that you learn in school, which adds up to nothing.) I restudied all the old masters, and concluded the obvious: They were unforgettable. But why? Beethoven's Fifth Symphony: bam-bam-bam-baaaaaaam. That's the most banal thing I've ever heard. Be honest: What is it? Nonsense, it's a nothing. But what he did with it! My God, I'd give my right arm to have done that. So I came to the "it is" formulation about my own music: I've said it many times--"You might hate it, but you're not going to forget it."

So it is with music--or any art form, painting or writing-- if you hear it, look at it, read it once, and you have no reason to go back to it, then it's failed. That's it. But if there's something there that aggravates you to the point that you want to hear it again, you want to look at it again, you want to read it again, then it's succeeded. It's gotten hold of you.

You listen to a piece of music on a record, and you say that the more you listen, the more things you find there. Do you think some gremlin came in and changed your record in the middle of the night? No! It's all been there all of the time. What happened is this: Hearing something the first time, you're involved with the top layer--the melody, let's say, or the emotional impact. If it draws you back to hear it again, for whatever reason--whether it annoyed you, or was pleasant, what's the difference? You feel the need to listen again and again; your mind, after a certain amount of listening, finally accepts the so-called obvious things. Then, all of a sudden, you begin to hear something else. You hear the under-layers; you begin to hear the harmonies, the counterpoint, the other things that had been there all along. They come up to the surface. Hearing more things proves that the particular composer--in my terms--built an architectural structure. That's why it stands up. An example: The worst performer cannot kill a Beethoven work. And it's not only because we hear Beethoven so much, or we know good performances. It's because there's an architectural structure there that cannot be destroyed.

One year may not be a long time, but it was a very intensive year of looking and searching until I formulated for myself that which I knew I was doing, but had not yet come to clearly under-stand. If that's a so-called "break" in my writing, fine, I don't care. We have Beethoven and other masters in periods, "the early," "the middle," "the late." I don't know if I'm in my middle or late period, I haven't the slightest idea! Some musicologist will figure that out someday!

Q: One remark of yours is frequently quoted: "I work with the concept of 'it is' instead of the traditional 'it becomes.'" "It is" is clearly the compositional approach that is richest for you, but do you feel that "it becomes" has become exhausted by now?

SHAPEY: I got tired of the nineteenth-century developmental ideas. They became like a dog running after its own tail. The "becoming" factor for me was nothing more than taking a seed and showing its constant growth. I don't deal with that any longer. To me, the seed has been planted and now we have the thing, whatever it is. I'm dealing with that and its relationships through its lifespan. I'm dealing with the constant juxtaposition of forces against each other, creating new developments of their own through their relationships.

Here's a simple example: You sent me a letter. I wrote back. Then I came to New York. I stood on a street corner, you walked over, we met. We got into a taxi and while coming here we talked. All of these are different relationships between three people. Now we're in this room, the two of you sitting in front of me and questioning me: a totally different kind of relationship. In the last half hour, we have assumed several different relationships. By the time we're finished, we will have had many different kinds of relationships. That's what I'm dealing with.

Q: In some of your works, you've incorporated tape, but it's usually been a tape of other musicians, rather than electronic music. Have you been interested in writing purely electronic music?

SHAPEY: No, I have not. In all my lectures, I've always defended electronics; to me, it's just another sound source. Any sound source is viable if you make something out of it. However, all the sounds in our basic orchestra are plenty for me, I've not yet lost interest in them, I still can use them.

I've heard certain people say, unfortunately, that they use electronics because they're fed up with the other sounds, that there's not enough notes for them; eighty-eight keys, that's not enough. To me, that's more than I need.

In my Songs of Eros, I do use electronic sounds on tape. As I say, it's a viable source, so why not use it? To me, the orchestra is still the greatest sound possible.

Q: The second movement of Rituals has aleatoric parts for the piano and three saxophones. How much freedom have you given those players? How precisely notated are their parts?

SHAPEY: It's hardly aleatoric. They're given a lead sheet (like the old jazz idea), containing all the ideas that the orchestra had been playing in the first movement, of which they themselves had been a part. They're improvising on that. For the recording of Rituals, the four musicians and I had a five-hour rehearsal the day before the rehearsal with the orchestra. A five-hour rehearsal with the improvisors is hardly aleatoric! One hears, "Ralph went into a jazz-kind of thing, improvisation." Rituals is the only piece of mine that includes improvisation. In the score and parts is the lead sheet, and I did a five-hour rehearsal with them; that's very non-aleatoric as far as I'm concerned!

Now, you might ask me, why didn't I just write the whole thing down? The point in this piece is that only the basic ideas are written down, allowing the players to recompose the material.

Q: By giving this kind of freedom to these particular instruments, you can't help but raise the spectre of jazz. Is this an association you want made by either the musicians or the audience?

SHAPEY: In the score I say that it's not to be jazz in the sense of "jazz." But when you're dealing with sax players, their big thrust in the learning of improvisation is in the jazz field. However, I try to get them as far away from that as possible.

On the record of Rituals, the first sax was kind of jazzy. If

you listen carefully, you'll hear how they got farther and farther
away, until my friend Richard Fudoli went completely nuts on that
tenor sax of his. He got up, put his foot on the chair, leaned back,
closed his eyes, and he started to go! At the end, the whole orchestra cheered him; it was sensational. He was sensational, he's
absolutely fabulous. He knew exactly what I wanted, and he climbed
to the stars. And he wasn't playing jazz.

Q: Presser has begun to publish your music, but it's still very difficult to get any scores.

SHAPEY: You know what publishers are like today; there's no sense
in being with one. The only reason for being with a publisher is
distribution. Most of my music is on rental, from Presser; everything is at Presser, all of my music. A couple of things they finally put out as publications, but I don't think of them as publication: They take my own manuscript, and Xerox it or whatever, and
stick a lousy cover on it. They call that publication; I don't. But
there's nothing you can do about that.

Q: For a long time none of your music was published. How did
you finally manage to break through?

SHAPEY: Oh, I could tell you lovely stories about me and publishers. I tried to get published. Many years ago, I went to see
Hinrichsen at Peters. I'd made an appointment, and showed up
with a load of scores under my arm. "Oh, Ralph Shapey, I'm so
glad to meet you, I've been wanting to meet you, I know your music, I've seen you conduct, blahblahblah, what can I do for you?"
I said, "Well, here, I need a publisher." So he opens up the music, looks at a page, the next page, and the next; finally, he closes
it up, turns to me and says, "Well, I'll tell you the truth, Ralph.
You're a genius, and we have no time for geniuses nowadays." So
I calmly picked up the scores, put them under my arm, looked back
at him, and said, "**** you," and walked out. Now, in all honesty,
what can you say to a stupidity like that? Or Boosey & Hawkes,
"When you're dead and buried we'll print you." So I said, "****
you," again.

What happened with Presser is very simple. Several years
ago there was a big article in The New York Times which was written by my colleague, Shulamit Ran. After that, Arnold Broido,
President of Presser, wrote to me, we talked, and Presser took
me on. That was only several years ago. But finally I got a so-
called publisher. I say "so-called" because they don't publish!

Q: In the late sixties you declared a moratorium on all performances of your music. We know about all the difficulties you'd had
with publishers and musicians, which in part led you to this decision.

But you've also been quoted as saying that you stopped for "personal and religious reasons."

SHAPEY: I don't know why they get "religious" in there; that one always puzzled me. To be perfectly honest, I never said "religious."

But personal, yes. I was completely fed up. In simplistic terms, you could say I went out on strike.

The trouble with this question is not that I don't want to answer it, but it would take hour after hour after hour to do so, for now it becomes a series of headline statements.

But I think, in essence, that I went out on strike. My children--namely, my music--I think are beautiful. That's my problem, OK. And I didn't want to give them to the human race because I despise the human race. I don't think it's worth a damn. It's nature's worst mistake, and nature's going to get rid of us, unless we get rid of ourselves first--one or the other's going to happen. I still despise the human race.

Q: Not just music publishers?

SHAPEY: No. You're both young, and--I hope--filled with optimism, etc. You should be. But don't look too deeply at the human race because you can get pretty disgusted with it. I have.

Q: Then why did you end your moratorium?

SHAPEY: Well, various persons--some friends, even some enemies--would write to me, or call me, and say, "Come on, Ralph, you can't do this, this is silly!"

My very dear friend, Paul Fromm, of the Fromm Foundation, would bitch at me over and over: "Ralph, you must end it." Finally, at one point he said to me, "Ralph: You yourself, in all your teaching, tell your students that a work is not fully alive until it is performed." I said, "Sure." He said, "Then at least let the work live! There are a few people who like your music; no matter where they are or who they are, there are those who do, who are interested and want to hear it. So why don't you get to be selfish like everybody else, and do it purely for selfish reasons?" Somehow or other, I guess that turned the final trick. I said, "All right, what the hell's the difference, let them play it." So I came back in when I did the performance of Praise in the bicentennial year--although it had nothing to do with the bicentennial, that was just a coincidence.

Q: You were composing throughout your moratorium.

SHAPEY: Yes. For public consumption, I said I wasn't writing anymore, but that was nonsense--I was writing all the time. It's my neurotic compulsion; I admit it, I can't help myself.

It's neurotic because this world has no use whatsoever for us, let's face it! Beethoven, Mozart, etc., the old masters, were part of their society. You might say it was a very special society, and it was: It was the elite of their day. But we don't have any elite today. Unless you want to call the intellectuals the elite. But intellectuals, if they are the elite, are just as bad as the rest of the human race, because they have to have their rear ends tickled all the time. They're so sophisticated. I'm not interested in tickling them with a feather; I'd rather jam a hot rod into them!

Q: Did you find, during the moratorium, that it was having an effect on your composition?

SHAPEY: Maybe. The only influence it might have had--and again, this is in retrospect--is that since I didn't give a damn about whether they were performed or not, it became almost a sort of Ivesian thing: I just sat in my place, and I just wrote music, and to hell with everybody. I've always done that, all my life, but maybe this had a greater effect on that level--I'm not sure. Again, this is one of those questions about "what influenced you?" Everything influences you, including things of which you're not even aware.

Q: You began to compose Praise, and then set it aside for a number of years.

SHAPEY: There's a simple explanation for that. I started it here in New York, when the Convocation was written. Then I went to Chicago, and there was a new job, and the Contemporary Chamber Players: performances, rehearsals, teaching, etc. Also there were a certain amount of commissions and other works--it all interfered. And since I knew Praise was going to be a big work, I just said, "Well, I better put it aside." Then finally, at one point, I said, "God damn it, this is it; I've got to finish that piece." It was in the summer, and I was in East Hampton, and I just decided: This summer I have to finish this piece that's been laying dormant for all these years. So I just set that time apart and wrote it.

Q: Since so many years had elapsed, did you have to significantly rework the earlier material for Praise?

SHAPEY: No. I just went right on from where I stopped. The work was in my mind all along; it never left my mind.

Q: Could you tell us why you decided to repeat the opening three movements of Praise during its intermission?

SHAPEY: Well, it can be played without that. But there's a staging factor in the music. It starts with the Convocation which, after all, is the calling of the people together.

We did Praise at the Rockefeller Chapel: We did the whole first section, and then we had an intermission. Everybody went offstage. Then they came back onstage. But instead of signalling, as one does in a concert hall, "Intermission is over, go to your seats," using lights, bells, and all that junk, I walked out and hit the downbeat. And of course everybody began scuttling for their seats--"What's happening? What's happening?" I could hear them behind my back! But that's what I wanted, the convocation, calling the people together.

Q: Do you have complete control over the music you conduct with the Contemporary Chamber Players?

SHAPEY: Oh, yes, I'm the music director; I pick my own programs. I will have to take the blame. If a composer sends me a score, and I don't put it on, I'm not going to hide behind a clique or a committee. I'm not going to say, "I'm sorry, my committee rejected your score." No. I'm sorry, I rejected your score, at least for the moment.

Q: Do your activities as a conductor work together well with your composing? Do you think you'd rather set conducting aside so you could have more time to compose?

SHAPEY: I started out first as a violinist, then as a conductor. When I was sixteen or seventeen years old, I had a conducting post, so I've always been an active, performing, interpretive musician. Of course, I specialize as a conductor in twentieth-century music. When I walk offstage after we've performed a new, difficult work that we've been able to figure out, we've had all the rehearsal time we need, and it was played as though it was Mozart. We knew it that well. I get a charge out of that. I don't get a charge out of doing Beethoven or Brahms, only because everyone else does them. You can't kill a Beethoven or a Brahms, they'll stand up anyhow.

In 1965 or '66 I brought the Contemporary Chamber Players to New York for a concert at Hunter College. And the mishpucha was there, every composer on the East Coast. At the end of the concert, people came backstage. Aaron Copland and I were yakking, and he said, "Ralph, do you remember the days when a composer got up at a concert, turned to the audience, and said, 'You didn't hear my piece'?" I said, "Oh, yes, Aaron, I remember." He had been floored by the concert, and said, "You must have performed these works at least six times; the performance was unbelievably wonderful." I said, "Thanks, Aaron, but this is the second time we've performed them." He said, "My God, that's unbelievable," and I said, "Not so, because that's the way I rehearse them."

That gives me a charge. This may sound egotistical, but I'm not so sure it is; I think it's a fact (and there's more than one musician in New York who might admit it--although several conductors might not want to admit it). As Sam Baron said to me, "You're the yardstick; you've set up a standard for the performing of contemporary music which is still the yardstick."

There's no reason under the sun why twentieth-century music can't be played as marvelously well as Bach, Beethoven, or Brahms. This has been the thrust of my life as a performer. When we walk off that stage--I don't give a damn how tough the piece is--it went as though we were playing the old masters.

This is one of the reasons why the bad critics are sore at me. They can't write in their papers, "Obviously, this performance was very bad, so we'll have to wait to give a criticism of the work." They can't hide any longer; not with me. They have to show that they either know or don't know what they're talking about. But critics are a necessary evil. I'm not even so sure they're necessary!

Q: So there's almost a polemical purpose to conducting for you, in terms of bringing this music out and changing the habits and tastes of people who go to concerts.

SHAPEY: To me, music is a living art. (Let's forget my moratorium.) This is a fact, and there are as many great composers of the twentieth century as there were of the nineteenth and eighteenth centuries. I know, we'll have to wait until we're all dead a hundred years before they say, "Oh yeah, that's right, there were some great ones then too, how about that!"

When Jean Martinon was conductor of the Chicago Symphony, he said to me, "Ralph, when I do contemporary music, my audience walks out!" I said, "But Jean, they walk back in again." You must know the Slonimsky Lexicon of Musical Invective; I tell my students, "You have to read it every day!" There it is, in black and white: "Beethoven's Third Symphony is a monstrosity and will never be heard again in a concert hall." I should write such a monstrosity!

There's great music around today. The unfortunate thing is
that most performers don't want to bother with it, largely because
most conductors are jackasses: They can't even read music. All
they can do is wiggle their ass around and put on a big show up
there. And if the orchestra paid any attention to the conductor,
they'd get lost and not know what the hell they're doing, so they
never look at the conductor. So why the hell should they do twentieth-century music, when it demands that they use their brains a
little bit?

I can tell you a wonderful story. (I've lots of stories! and
they're all true, they all happened to me.) I was conducting my
Invocation with the Chicago Symphony, and there was the fight going
on with Martinon; they were also doing the Carter Piano Concerto,
and they were mad--all kinds of crap. (Let's face it, American
orchestras are the biggest bunch of babies alive!) So they told me
that they were going to give me a hard time--I was the guest conductor, so they could let me have it; they couldn't let Martinon
have it, he was their boss! Well, at one point I got fed up and
walked out of the rehearsal. I said, "OK, I'm canceling my piece.
The hell with it, I'm not going to take this God damned crap!"
Well, the committee and Jean: "Who insulted you? Blahblahblah,"
and they convinced me to go back on again. At intermission, the
concertmaster came up to me and said, "When we play a work of
yours, we should get double pay." I said, "Well, that's a very
interesting idea, and if I had the money I'd be glad to give it to
you, but why?" He said, "You know why." I said, "I know why,
but I want to hear you say it!" He said, "Well, for a work like
yours, we have to think, and we're not used to thinking. We don't
want to think. Pay us double, and then we can think."

On the tenth anniversary of the Contemporary Chamber Players, we figured out that I'd done 250 new works. Now I'm in my
sixteenth year, so that must be about 350 new works that I've conducted. Never did I do what Georg Solti did. A week before he
went into rehearsal for Sessions' When Lilacs Last in the Dooryard
Bloom'd: He called in the critics and notified them that the Sessions work had ruined his entire vacation. He didn't know what
the hell he was doing; he murdered it--it was one of the worst performances Sessions ever had.

Is this a conductor? Who's kidding whom here? This is a
joke, the whole thing is an obscene joke. I've been saying, for
God knows how many years, and finally now others are saying it,
including Lenny Bernstein: The orchestras--especially American
orchestras--are museum pieces. Put them in a glass case in a
museum, and forget about them. Of course, what they're going to
do is destroy themselves.

Where does the fault lie? I think a lot has to do with the
whole star system; we've got to get rid of that. There's a million
things which have to change and which obviously are not going to
change.

Yes, I believe in an elitist society, I believe that great art is an elitist thing. But as far as I'm concerned, the doors are open to anybody. To me, great art is still the <u>Holy of Holies</u>--a very old-fashioned idea. You have a right to come to it; it does not come to you.

Music, art, do not make money. The old civilizations knew it. The first elite that supported it was royalty. When they were finished, it went into the church and they supported it; the church was the new elite. Then the state took over. That's what we need in America, the same damned thing. But of course, in this so-called "democracy" it'll never happen, not the way it should happen.

What's going to happen? I do not have a crystal ball. But what's going on is devastating. That's a hard word, but it is devastating. I think the human race is destroying itself in more than one way.

Q: Are there any conductors on the scene today whom you really respect?

SHAPEY: I really don't know how to answer that. I've gone far away from that scene because it disgusts me so. When it comes to twentieth-century music, you cannot get up there and put on a show. The composers of today are writing very difficult things, and you have to really be a conductor with baton technique, à la Fritz Reiner. And conducting the old masters? Look, there's not one conductor who could have possibly conducted a given Beethoven symphony as many times as the orchestra has played it over the years under different conductors. So he gets up, gives a downbeat, and goes to sleep. He lets them play it, they know what the hell they're playing. They don't bother with him, they don't even look at him.

The conductors are not conducting. They're a bunch of prima donnas who sell themselves; they're not selling music, they're not really interested in making music. Yes, sometimes they do inspire the orchestra, but the orchestra plays it the best they can, for their esprit de corps. It's not like Toscanini (who had an extremely limited repertoire, so I condemn him for that). With Toscanini, the baton was there. There wasn't any crapping around; he knew what he wanted and he got it out of the men. The same with Bruno Walter, or what history says about Mahler.

We don't have giants today. But I think America doesn't want that kind of giant. They don't want real music making. All it is now is a Madison Avenue sell-job. I weep because I believe that's the end of music making.

Q: Have you wanted to write about music?

SHAPEY: I'm not one of those who writes articles and books. I have a very strange idea: I think that the music has to speak for itself. In the future, you're not going to have Milton Babbitt giving lectures that nobody understands. (Sometimes I wonder if he understands what he's saying, and I've told him that. I've told him that some of my students have translated his articles into English! He said, "Oh, I'd like to see it," and I said, "Why, do you want to find out what the hell you were saying?") Seriously, you're not going to have John Cage there giving his lectures about mushrooms as a personality. In other words, someday we're all going to die. Believe me, every one of us will be gone. And if the music is played a hundred years from now, it's going to have to speak for itself. You're not going to have Babbitt, Cage, or anyone else telling you what to listen for. The music is going to have to speak for itself.

Q: In your program notes, you've written a description of what great art is: "a work which transcends the immediate moment and that moment becomes a moment of eternity; as one seems to live in a space of timelessness...." There's a mystical feeling to that, like a description of a religious experience. Do you think that that finally is the value of great art, that it affords us a form of religious communication?

SHAPEY: To answer that, I would then have to ask you, what is religion? We'd have to define every word.

But if you've experienced--great music, a great book, a great painting, great opera, theater--something through which you lose all track of time, then you know.

I received a wonderful compliment when I did Praise: Somebody came up to me and said, "But it was so short, Ralph." I said, "Really? You've just listened to an hour of music." "What? No, you're crazy! It was too short!" Time stood still for that person.

If you want to call it religious, OK, call it religious, because for me, yes, great art is a miracle. Now if you've experienced these things, whether it's with art, religion--you call it a religious experience. I don't like the word "religious" because it has connotations which I don't want. I'm talking about an experience in which for that moment, you have lost control of your basic life, and lived in a different time-element, a different sphere. You receive something so marvelous that you cannot define it. You want it again--despite an element of fear, you remember it as a moment beyond yourself! It's one of the most marvelous experiences of your life. If you've experienced that, then you know what I'm talking about.

Isn't that the thing that we're all striving for, in our daily lives? Otherwise, what the hell are our daily lives anyway? Pretty damned nasty. Then what the hell are we living for? Aside from the fact that your mother and father gave birth to you, what are you living for? Isn't it to have lived some kind of marvelous experience? I believe that great art can do that to you. I've experienced it. If you haven't, I'm sorry. I hope someday you will.

CATALOG OF COMPOSITIONS

1946	Piano Sonata	Presser
1946	String Quartet No. 1	Presser
1947	Piano Quintet	Presser
1949	Three Essays on Thomas Wolfe for piano	Presser
1949	String Quartet No. 2	Presser
1950	Violin Sonata	Presser
1951	Seven Little Pieces for piano	Presser
1951	Cantata for soprano, tenor, bass, narrator, chamber orchestra, and percussion	Presser
1951	Fantasy for orchestra	Presser
1951	String Quartet No. 3	Presser
1952	Symphony No. 1	Presser
1952	Oboe Sonata	Presser
1952	Quartet for Oboe and String Trio	Presser
1952	Suite for Piano	Presser
1953	Cello Sonata	Presser
1953	String Quartet No. 4	Presser
1954	Sonata-Variations for piano	Presser
1954	Concerto for Clarinet and Chamber Ensemble	Presser
1955	Piano Trio	Presser
1955	Challenge--The Family of Man for orchestra	Presser
1956	Mutations No. 1 for piano	Presser
1957	Duo for Viola and Piano	Presser
1957	Rhapsodie for oboe and piano	Presser
1958	Ontogeny for orchestra	Presser
1958	Walking Upright for female voice and violin	Presser
1958	String Quartet No. 5 (with female voice)	Presser
1959	Evocation for violin, piano, and percussion	Presser
1959	Soliloquy for narrator, string quartet, and percussion	Presser
1959	Form for piano	Presser
1959	Rituals for orchestra	Presser
1959	Invocation for violin and orchestra	Presser
1960	Movements for woodwind quintet	Presser
1960	De Profundis for contrabass and chamber ensemble	Presser
1960	Five for violin and piano	Presser

1960	This Day for female voice and piano	Presser
1960	Dimensions for soprano and twenty-three instruments	Presser
1961	Incantations for soprano and ten instruments	Presser
1961	Discourse for flute, clarinet, violin, and piano	Presser
1962	Piece for violin and instruments	Presser
1962	Chamber Symphony for Ten Solo Players	Presser
1962	Birthday Piece for piano	Presser
1963	Brass Quintet	Presser
1963	Seven for piano four-hands	Presser
1963	String Quartet No. 6	Presser
1964	Sonance for carillon	Presser
1965	Configurations for flute and piano	Presser
1965	String Trio	Presser
1966	Partita for violin and thirteen players	Presser
1966	Poeme for viola and piano	Presser
1966	Mutations No. 2 for piano	Presser
1967	For Solo Trumpet	Presser
1967	Partita-Fantasy for cello and sixteen players	Presser
1967	Reyem for flute, violin, and piano	Presser
1967	Songs of Ecstasy for soprano, piano, percussion, and tape	Presser
1967	Deux for two pianos	Presser
1971	Praise for bass-baritone, chorus, and chamber orchestra	Presser
1972	Three Concert Pieces for Young Players for violin, viola, cello, and percussion	Presser
1972	String Quartet No. 7	Presser
1973	Fromm Variations for piano	Presser
1975	Songs of Eros for soprano and orchestra	Presser
1975	Oh Jerusalem for soprano and flute	Presser
1977	The Covenant for soprano, sixteen players, and tape	Presser
1978	21 Variations for Piano	Presser
1979	Song of Songs No. I for soprano, fourteen players, and tape	Presser
1979	Evocation No. 2 for cello, piano, and percussion	Presser
1979	Three for Six for violin/viola, cello, piano, flute/piccolo, clarinet/bass clarinet, and percussion	Presser
1980	Four Etudes for Violin	Presser
1980	Song of Songs No. II for bass, fourteen players, and tape	Presser
1980	Song of Songs No. III for soprano, bass, fourteen players, and tape	Presser

CHARLES WUORINEN ☐

photo: Gene Bagnato

Charles Wuorinen was born on June 9, 1938, in New York City. He received both his B. A. and M. A. from Columbia University. He studied composition with Jack Beeson, Otto Luening, and Vladimir Ussachevsky. Wuorinen has taught at Columbia University and the Mannes School of Music. He has also been extremely active in the performing world of contemporary music. With Harvey Sollberger, Wuorinen is co-founder and co-director of the Group for Contemporary Music. He is widely admired as both a pianist and conductor, and in these capacities has performed both his own works and the music of many twentieth-century composers in concert and for records.

Wuorinen's first works had their basis in the more tonal compositions of Igor Stravinsky. By the early 1960s, he began to combine Stravinskian technique with the serial developments of Arnold Schoenberg and Milton Babbitt. He has written a vast amount of music, covering virtually every medium. They all display the complex structuring and occasional flashes of subtle wit which have come to characterize his music.

Cole Gagne interviewed Charles Wuorinen in his Manhattan apartment on July 14, 1975. It was a brief visit which the composer dominated with the formal, somewhat reserved directness that he brings to his activities as a performer. With the exception of a brief attempt by one of his cats to gain admittance, the interview was conducted without interruption.

Q: How did you first become involved with electronic music?

WUORINEN: I studied with Vladimir Ussachevsky and Otto Luening. Both of them at the time were involved with the first American developments in electronic music. Naturally, therefore, I was close to those initial developments and was around the first studio at Columbia; and remained associated in one way or another for many years thereafter.

Q: What was there about the medium itself that attracted you to it?

WUORINEN: I don't know if "attraction" is the proper word to use. I regard whatever there is on the musical scene as part of the pro-

fessional composer's domain, and it certainly seemed to me that
the electronic medium represented a significant addition to musical
resources, one which I should investigate as thoroughly as suited
my purposes. In the course of that investigation I found what to
me were a number of serious problems--still largely unresolved--
in the nature of the medium itself.

Q: I'm curious about that, because you haven't written a large body
of electronic works. What are the problems with electronic music?

WUORINEN: Perhaps I shouldn't say there is a problem with the
electronic medium, so much as there is a question in my own mind.
It has two parts. The first concerns the permanence of the compositional result. That is in a way secondary to the second, which
concerns the reproducibility and interpretability of what is composed.

To take care of the first problem in a summary way: I'm
a little nervous about works existing in one physical--and no doubt
deteriorating--form. Since our experience with plastic is that it
doesn't last very long, and our experience with the physical products of this age is that they tend to disintegrate rather rapidly,
to have a compositional effort which is enshrined entirely on a
length of magnetic tape seems to me a little precarious.

I don't think that the electronic medium has anything particular to do with new sounds. Nor do I particularly agree with certain composers who believe that the resources of the electronic
medium as respects the articulation of complex rhythmic or temporal patterns, or the synchronization of elaborately, subtly related components which could not be, perhaps, practically performed,
represent a major advance. I don't think that stretching the limits
of the physical bounds of musical perception is necessarily of any
great significance. It may be interesting, but I don't think that it
represents necessarily a net expansion in resources of musical significance.

So those two claims for the electronic medium have never
been of particular interest to me. What is far more important is
something I have felt as a limitation of the medium, and that is
simply that what is done within it remains exactly as it was first
conceived. I have claimed for a long time that at least up until
now--and I think including now as well--what appears as compositional exactitude is in fact generality. That is to say, when one
writes a specific note in a specific temporal and dynamic position,
it appears that that is a precisely specified event. Well, from an
acoustical point of view it is not at all, because as we know there
are an infinity of ways of performing that note, both temporally,
dynamically--sometimes even in terms of minor pitch variations--
all of which we can easily regard as that note at that dynamic level
in that time slot, but which are all in fact quite different entities.
It is that capacity of music, within a very limited temporal frame-

work to admit an infinity of possible representations, all of which can be agreed to denote the same notated phenomenon, that makes musical interpretation--that is to say, musical expression--possible.

When one removes that flexibility and that resource, and presents one and only one representation of the compositional idea electronically--whether it is synthesized, or analog-studio-produced, or what have you--one is in effect making the claim for the composition that there is one and only one way to represent the musical relations which it contains, and that the way which the composer has presented in his finished electronic work is the best or only way available. Now that claim also contains, it seems to me, some very deep problems, because no composers in the past have ever been called upon to provide the one and only, permanent and eternal most valid representation of their compositional thought. No score, past or present, no matter how detailed and exact it seems, ever has done so, and I don't think there's any reason why it should. It's certainly not a goal to be sought after. But be that as it may, it never has been before, and therefore it seems to me that the entire weight of Western musical tradition--not to mention that of the rest of the world--lies against trying to make an exact, for-all-time, single sonic representation of the work.

What I'm saying has nothing to do with the physical resources of the electronic medium, nor with a roundabout way of raising the old "machine-music" bugaboo. But it does seem to me to be a very important concern, and it may arise as powerfully as it does in my mind because of my experience as a performer, and what I think of as my awareness of the multiplicity of possible representations of the same musical event. I think that is one of the astonishing things about music, and that is one of the characteristics of music which makes it possible to compress into a limited time frame and dynamic range so much relational information--which, of course, is why we regard music as such a profound phenomenon, and why we can ascribe so much significance to it (whether it's expressive, connotative, denotive, or relational significance doesn't matter).

This problem has always confronted me in the making of electronic music, and it is the reason I have done so little. At the moment I have 110 works, and I think only four of them are electronic. It is also the reason, I think, why so much electronic music tends to deal with vaguely specified events--that is to say, events whose initiation and termination are temporally vague, things that start softly and die away, things that reverberate, events which are often not recognizable as specific pitches. I think that that tendency is perhaps the instinctive response of composers to this problem; because when, for example, the initiation of an event is not really exactly located in time by a sharp attack, then the question of shifting the beginning of the event around for interpretive purposes to slightly different temporal locations is not so much of an issue. That's why a lot of electronic music has that kind of whoosh quality to it.

Q: In an interview you gave in 1962, you remarked that you couldn't love your past works. You said that they seemed frozen and detached, and that you could only objectively like them as you would like somebody else's music. It would seem that the past electronic pieces would be doubly frozen, being earlier works which cannot permit reinterpretation. Does it bother you to be represented by Time's Encomium? Is that the old Charles Wuorinen?

WUORINEN: Oh, no, not at all. I never present myself as a reformed version of my former self. I have found that my interests as a composer (as with every composer) necessarily concentrate on present work. But, after all, the function of composing as far as the outside world is concerned--not as far as one's self is concerned, of course--is to produce works which can be of use to other people. I have never felt any proprietary attachment to the works that I have already composed. In effect, I give them out, to be used as people want to, and therefore a work like Time's Encomium I certainly don't reject or accept any more or less than any other work of mine. I'm simply making observations on what I regard as the nature of the electronic medium, as if I were writing a piece for double bass alone (which I also have done at one time).

Certain pieces are inevitably of greater interest to me than others; certain works which have been played a lot may be of less concern to me than other works that don't get played, but none of this has to do with rejecting old attitudes. That's a kind of disingenuousness which I would like to avoid, because my compositional concerns, my artistic concerns, are always (and always have been) so focused on the immediate, on what I'm working on at the moment, and the general surroundings of attitudes and dispositions that that work represents, that I practically never think of the past in that sense.

Q: There's just one other aspect of Time's Encomium that I'd like to touch on. In your liner notes to that piece you discuss the advantage the electronic medium gives you in controlling time and rhythm. It seemed to me that in the bulk of the work there is nothing really superhuman; certainly in Part One those rhythms could have been performed by very skilled musicians.

WUORINEN: I don't think that's really true. We're speaking now of the synthesized core, not the analog-studio transformations which make up most of the work, because those of course can only be electronic. But there are, in the synthesized sections of Time's Encomium, attacks which proceed at 32 per second, and they could not possibly be performed by human instrumentalists. Moreover, if one wants to descend to a slightly more mundane level, even those things which might possibly be done by human beings could be achieved only at the cost of enormous rehearsal. (Not that I'm

against enormous rehearsal! I've spent my whole life rehearsing.)
Nevertheless, I think that to present such a problem to performers
in rehearsal is not necessarily the most germane and pointful use
of players.

But quite apart from that, there are certainly a great many
parts of that synthesized core of material which could not possibly
be represented "live." As a matter of fact, the question you raised
invokes a rather interesting point: Even though the 32 per second
sections of that work for the most part feature very sharp attacks,
to make the location of each event as clear as possible, I don't believe that one hears more than a kind of general intervallic sound
in those parts of the work. Thirty-two per second is the point at
which the ear begins to hear individual attacks, even if they're very
sharp, as continuity. After all, with the low A on the piano, the
fundamental is vibrating at $22\frac{1}{2}$ cycles per second; you think of
something that's faster--actually, 32 is around the low C--and you
think of those representing not periodic vibrations for a single pitch,
but rather individual events, you see what a marginal thing it is
perceptually.

The point I want to make is that it seems (although I've never demonstrated it and I don't know if anyone else has) that the
limits of what can be performed are approximately the same as
those of what can be perceived. In the synthesized sections of
Time's Encomium, when there are attacks coming at the rate of
32 per second, one finds an inability to perceive them as separate
events. They squish together as something composite. By the
same token, we know that performers cannot manage attacks that
fast. Even if the instruments are physically capable of producing
and responding that quickly, one couldn't do it. The fastest trill
that one can play is only about twelve articulations per second.

I've always maintained that the limits of perception are the
same as the limits of performance capacity. What can be heard
by a performer is what can be played by a performer. "Heard"
meaning the complex received and understood, grasped and organized in the mind. It's inconceivable to me that one could hear
something and not be able to execute it. There have been asser-
tions made that there are perceptual boundaries that extend beyond
what can be performed. I question that. Of course, if one is
speaking again of a double bass player attempting to articulate rapidly, the physical nature of his instrument and the frequency range
within which he performs makes it impossible. But I'm assuming
an instrument of sufficient physical efficiency and quickness of response.

Q: In the old interview, you said that musicians were fifty years
behind composers. Is that still true?

WUORINEN: It depends on which musicians you mean. It's cer-

tainly changed a great deal in these parts, and since these parts
are the world music center, I suppose one could say that the world
at large has changed too. Certainly, there was not even so recently as 1962 the kind of incredible flowering of performance activity
and the amazing appearance of so many really expert young players
that we see at present--although the development was beginning then.

When I began my career in the middle fifties there was nothing like what there was in the early fifties, and no comparison at
all with the way things are now. One hesitates to make absolute
claims, but it's hard to believe that we are not living in one of
the greatest ages of performance, if not the most distinguished that
has yet appeared for Western music. The irony is, of course, that
so many people, both inside the musical profession and outside,
seem totally unaware of it. Then when you add the twin evils of
excessive publicity for the wrong thing, and the ignoring of the
right thing, you are left with a totally distorted picture. One has,
for example, the picture of "distinguished" conductors who claim
to be "bringing" contemporary music to New York, and playing
badly, under circumstances of enormous public prestige and great
journalistic attention, works which are played constantly for much
smaller audiences with no journalistic coverage whatever, and
played superbly. This is an anomaly of the age, and it's characteristic of many other contradictions of the age. I suppose we
should be in a certain sense resigned, as well as resentful.

But there is no doubt in my mind that performers now are
capable of playing their contemporary music much better than the
contemporaries of Beethoven could play his. It's also hard to believe, since everything healthy in music comes out of contemporary
musical practice, that the old music is not being better played now
than it ever has before. I'm quite sure of that. Certainly we owe
the past no apologies. At the same time again, however, there is
an irony in that the most publicly renowned performances of old
music are usually the worst. The most revolting travesties and
excesses taking place in the world of opera, for example, are perpetrated by singers who are regarded as the most significant musical
figures of the age. But this is one of the contradictions with which
we live.

There is a more serious question involved here, and that has
to do with training. It should be carefully noted that the younger
generations of performers that I am talking about are not people
emerging from schools of music which have decided to train performers in the music of their own time. These are people, for
the most part, who come to their interest in contemporary music
on their own, frequently over the active opposition of their teachers; and that makes the phenomenon all the more remarkable. In
spite of the incredible backwardness of conservatories--and to some
extent of university music schools and private teachers--this un-
stoppable development has taken place. It is equally remarkable
that despite the vilification, indifference, and hostility that has been
visited upon contemporary musical activity by the press, especially

in New York, the audience has nevertheless grown. This music cannot be denied, and it is not being denied. I suspect that many of the anomalies and contradictions I have referred to will simply go away as the appropriate people die.

There is, however, a great deal of concern that is justified, I think, over the persistently reactionary nature of conservatory teaching. The most gifted will always find a way to overcome the limitations of their environment and the hostility of their instructors, but that is not enough. A genuinely healthy artistic culture requires a host of lesser practitioners as well. There must be a solid body of reasonably qualified, competent, cultivated, intelligent professionals, who may not all be the greatest geniuses of the age. Without them, each individual genius-type lives in a very unhealthy and very counterproductive isolation. I cite you Charles Ives for an example, an extreme case of that person who tried to function entirely on the outside, and I think that his work is seriously flawed because of it. One must therefore have a great deal of concern over the general level of training which is provided in conservatories, and its effect on the general kind of student.

As a counter-example, I can cite the activities of Raymond DesRoches, a very distinguished professional and long-time colleague of mine who teaches at William Paterson College in New Jersey. That institution is not well known in the Ivy League, but due to his own intensity and energy in the training of a percussion ensemble which he's had there for many years, he has produced an entire generation of players, a very healthy handful of absolute masters by now--all very young yet--and dozens of extremely well-qualified, literate, intelligent, and responsive performers. That simply shows you what can be done with a teacher of minimum decency.

There is one other educational matter I'd like to touch on while I'm on this subject, and that is the general state of music education in the United States. It is, as you know, appalling. I think a good many music educators know it too. I don't want to launch into an elaborate diatribe about it, but I do think that, in elementary and secondary schools, the horrors perpetrated in the name of music--the football band in the fall, the musicale in February, the spring concert which is the art moment of the year, the incredible incompetence of most of the teachers--have a very bad, a very damping effect upon the development of the public. Again, however, what is astonishing is that in spite of that monumental turn-off, so many people over the whole country buy records of contemporary music when they come out--when they are well distributed. You can see this with the enormous success of Nonesuch, the only label seriously involved with contemporary music which has an efficient and wide-spread distribution system.

Q: I'd like to discuss a rather iconoclastic statement you made to the effect that Schoenberg had more to offer to the new generation of composers than Webern--who was the god for composers after

World War Two.   You emphasized Schoenberg's polyphony in particular, and it's obvious how important polyphony is for you in such
works as the Chamber Concerto for Cello and Ringing Changes.   In
those scores, an ensemble of instruments can be one voice in the
polyphony.   Is that technique related to Schoenberg's notion of klang-
farbenmelodie?   Is that where Schoenberg's importance is greatest?

WUORINEN: Well, that kind of instrumental practice is something
which Schoenberg--and Webern, too, to an extent--were primarily
responsible for introducing as ordinary and regular in Western music.   It is out of that tradition that I operate, but I think that it's
become somewhat more ramified and complex in my works.

I would like to respond to what you said about Schoenberg.
First of all, you say Webern was the god.   Webern was the god
in Europe, for a group of well-financed, highly publicized post-
World War Two composers, of whom Boulez and Stockhausen are
the best known.   They "discovered" Webern, and never knew Schoenberg at all, in an environment in which musical tradition and
practice had been destroyed.   That is something most important
to remember.   When these gentlemen began their panegyrics on
Webern, the Americans of course all slavishly followed (since Americans know in their hearts that they cannot have a real opinion of
their own), although Webern's music was continuously known here
already since the '20s.   That was the reason for the enormous publicity which Webern received then.   You notice, it's died down a
good deal now, because it is just puffery for the most part and
cannot sustain itself.   This is not, by the way, to minimize Webern's significance as a composer.   I think he's a very good composer, and a very pleasant one to listen to, but the idea that his
work contains the kernel of a new world I think is really absurd.

On the other hand, it seems to me that Schoenberg's mind
offers an infinitely greater depth.   He was, after all, the teacher,
and it seems to me that Webern represents only one idiosyncratic
development of something which Schoenberg's music encompasses
in a much larger way.   Those who have followed the invaluable
work of Milton Babbitt in developing, rationalizing, and explicating
the twelve-tone system--mostly originally, out of the works of Schoenberg himself--can begin to understand what enormously significant
relations Schoenberg formulated and touched on.   He did so in terms
somewhat different from the ones we would perhaps use today, his
rhetoric is not ours, but that really makes no difference at all.   As
for the charge that was so lightly yet so pompously leveled at Schoenberg by the Europeans a few years ago, that there was "something wrong" with his rhythms--also absurd.   If one bothers to make
a non-ideological examination of his works, one finds that even though
the larger phrase shapes seem to have a relationship to certain older kinds of music, the notes that make up those phrases are the
real determinants of those shapes, as well as the time-locations of
the articulations that are those notes.   This becomes too technical
to pursue further, and I don't wish to; but I simply want to make

that point, because it is representative of a larger concern of mine: not to take the immediate superficial characteristics of an art-phenomenon and assume them to be the realities that underlie them. Nowhere is this more dramatically illustrated than in the case of Schoenberg, whose music, to the indifferent and uneducated listener, may simply seem like "wrong-note" Romantic music, even today. But it's not at all that way, far from it.

I would also say, by the way, that in my own work there is not what you may call a direct idiomatic or sonic influence from Schoenberg. There's an ideational influence of great significance, but as for sound and articulation, I think I owe a great deal more to Stravinsky.

Q: I'd like to return to the subject of polyphony. It seems that in certain works polyphony is the dominant concern, even over tone color. If you compare Ringing Changes to something like Ionisation, the fascination with the sheer sound of the percussion instruments and their rhythms has fallen away, and now it's a matter of polyphonic patterns, even with non-pitch instruments. Is polyphony of greater interest to you than something like tone color?

WUORINEN: No. It's not possible to compose that way. One doesn't decide to ignore certain things and not to ignore other things. What you refer to may be a manifestation of my belief in the very inseparability of all these components, which are normally talked about as if they were different things. Rhythm, pitch, tone color, dynamic level, are all verbally separable attributes of a single, unified phenomenon, but they cannot be artistically separated. The sound, the color of a given orchestral or instrumental chord, comes as much from its pitch content as from the instruments that are playing it. Consider an example I always use, the opening chord of the Symphony of Psalms. The main reason it has its characteristic sound is that it is an E minor chord with four Gs in it. In other words, the third of the chord is given the greatest prominence, the presence of the root and the fifth being minimized. That's why it has the color it does, as much as because of the instruments that play it.

Now, Ringing Changes. First of all, remember that Ionisation--which I think is a marvelous work, one of Varèse's best--is only four minutes long. Imagine that multiplied by four or five, and think where you would be. In Ionisation, continuity is achieved by the assertion of different kinds of articulations, different kinds of timbral groups, and a rough contrast of highs and lows and middles--because, of course, there is no exact pitch, and the few instruments in that score that are of exact pitch play clusters, so they are also "noise" instruments. In Ringing Changes, the problem was a very different one for me. To begin with, I didn't want to write a percussion piece that contained only pitched instruments. What I wanted was to write a piece in which relative pitch played

as much of a role as absolute pitch. I wanted to avoid limiting the
interpretive possibilities of a performance of the work by becoming
overly specialized and overly detailed in my designation of instrument types--for example, choice of mallets, and other similar details. At the same time, however, I wanted to create an environment in which the elements of pitch that were present would not
unfold so quickly that they would seem to take the major role. As
you can see, I'm answering your question in a way that points the
whole concern into a different area from what you were talking about
before. I intend Ringing Changes to be heard as a work in which
there is not much of a distinction between exactly fixed pitch, and
less precisely fixed pitch--what we normally regard as "noise" or
"relative pitch." For this reason, the number of noise events is
much greater in the work than the number of pitched events, and
the pitched events have repetitious characteristics. Those were my
concerns in Ringing Changes.

As for polyphony, I don't see how one cannot be concerned
with polyphony, unless one sets out to be a monophonic composer.
Polyphony is there, in our perception, indeed, even of monophony
by now. We don't hear single lines--I don't know how people did
before the development of polyphony--we hear a one-at-a-time representation of a number of different levels. Any tonal or post-
tonal melody has that characteristic.

Q: You've used the notion of pitch centricity in works like Ringing
Changes and Flute Variations II. Do you see it as a throwback to
your earlier, more tonally oriented music?

WUORINEN: It's a throwback, in a certain sense, but mainly it's
an attempt to deny what has been an almost universally accepted
assertion about twentieth-century music: that there's a sharp cleav-
age between old music and new music; that the period around The
Rite of Spring and Pierrot Lunaire (and those works) represents a
major breaking point, and the past is all past. This I reject entirely, for a number of reasons--musical, structural, aesthetic,
and historical. But without rambling off into those pastures, let
me simply state my belief that from the vantage point of almost
seventy-five years, the twentieth-century musical revolution doesn't
seem so revolutionary anymore. The alleged gulf between the music that was written around 1910 and the music that went before
does not seem all so enormous. The tonal system does not seem
to hold sway until 1899, but seems to disintegrate already in the
1820s. (Certainly with Liszt and with Wagner, it's often rather
begging the question, I think, to call these works tonal. The fact
that those composers may have thought they were tonal is of no
more significance in my view than the fact that composers of the
early twentieth century thought they were writing music of an entirely new sort.)

It is my profound conviction that the twelve-tone system in

all its ramifications is the legitimate successor to the tonal system. We do not exist, therefore, in the kind of pluralistic musical world that people would like to have us think we do. There is one main way of doing things, now grown so complex and so ramified that it includes all kinds of composers of highly chromatic music--for example, Elliott Carter, or even Stefan Wolpe--who never were for a minute twelve-tone composers, and never thought of themselves in that way. This enormous body of significant music, now seventy-five years in the making, is not only the direct successor of the world of tonal practice, but is also in unbroken continuity with it.

What this means for me is that, although I am primarily a twelve-tone composer and have been so for practically all of my career (even in those earlier works which appear tonally oriented), there is no contradiction between hierarchical pitch organization--that is, pitch centricity, of which the tonal system is a very clear exemplification--and the order-determined world (or one might say serial world) that succeeded it. In other words, it seems to me that it is now possible, from the vantage point that we have, to tie together certain attributes of older and newer music, and to regard ourselves not as path-breakers who move into an ever-expanding frontier--an old-fashioned, Romantic notion--but rather as the inheritors of an unbroken, whole, and wholesome artistic tradition in which we simply continue.

Q: Earlier, you were talking about Varèse and Ionisation. I understand that you knew Varèse. I'm curious as to under what circumstances you knew him. Was there a working relationship?

WUORINEN: I never had a working relation with Varèse. I knew him during the last years of his life, and we were on very cordial terms. I had a great admiration for him, both as a composer and as a person who had never capitulated to the exigencies of his circumstances.

I met him through the introduction of Carlos Salzedo, a close friend of his, in the middle fifties. Following that, he was around the studio at Columbia from time to time, where I had the opportunity to know him a bit. It was a very significant and meaningful association for me, but not a collaborative one in any sense.

Q: The other figure I'd like to touch on is Stravinsky. You've written a work utilizing the last fragments of music Stravinsky was working on at the time of his death.

WUORINEN: Madame Stravinsky made these sketches available to me a year ago last February. They are very fragmentary indeed. (We're not speaking here of the completion of a work, by any means.)

What they consist of is primarily his serial charts, which are about six pages, and about half a dozen very short fragments, ranging from about a measure to a couple of lines. What I did in the work, which I called Reliquary, was to incorporate these fragments and make use of them as generative material for the whole composition.

I first wrote a work, incorporating all of the fragments that survive. It is about five minutes long, and has certain character- istics like Stravinsky's Variations Aldous Huxley in memoriam. It is intended to contain music by me that is in his manner. Then there's a middle section which is a variation in my manner on the first one, including some other new material. Then there is a truncated reprise of "his" piece--most of the music is still mine-- and finally a concluding coda. It's a simple design which I thought was appropriate for the circumstance.

Q: How did you actually get the fragments?

WUORINEN: Robert Craft showed them to me on one occasion when I was at the Stravinskys'--this was, of course, after the old man had died--and the idea came to mind that it would be interesting to do something with them. I proposed it and Madame Stravinsky agreed, and we proceeded from there.

Q: I've read that you were very impressed with the Japanese mu- sical instrument the shakuhachi, and that it influenced your writing of Flute Variations II. What was it about the shakuhachi which ap- pealed to you?

WUORINEN: Well, it was not so much the instrument--which is very nice, very pleasant to listen to--as it was the remarkable mastery of the player I heard. It's very difficult to describe what it is about the combination of a performance, the musical idiom, and an instrumental timbre, that one finds engrossing. As you can imagine, with me, it was finally the sense of over-arching form and coherence in his performance. That is, to me, what is most expressive; the end of all expressivity is no contradiction of it, but rather an apotheosis of it. It was that in his performance that seemed so impressive. In writing the work for Harvey Sollberger, I tried to reproduce a memory of those impressions; the work has no melodic or pitch relational connection with the music that the shakuhachi plays. It also seemed to me that the integration of a large number of disparate instrumental sounds into a continuous melody was something not normally in the West associated with the playing of a given instrument, and was worth attempting for an artist of the skill and achievement of Harvey Sollberger. That is why there are a number of "effects," of which the buzz-tones be- low the normal range of the flute are the most noticeable, that are in this work but are not normally in my other flute music. I don't mean to propose this as in any sense unusual now, because everybody puts bloops and bleeps into what he writes, but for me it represents something different, something rather special.

Q: You've said that it was the sense of over-arching form which impressed you. Is it that concern of yours which has made you reject aleatory and jazz?

WUORINEN: I've never rejected jazz, it's just that most of what I've heard has never seemed very interesting. I don't know enough about it to speak intelligently of it, of course, but jazz which is really improvised on a coherent set of conventions I think can be extremely worthwhile.

The so-called aleatoric doesn't interest me, but not because of its alleged formlessness. It isn't formless, nothing is formless. Everything has shape. The question is whether the shape is of any significance. The mere fact that it changes every time is also not the issue, because so does figured bass realization, and one doesn't criticize that. No, the problem is a different one for me: A highly indeterminant or unspecified compositional environment deprives the individual pitch of its unique, atomic function. In other words, the individual note or sound in such music is no longer the atomic unit that goes to make up the piece, it's no longer the smallest thing that can be used to define a relationship. Rather, you deal with textures, gestures, much larger blobs of acoustic material. What that means, in turn, is simply that the work, whether it's of indeterminate length or not--unless it is of infinite length, as some of them seem to be--contains far fewer "atomic units" than a normal piece of music does. Instead of thousands and thousands of notes, all coordinated and defining relations amongst each other, you have a much smaller number of acoustic blobs (which are internally highly complex, perhaps, but that internal complexity is entirely irrelevant). Therefore, such music is relationally impoverished, and it is impossible for it to achieve more than the most primitive kind of structural communication. (Or communication of any sort, since I think all communication is in some sense structural.) Whether the structure is deliberate or intuitive is not the point; it's there--just as the plant does not intend to come out that way, but does anyway. It's the catastrophically limited nature of that compositional approach which makes it of no interest whatever to me.

For a long time, I thought it would be nice to have a practice of contemporary improvisation, in the same way that there existed in figured bass realization, but I've not been convinced by any of the attempts at that that have been made over the years, and I've never been able to think of a way, myself, to do it. I think that's because it requires a set of very specific and widely accepted, detailed conventions as a ground. When one has that, one can proceed. Perhaps if composition becomes more standardized than it is now, such a practice will emerge.

CATALOG OF COMPOSITIONS

1953	Scherzo for piano	ACA
1954	Te Decet Hymnus for mezzo-soprano, bass, mixed chorus, two pianos, and timpani	MS
1955	Hommage à Bach for organ	ACA
1955	Prelude and Fugue for percussion	Music for Perc
1956	Song and Dance for piano	ACA
1956	Into the Organ Pipes and Steeples for orchestra	ACA
1956	Music for Orchestra	ACA
1956	Sonatina for flute, oboe, clarinet, and bassoon	Presser
1956	Two Tranquil Pieces for piano	ACA
1956	Woodwind Quintet	MS
1956	Concert Piece for piano and strings	MS
1956	Subversion for two violins, two violas, two cellos, and contrabass	MS
1957	Concertante No. 1 for violin and orchestra	MS
1957	Three Mass Movements for violin	MS
1957	Triptych for violin, viola, and percussion	MS
1957	Alternating Currents for chamber orchestra	ACA
1957	Dr. Faustus Lights the Lights for narrator, clarinet, bassoon, saxophone, cello, piano, timpani, and percussion	ACA
1957	Wandering in This Place for mezzo-soprano	ACA
1957	Be Merry All That Be Present for SATB and organ	ACA
1958	Three Prepositions for piano	Presser
1958	Movement for woodwind quintet	Presser
1958	Three Pieces for String Quartet	ACA
1958	Spectrum for violin, brass quintet, and piano	ACA
1958	Piano Sonata	MS
1958	Symphony No. 1	MS
1958	Concertante No. 2 for violin and orchestra	MS
1959	Concertante No. 3 for harpsichord, oboe, violin, viola, and cello	MS
1959	Concertante No. 4 for violin and piano and chamber orchestra	MS
1959	Trio Concertante for oboe, violin, and piano	MS
1959	Musica Duarum Partium Ecclesiastica for brass quintet, piano, organ, and timpani	MS
1959	Symphony No. 2	MS
1959	Symphony No. 3	ACA

1960	Sonata for Flute and Piano	ACA
1960	The Door in the Wall and On the Raft for two mezzo-sopranos (or one mezzo-soprano and one soprano) and piano	ACA
1960	Madrigale Spirituale for tenor, baritone, two oboes, two violins, cello, and contrabass	ACA
1960	Turetzky Pieces for flute, clarinet, and contrabass	ACA
1960	Concertone for brass quintet and orchestra	ACA
1960	Eight Variations for violin and harpsichord	ACA
1960	Consort for four trombones	ACA
1961	Symphonia Sacra for tenor, baritone, bass, two oboes, two violins, contrabass, and organ	ACA
1961	Consort from Instruments and Voices for magnetic tape	ACA
1961	Tiento Sobre Cabezon for flute, oboe, violin, viola, cello, harpsichord, and piano	ACA
1961	An Educator's Wachet Auf for orchestra	ACA
1961	Evolutio for organ	ACA
1961	Evolutio Transcripta for chamber orchestra	ACA
1961	Concert for contrabass	McGinnis & Marx
1961	Trio No. 1 for Flute, Cello, and Piano	ACA
1962	Octet	McGinnis & Marx
1962	Invention for piano and percussion quintet	Music for Perc
1962	Duuinsela for cello and piano	McGinnis & Marx
1962	Bearbeitungen über das Glogauer Leiderbuch for flute, piccolo, clarinet, bass clarinet, violin, and contrabass or cello	CF Peters
1962	The Prayer of Jonah for SATB and string quintet	ACA
1962	Trio No. 2 for Flute, Cello, and Piano	CF Peters
1963	Chamber Concerto for Cello and Ten Players	CF Peters
1963	Piano Variations	McGinnis & Marx
1963	Flute Variations I	McGinnis & Marx
1964	Composition for Violin and Ten Instruments	CF Peters
1964	Chamber Concerto for Flute and Ten Players	CF Peters
1964	Super Salutem for male voices and instruments	CF Peters
1964	Variations A 2 for flute and piano	ACA
1965	Composition for Oboe and Piano	CF Peters

1965	Orchestral and Electronic Exchanges for orchestra and tape	CF Peters
1965	Chamber Concerto for Oboe and Ten Players	CF Peters
1966	The Bells for carillon	ACA
1966	Concerto for Piano and Orchestra (No. 1)	CF Peters
1966	Janissary Music for percussion	CF Peters
1966	Harpsichord Divisions for harpsichord	CF Peters
1966	Making Ends Meet for piano four-hands	CF Peters
1966	Duo for Violin and Piano	CF Peters
1966	Bicinium for two oboes	CF Peters
1966	John Bull: Salve Regina Versus Septum for chamber ensemble	CF Peters
1967	The Politics of Harmony masque for alto, tenor, bass, two violins, two contrabasses, two flutes, two tubas, two harps, piano, and percussion	CF Peters
1968	String Trio	CF Peters
1968	Flute Variations II	CF Peters
1969	Time's Encomium for synthesized sound and processed synthesized sound	CF Peters
1969	Adapting to the Times for cello and piano	CF Peters
1969	The Long and the Short for violin	CF Peters
1969	Contrafactum for orchestra	CF Peters
1969	Nature's Concord for trumpet and piano	CF Peters
1969	Piano Sonata (No. 1)	CF Peters
1970	Ringing Changes for percussion ensemble	CF Peters
1970	Chamber Concerto for Tuba, Twelve Winds, and Twelve Drums	CF Peters
1970	A Message to Denmark Hill for baritone, flute, cello, and piano	CF Peters
1970	Cello Variations I	CF Peters
1970	A Song to the Lute in Musicke for soprano and piano	CF Peters
1971	String Quartet	CF Peters
1971	Canzona for twelve instruments	CF Peters
1971	Grand Bamboula for string orchestra	CF Peters
1972	Concerto for Amplified Violin and Orchestra	CF Peters
1972	Harp Variations for harp, violin, viola, and cello	CF Peters
1972	Bassoon Variations for bassoon, harp, and timpani	CF Peters
1972	Violin Variations	CF Peters
1972	On Alligators for eight instruments	CF Peters
1972	Speculum Speculi for flute, oboe, bass clarinet, contrabass, piano, and percussion	CF Peters
1972	Trio No. 3 for Flute, Cello, and Piano	CF Peters
1973	Grand Union for cello and drums	CF Peters
1973	Arabia Felix for flute, bassoon, violin, electric guitar, vibraphone, and piano	CF Peters

1973	Concerto No. 2 for Piano and Orchestra	CF Peters
1973	Mannheim 87. 87. 87 for unison chorus and organ	CF Peters
1973	Twelve Short Pieces for Piano	CF Peters
1974	An Anthem for Epiphany for chorus, trumpet, and organ	CF Peters
1974	Fantasia for Violin and Piano	CF Peters
1975	A Reliquary for Igor Stravinsky for orchestra	CF Peters
1975	TASHI for clarinet, violin, cello, and piano (alone or with orchestra)	CF Peters
1975	The W. of Babylon opera in two acts	CF Peters
1975	Hyperion for twelve instruments	CF Peters
1975	Cello Variations II	CF Peters
1976	Piano Sonata No. 2	CF Peters
1976	Percussion Symphony for twenty-four players	CF Peters
1977	The Winds for eight wind instruments	CF Peters
1977	Six Pieces for Violin and Piano	CF Peters
1977	Six Songs for Two Voices for countertenor (or alto) and tenor with chamber group	CF Peters
1977	Fast Fantasy for cello and piano	CF Peters
1977	Wind Quintet	CF Peters
1977	Archangel for trombone and string quartet	CF Peters
1977	Self-Similar Waltz for piano	CF Peters
1978	Ancestors for chamber orchestra	CF Peters
1978	Two-Part Symphony for orchestra	CF Peters
1978	Archaeopteryx for bass trombone and ten players	CF Peters
1979	Three Songs for tenor and piano	CF Peters
1979	Psalm 39 for baritone and guitar	CF Peters
1979	Percussion Duo for mallet instruments and piano	CF Peters
1979	Fortune for clarinet, violin, cello, and piano	CF Peters
1979	Joan's for flute, clarinet, violin, cello, and piano	CF Peters
1980	The Celestial Sphere for SATB and orchestra	CF Peters

APPENDIX

Key to Publishers' Abbreviations

ACA   American Composers Edition
                             170 W. 74 Street
                             New York, NY 10023

American Music   American Music Edition
                             263 E. 7 Street
                             New York, NY 10009

AMP   Associated Music Publishers, Inc.
                             866 Third Avenue
                             New York, NY 10022

Apogee   Apogee Press, Inc.
                             2145 Central Parkway
                             Cincinnati, OH 45214

B&H   Boosey & Hawkes, Inc.
                             24 West 57 Street
                             New York, NY 10019

Belwin-Mills   Belwin-Mills Publishing Corp.
                             25 Deshon Drive
                             Melville, NY 11747

BMI   Broadcast Music, Inc.
                             (see G Schirmer)

Boelke-Bomart   Boelke-Bomart, Inc.
                             Hillsdale, NY 14214

Bowdoin   Bowdoin College Music Press
                             Bowdoin College
                             Music Department
                             Gibson Hall
                             Brunswick, ME 04011

Broude Brothers

Broude Brothers Ltd.
56 W. 45 Street
New York, NY 10036

Carl Fischer

Carl Fischer, Inc.
62 Cooper Square
New York, NY 10003

CF Peters

C. F. Peters Corp.
373 Park Avenue South
New York, NY 10016

CPE

Composer/Performer Edition
Source
2101 22 Street
Sacramento, CA 90046

Dunvagen

Dunvagen Music Publishers, Inc.
c/o Performing Artservices, Inc.
463 West Street
New York, NY 10014

EAM

European American Music Distributers
Corp.
195 Allwood Road
Clifton, NJ 07012

EB Marks

Edward B. Marks Music Corp.
(see Belwin-Mills)

EC Schirmer

E. C. Schirmer Music Co.
112 South Street
Boston, MA 02111

Elkan-Vogel

Elkan-Vogel, Inc.
(see Presser)

Fostco

Fostco Music Press
P.O. Box 783
Marquette, MI 49855

Galaxy

Galaxy Music Corp.
2121 Broadway
New York, NY 10023

G Schirmer

G. Schirmer, Inc.
866 Third Avenue
New York, NY 10022

Hargail

Hargail Music, Inc.
51 E. 12 Street
New York, NY 10003

Henmar	Henmar Press, Inc. (see CF Peters)
Hinshaw	Hinshaw Music, Inc. P.O. Box 470 Chapel Hill, NC 27514
HW Gray	H.W. Gray Co., Inc. (see Belwin-Mills)
Impero	Impero Verlag (see Presser)
Lawson-Gould	Lawson-Gould Music Publishers, Inc. (see G Schirmer)
Leeds	Leeds Music Corp. (see Belwin-Mills)
Lingua	Lingua Press P.O. Box 481 Ramona, CA 92065
MCA	MCA Music (see Belwin-Mills)
McGinnis & Marx	McGinnis & Marx Music Publishers (see Marx)
Marx	Josef Marx Music Co. P.O. Box 229 Planetarium Station New York, NY 10024
Media	Media Interstellar Music Box 20346 Chicago, IL 60620
Mercury	Mercury Music Corp. (see Presser)
Merion	Merion Music, Inc. (see Presser)
MS	unpublished manuscript
Music for Perc	Music for Percussion, Inc. 17 W. 60 Street New York, NY 10023
New Music	New Music Edition (see Presser)

NY Public Library	The New York Public Library & Museum of the Performing Arts 111 Amsterdam Avenue New York, NY 10023
Orchesis	Orchesis Publications, Inc. 200 W. 57 Street New York, NY 10019
Pagani	O. Pagani & Bro. Inc. 289 Bleecker Street New York, NY 10014
Peer	Peer-Southern Organization 1740 Broadway New York, NY 10019
PNM	Perspectives of New Music Annandale-on-Hudson, NY 12504
Presser	Theodore Presser Co. Presser Place Bryn Mawr, PA 19010
Salabert	Editions Salabert, Inc. (see G Schirmer)
Schott	B. Schott's Söhne, Mainz (see EAM)
Smith	Smith Publications--Sonic Art Editions 1713 Adams Street Madison, WI 53711
Soundings	Soundings Press 984 Canyon Road Santa Fe, NM 87501
Southern	Southern Music Co. P.O. Box 329, 1100 Broadway San Antonio, TX 78292
SPAM	Society for the Publication of American Music (see Presser)
Summy-Birchard	Summy-Birchard Music Box CN 27 Princeton, NJ 08540
Suvini Zerboni	Edizion: Suvini Zerboni, Italy (see B&H)

Tempo	Tempo: A Quarterly Review of Modern Music (see B&H)
Universal	Universal Editions Publishing, Inc. (see EAM)
Valley Music	New Valley Music Press Sage Hall, Smith College Northampton, MA 01060
Visibility	Visibility Music Publishers c/o Performing Artservices, Inc. 463 West Street New York, NY 10014
Volkwein	Volkwein Bros. Inc. 117 Sandusky Street Pittsburgh, PA 15212
Waterloo	Waterloo Music Company (see AMP)

INDEX